D0216261

ENGINEERING MANAGEMENT

ENGINEERING MANAGEMENT

Robert E. Shannon

The University of Alabama in Huntsville

JOHN WILEY & SONS

New York · Chichester · Brisbane · Toronto · Singapore

Library of Congress Cataloging in Publication Data:

Shannon, Robert E   1932–
  Engineering management.

  Includes indexes.
  1. Engineering—Management. I. Title.
TA190.S5   658   79-14721
ISBN 0-471-03408-8

Printed in the United States of America

10 9 8 7

**Dedicated to my beautiful wife Marion
and my children, Kelly and Ted.**

This book is about the management of technical organizations. Engineers typically find themselves in a dilemma 4 to 6 years after graduation, when technical management positions become available to them. They quickly become aware that such positions require new knowledge and skills that their previous professional training has not provided. At this point they either frantically try to discover on their own the methods and concepts that will allow them to understand the management process, or they read management texts and return to school. Although dozens of books have been written on managing almost every other business function, only a handful of books have recently appeared dealing with managing technical functions.

Statistically, 80 percent of all engineers will end up in some sort of managerial position during their working careers. In most of these positions engineers will manage professional personnel who perform technical functions. Technical functions are not managed the same way as an operating business or as nontechnical functions are. Technical functions are concerned with creating something new or improving the old. This is a future-oriented, "one-time" activity directed toward innovation and change. The resources required and the end results are highly uncertain and unpredictable. The technical manager must handle, motivate, and control highly trained, creative people in an uncertain environment that requires flexible planning, policies, and procedures. The activities of a technical group must be planned and controlled just as much as the other operational business activities. However, there are some significant differences. These differences form the rationale for this book.

The dilemma faced by anyone writing on engineering management is to determine whether one is writing about the management of engineers or the management of engineering. There are two aspects to any type of management, which I think of as the formal and informal aspects of management. The former deals with the official chains of authority, policies, procedures, forms used, etc. The latter deals with the interpersonal relationships among peers, managers, and subordinates. I firmly believe that these two aspects of management are equally important and interrelated. They are either mutually supportive or in conflict with each other. In this book I show this interrelationship.

The book is divided into four parts. Part One deals with the strategic level of management, the long-range, continuing problems faced by the technical manager. Chapter 1 is an introduction that sets the tone and scope of the book by discussing the environmental context within which the engineering manager operates and the functions and roles of the engineering manager as they relate to the unique characteristics of technical functions. The discussion centers on the conflict between the need for management controls versus the need for freedom of the creative individual; also stressed are the uncertainties faced and the nature of the output of a technical organization.

Chapter 2 reviews the problems associated with planning the work of technical groups, which includes technology forecasting, needs research, sources of ideas, and environmental monitoring. The types of planning required and suggested approaches are presented.

Chapter 3 considers the important function of organizing the technical group. Various possible forms of organization and their strengths and weaknesses are discussed. The dynamic nature of organization and formal and informal organizational structures are examined.

Chapter 4 goes into various staffing and training concerns. The difficulties of soliciting and selecting the right kinds of people and then maintaining them as viable, productive workers are discussed. Problems of new employees and those of midcareer employees and technical, managerial, and organizational obsolescence are analyzed.

Part Two deals with the personnel level, including the interpersonal relationships among peers, managers, and subordinates. Chapter 5 is about the "care and feeding" of creativity. The creative process and the personal and organizational barriers to creativity that must be guarded against are discussed. Some suggested techniques for enhancing creativity are offered.

Chapter 6 presents the problems associated with the motivation of engineers, scientists, and technicians. Behavioral science theories on motivation are evaluated from the technical manager's viewpoint. The effects of aging, both on the individual and the organization, are discussed.

Chapter 7 is about the problem of choosing a leadership style. Much of the discussion resolves around whether there is one best leadership behavior. The effects of environmental factors and the personalities and expectations of the followers are presented.

In Part three we learn about the tactical level of management, that is, some of the day-to-day operational problems. In Chapter 8 the problems of deciding what projects are to be pursued by the technical group are explored. Both quantitative and qualitative methods are evaluated, and the limitations of quantitative methods and current practice are presented. A mixed approach to project selection is suggested.

Chapter 9 studies the various aspects of managerial control. The criteria for a good control system and suggested approaches for implementation are proposed. Management by objectives and methods for the planning, reporting, and appraisal of individual projects are discused.

In Chapter 10 we consider the unique problem associated with the management of complex systems projects and the utilization of the work breakdown structure and network analysis methods for the planning and control of complex systems projects.

Part Four consists of Chapter 11, which reproduces a series of papers written by W. J. King. This chapter offers some of the best advice I have ever seen to the new engineer just beginning his or her career and to the engineer who has just been promoted to management.

Management today is more of an art than a science. Consequently, any book written on the subject reflects the personal views and value system of the author. This book is no exception, and many individuals have greatly influenced my ideas. Teachers such as H. G. Thuesen, Wilson J. Bentley, and Paul E. Torgerson shaped my early thinking. I later was privileged to work under Dr. William R. Lucas, Director of the George C. Marshall Space Flight Center, from whom I learned a great deal while gaining invaluable first-hand experience. Associations with other technical executives, such as Dr. John L. McDaniel, former director of the Research Development and Engineering Laboratory of the U.S. Army Missile Command and Dr. Rudolph Hermann, former Director of the University of Alabama Research Institute, have also influenced my thinking. Finally, I am especially grateful to my late friend, Alexander T. Flynn, whose great depth of understanding taught me the importance of honesty, fairness, and compassion.

I also thank the many individuals who have made it possible to complete this project, particularly Dr. Jafar Hoomani, Dean of the School of Science and Engineering, Dr. Robert A. Brown, Chairman of the Department of Industrial and Systems Engineering, and my colleagues at The University of Alabama in Huntsville for their help, understanding, and encouragement, my mother-in-law, Mrs. Maybella Day, for typing the basic manuscript, and Mrs. Judy Duvall, for typing the case studies.

ROBERT E. SHANNON

Huntsville, Alabama 1979

CONTENTS

ENGINEERING MANAGEMENT

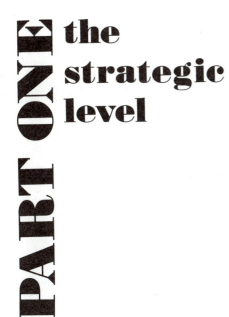

PART ONE

the strategic level

CHAPTER 1 environment of engineering management

1.1 Societal Changes

The search for knowledge and the means to utilize it to benefit humanity have occupied our minds almost from the very beginning of time. One of the most significant characteristics and phenomenon of modern society is the increasing rapidity with which nature is being made to serve the needs of people. Of all the forces that shape and reshape life in America, none is more insistent and powerful than those that spring from engineering and science. Our standard of living depends on technology to find new ways of using the resources we have, to find new products among the old raw materials, and to make life longer, safer, easier, and more productive.

The nation's two-hundredth birthday was celebrated with massive fireworks displays, historical reenactments, and thousands of other Bicentennial activities. During these first 200 years, world population increased sixfold, *but* real-world production multiplied 80 times over. At the same time, the distance a person can travel in a day stretched by a factor of 1000, the amount of energy we get from a pound of matter multiplied by 50 million, and our capability for instant communication multiplied several billion times. Technology was responsible for these changes.

In addition, during the last 100 years or so, American society went from an agriculturally based economy to an industrial economy and now to a service-oriented economy. Mainly because of the benefits of technology, for the first time in history, a nation now employs more than half of its working force in services. The

3

percentage of the U.S. labor force engaged in agriculture decreased from 90 percent in 1790 to 4 percent in 1970 and stabilized at that point. As employment in agriculture declined during the nineteenth and early twentieth centuries, there was a corresponding rise in the percentage of the work force engaged in manufacturing and construction. But, according to the Bureau of Labor Statistics, since the end of World War II, the percentage engaged in manufacturing has also been declining from 30 percent of the labor force in 1947 to an estimated 22.4 percent by 1980. It is even projected by one RAND Corporation study that by the year 2000 perhaps as few as 2 percent of the labor force will be required to turn out the necessary manufactured goods required by this country.

If we define an industrial society as one in which manufacture is the controlling force that shapes the characteristics of its labor force, then the United States today is *not* an industrial society. Although there is little agreement as to what to call the era on which we have embarked, there is general consensus as to its characteristics. These include:

1. *Economic Sector:* The change from a goods-producing to a services-producing economy.
2. *Occupational Distribution:* Increasing education for all citizens and the preeminence of the professional and technical class.
3. *Resource Base:* The centrality of theoretical knowledge and innovation as the source of power and policy formulation.
4. *Change:* Rapid technological change propelled by the explosion of knowledge.
5. *Decision Making:* The creation of a new "intellectual technology" to provide dynamic adaptation to the rapidly changing social environment.

As a part of the 1976 Bicentennial celebration, the Museum of Science and Industry in Chicago conducted a survey among leading engineers, scientists, and historians to select America's 10 greatest scientists, engineers, inventors, and innovators [3]. They also selected the 100 most significant American scientific discoveries, technological inventions, and industrial innovations. The selections were based primarily on the development's impact on its field and scientific, social, or economic progress. The results are shown in Appendices A and B.

Even a casual reading of these lists should be enough to convince the most skeptical reader that the fruits of American innovation have done more than anything else to shape the quality of this country's economy and national life. Technology has provided the gains in efficient use of labor, materials, and time. Innovation creates jobs and boosts productivity. Above all, innovation generates economic momentum and helps to guarantee American preeminence in a world where power and progress are often measured in terms of technological achievement.

It is also no exaggeration to say that technology and its products may very well decide the political and economic future of the world. Today, this country and its allies find themselves locked in a struggle with an antagonistic ideology dedicated to the destruction of the democratic and capitalistic way of life. The communist countries are devoting much of their energies and resources to this conflict in an attempt to surpass us economically and technologically. Efficient and effective management of technology may be the deciding factor in this race for supremacy in the technical and space age.

1.2 The Changing Process

Almost unnoticed during all of the excitement of America's Bicentennial celebration was the fact that 1976 also marked the centennial of the establishment of the first applied research and development (R&D) center, Thomas Edison's installation at Menlo Park, New Jersey, in 1876. The opening of this center is historically important because it marked the beginning of an entirely new way of doing applied research and engineering [11].

Until this time, new knowledge and new products were the result of individuals working in their homes, at universities, or in small factory areas. Here, for the first time, we find an organization with facilities and equipment devoted exclusively to the development of new products. Edison's installation was followed by the establishment of research facilities by General Electric (1900), DuPont (1902), and Eastman Kodak (1913).

The shift from the individual inventor to a team effort can be graphically seen in the *Book of Knowledge* (Grolier, New York). The 1966 edition of this work lists notable inventions, starting with the third century B.C. and proceeding through the twentieth century. Up to 1942, 237 inventions are listed that show one, two, or three individuals as the recognized inventors in each case. From 1942 to 1960 15 additional inventions are shown. Of these, 10 are attributed either to organizations or to anonymous groups such as "military scientists" or "group of physicists."

This is really not too surprising, since modern engineering and science require organization. Without organization, there is no such thing as engineering or science as we know it today. If an airplane is to be built, there must be an organized system to translate the engineer's design into drawings, orders to the shop, purchase requests to vendors, assembly instructions for workers, maintenance manuals for the crew, and procedures for the pilots. For better or for worse, except for very small companies, engineers and scientists are today hopelessly enmeshed with organizational bureaucracies.

Perhaps we can see the significance and need for doing business this way by looking at what it took to develop a useful product 100 years after the opening of Menlo Park. Since 1952, *Industrial Research Magazine* has held an annual international competition to pick the 100 most significant products brought on the market during the preceding year. It took an average of 37 months to develop a winning product in the 1977 competition [2]. This compares to 39 months in 1976, 40 months in 1975, 36 months in 1974, 35 months in 1973, 33 months in 1972, and 23 months in 1971. It required 23,000 man-hours of work in R&D to come up with the average winning product in 1977.

The average development cost per winning product in 1977 was $943,900, with a low of $6000 and a high of $15 million. This was well above the 1976 cost of $450,000 or the 1975 and 1974 costs both of which averaged $665,000. The average costs were $369,000 in 1972 and $419,000 in 1971. It is important to remember that these are products that have reached the market and are considered as significant. Surveys have shown that 80 percent or more of R&D projects never reach the market. The infant mortality rate of new product ideas is extremely high (see Figure 1.1), and the sponsor receives nothing for the investment.

With this type of inherent risk, coupled with high developmental times and costs, it is little wonder that the lonely inventor working in the basement is seldom heard from anymore. Technology is a big and expensive business. It requires vast investments of money and facilities and the best technical and managerial talent available. The continuous rise in R&D expenditures alone is easily seen in Figure 1.2.

Many decry the expense to our society and say "Enough." It is probably true that the golden age of relatively easy and low-cost inventions ended 50 or 75 years ago. However, there are still opportunities and needs. Jones [6] says,

> Those who would compare technology's challenges and opportunities today with those of our first 150 to 175 years, and bemoan the change have missed the point

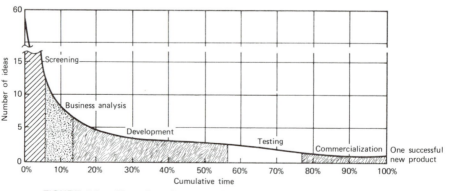

FIGURE 1.1   Mortality of new product ideas by stage of evolution for 51 companies. (Source: Booz-Allen & Hamilton Inc.)

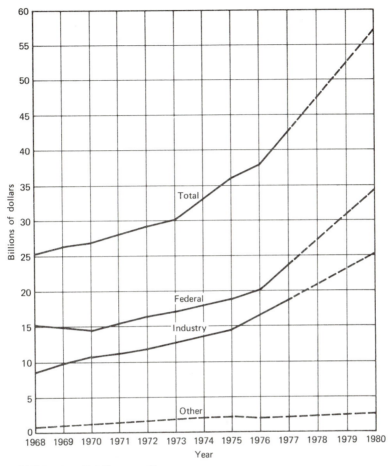

FIGURE 1.2   R & D expenditures.

entirely. It is technology's triumphs that have put us where we are. Our way of life, our standard of living, the benefits of modern culture—they too are technology's triumphs—and if the easy inventions have already been done, that is a small price to pay for what we have now.

1.3   The Technical Function

An organization supports technical personnel in order to achieve one or more of the following.

1. Provide technical expertise and consultation.
2. Extend, improve, or provide more differentation in its products and services.

3. Increase productivity and reduce costs by improving processes or methods.
4. Adapt existing technologies to new uses or markets.
5. Create new markets (or even industries) with new technologies and products.

In the remainder of this book the term ''technical function'' is used instead of ''research and development'' because we see the technical function as being broader than the usual context of R&D. The technical function is basically a supporting function, albeit an important and even critical one. Some of the technical functions found in most industrial organizations are shown in Table 1.1. As we will see throughout this book, the nature of these supporting technical functions presents the technical manager with unique challenges not faced by other managers.

Every author attempts to break technology into categories such as pure, basic, supporting, applied, development, etc. This becomes almost impossible to do in an unambiguous manner, since there is a great deal of fuzziness and overlap in such definitions. It is perhaps most useful to visualize technological activities as arranged in a spectrum (see Figure 1.3), with basic

TABLE 1.1   Technical Functions

Support of	Technical Function
Sales/Marketing	Development of new products, processes, and materials
	Technical service to customers
	Improvements in existing products and processed materials
	End-use testing and evaluation of products, processes, and materials
	Development of new uses for existing products
	Design and development of integrated systems
	Logistics engineering
	Maintainability engineering
	Reliability engineering
Production	Quality Control
	Design and modification of plant and processes
	Troubleshooting on plant and process
	Development of analytical and testing methods
	Safety engineering
	Design of work methods
Purchasing	Specifications for raw materials and components
	Acceptance testing
	Evaluation of alternative sources
Corporate	Centralized technical services
	Diversification studies
	Plant location activities

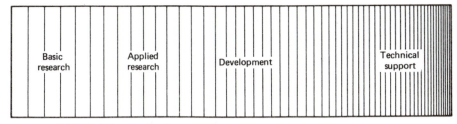

FIGURE 1.3   Technology spectrum.

or pure research at one end and process or product improvement at the other. It is neither possible nor necessary to draw a distinct line on this spectrum and say this is "applied research" or that is "basic research." However, because words must be used to communicate, the following general terms are defined.

Basic or Fundamental Research. Investigation and study of the fundamental laws and phenomena of nature in order to contribute to general knowledge. The hope is that a better understanding of the secrets of nature will lead to useful future results. End results are usually research papers.

Applied Research. Exploration of the practical possibilities of creating new products and processes through state-of-the-art or technology advancement. Practical objectives with preconceived notions of their utility are pursued. End results are usually in proof of technical feasibility and perhaps a patent.

Development. Converting ideas for new or improved products and processes into practice. End results are the detailed drawings, specifications, plans, testing, etc., required to make or use the product or process.

Technical Support. Providing the technical know-how for troubleshooting, improvements, customer support, etc., to maintain a competitive position and implement the results of the development phase. Technical services in the form of advice, improved designs, etc., may be provided to any part of the parent organization.

We should at this point also make the distinction between *discovery* and *invention*. You do not invent a fundamental law or phenomenon of nature but, if you are the first to see it, you have discovered it. For example, the human body has many enzymes that operate as catalysts. Someday a biochemist may discover an enzyme that is not yet known. This would be a "discovery," since evolution has already "invented" it. On the other hand, if the biochemist develops a way to synthesize the new enzyme for medical use, a process has been invented. The biochemist could patent the process, but not the enzyme. It is often said that basic or fundamental research is directed toward the "discovery" of the facts and laws of nature, while supporting or applied R&D are directed toward producing or inventing useful things for the benefit of humanity. Unfortunately, there is still great overlap between these areas.

Even though these and other terms are widely used, their ambiguity becomes readily apparent. There are two aspects of this problem that make meaningful word definitions difficult. The first of these is the fact that the motivation of the investigator for the work performed may, in fact, be different from the motivation of those providing the funding. One often finds that people provide the money in the hope of finding a solution to a real and immediate problem, whereas the researcher is interested in obtaining a fundamental understanding of some phenomenon. These mismatches of motivation can and do lead to serious misunderstandings and managerial problems.

Another confusion factor derives from the fact that elements of all phases of technology exist in all projects, no matter what the motivation. For example, even the most basic research often requires the invention and development of new instrumentation and techniques. In some cases these new instruments or techniques turn out to be the most useful outcome of the project, and they more than justify the entire expense of a project that failed in its major objective.

1.4 Product and System Life Cycle

By definition, technical executives are concerned with the management of engineers and other personnel who are engaged in the technology process. This process is devoted to the design, evaluation, and technical support of products and systems. Fundamental to the management of the technology process is a basic understanding of the life cycle that any product or system undergoes and the role of engineering during each phase. The life cycle commences with the recognition of a need and the conceptualization of a product or system to meet that need. It proceeds through the necessary research, design, development, and evaluation to the ultimate production, implementation, use, and phaseout of the product or system. Engineering plays an important and critical role in each of these phases. Figure 1.4 shows a conceptual model of this product or system life cycle. Each of the seven phases will now be briefly discussed.

Phase A: Conceptualization. In order to begin the cycle, the need for a new product or system must arise and be recognized. The identification of the need can arise from many sources and may be motivated by one or more of the motives specified in Section 1.3. The stimulation resulting in the needs recognition can arise from what Gerstenfeld [5] calls "demand pull" or from "technology push." Demand pull is defined as the idea originating from outside the technical group, such as from sales, production, quality control,

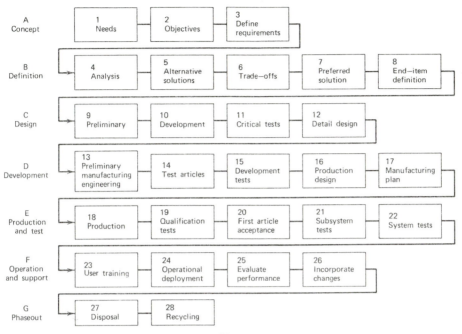

FIGURE 1.4   Product or system life.

etc. Technology push derives from ideas originating within the technical group, perhaps from basic and applied research being conducted. In Chapter 2 we will discuss research that indicates that approximately 75 percent of all successful innovations are stimulated by market demand or a production need, whereas only about 20 percent arise from someone saying "Maybe we can find a use for this technical idea."

Phase B: Definition.   After a need has been identified, the technical group begins to define the objectives and requirements for the new product or system. This leads to a search for and evaluation of alternative ways to meet the perceived need. Feasibility studies and tests are conducted on both market potential and different technical ideas. The definition phase ends with the determination that there is indeed a need or market, the selection of one or more preferred solutions, and the definition of what the end item should be and do. At the end of this phase, we usually have an established official project and a definite commitment of resources. This is ordinarily accomplished by the preparation and approval of a formal proposal.

Phase C: Design.   During this phase the concepts of the preceding phases are turned into concrete ideas in the form of drawings, schematics, specifications, breadboards, and models. Component and subsystem tests and simulations may be performed. Preliminary plans for manufacture are considered, and trade-off studies are conducted. In addition to functional capability or performance considerations, reliability, maintainability, human factors, safety, and producibility are of concern. Certain critical tests are generally conducted during this phase to demonstrate and prove out the design concepts. At the end of this phase, we generally have a critical design review, and all engineering documentation is released to the development team.

Phase D: Development. With the release of the detailed design of the product or system, there is still a great deal of engineering to be done. Facilities for fabrication and the manufacturing process, special tools, test equipment, transportation equipment, handling equipment, and work methods must be designed. Modifications to the design to improve fabricability and articles manufactured under developmental conditions must be tested. Market and user tests are generally conducted before committing to full-scale production.

Phase E: Production and Test. As the manufacturing plan is put into effect and the first production takes place, qualification and acceptance tests usually uncover new problem areas. Logistics plans to support the product or system are completed and implemented.

Phase F: Operation and Support. Even after the product or system is deployed, engineering continues to provide field service or customer service support. New manufacturing problems may arise as weaknesses in the design of the product or system, manufacturing tools, test equipment, etc., become apparent.

Phase G: Phaseout. As the product or system loses its appeal or utility, there will come a time when it must be phased out. Engineering also provides support for the subsequent reclamation and recycling of components, materials, tooling, etc., during this phaseout and disposal of the product or system at the end of its life cycle.

1.5 Is Engineering Management Different?

You do not manage a technical function in the same way that you manage an operating business or function. Some people tend to say that "management is management," and standard operational management conventions can be applied to the planning and control of technical activities. This is not true, and adherence to this idea will inhibit the success of the technical group. The activities of a technical group must be planned, executed, and controlled just as much as the operational business activities. However, there are some significant differences.

First, technical functions are associated with creating something new or improving the current method of operation. It is oriented to *innovation* or *change* and is a one-time activity. Technical groups are involved with developing the new or changing the old; this includes the activities of machines and people. Operational groups, on the other hand, deal with more predictable, well-defined tasks. The emphasis is assuring adherence to procedures and plans. Most operational functions are repetitive, and unpredictable behavior by people or machines is unacceptable. Technical functions seek change; operational functions seek sameness. Thus, the technical manager must encourage and create an atmosphere that is conducive to creativity, innovation, and change; the operational manager must demand predictability and a pattern of behavior that is highly structured and precisely defined.

Second, technical functions usually deal with one-time activities. Once a study is done, a new machine designed, or a new system developed, the work is seldom repeated. Operational work, by contrast, is associated with routines that repeat themselves periodically (hourly, daily, weekly, etc.). Since it is an integral function of running the business, the operating routine is expected to perpetuate itself once it is developed.

Third, the costs of one-time activities are much more difficult to estimate ahead of time. Estimates of operational costs can usually be predicted based on historical data. In operational work we are much more likely to have similar operations on which to base estimates of a new operational job. In technical work, since we are more apt to be dealing with first-time endeavors and creative or innovative tasks, estimates are obviously subject to higher estimating errors. Because first estimates are generally incorrect, a more dynamic and flexible planning philosophy is necessary.

Fourth, there are differences in the way we can expedite work. We can generally increase the production of an operational activity in proportion to the resources applied. However, we find that diminishing returns may be reached very early, with the addition of resources to expedite technical project activity. Too many people on a technical project may be less efficient than not enough people.

Fifth, our ability to measure performance is different. If 50 percent of the time and resources planned for a technical project are expended, we do not know whether that project is in trouble or not. We must know how much effort and time are needed to complete the activity and what effect a schedule slippage or cost overrun will have on the total project objectives. Furthermore, most technical functions do not directly bring about increased sales or reduced costs. Their work results in a payoff only when an operational group implements it. If a technical project does not have the desired result, was it the fault of the project or of its implementation by others? Project performance should be measured on project profitability or return on the invested cost of the technical work, but the profitability is often outside the control of the technical manager.

We can, therefore, sum up the major differences as follows. The technical manager is concerned with one-time, future-oriented tasks directed toward innovation and change. The resources required and end results are highly uncertain and unpredictable. The operational manager, on the other hand, is concerned with present-oriented, periodically repetitive tasks; strict adherence to predetermined policies, procedures, and methods is the desired goal. The technical manager must deal with, motivate, and control highly trained, creative people in an uncertain environment that requires flexible planning, policies, and procedures. The operational manager must deal with the enforcement of plans, schedules, policies, and procedures where the results of decisions are much more predictable.

The technical manager has an immensely difficult job, one that is less similar to other types of management than is commonly realized. As managers, they sit directly astride the problem of how to achieve a workable accommodation between the technical and business personnel. As we will see later, this is not easy to achieve. Furthermore, the technical manager carries a personal psychological burden created by an ambivalence between an earlier career in technical work and a present career in management. This ambivalence derives from the distinction (and it is a real one) between *doing* engineering and research and *managing* engineering and research. The work of the technical manager is not that of the organization; it is the specialized task of maintaining the organization in operation. That is, the manager does not personally perform the technical tasks required, but serves predominately as a planner, facilitator, and communicator.

Some people may object that a solid grounding in science or engineering and personal experience in technical work are absolute prerequisites for any successful technical manager. True, but the fact remains that the manager's concerns deal with three basic elements: (1) organization (the people physically involved in the operation); (2) facilities (all the tangible assets of the operation, such as buildings, tools, equipment, inventory, and cash); and (3) information (the bond that allows the organization and its people to use the facilities at their disposal effectively). The manager must be concerned with the basic purpose and goals, with obtaining the necessary resources, and with seeing that the group's outputs are utilized. These things are apart from the engineering and research itself.

Some technical managers try to deny that the managing and doing are separate and distinct; they insist that their main responsibility is to guide and direct the technical work while providing personal inspiration to their people. This concept may be true at the very first level of management but, in the long run, it is possible only if someone else assumes responsibility for the other management functions. Such managers are trying to keep a foot in both camps without declaring themselves. By continuing to do personal research and engineering design, such a manager fails to delegate responsibility properly and neglects some of the important management functions.

The decision to move into management is often a difficult one that has significant consequences on one's career and life. The engineer or scientist has spent many years in intense preparation for a given career. By moving into the management ranks, they are abandoning that career and starting a new one, where the skills required and concerns are very different. The engineer or scientist who enters management will no longer be judged and rewarded for technical skills, but for managerial skills.

1.6 The Functions of Management

We can approach a discussion of management from two viewpoints.

1. The functions to be carried out.
2. The roles to be played.

In the remainder of this section, we will discuss the functions of management; in Section 1.7 we will discuss the roles needed to carry out these functions.

Barnard [1] suggests that the function of managers is to (1) formulate and define purpose, (2) provide the system of communications, and (3) promote the securing of the essential efforts of the required members of the organization. He sees the manager as predominantly a planner, facilitator, and communicator. Various other authors have presented the managerial functions in different ways and using varying classification schemes. The approach we like is to consider the functions of the manager to be:

1. *Planning.* Anticipating future events and making preparations to meet them effectively. It is based on forecasts of alternative future events.
2. *Organizing.* Defining and grouping the activities required, establishing the responsibilities for the people who will carry them out, and setting forth the working relationships among these people.
3. *Staffing.* Securing the services of people with the knowledge and skills to carry out the necessary activities.

4. *Motivating*. Offering the inducements and incentives to the individuals in the group to get them to put forth their best efforts.
5. *Communicating*. Seeing that all required information is passed among and between the group members and integrating the needs of the individuals with the purposes of the group for their mutual benefit.
6. *Measuring*. Evaluating whether or not the activities of the group are accomplishing the desired purposes and goals.
7. *Correcting*. Revising the planning, organization, staffing, motivating, and integrating, processes as necessary.

With a little thought, it is readily apparent that these seven items are merely an elaboration, in different terms, of Barnard's three managerial functions. These functions are true for any manager, regardless of the nature of the activities of the group. They are carried out predominantly through communication and secondarily through decision making. Let us briefly consider each of these managerial functions.

One of the manager's most important responsibilities is to guide the organization toward desired objectives or future states. This entails both the consideration of which future events or states are possible and which are most desirable. Once the future possible states have been defined and evaluated, goals for the organization can be formulated and plans for achieving the goals prepared. *Planning* basically consists of deciding, in advance, what to do, how to do it, where to do it, when to do it, and who is to do it. It involves strategic (long-range) planning, tactical (short-run) planning, and planning for operational control. This is a continuing, not one-time, responsibility. Plans must be continually modified to accommodate changes in the operating environment, and new plans must be prepared as circumstances evolve. The effort that must go into good planning and the value derived make it imperative that the manager deal with planning in a conscious and systematic manner.

The purpose of *organizing* a group of individuals is to achieve the most effective utilization of the available resources (people, facilities, equipment, and money). This is accomplished by establishing decision-making and communications processes designed to facilitate and activate the full potential creativity and productivity of the members of the group. Organizing consists of much more than just drawing up an organizational chart. It consists of assigning roles and responsibilities as well as facilities and equipment. It relates to aspects of the physical environment, the social environment, the prestige and status environment, and the authority relationships. It is now established that there is both a formal and informal organizational structure. But it is also known that the informal organization can be greatly influenced by the design of the formal organization. For example, we can encourage or discourage social and professional interaction between people by where we locate their offices or laboratories and by how we arrange the furniture. Planning and organizing are inseparably tied together.

Staffing consists of deciding what kind of people with what skills we need to carry out the plans laid and then finding and recruiting them. This is not as easy as it may sound, since the National Research Council now lists more than 150 distinct scientific and engineering disciplines. There are also technician, clerical, and administrative positions to be filled. A person will choose whether or not to join a particular organization based on (1) the individual's goals, desires, and impulses of the moment, and (2) the alternatives recognized as available. There must be an identifiable matching of needs between the organization and the individual. Staffing may be facilitated by an outside group such as the personnel office, but the primary responsibility rests with the manager. Success in this function is critical. The manager who can identify and attract good people is well on the way to success.

Of course, attracting highly skilled people into the organization is a necessary but not sufficient condition for success. Having induced the individual to join the group, the manager must proceed to provide the incentives and environment that will allow and cause the person to put forth his or her best efforts. An individual's actions are very much determined by desires, impulses, and wants, which we call "motives." They are chiefly the result of forces in the physical, biological, and social environments, past and present. *Motivation* is usually described in terms of the end sought. The specific ends sought by people are of three kinds: physical, social, and psychological. Physical ends are material objects and physical conditions such as warmth, shelter, food, etc. Social ends are contact, interrelationships, and communications with other people. Psychological ends include recognition, praise from others, and internal feelings of accomplishment, growth, and self-satisfaction. A person will cooperate and put forth effort when he or she perceives that the sum of the benefits derived outweigh the burdens. The manager provides motivation by increasing the perceived benefits or reducing the perceived burdens.

Strictly speaking, the purpose and goals of the organization have no direct meaning for the individual. What does have meaning is the organization's effect—the burdens it imposes and the benefits it confers. *Communication* is the process by which the possibility of accomplishing a common purpose is integrated with the individuals whose desires might constitute motives for contributing toward such a common purpose. Obviously, a common purpose must be commonly known and, to be known, must be communicated in some way. Similarly, offering inducements to people depends on communicating with them. The methods, techniques, and content of communications are a critical part of every manager's job and the major problem of many managers. Through communications the manager must (1) make known the common purpose, (2) convince the individuals that they should put forth their best efforts to meet the common purpose, and (3) provide the necessary information to the group members that will allow them to do their jobs most efficiently and effectively.

Unfortunately, the manager is always operating to a greater or lesser degree from a state of ignorance. Very seldom is it possible to make a decision where all of the facts and potential outcomes are known with certainty. Even if such an ideal situation were possible, conditions are continuously changing, so the manager must *monitor and evaluate progress* and determine if the goals and purposes are being met. In order to do so, he or she must attempt to measure both the effectiveness and efficiency of the group's effort. An organization is effective if it accomplishes its specific aim, and it is efficient if it minimizes the expenditure of resources in so doing. As the work progresses, new unforeseen circumstances will arise, things thought possible will be found to be impossible, and conditions beyond our control will change. All of these factors will influence how successful the groups' efforts are. Therefore the manager must continuously measure and evaluate whether or not the activities of the group are leading to the accomplishment of the desired goals and purposes.

As the work progresses and new limitations to accomplishment appear, the organization must adjust or fail. As each new limitation is overcome (or not), new purposes and goals appear or old goals are abandoned. Plans are revised, organizational structures are modified, personnel are promoted, demoted, or dismissed, communication methods or channels are changed, and resources are redistributed. Every organization is a dynamic, living, ever-changing being. Managers must constantly cope with changes in their own jobs, in their departments, and in their companies. Some of these changes will be evolutionary, but some will be revolutionary, some will be directly under the manager's control (i.e., the manager will be the change agent), and some will not. The good manager must constantly *correct, modify, and adjust* the planning, organization, staffing, motivating, and communicating processes as necessary.

We can perhaps conclude this preliminary discussion of the managerial functions by classifying the problem areas of concern and the types of management decisions required. The problem areas are:

1. Technical program.
2. Personnel.
3. Organization structure.
4. Incentives.
5. Financial.
6. Service and support activities.
7. Facilities.

The types of management decisions required can be classified as:

1. Determination of long-range objectives.
2. Determination of immediate objectives.
3. Operating decisions and actions.
4. Evaluation of progress and results.

One very important fact to recognize, however, is that in a technical organization whose main goal is research or engineering, these functions and decisions are widely shared and carried out by everyone in the group. In other words, some of the most important planning, communicating, evaluating, and decision making is done by nonmanagerial scientists and engineers. As we will see throughout later discussions, the very nature of the engineering and research process mandates a highly participatory concept of management.

1.7 Managerial Work Roles

Having briefly discussed the managerial functions (or what a manager is supposed to do), we now consider the managerial roles (or how they are carried out). Social scientists like to classify behavior into roles [4]. Roles are organized sets of behavior that belong to incumbents in certain offices or positions. The manager is predominantly a communicator and decision maker, but Mintzberg (after extended observation of managers) has broken this down into the following nine roles [8].

Leader. Leadership is the most widely recognized of the managerial roles, even though its definition is the most nebulous. It describes the manager's relationship with subordinates, including attempts to influence their behavior through motivation and guidance. Every time a manager encourages, reprimands, suggests, or demands, leadership is being exerted.

Figurehead. As the legal authority of the group, the manager also becomes its symbolic representative. In this role the manager is required to represent the group on ceremonial occasions and in welcoming special visitors. This entails presiding at ceremonial events such as retirements or special awards presentations and attending certain social functions.

Liaison. The manager provides a focal point for the exchange of information with outside groups. Over a period of time, a network of contact is established with other people both within and outside of the parent organization that brings information, tasks, and favors to the group. The manager provides time, information, and favors in return for the same from others.

Disseminator. The information that the manager gathers from outside sources must be passed on to subordinates. Some of this information is of a factual nature, and some of it is value interpretation (i.e., preferences or value judgments).

Spokesperson. The manager is responsible for informing upper management and other interested parties about the performance, accomplishments, policies, plans, and needs of the group.

Change Agent. The manager should be the designer and initiator of controlled change in the organization. Both the external and internal environment in which the group is working is in a constant state of flux. This creates the need to improve and adapt the way things are done.

Disturbance Handler. While the change agent role focuses on voluntary or self-initiated change, the disturbance handler role deals with corrections forced on the manager by others. Periodically, large and small crises occur that threaten the stability of the group's operation. These disturbances may be personal conflicts between group members, problems with outsiders, new situations not faced before, or confusion as to who is responsible for a new task. Most managers refer to this activity as "firefighting" (i.e., putting out this little blaze, then another and another).

Resource Allocator. The major means by which a manager controls and directs the group is through the allocation of its resources. By deciding who gets what and who does what, the manager sets the course and direction of the organization. This is primarily a decision-making role that strongly influences the motivational system and group productivity.

Negotiator. The final role deals with the critical job of negotiation. Since the manager is responsible for obtaining and disbursing the resources of the group, negotiating becomes almost a way of life. Negotiation is carried out with groups to whom services are being sold, those who are providing supporting services, and those who are setting standards for the group's work. As the group's legal authority, spokesperson, and resource allocator, the manager must do most of the important negotiating or resource trading.

These nine roles constitute the means by which the manager carries out the functions discussed in Section 1.6. Each role is very demanding and time consuming and requires careful thought and the allocation of the manager's personal time.

1.8 Definition of the Control Problem

The problem faced by management is to develop a product or to provide knowledge or the solution to a problem that is desired by a customer by a date dictated by a maximum payoff and minimum expenditure of resources (people, money, and facilities). Ideally, we would like to have a methodology that could be applied to any organization that could assure the optimal use of resources to provide this maximum payoff. Unfortunately, such a methodology is still only a fond hope.

Every manager of an organization engaged in technology is faced with the same basic problem: how to obtain the maximum benefit from the available resources. In every technical group there are more desirable projects than resources available to pursue them. The resources of time, money, facilities, equipment and, most important, competent, creative personnel are always limited. The apparently desirable projects on which to expend them are not limited. The technical manager is therefore faced continuously with a painful problem that consists of three parts.

1. Have the projects that have the highest potential payoff or value been considered?
2. Of the projects considered, on which ones should resources be expended?
3. How should the available resources be divided among these projects to obtain maximum benefit?

The generation of ideas, the initial examination of them for feasibility, and the choice of which ones to support and to what degree are critical to the overall effectiveness of the program. The decisions that result from these phases will allocate resources in a pattern that is costly to modify or reverse. When large efforts are involved and choices are mutually exclusive, these decisions may, in the short run, be irreversible.

The manager of a technical activity seeks to avoid two general types of errors: (1) failing to undertake "good" projects, and (2) undertaking "bad" projects. The reasons for the difficulty most technical organizations have in avoiding these errors are inherent in the technical process itself.

1. The outcome of individual projects and programs is highly unpredictable. That is, for other than technologically trivial projects, project selection involves decision making under (at best) risk—where probability distributions can be associated with outcomes—or (at worst) uncertainty—where such probability distributions are not available.
2. The outcome of an individual project occurs with time lags of months or years, during which period some of the factors that enter into the initial project selection decision (market demand, material price, competition, available supporting technology, etc.) may change significantly.

Particularly in projects that entail specific objectives, time constraints, limited manpower, and limited funds, the point of greatest flexibility in resource allocation occurs in the project selection phase. In later phases, when work is already in progress, it becomes more and more difficult to change direction or reallocate resources without great loss. This is particularly true for large systems projects.

Any system for the management of technical activities must provide in some way for project initiation, selection, evaluation, and periodic review. If the system is effective, it should result in a smooth flow of well-chosen projects whose statuses are updated and reviewed periodically. In other words, of all projects considered, those that have the best expected payoff to the organization within budget, manpower, and other limitations should receive the necessary technical effort.

1.9 Importance of Time

One of the key factors seems to be time. Try as one may to separate the time factor from the allocation of resources and the reaping of profits or payoff, the separation cannot be made. Technological decay (obsolescence), environmental decay (changing situation), and the present worth of future dollars further dictate the consideration of the time factor in evaluating costs and payoff. Part of the problem is that any project in a rapidly changing or competitive technology may be obsolete by the time it is designed, developed, or the results ready for publication or dissemination.

Before the influence of time on value and costs is discussed further, it is important to consider briefly another aspect of the problem: probability of success. In any discussion of technology, one frequently hears the terms "state of the art," "degree of newness," and "risk or probability of successful conclusion." I feel that misunderstanding of such terms has seriously retarded progressive and dynamic thinking in the solution of the evaluation and selection problem.

Some contemplated projects are recognized as having very little prior experience for guidance in exploration, design, production, or use. The state of the art is considered low, and the degree of newness is considered high. With such a project it is also likely that the probability of successful conclusion is considered very low. What is really meant by such terminology? Is it not that insufficient knowledge, facts, and experience are available to feel really confident about the future? Similar situations exist to a greater or lesser degree with all but the very simplest of developments. The truth is that all unknown facts and experiences *can be obtained* at some cost from applied research, pilot plant lots, market analysis, and thorough testing. Any project (other than basic research) can be technically successful—if management is willing to pay enough in dollars and manpower.

Keeping in mind the meaning of the risk of being unsuccessful, we again discuss time and its influence on value and cost. Consider first the relationship between value and the results of technical projects versus time of project completion. The true value of a project is the value that would be attached to it if the total contribution it would make toward the objective of the organization were known. Figure 1.5 shows a typical plot of true value as a function of time. For a commercial concern, this may represent monthly revenues to be derived from a new or improved product; for the military, it may represent the deterrent value of a proposed weapon system; and for the space agency, it may represent the international prestige derived from accomplishing a certain mission or knowledge gained.

One can conceive of projects whose results are available too early. This is especially true of projects that result in a tangible product. Prior to point A, the need for the results or the surrounding circumstances necessary for their use have not yet arisen. If the results are available prior to point A, invested money, personnel time, facilities, etc., without a payoff represent a negative value. For example, Charles Babbage, the British mathematician, invented the basic principles of the digital computer between 1820 and 1830. He finally abandoned effort on it in 1842, when he could derive no value from his brilliant conception because the technology of his day was incapable of utilizing it. Not until the advances of the electronics industry 100 years later provided appropriate technological circumstances did the true value of his concept achieve a positive value. It is probably a misstatement to say that the project had a negative value to humanity but, from Babbage's viewpoint, that was the result.

After point A, the value rises to some peak, such as B, after which the need declines or the product becomes obsolete and is superseded by later develop-

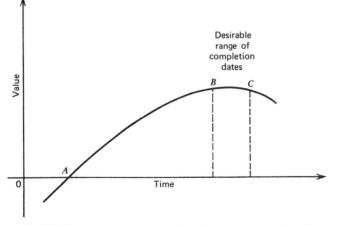

FIGURE 1.5   Value as a function of project completion date.

ments. The true value is usually not known at the time that planners must make their decisions. They must proceed on the basis of estimates of value. It is characteristic of most planners that they initially underestimate the value of a project until they see the sudden rise sometime after point A. Then there is a tendency to overestimate the peak true value and underestimate the rate of decline. In practice, the estimates of the true value curve are sometimes in error by a factor of 10 or 100. Even though it is not usually possible to have accurate numerical values available for a curve such as that in Figure 1.5, it does focus attention on a basic parameter of the problem.

The relationship of project duration and cost of completing the project is shown in Figure 1.6. A crash program to obtain the results in the shortest possible time is always very costly. If a project is stretched out over too long a period, the total costs will rise again as enthusiasm lags, personnel come or go, and momentum is lost. Note that there is a minimum project duration below which the project cannot be accomplished. Costs increase exponentially and are prohibitive as this lower bound is approached. Thus the time to complete a given project can sometimes be reduced by the use of additional resources, but only up to a certain point. Unfortunately, true cost is as hard to accurately pin down quantitatively as is true value. However, even government managers must somehow keep true cost in mind to achieve optimized output.

1.10 Necessity of Management Controls

Management controls are an essential part of every organized activity. There is a saying that "Action without direction or control is simply a faster form of drifting." Technical activity is expensive. With engineering and science cost-

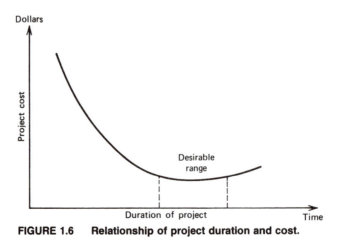

FIGURE 1.6   Relationship of project duration and cost.

ing an average of $75,000 or more per man-year (including salary, facilities, and support), it is imperative that technical management insure that the money is spent in ways most likely to benefit the organization that is supporting the activity.

The time advantage that can be gained with an innovation by an industrial organization is of vital importance, since this advantage may determine the profitability of exploitation. One or two years is about all the time advantage a modern sponsor can expect out of the investment. This means that the development phases must occur rapidly once an idea is conceived, and that the idea or item must be capitalized on at the earliest practical time. This requires good coordination among the various segments of the organization and timely decisions all through the development phases. Such coordination and decision making can only occur through the presence of and proper use of the communication system, which is the heart and purpose of management controls.

There are many balancing and counterbalancing factors at work in a technical organization. An excess in one factor may be accomplished at the cost of a deficiency in others. Figure 1.7 graphically shows the problem presented by the paradox of control. With no control, the curve starts at a low value of useful productivity. It does not begin at zero, because even with no control whatever, technical workers would still come up with some useful results. As control increases, the productivity rises gradually until a critical point is reached. At this point, something occurs in the mind of the worker that convinces him or her that they are being regimented. Beyond this point, increased control causes frustration and a rapid drop in productivity. Further increases in the degree of control will result either in the worker seeking another position or in the worker compromising individualism and losing the

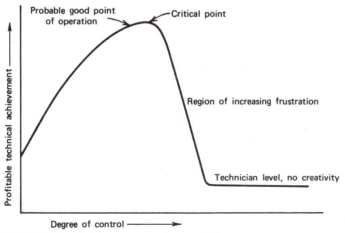

FIGURE 1.7   Achievement versus control.

creative urge, thereby reducing the level of work. It is evident that a certain degree of control is necessary, but overcontrol is suicidal.

The thing that further complicates the management problem, is that each individual in the organization has a different curve, just as each one has a different level of creative ability. What is excessive control for one individual is optimum control for another. Apparently the peak of the curve shifts with individuals in proportion to their creative capabilities; it shifts to the left as creativity increases and to the right as creativity decreases.

It is a demonstrated fact that a few individuals possess creative capability out of all proportion to their number. The distribution of intelligence in the population has been found to be normal. This is not the case with creativity, which is concentrated in a very small number of individuals. Shockley has made a careful study of this, using rate of publication as a measure of creativity. Figures 1.8 and 1.9 are reproduced from his report to demonstrate some of his findings. He found the same pattern (i.e., creativity centered in just a few members) in every laboratory he studied [9]. Tangerman estimates that perhaps 100 Americans are capable of doing basic research at the Nobel Prize level, and perhaps 1000 are capable of high-level innovation and discovery [10].

It is therefore the prime responsibility of management to recognize these highly creative individuals and match their natural inclinations to the requirements of the job. In most technical organizations there is a spectrum of work ranging from basic research to straight development. At the basic research end, control is difficult, and any breakthrough or useful result is still likely to have value, even though it is not quite on target or as planned. At the other end, control is mandatory with product or process development. Such projects must be completed on time and according to a schedule, or the development

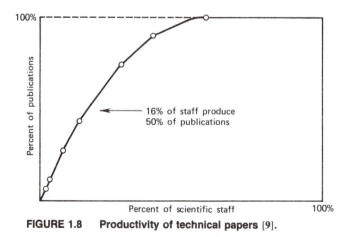

FIGURE 1.8   Productivity of technical papers [9].

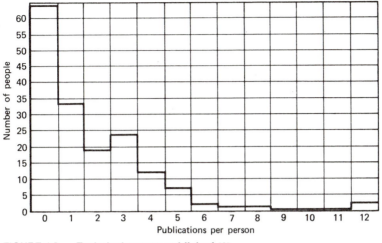

FIGURE 1.9   Technical papers published [9].

may be a total loss. It is clear that the degree of control necessary in the first case is minimal and that the opportunity for creativity is very great. In the case of the new or improved product or process development, the objective is accurately defined, constraints to conform to the definition are rigid, and less opportunity for creative thinking exists.

The degree of control and the level of creativity required for any project are *inversely* proportional. Furthermore, it is generally agreed that the individual's level of creative capability and the desire and need for freedom from rigid controls are *directly* proportional. Therefore, control and productivity are optimized when the individual's creative capabilities are matched to the demands of the project and when the minimum level of control necessary to assure profitable achievement is exercised. This theory is sound but over-simplified. Creative requirements and creative capabilities are presently difficult, if not impossible, to assess. Therefore technical worker versus manager conflicts will unfortunately arise.

Follett states that such conflicts may be resolved by three means: domination, compromise, or integration [7]. If they are settled by domination, only one side gets what it wants; if they are settled by compromise, neither side is wholly satisfied; and if they are settled by integration, each side may get what it wants. The integrative process or approach requires the abolition of the "either-or" psychology prevalent in most conflicts (i.e., the attitude that there are only two alternatives). In its place it substitutes the belief that by proper study and the cooperation of the parties in conflict, a solution may be found that is mutually advantageous and beneficial. Providing for the integration of the technical worker versus manager conflicts, which will result from the paradox of control, is the only feasible way to optimize our management controls.

1.11 The Dilemma of Evaluation

Two aspects of the technical function's activities make decision making particularly difficult. The first (already mentioned) is the uncertain outcome of individual projects; this ranges from the question of the cost and time required for a project or program to be successful to the question of whether it will prove to be successful at all. The second is the difficulty, even after a project has been "successfully" completed, of telling just how successful it has been and how much of the success is due to the efforts of the technical organization itself. The output of a technical organization falls into two categories.

1. *The Direct Products—Information.* This includes all of the new knowledge, formulations, patent applications, operating instructions, product specifications, advice, diagnosis of difficulties, service reports, and other information turned out in accordance with the objectives of the technical program. This is an intermediate step in the accomplishment of tangible results.
2. *The Indirect Products—Tangible Results.* Few technical departments have the direct opportunity to bring about tangible results such as increased revenues, decreased costs, and increased profits. These ultimate results are brought about by other organization activities, supported by the information that is provided by the technical group. Although the ultimate success of engineering and research thus depends heavily on the quality and usefulness of the technical findings, it also depends on the ability and willingness of the rest of the organization to apply the supplied information.

This situation leads to the dilemma that confronts many technical groups. The direct product of the group is information, but management is interested in evaluating its tangible results. However, it is difficult to attribute results to the technical function on a logical and equitable basis. Having a *potentially* useful result, such as a new product design or new information from the technical organization, does not assure a payoff for the parent organization. The influences of the comptroller, production engineering, manufacturing, and marketing can still make or break the end results. There are numerous and well-known instances of very poor or marginal products developing into tremendous financial successes because of brilliant exploitation and of financial disaster of technically sound and brilliantly conceived products that have been poorly commercialized.

1.12   Factors To Be Controlled

The basic purpose of management controls is to insure that the organization is working toward the fulfillment of the goals set up by management. Without these controls, there is no way of ascertaining if persons in the group are working toward the objectives of the organization or if they are even aware of these objectives. The effective control of technology entails securing maximum results from minimum dollar expenditures.

As pointed out earlier, since the major product of the technical group is primarily ideas—new concepts, designs, or evaluations—the major productive force is the mind of the technical worker. The salary of the engineer or scientist constitutes better than 50 percent of the cost of pursuing technical activities. It is therefore obvious that the primary factor that we must control is the utilization of the professional's time.

Most organizations strive to effect this control through an annual budget, current approval of individual projects, or both. It is literally impossible to control *costs*. One can only control the actions of persons who incur costs. On the other hand, control of projects without relationship to the costs being incurred provides no method of evaluating the profitability of the effort. For these reasons, the only adequate approach seems to be a control system oriented from both a budget and manpower utilization approach. In order to insure maximum profitable achievement, the control system must provide the means of continually evaluating the progress and value of the projects being pursued against the costs being incurred.

There are undoubtedly many factors that contribute to or influence the value of technical activities. Many of these, no doubt, are not even recognized, or we are at best only dimly aware of them. Yet it is possible to identify the prime considerations that should affect project selection and control. The following ones come to mind immediately.

Cost. Money, as just discussed, is one of the limited resources, even for a government organization, and is also a measure that everyone understands. Since cost consciousness permeates the entire economic structure, there can be no question that cost does, and must, play a role in the planning of technical operations. Cost—either initial investment or operating—must be viewed as a significant factor in project selection.

Manpower. Two aspects are involved here. First, the American people attach considerable value to human life. Substantial expense will be incurred to minimize waste of life, whether of consumers, workers, military personnel in war, or astronauts in peaceful exploration of space. Therefore costs may be subordinated to safety and reliability. Second, manpower is also a limited resource, especially highly trained, creative persons. In the face of such a limitation, conservation of trained manpower for use only where critically needed is an important factor.

Time. The importance of time was discussed in detail earlier. But time has another significant aspect to some government organizations. The decisive results that may accompany the employment of a new military weapon against an enemy whose defense is ineffective against it are well recognized. Also, to avert disaster, time can be crucial in the development of countermeasures, both in the military sphere and in the area of public health and welfare. Even in the area of peaceful exploration of space, time has great significance. No prestige or propaganda advantage is accrued by those who are in second place; this was demonstrated well by the impact of the launching of the first space satellites. For these reasons, and for the reasons discussed earlier, time may overshadow both cost and manpower.

Need. This factor is akin to time in that the need for an item becomes acute where limited time is available to get it. But need here is meant to be a strong motivation in its own right. Need is a concept different from cost, manpower, and time. It is a measure of how badly something is wanted, for whatever reason. Need is satisfied, cost is incurred. But the cost in personnel, time, and dollars may indicate that the price is too high, that the need is overvalued. Thus, it is believed that need is a consideration along with the other three.

These four factors seem to be the fundamental parts of any measure of effectiveness that may be applied to technical operations. The relative weights to be assigned will change from one situation to another but, in almost every case, one factor will generally overshadow the others and, in a sense, become the predominant consideration. Therefore any methodology or system for selecting, evaluating, or controlling projects on the basis of only one of these factors is not sufficient.

1.13 The Management of Uncertainty

The preceding sections stated that the manager of any technical function is faced with many uncertainties. The nature and scope of these uncertainties distinguish the management of technical functions from the management of operational functions. Some of them deal with internal relationships; others deal with external ones. We can perhaps categorize these uncertainties as (1) threat, (2) technical, (3) internal programs, and (4) external relationships.

Threat uncertainties are the physical and performance characteristics that the product or system must have to accomplish its purpose. What do we need to meet the needs of the parent organization? Here we must also be concerned about the actions of competitors. What new processes, products, and systems are they developing? Can our group and products compete effectively in terms of cost and performance? What is the nature of the environment in which we will be competing in the future? What counteractions can or will the competition take?

Technical uncertainties determine the degree of technological advancement necessary to accomplish the performance goals within the cost and schedule constraints. Here we are concerned with whether we have really anticipated all of the technical problems and really understand the current state of the art. It involves the analysis of where technical problems will arise and how they can be surmounted. Can we count on suppliers to meet our specifications on time and for the cost we have allocated? Are other organizations pursuing work that will overcome our problems in time? Is there a faster, cheaper way to accomplish a task or function?

Internal program uncertainties originate within the group as a result of the way it is organized, planned, and managed. It includes questions such as the reliability of the technical, cost, and schedule estimates. We are also concerned with questions of how we can organize to minimize areas of high risk. For example, should we institute parallel projects in certain areas? How much internal checking should we institute? How can we assure that problems are exposed instead of being hidden? Who can be counted on to get the job done? What trade-offs can we make to reduce the uncertainties?

External uncertainties are outside the immediate purview of the manager, but they can have an impact on the successful accomplishments of the group. This area of uncertainty deals with questions of availability of resources and support, relationships with supervisors and customers, and competing projects in other organizations. Not all of the factors needed for a successful project are under the control of the manager. Funds can be cut off or reduced, customers can change their minds, and other groups can object that they should have the responsibility.

All of these uncertainties exist in the technical manager's environment. They must be dealt with and minimized if success is to be achieved. In this chapter, we cursorily explored the environment faced by the modern manager of a technical function. In the following chapters we will explore some of the means for minimizing and controlling these uncertainties.

References

---

1. Barnard, C. I., *The Functions of the Executive,* Harvard University Press, Cambridge, Mass., 1960 p. 217.
2. Burkholder, T., "About the Products—I.R. 100," *Industrial Research,* 19 (10), October 1977, pp. 39–40.

3. Danilov, V. J., "America's Greatest Discoveries, Inventions, and Innovations," *Industrial Research, 18* (12), November 1976, pp. 21−24.

4. Sarbin, T. R., and V. L. Allen, "Role Theory," *The Handbook of Social Psychology,* Vol. 1, 2nd ed., G. Lindzey and E. A. Aronson, Editors, Addison-Wesley, Reading, Mass., 1968, pp. 488−567.

5. Gerstenfeld, A., "A Study of Successful Projects, Unsuccessful Projects, and Projects in Process in West Germany," *IEEE Transactions on Engineering Management, EM-23* (3), August 1976, pp. 116−123.

6. Jones, Robert R., "Technology Triumphs," *Industrial Research, 18* (12), November 1976, pp. 10−16.

7. Metcalf, H. C., and L. Urwick, Editors, *Dynamic Administration—The Collected Papers of Mary Parker Follett,* Harper & Bros., New York, 1940.

8. Mintzberg, H., "Managerial Work; Analysis from Observation," *Management Science, 18* (2), October 1971, pp. B97−B110.

9. Shockley, W., "On the Statistics of Individual Variations of Productivity in Research Laboratories," *Proceedings of the IRE, 45* (3), March 1957, p. 281.

10. Tangerman, E. J., "Creativity . . . the Facts Behind the Fad," *Product Engineering, 30* (34), August 24, 1959.

11. Vanderbilt, B. M., "America's First R and D Center," *Industrial Research, 18* (12), November 1976, pp. 27−31.

──────────────────── **Discussion Questions** ────────────────────

1. It is often said that management is the art of getting things done through people. Is this an adequate definition?
2. Is there a difference between management theory and management principles?
3. Discuss the terms manager, leader, and decision maker. Are they the same?
4. Is there a difference between the functions of management and the managerial roles?
5. Does the management of a technical group require different skills and approaches from the management of:
   (a) An advertising department?
   (b) A sales group?
   (c) A personnel department?
6. Is management an art or a science?
7. Discuss how the various management functions are interrelated.

──────────────────── **Case Study I** ────────────────────

A DAY AT SEAGRAVES

Dr. David Pope arrived at his office at 8:10 A.M. in a foul mood. One of his children had kept him up half the night with the flu. He was usually able to spend a couple of hours in the evening at home reading reports from his department heads, but the sick child had precluded that last night. His secretary greeted him cheerily and handed him three phone messages that had come in already.

Dr. Pope was the director of engineering for the Seagraves Corporation. Two of the messages were marked urgent; he decided to return George Jamison's call first. Jamison was the head of plant engineering. "Dave, we had a bad fire at the North Plant last night. It started in the window air conditioner checkout line. Looks like they'll be out at least a couple of weeks unless I can work my people overtime," reported Jamison. After some discussion, Pope authorized Jamison to work as much overtime as necessary to get the line going again. Jamison promised to keep Pope posted on progress. Next Pope called Dr. John Bush, the director of research and development.

BUSH: Thanks for returning my call so promptly, David. I was talking to Pat Wright at a cocktail party last night, and he told me that there is going to be trouble at the new products committee meeting tomorrow morning. Seems Sherry Smith has decided that our waste treatment plant is inadequate to handle the additional load from the degreasers needed for the new refrigerator line. I knew we'd have nothing but trouble putting a consumer advocate on the committee.

POPE: What brought about her concern?

BUSH: Seems she read an article about river pollution and went down and talked to one of the operators at the treatment plant.

POPE: Okay, John, don't worry. I'll bring a copy of that study Jamison's people did. That ought to satisfy everyone's concerns. Maybe you should call on me at some appropriate point in your presentation, and I'll say a few words in this regard.

BUSH: Great. I'm sure glad I went to that party and ran into Wright. That would have been a nasty shock to have gotten hit cold.

As he hangs up, Janice, his secretary, enters and reminds him of his 10 o'clock appointment and his intention to call the company patent attorney.

JANICE: Here's the mail. Nothing much except a budget request from industrial engineering and a research proposal from materials engineering. Oh, yes, Joe Land stopped by and wants to see you when you're free. He said it was something to do with that new engineer he wants to hire. I almost forgot; the flight you wanted to Washington was booked, so I put you on the 4 P.M. flight on the tenth.

Pope quickly went through the mail. He signed without reading the proposal from the materials group to a government agency; dictated on his recorder a negative reply to an invitation to speak to a regional meeting of ASPE, on the excuse that he would be out of town; noted on his appointment calendar the date of the United Way (of which he was a member) board meeting; and read the request from the Industrial Engineering Department for a new minicomputer and made some notes on it requesting clarification of certain portions and a further justification for why they could not use the company's CDC 7600 computer.

It was now 9:15; he called Janice in and asked: "Who is this meeting at 10 o'clock with?" Once told, he asks Janice to arrange for his administrative assistant to be present at the meeting. He also told her to call Joe Land and tell him to come on up. Picking up the phone, he returns the call of George Wallace, the general sales manager. Wallace's secretary says he is out of the office but will call back. As Pope hangs up, Joe Land enters his office. For the next 30 minutes they discuss the pros and cons of two applicants who have been interviewed for a lead engineer's job. They finally agree on one of the applicants, and Pope tells Land to get together with personnel on the salary to be offered but to check with him first before the letter of offer is sent.

At 10:05 the two management consultants hired by the president and Pope's assistant are ushered into his office. The consultants explain that they have been hired to design a formal uniform wage and salary plan. The next 1 hour and 45 minutes are spent discussing the general form of such a plan and the inputs that will be needed from the engineering division. Pope assigns his assistant to work with them and instructs him to introduce the consultants to the department heads. It is agreed that Pope will first discuss the situation with his department heads at the Friday staff meeting and that the consultants can start the next Monday.

As his visitors leave, his secretary buzzes Pope for a phone call. It is George Wallace, and they decide to meet in the executive dining room for lunch. During lunch, Wallace complains that customer service engineering is not being responsive to his field representatives. He claims that it is sometimes a week before engineering comes back with an answer to customer complaints. Pope asks Wallace to send him a few specific documented instances and promises to look into it. He then tells Wallace about his phone call from John Bush and asks for strong support from sales in the new product committee meeting the next day. Wallace assures Pope that sales wants the new refrigerator line as much as anyone and that R&D and engineering can count on his strong support.

As Pope returns to his office from lunch at 1:30, he notices that four engineers are still playing bridge in one of the laboratories. He makes a note to himself to remind the department heads at the Friday staff meeting to be sure their people are not taking more than an hour for lunch. As he gets to his office, the personnel director and Glen Sanford are waiting for him. "Well, Glen, what are you going to do with all yor free time after you leave us?" queries Pope. After some discussion of Sanford's farming plans, he is presented with a plaque commemorating 30 years of service as a model maker with the organization.

At 2 o'clock, the president's secretary calls to ask Pope to come to a 2:30 meeting to discuss next year's budget. As he walks toward the president's suite, he is stopped in the hall by Oscar Ford, the head of quality control (whose morning phone call he had not returned). Ford explained that while the room air conditioner line was down because of the fire, he wanted to redesign the final inspection station, but he would need the help of two industrial engineers full time for a week. He further explained that Bill Binford, head of industrial engineering, had confirmed that he had the available personnel, but needed Pope's approval, since this was a new project. Pope gave his okay and made a note to himself to tell the department heads that they did not need his concurrence on such little projects. "I probably should set some guidelines," he thought to himself.

The meeting in the president's office lasted until 5:30 P.M. Corporate Planning explained the guidelines and timetable for preparing the budget requests for next year. Pope had been disturbed when given the guideline of an overall increase of 10 percent for engineering. Since the cost of living had gone up 9 percent during the past 12 months, he had hoped to be able to grant an across-the-board increase of at least that much plus merit increases. He had requested a meeting with the president and comptroller to discuss the matter, and it had been set up for 2 P.M. the next day.

Upon arriving back at his office, he immediately phoned his wife. She told him the doctor had put their daughter to bed for 3 days and prescribed some medicine. Because of this, she informed him, he would have to go to the executive vice president's cocktail party by himself. Pope groaned. He hated cocktail parties anyway, but they were even worse when he was alone. At least if his wife was there, he could make the excuse that he had to look after her if he got into a boring or embarrassing conversation. To make matters worse, the party meant he would not be able to catch up on reading reports. "Well, maybe I can get caught up tomorrow," he thought to himself.

As he was leaving the building at 6:30 P.M., the security guard smiled at him and said, "Have a good day, Dr. Pope?" Smiling wearily, Pope replied, "Just about like usual. Just about like usual."

Case Study Discussion Questions

1. Can you classify each of Dr. Pope's activities as to role or function?
2. How much of his time expenditure was dictated or controlled by others?

CHAPTER 2 planning

2.1 Planning Defined

It is impossible to overemphasize the importance of good planning to the success of any organization. Planning provides direction and focus to the group's activities and results in the:

1. Clarification of purpose.
2. Achievement of better communication.
3. Proper allocation of resources.
4. Establishment of a basis of control.
5. Advance recognition of problems.
6. Establishment of a basis for diagnosis.
7. Avoidance of wasted or duplicated effort.

Planning precedes all other management functions. In order to organize group activities, planning must be done first. To direct, motivate, or integrate, the manager must first plan.

The terms forecasting and planning are often used synonymously, but in this chapter they will be given different meanings. We will use the term *forecasting* to mean prediction—the act of anticipating future events in some formal and quantitative way. This entails both the consideration of which future events or states are possible, what their probability of occurrence is, and which are most desirable. Once the future possible events or states have been defined and evaluated, goals for the organization can be formulated and plans for achieving the goals prepared. *Planning* basically consists of deciding in advance what to do, how to do it, where to do it, when to do it, and who should do it. It involves strategic (long-range) planning, tactical (intermediate-range) planning, and planning for operational control.

A number of developments are forcing technical managers to plan 5, 10, or even 20 years ahead. These include:

1. The increasing rate of technological change.
2. The increasing time span that separates beginning a task and reaping the benefits.
3. The increasing cost of facilities, equipment, and specialized personnel.
4. Decisions on the commitment of time and money tend to be inflexible. Decisions made at one stage may preclude various options later.
5. Intense worldwide competition.

Technological change is greatly shortening the life cycle of products to the point where an organization must continually plan for new or improved products and services in order to survive. A single new development may propel a firm to great success or to failure and bankruptcy. For a single-product firm or one that receives most of its revenue from only one of its products or services, an unforeseen technological innovation can be devastating. The shortening of the life cycle of products, coupled with rapid technological change, requires quicker management decision making and much more careful planning. It is less and less possible to watch what others are doing and then imitate them. By the time the imitators get into the field, the product use may be reaching the saturation stage or approaching the end of its life cycle.

Another difficulty is introduced by the time lag between the completion of an engineering or research project and its commercial introduction or operational use. Investigations such as the TRACES study [24] and Project Hindsight [20] have shown that the median time lag between completion of a feasibility demonstration and application was about 6 years. This time lag presents a serious problem to the technical manager, who must first recognize the median lag of 6 years between the end of a successful project and the operational use of the result and then add to this the time to carry out the project; this will typically be about 3 years (see Section 1.2). Thus a decision to initiate immediately a project must be based on estimates of the problems that will exist 9 years in the future.

Analysis of recent technological change clearly identifies two related phenomena of great importance to the technical manager's planning. One is the increasing competition from foreign countries and the application of foreign technology in the process and product areas. The other is the erosion (often the disappearance) of traditional industry and product boundaries. Some of the most significant developments affecting both production and marketing are likely to be spawned by companies operating in other areas of technology.

One of the main purposes of long-range planning is to insure that the organization replaces itself instead of waiting for someone else to replace it. But a long-range plan is also necessary to insure that there will be time to take the steps needed to provide new products or services or to meet the increased demand for an old one. Every technical manager is faced with the same basic problem—how to obtain the maximum benefit from available resources. In every technical group there are more apparently desirable projects than resources available to pursue them. The resources of time, money, facilities, equipment and, most important, competent, creative personnel are always limited. The apparently desirable projects on which to expend them are not.

We are faced with a dilemma. Management must commit its available resources so as to optimize the payoff, but the outcome and required resources for individual projects are unknown and unpredictable. If management does not know for sure what the outcome of each project will be, how can it assure optimum utilization of resources? The answer, of course, is that they cannot. But, by having a formal program for technological forecasting, needs identification, project selection, and program planning, they can help to assure that they are doing as well as possible.

2.2 Organizational Goals

Before any kind of planning for the technical activities can occur, the parent organization should provide answers to several questions, which will define the goals of the technical groups. For example, does the parent organization want to be:

1. A creative technological leader, the first in the industry to discover, develop, and market new products at the leading edge of a dynamic technological area?
2. An early imitator and adapter of the successful innovations of the industry's creative leader?
3. A low-price, mass producer of established products and services, thus avoiding the high risks of innovation while going for the limited risks of high-volume, low-price imitation?

Each of these approaches is valid, although they will certainly lead to different corporate images and strategies. The approach that is chosen will have a direct and significant effect on the type of planning required and the kind of investment in product, process, and market research, the organization structure, the type of technical personnel hired, etc.

Equally important is the need for management to decide what our basic business is. Among the questions to be answered are:

1. Is our basic business to be narrowly or broadly defined? For example, are we a steel company or a materials company, a petroleum company or an energy company, a business machine company or a communications company?
2. Are we concerned with the sale of a product or service, or are we interested in the delivery of a complete system of values to the customer? For example, should an airline market packaged vacations; should a computer hardware company market software for integrated management information systems?
3. Are we interested in diversification? If so, should it be:
    (a) Unrelated or accidently related companies, products, or services anchored to a central core of strong management competence?
    (b) Aimed at exploiting complementary technologies, production resources, or market systems?
    (c) Aimed at balancing high- and low-risk ventures, fluctuating and stable industries, or cyclical and seasonal variations?
    (d) Aimed at vertical integration to gain control of raw materials, supplies, etc.?

Again, the answers to these questions are vital to good planning and will have a significant effect on the types of projects undertaken by the technical groups. If these questions are not answered early, a great deal of the planning effort will be misdirected and wasted.

In addition to answering questions related to the basic attitude toward technological innovation and defining the basic area of activity, numerous decisions related to production will also affect planning. Some of these critical trade-offs have been identified by Skinner [22] and are shown in Table 2.1.

TABLE 2.1   Typical Trade-Offs Possible

Decision	Alternatives
Span of process	Make or buy
Plant size	One big plant or several small ones
Equipment	General purpose or special purpose
Tooling	Temporary minimum or production tooling
Quality control	High reliability or low costs
Design stability	Frozen design or many engineering change orders
Job specialization	Highly specialized or unskilled
Size of product line	Many customer specials or fixed

As Skinner points out, the answers to some of these questions can limit a corporation's strategic options by locking it to facilities, equipment, personnel, policies, and controls that may take years to turn around.

2.3 The Phases of Planning

The manager concerned with technical programs must plan for five components: major technical areas, facilities, specific projects, personnel, and funding. All of these components strongly interact and cannot be considered in isolation. A more or less logical plan of events is depicted in Figure 2.1; however, it is important to realize the mutual dependence and interaction among the components that require iteration back and forth in order to obtain a consistent set of plans that matches the goals and constraints.

Starting with the basic socioeconomic purpose of the parent organization and the values of the top executives, we must first set the organizational goals of the technical group. Any technical group that conducts research or development must select a limited number of technical areas in which it wishes to achieve a high level of competence. Building up such competence is an expensive proposition and takes time, since facilities must be built or bought, people hired, and experience gained. Moreover, once a high level of competence is obtained, it cannot be terminated quickly except by scrapping a large

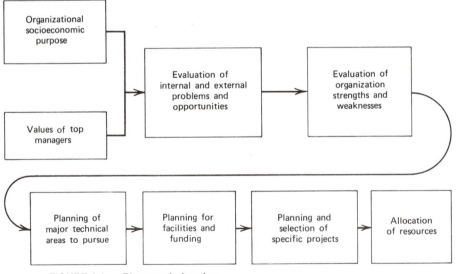

FIGURE 2.1   Phases of planning.

investment in people and facilities. The decision to enter a major technical area involves a long-term commitment.

Because the choice of a major technical area does involve a long-term commitment, it must be based on the goals of the parent organization. However, the establishment of these goals cannot be separated from an evaluation of the external and internal strengths and weaknesses. Examination of the problems and opportunities can be accomplished through technological forecasting and needs research. Both of these areas will be discussed in more detail in succeeding sections. Even if the goals of the parent organization remain constant, a change in technology may require a change in the major areas of pursuit (i.e., a new technology may be needed to achieve an old goal).

The facilities and equipment used by technical groups tend to be one of a kind and highly specialized. If a group is going to be working at the frontier of knowledge and the state of the art, the special equipment it will need is generally not available as a standard item. In addition to special equipment, there may also be a need for construction of special buildings or rooms peculiar to the needs of a specific group. These might include facilities such as rooms with special atmospheres, anechoic chambers, and rooms that are shielded from electromagnetic radiation.

If a group is going to work in some major technical area, it must expect that special facilities and equipment to work in that area will have to be built or bought especially for that purpose. The manager must thus allow adequate lead time for ordering, fabrication, and construction of the required facilities and equipment. In some cases it may even be necessary to undertake a R&D project for the equipment or facilities design. If this is the case, even more lead time will be required. The technical manager must plan well ahead of time for the facilities and equipment needed to carry out the projects appropriate to meet the goals of the organization.

Since it is not possible simply to "work" in some general technological area, specific projects must be planned. Each project must have its own goals, stated in terms of end result desired, time to complete, and resources to be expended. The objective of the problem-oriented projects will be to produce a material, process, device, technique, procedure, or understanding that solves a specific problem. Further discussion of this important aspect of planning is deferred until Chapter 8.

In one sense, funding considerations should be considered prior to the others, since funds available constrain everything else. It is obvious that the number of major technical areas pursued, the extent and type of facilities built, and the number of projects started will all depend on the funds available. On the other hand, it is also true that the funds made available should come as a result of the previous planning. Technical programs are not planned simply to expend the money available. They exist for specific purposes, to meet the goals of the parent organization. Therefore, ideally, we would like to plan what should be done and what it would take to do it and *then* secure the necessary funding.

Unfortunately, the parent organization may not have sufficient funds available because of other demands. Then the manager must decide if funding might be secured from other sources, such as government contracts, etc. Since the technical group does not generate its own funds and is totally dependent on selling its efforts either to its parent or some other organization, careful planning and skillful sales techniques are required of the manager. The technical manager must be able to demonstrate a clear connection between the goals of the solicited sponsor and the activities of the technical group. If the program needed to achieve the goals of the parent organization cannot be funded fully, the goals and plans themselves must be reduced to be compatible with what funding is available.

We will discuss some of the problems associated with staff planning, such as recruiting and career development, in Chapter 4. Recruiting involves bringing in people who have the skills required to pursue the planned programs. This means not only the skills needed in the immediate future, but also the skills that will be useful over a long period of time. Recruiting top-notch people who will continue to be valuable to the group requires having some idea of what the group will be doing 5 or 10 years from now.

Staff planning also entails striking a balance between recruiting people trained in narrow specialties that might be rendered obsolete by technological change and those whose background is broad enough to survive technological change but who might need specialized training in certain specific skills.

In Chapter 4 we will also discuss the problem of technical obsolescence of staff members. One of the responsibilities of the manager is career development, to assure that the professional staff does not become obsolete but stays abreast of work being done elsewhere. This presents the problem of deciding what new skills the engineers and scientists should acquire based on some idea of those with a high likelihood of being needed in the future.

Finally, the manager must face the fact that if technology changes drastically enough, some of the staff may not be capable of being retrained to work in the new areas. It may be necessary to purge the staff of people who are highly skilled in areas that are no longer needed and who cannot easily be retrained into new areas that are required. Early recognition of the problem and planning will allow an orderly cutoff of recruiting, phasing out of career development plans, and phased termination of such employees without a sudden, massive layoff.

Making plans and decisions about each of the factors discussed up to this point requires a good estimate of future needs and requirements. In the next section we will discuss the role of technological forecasting in providing the information needed to make such plans and decisions.

2.4 Technology Forecasting

Technology forecasting is the prediction of changes in the technical parameters, attributes, capabilities, or needs of an area of technology as a function of time. It involves the preparation of a statement about uncertain or unknown events that lie in the future. The main purpose of forecasting is to gain knowledge about uncertain future events that are important to our present decisions.

The basic justification for technological forecasting is to provide information for planning and guidance of decisions. Specifically, such forecasts should:

1. Identify technological limits.
2. Establish possible rates of progress.
3. Describe alternatives and possibilities.
4. Provide warning signals that present activities must change.

Technology forecasting is based on three premises. The first is that technological events and capabilities (meaning things such as speed, pounds per horsepower, tensile strength, etc.) seem to grow in an astonishingly orderly manner over time or through experience. The basic hypothesis is that there is a consistency or pattern in technological changes and that abrupt, major deviations, although extremely important when they occur, are not common. This consistency provides a basis for trend extrapolation from past data.

The second rationale is that technology responds to needs, to opportunities, and to the provision of resources. If these supporting forces can be identified, the technology change can be anticipated as a response to their pressure and support. There has been a growing willingness on the part of the American public to use national resources to support the technology that leads to desirable social goals. It is assumed that technology can and will respond to these needs and this commitment of resources.

A third premise or rationale of technology forecasting methods is that new technology can be anticipated by understanding the process of technological innovation (a process that takes time that is measured in years and decades). In other words, understanding the innovative process allows one to anticipate new applications that are made possible by current breakthroughs.

Managers must understand and recognize several characteristics of technology forecasts if they are to aid and not mislead. Among them are:

1. A key to realistic forecasting is the inclusion of the best available informed judgment and intuition and sound scientific methodology.
2. Forecasts are usually incorrect. Everyone recognizes this, but few really prepare to react to errors that inevitably arise.
3. Forecasts are less accurate the further into the future they are projected.
4. Forecasts should reflect the degree of uncertainty associated with them, there should be a range of possible values or a probability of occurence associated with each forecast.

Finally, any formal technology forecasting system should include and make provision for (1) gathering and evaluating pertinent information and data, (2) preparing the forecast, and (3) monitoring the performance of the forecasting system.

2.5 Forecasting Methods

Technological forecasting is used to predict future conditions and needs from a study of the past behavior of a number of contributing factors. The methods of technological forecasting can be used to predict developments in the areas of economic, sociological, and demographic change and to forecast changes in technology. There have been a number of comprehensive descriptions of the methods of technological forecasting; refer to them for a detailed description of the methodologies [1, 4, 17, 23].

Technological forecasting methodology has been structured into various classifications by different authors in the field. We will now discuss the most widely used types.

Persistence. This type of forecast assumes that what is happening now will continue indefinitely as it has been experienced in the immediate past. If technology moves on a fixed track, only upward, then the future will be like the past, only more so. It is really a form of nonforecasting, and this requires no procedural techniques or methodologies.

Trend Analysis. This type of forecasting assumes that future technology will have some sort of predictable relationship to past performance. The trend concept consists of modeling the past and then extending into the future assuming continuity. Various graphical and mathematical methods have been used to portray the trend of the existing data and to serve as a basis for extrapolation. Among those used are (1) linear regression, (2) multiple linear regression, (3) nonlinear regression, (4) moving averages, and (5) exponential smoothing [17].

Trend extrapolation is unreasonable if there is a natural limit to growth or if the conditions that originally produced the available trend are likely to change. It has been observed that a number of technology areas have displayed similar S-shaped growth curves, based on a slow start, exponential growth, and then a leveling off against some limit. Two mathematically defined growth curves widely used in technology forecasting are the Pearl curve and the Gompertz curve. The choice between these curves is partly subjective, based on an estimate of the goodness of fit of the past data [17]. Trend analysis techniques have fairly good accuracy for the short to medium term (up to 2 years).

Cyclic. These forecasting techniques are based on present data that are assumed to be cyclic in nature, such as seasonal variations. This type of forecast uses time-series analyses such as those of Box-Jenkins [3]. These techniques help to identify and explain any cyclic regularity or systematic variation in the series and general trends and growth rates. Since most technology is not cyclic (i.e., it does not retrogress), these techniques are most useful if the technical manager is interested in forecasting sales or demands for certain products or services.

Associative. If an area of technology changes through a blend of many logical factors of performance, cost, or usage of other materials or devices, forecasts of these other areas may be useful. For example, there may be a substitution effect (i.e., one technology that exhibits a relative improvement in performance over the conventional technology will eventually substitute for the technology of lesser performance).

Trend extrapolation, S curves, or envelope curves may be used in the development of curves that show the phasing out of an old technology and its replacement by the new technology (i.e., aluminum may replace steel, and plastics replace aluminum in certain areas). Techniques such as correlation may be useful in showing the relationship of one technology to another.

Analog. Technology forecasting by analog methodologies consists of using simulations of the technology area applications. A valid model of interactions enables the forecaster to vary components of the system in order to provide descriptions of future states. The forecaster must first generate the alternatives to be considered; then the simulation model is used to predict the impact or outcome. Simulation techniques are widely used for corporate planning [19] and national economy models. They have also been proposed for use in urban planning [9] and even world planning [18]. For an overview of the use of dynamic simulation models, see Blackman [2].

Normative Forecasting. Normative or goal-oriented forecasting assumes that the technology will materialize to fill needs. Therefore, the techniques used in normative forecasting are directed toward (1) the discovery and evaluation of future needs, (2) the evaluation of the importance or likelihood that a specific area of technology will help fill those needs, and (3) the likely direction in which a specific area of technology will develop in order to respond to the opportunity. Dathe [6] has argued that normative forecasts, in which the course of technological development is derived from social-economic demands and social objectives, will become of increasing importance.

The normative methods have their foundation in systems analysis techniques. They establish the elements of a system and examine the relationship between the elements, costs, capabilities, limitations, and bottlenecks. The objective is to determine the technological capability that will be required to carry out some function, based on a projected demand. Whether normative forecasting is forecasting or planning (although of concern to forecasting purists) is a moot point. It is an attempt to design technology to meet proposed future needs. Methodologies proposed for this type of forecasting include morphological analysis, social technological plans, mission flow analysis, and relevance trees [17].

Expert Opinion. This type of forecasting is sometimes classified as intuitive forecasting. It is the use of systematic assessment of informed opinion. It is commonly believed that a committee of experts is superior to the use of a single expert because (1) it integrates a broader range of skills and experience, and (2) the experts supposedly challenge each other to develop better reasoning and improved use of data. However, it is also recognized that face-to-face committee deliberations can be strongly influenced by interpersonal relationships such as undue persuasiveness, bandwagon effects, and authority figures.

In the early 1960s RAND researchers Dalkey and Helmer and their colleagues introduced the Delphi technique [5]. This technique is designed to improve the use of expert opinion through polling based on three conditions: anonymity, statistical display, and feedback of reasoning. The interrogation is conducted anonymously through formal questionnaires submitted to the individual members of the group of experts. The experts do not know who is on the panel or, at the very least, do not know what predictions and critiques are being made by each individual. The questions are formulated so that respondents reply with a numerical number, such as the year of occurrence or the predicted sales rate for a specific time period. The results are collected by a central authority, and the median and interquartile range (IQR) are computed. The results are fed back to the participants, who are urged to challenge or support predictions that fall outside the IQR and make new predictions. The new predictions, arguments, and counterarguments are circulated again to the participants, and another feedback cycle starts. This continues for several iterations until a consensus results or no further convergence takes place. The Delphi technique is very widely used in technological forecasting. An excellent example is its use by Goodyear Tire to forecast the future needs and performance of automobile tires [14].

Another form of intuitive or expert opinion forecasting is *futures creation*. The futures creation method uses the scenario technique to establish a basis for forecasting. The concept of using alternative scenarios for planning was popularized by Kahn in his writings about the future [13]. The method begins by construction of a number of different scenarios (situations or conditions) that represent possible future states. The forecaster uses scenarios that include significant differences (based on different assumptions) and that span a wide range of changes in economics, politics, and society and in technological areas. After several scenarios are defined, the technological implications of each are studied. The results are compared for similarities and differences and for desirability and likelihood of occurrence. An example of this type of forecasting is the U.S. Federal Aviation Administration's forecast [21] through the year 2000.

Even after some forecast of future events is prepared through the use of the Delphi technique or futures creation, it is difficult (but necessary) to consider explicitly the interrelationships among events that shape the future. In 1968 Gordon and Hayward proposed a technique they called the *cross impact matrix* [11] for considering these interrelationships. The events are listed in chronological order, across the top and down the left side of a matrix. Then the intersect boxes between two events are the interaction effect that would happen to the column event if the row event actually occurred. This can be expressed in terms of the increase or decrease in the probability of occurrence of the column event produced by the previous occurrence or nonoccurrence of the row event. What the analyst is looking for is the events that seem to be unaffected by other events and a feel for how the occurrence or nonoccurrence of a certain event is likely to affect other projected events. An example of this type of forecast is given by Enzer [8]

2.6 Environmental Monitoring

By this point, the reader may be wondering, "Can you really predict a technological breakthrough?" The answer is a qualified yes. Obviously, it is logically impossible to predict something that is truly unpredictable; however, technological breakthroughs are not unpredictable. They are always the result of a sequence of scientific discoveries and precursor inventions and events. A breakthrough is an advance in the level of performance of some device that significantly transcends the limits of prior devices. A strong case can be made for the view that inventions are inevitable and that breakthroughs almost come on schedule. Studies of the history of inventions have shown that in every case, precursor events could have been used to warn of the ultimate achievement. Therefore, it should be possible to set up a deliberate program of monitoring the environment for precursor events that can serve as signals of coming breakthroughs and significant changes.

This looking for signals has been termed "monitoring the environment" by Bright, a leader in developing the technique [4]. Monitoring consists of, or is based on, assessing events in being. Bright lists the following four activities as being necessary.

1. Searching the environment for signals that may be forerunners of significant technological, social, or economic change.
2. Identifying possible alternative consequences if these signals are significant and if the trends that they suggest continue.
3. Choosing the parameters, policies, events, and decisions that should be followed in order to verify the speed and direction of the technology.
4. Keeping management apprised of any events or trends that appear pertinent.

This monitoring is an attempt to identify technology changes in its early stage, recognize signals that will influence its direction, and follow the appropriate phenomena in order to determine the rate of progress and the true character of the impact. For example, Martino [16], in pointing out the importance of societal attitudes on technology, discussed the legislative banning of DDT and phosphates as follows.

In a nation as large as the U.S., such events do not happen overnight. There are almost always precursors indicating changes. For instance, the DDT ban was not a bolt out of the blue. At least as early as the publication of Rachel Carson's "Silent Spring," there were indications that a segment of the population was unhappy with DDT. Although this one signal was not proof a change was coming, it should have been a warning to watch for confirming signals. Was this book followed by similar books and articles? Did newspapers begin to play up fish kills? Did conservation groups begin to make demands for restrictions on DDT? Did politicians begin to take notice of this shift in public opinion?

All these signals, and more, would have been caught by a forecaster or decision-maker who was "monitoring the environment." He might not have been able to predict exactly when a ban would come, but should have been able to anticipate significant restrictions.

Similarly, the current concern about the overall environment did not develop overnight. A forecaster might not have predicted that phosphates specifically would be a target, but he could have predicted that the dumping of industrial wastes would become an issue.

Technological forecasters do not claim that monitoring will eliminate all surprises. There will continue to be details that will remain unpredictable, such as the opposition to phosphates rather than to some other chemicals. Nevertheless, systematic monitoring for signals can go a long way towards eliminating surprises.

As Martino points out, it is not just the technological innovations with which we must be concerned, but the economic, societal, and demographic spheres as well. Forecasting of social and demographic trends covers topics such as changing social structure (including racial and ethnic components), the evolution of living patterns, and shifting values and priorities (e.g., shifts between work and leisure time and between risk and security). Political forecasting includes predicting the shifting boundary between the private and public sectors of the economy, increasing government regulation, and using governmental incentives to produce change. A wide variety of sources must be monitored and interpreted for clues of important changes. Sources of such evidence are: (1) trade journals; (2) technical conferences and journals; (3) patents granted; (4) salespeople's field reports; (5) financial journals and newspapers; (6) speeches and testimony before Congress; (7) government requests for proposals; (8) nonfiction books that receive a lot of attention; (9) TV documentaries and newscasts; (10) census data; and (11) newspapers and popular magazines.

The output of basic research laboratories and universities is an obvious source to monitor, but one must know what evidence to seek. A new reaction or chemical or a better understanding of some phenomenon may point to a new product or a new way of making an old one. Likewise, one should watch for inventions or discoveries that did not quite work or whose performance is now too low to be competitive but that might be improved. In many cases the successful implementation of an innovative process or product that did not quite work or was not yet competitive merely awaits a single advance in some other field. For example, the transistor was patented twice in the 1930s, but the devices that were patented did not work because materials of the required "impurity" were not yet available. The first commercialization appeared in 1954. If forecasters detect such a process or product, which has a large potential impact if it is made to work, the question becomes, "What would it take to make it work?" The answer tells forecasters what technological areas to monitor or watch.

One very important source of environmental monitoring is sales or field service personnel who are in contact with customers. Remember that these customers are also in contact with your competitors, and a casual comment such as "Are you all working on a . . .?" or "When will you have a . . . available?" may well be precipitated by knowledge that another group is working on such a product or process. It is very important that field personnel be encouraged and constantly reminded to keep a sharp watch on the competition and report any indications of potentially detrimental activity.

2.7 Pitfalls in Forecasting

Since hindsight is almost always $20-20$ and it is easy to be a Monday morning quarterback, it is useful to consider briefly common errors of past forecasting efforts. Probably the most common error is the lack of imagination, by failing to see the convergence or impact of the interaction of several technological advances in diverse areas. A common failure of forecasters is to ignore developments in other fields and countries. Most of the major breakthroughs occur through the impingement of one technology on another, and they are often brought about by groups outside of the current industry.

A second major error derives from the failure of forecasters to recognize the important influence that political, social, economic, and demographic changes often have on technology. Concerns about the environment, energy, consumer safety, and chemical additives to the food supply impact almost every industry and organization. Failure to consider such concerns can lead to gross errors in forecasts and unpleasant surprises. Such concerns usually lead to restrictive legislation, changes in funding priorities, and major shifts of technologies.

A personal, vested interest in a particular way of doing things or satisfying a need can lead the forecaster to be blind to the obvious, inevitable truth. A prevailing psychological mental bias toward an existing environmental condition can excessively distort a forecast. Forecasters tend to predict what they would like to see happen, not what is most likely to occur. This is particularly true if a forecast projects the necessity of an unpleasant course of action.

Finally, there is the failure to recognize the importance of developments, particularly in their early stages. This is usually due to the acceptance of present trends as rigidly continuing and vested interests in the technology now in use. It is usually difficult to conceive that an area of technology that is currently in wide use might rapidly become obsolete, particularly if your organization is a leader and is in the forefront of that area of technology.

Technological forecasting can improve planning and decision making through clearer delineation of future technological opportunities and threats. Forecasts need not provide perfect information about the future. To be worthwhile, forecasts must simply allow a better-informed opinion than could be achieved without them. Since technological uncertainties are among the most important challenges facing managers today, forecasting must be an integral part of the planning function.

2.8 Needs Research

Once a technological forecast has been prepared, the next step in planning is to perform needs research. Figure 2.2 shows an overall view of the technical function planning process. The determination of the needs of the parent or-

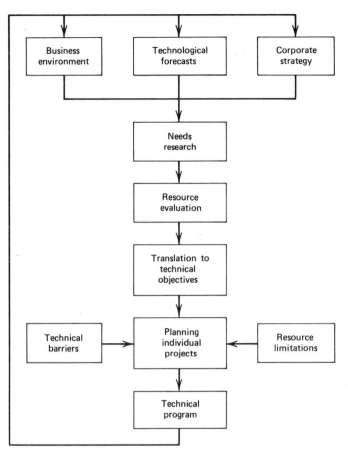

FIGURE 2.2   Technical planning process.

ganization and the assessment of the feasibility and desirability of meeting those needs constitute the strategic planning for the technical group. This strategic planning must be based on the assessment of the external environment, present and future technology, and the goals or objectives of the parent organization. Almost all technical organizations are predominantly information generators and processors. They take information from internal and external sources and produce information in the form of engineering design, specifications, reports, process instructions, etc. This process is usually planned and controlled in the form of individual projects.

Thus, needs research planning consists of:

1. Evaluation of possible alternative fields of endeavor that should be considered.

2. A search for project ideas to meet organizational objectives.
3. Screening of the ideas for technical feasibility.
4. Evaluation of the ideas from economic and desirability viewpoints.

The ideas for the conception of individual projects can arise from a wide spectrum of external and internal sources. Gerstenfeld [10] has suggested classifying projects as being either "demand pull" or "technical push." Demand pull can be defined as the idea originating from outside the technical group, as opposed to technical push, where the idea originates within the technical group. Contrary to previous beliefs, recent research indicates that the largest percent of successful projects result from demand pull.

In a study of 567 innovations, Marquis [15] found that 75 percent of the successful projects were stimulated by a market demand or production need. Only 20 percent arose from someone saying, "Aha, maybe we can find a use for this technical idea." Gerstenfeld [10] studied both successful and unsuccessful projects in the chemical, electronic, and automotive industries in West Germany. He found that of the successful projects, 73 percent resulted from demand pull and 27 percent from technical push. On the other hand, 80 percent of the unsuccessful projects originated from technical push. The danger and problem with technical push innovations seems to be that the innovators often misread the market or need.

Of perhaps even greater interest is the research indicating that most successful innovations have been conceived, prototyped, and first field-tested by users instead of by the manufacturer or commercializer. These studies deal with situations where the user of an innovation was different from the manufacturer. Von Hippel [25] found that 80 percent of the scientific instruments judged by users to have offered them a significant improvement were, in fact, invented, prototyped, and first field-tested by users of the instrument and not by the instrument manufacturer. In this study and several others, an innovation was considered to have been user dominated if the initial user:

1. Perceived the need for the innovation.
2. Conceived of a solution.
3. Built a prototype.
4. Proved the value of the prototype by using it.
5. Diffused the detailed information to other potential users and potential manufacturers.

Typically, the manufacturer's contribution was to:

1. Perform product engineering to improve appearance, reliability, convenience of operation, etc.

2. Manufacture, market, and sell the innovation.

When Von Hippel conducted another study on innovative process equipment for the semiconductor and electronic subassembly industries, he found that 67 percent were user devised, 21 percent were manufacturer devised, and 12 percent were jointly devised [26]. This agrees very closely with Hollander's [12] findings in the rayon production industry of 67 percent user devised, 33 percent joint devised, and 0 percent equipment manufacturer devised. Finally, Enos [7] studied the petroleum refining industry and found that 42 percent of the process innovations were user devised, 42 percent were jointly devised, and only 6 percent were equipment manufacturer devised. Apparently there is still great truth in the saying ''Necessity is the mother of invention.''

Thus we can see very clearly that a technical group cannot afford to depend on themselves alone for new project ideas. A major problem is how to find ideas created by others, both recorded and unrecorded. To achieve this goal, the group must search among its employees, its customers, and other outside sources, foreign and domestic. This is where environmental monitoring (as discussed in Section 2.6) again becomes critical to the well-being of the technical group and its parent organization.

2.9 Internal Sources of Ideas

Very few technical groups make a systematic effort to seek ideas for new or improved processes and products from all employees of the company. Employee suggestion systems are generally ineffective and are not really designed to turn up the type of project ideas we are seeking. In the following sections we will discuss some of the more obvious internal sources of ideas.

Sales Department.   Sales personnel are in a unique position to assess market needs. They have numerous opportunities to talk to customers about new applications of existing equipment, modifications that the customer feels should be made, and innovative solutions that the customer has developed for problems. Some companies ask each salesperson to visit a specified number of customers each year and work through a questionnaire specifically designed to discover needs for improvements in existing products and new product ideas. It has been found that the very fact that a company is interested in the ideas and suggestions of a customer creates a great deal of goodwill and many new ideas. It is also suggested that there be a specific place on each salesperson's report form for new ideas, suggestions, customer complaints, and reports on competitors' activities. All such questionnaires and reports should be sent to the technical planning group for careful evaluation.

Service Department. Company service people are also intimately in contact with customers and users. Almost all of their work deals with correcting weaknesses in the product. They also hear the customers' complaints about convenience, safety, maintainability, etc. Thus they are often in a position to suggest the need for modifications or improvements. Another excellent source is a monitoring of the frequency of different types of repairs, failures, etc. The service personnel are also in a unique position to discover or observe an adaptation of a company's product by an ingenious user to fit a peculiar operating condition or job requirement. Such adaptations may suggest new markets or the need for new products. Again, it is suggested that there be a formal mechanism for querying service personnel on a systematic basis and that a special place be provided on the service report to list unusual uses or applications of the company's products.

Credit and Collection Departments. This group is usually not even considered or consulted when looking for new ideas. A significant number of a firm's delinquent accounts derive from perceived deficiencies in a company's products. Customer complaints explaining why a bill is not being paid provide an excellent source of ideas for improved and new products. Such complaints are usually sent to the sales and service departments, but the technical planning group also must be aware of them.

Manufacturing. An obvious source of ideas are the people engaged in the manufacture and inspection of products. Some technical groups have specific people whose job it is to walk around the manufacturing facility, talking to people and seeking out problem areas and new ideas. Things they should be looking for are: (1) what safety devices are needed; (2) what new equipment, gadget, or device the worker would like to see developed to make the work easier; (3) what operations seem unnecessarily difficult or time consuming; (4) what equipment is not performing correctly; (5) what the most expensive operations or materials are; and (6) what new or innovative solutions the employees have devised that solve particular problems.

If properly approached and motivated, *every* employee is a potential source of good ideas. The technical manager should seek out the creative individuals throughout the organization, in all departments and at all levels. One way to do this is by polling employees as to who they think are the most creative among their fellow employees. Once identified, they should be encouraged, motivated, and stimulated to participate in the generation of new ideas. Creative, innovative people with ideas for new products, new processes, or ways to improve old products and processes are scattered throughout every organization. The challenge to management is to find them and then remove the bureaucratic organizational obstacles that dry up and discourage new ideas.

2.10 External Sources of Ideas

As indicated in Section 2.8, there is strong evidence that a large proportion of products and processes are invented by user organizations and are then commercialized and manufactured by other groups. Thus the constant search of external sources for project ideas is mandatory and should not be left to chance. Section 2.6 mentioned that the technical group should keep a constant watch on (1) technical and trade conferences and journals, (2) patents granted (both foreign and domestic), (3) output from university and nonprofit research groups, and (4) government reports.

Since the federal government sponsors a major portion of the R&D done in this country, it obviously controls an increasing number of patents. In general, the government is eager to see these patents used, although an exclusive license cannot usually be granted. The U.S. government has set up a number of mechanisms to aid in the transference of its technology to industry. For example, the National Aeronautics and Space Administration (NASA) has the Office of Technical Utilization to help speed their developments into industrial applications. Likewise, the Commerce Department's Office of Technical Services and Small Business Administration provide several publications and services to help make information about available government patents readily accessible.

Another lucrative source (although much harder to tap) is other industrial firms that have patented products or processes outside the area of their normal or desired sphere of operation. A research group will often come up with a new idea for a product or process that, for various reasons, the parent organization does not or cannot exploit. The companies holding these patents may be perfectly willing and even eager to license others to use them, since this allows them to recover part or all of their R&D investment in the idea. The difficulty is in finding a way to get the patent holder and potential licensee together. Many of the country's educational institutions also hold potentially useful patents that are available for license agreements. Many universities have separate research institutes that frequently produce patentable ideas that can derive substantial income from royalties when licensed; these universities are eager to provide information on their patents, but they must be solicited.

Obviously, technical and trade journals (both foreign and domestic) should be screened carefully. Many of these journals carry advertisements offering new products and processes for sale or license. Similar advertisements often appear in financial newspapers and journals. In addition to direct offers, these journals usually have a new products section. The products that are shown may precipitate ideas of how they can be used to improve existing products or processes. Likewise, the technical group may see how they can improve someone else's product by incorporating into it some developments they have already made or adapting it to a new use.

Finally, products developed in foreign countries should not be overlooked as a potential source of ideas. The trade fairs held in many European and Asian countries are fertile ground for new ideas. Many foreign companies are highly receptive to licensing agreements with American companies. Foreign patents and technical and trade journals should also be reviewed. Many companies have even found it advantageous to use a foreign technical representative to seek out ideas in foreign countries.

2.11 Screening Ideas

Any system for the management of a technical group must provide in some way for project initiation, selection, evaluation, and periodic review. If the system is effective, it should result in a smooth flow of well-chosen projects whose statuses are updated and reviewed periodically. In other words, of all the projects considered, those that have the highest expected payoff to the organization within budget, manpower, and other limitations should receive the necessary effort.

If a technical organization is properly monitoring the internal and external environments, there should be no dearth of ideas for new projects. The next step in needs research is to screen these ideas for compatibility with the parent organization's objectives and for technical and economic feasibility. The appropriate criteria to use will, of course, depend on the nature and type of projects being considered. Among the questions to be answered, will the project if successful:

I. Support company objectives?
   A. Be within the field of interest and growth objectives?
   B. Be compatible with company images and policies?
   C. Be compatible with present marketing capabilities and channels?
II. Satisfy a need?
   A. Fulfill a real market and need (i.e., will the customer buy?)
   B. Require development of a new market?
   C. Provide savings from improved processes, methods, or raw materials?
   D. Provide increased safety, reliability, maintainability, or usability?
   E. Provide improved external relations and goodwill?
III. Be Implementable?
   A. Fit within present manufacturing capabilities?
   B. Be affordable in terms of capital investment?
   C. Be compatible with available staff and facilities?
   D. Be achievable within a useful time frame?

IV. Be Profitable?
  A. Provide an adequate return on investment?
  B. Represent an acceptable risk?

2.12 Types of Planning

In order to be really meaningful, planning must eventually become quantified (result in numbers such as dates, dollars, man-hours, etc.). The goal of management in any technical project is to use the resources of materials, facilities, time, funds, and people to accomplish a specified task, for a reasonable cost, and within a reasonable schedule. Thus the planning domains of interest are cost, schedule, and performance. A meaningful overall plan must contain all three dimensions (i.e., what are we going to do, when will we do it and how long will it take, and how much will it cost?)

All of these dimensions are important and need careful consideration. We have previously discussed part of the problem of what are we going to do in the sense of setting objectives, technological forecasting, and needs assessment. We will postpone a detailed discussion of selecting and planning individual projects until Chapter 8. As far as time or timing is concerned, plans can be categorized relative to the planning horizon or calendar time. Thus, we have long-range plans (5, 10, or 20 years), annual plans (next year), and current operational plans. All three contribute to providing guidance, direction, and focus to our activities.

Plans can be developed, in a number of ways, including conference planning, directive planning, and bottom-up or top-down planning. *Conference planning* is based on the committee approach, whereby a group of cognizant individuals collectively considers the problems of the future and collectively decides on a future course. Opinions, feelings, and joint participation are highly stressed. This method is almost the direct opposite of *directive planning,* in which almost all of the major decisions relative to the future are made by a single individual. The plans are then communicated to subordinates for implementation. Directive planning is usually associated with a highly authoritarian method of leadership or management. In the so-called *bottom-up planning* approach, plans are first generated at the bottom of the organization. These plans are then passed up through the various levels of management; each level consolidates and integrates the plans submitted to it. Generally, this type of planning is based on what is available and what can be done with what already exists. It may also contain a "Christmas" or "wish" list of new equipment, personnel, etc., desired and what could be done if these new resources were made available. Opposite to this is *top-down planning,* in which major goals are set by the top level of management and passed down the hierarchical levels. At each level of management, plans are made as to how to accomplish those goals. Such planning is based largely on intelligence as to what is necessary and possible to accomplish. Thus, top management may specify certain sales goals, cost reduction goals, new areas of endeavor, etc., toward which plans are to be directed.

In identifying these methods there has been no intent to make them independent or imply that one is better than another. In almost any organization, some mix of all of these methods is used. In technical organizations it is not unusual for the planning process to start with a bottom-up approach. Top management then examines and evaluates the result, establishes goals and objectives, and sends the plans back in a top-down method. Planning may then iterate back and forth, up and down, until a mutually agreeable consensus is arrived at. Such plans will generally consist of individual project plans (showing goals, schedules, manpower planning, and budgets) and overall budgets (by organizational group). Budgets will be of two types: expense and capital. Expense budgets cover salaries, materials, and minor tools needed for the planning period. Capital budgets cover major facility or equipment acquisitions.

2.13　Responsibility for Planning

Some organizations maintain special groups whose sole mission is planning. Such groups can serve two purposes. First, they are the focal point for technological, economic, social, and political forecasting. Second, they can be made responsible for developing a planning mechanism, installing and coordinating the planning process (i.e., integrating, analyzing, and recommending), maintaining the plans, and educating personnel on the importance of planning and its bases and intent. Management cannot, however, abdicate the responsibility for seeing that each activity has a plan, that it is being followed, and that it is revised when necessary. Naturally, management must retain the prerogatives of altering plans, approving plans, and controlling the objectives of the plans.

As we will see in Chapter 6, it is very important to engineers and scientists that they play a major role in planning their work. Every individual in the organization must recognize his or her role in, and responsibility for, planning. This does not imply that every individual must know all the details of the organization's plans; instead, it means that the individual must be informed relative to objectives and expected contributions. In effect, each individual must have his or her own goals and program for achievement of those goals and must know how those goals fit into the overall picture.

The important point is that planning is everybody's business and not just the responsibility of some central planning group. Planning is the basic tool for gathering, integrating, interpreting, and disseminating available information with respect to objectives, manpower, materials, facilities, cost, and schedules.

2.14 Achieving a Balanced Program

Another aspect of the problem of planning is that associated with achieving a balanced program. As would be expected, programs of all but the smallest technical organizations are composed of projects of varying complexity. In very general terms, these may be classified as long- and short-term projects, depending on the length of time required for a reasonable obtainment of results. An arbitrary system of classifying projects according to duration that I find useful is shown in Table 2.2.

Determining how much effort to put into the solution of present problem areas and how much effort to put on problems of the future is one of the enormous challenges confronting the technical manager. An overemphasis in either direction can be disastrous. It makes little sense to concentrate on solving day-to-day problems while the parent organization is left hopelessly behind technologically. On the other hand, there is no point at all in solving tomorrow's problems if the parent organization should fail before tomorrow comes.

In the business world, the technical manager knows that long-term projects are needed to develop the new or improved products and processes that insure the future health of the company. Because of their long-term nature, however, concrete results are slow in coming. A program made up of a preponderance of such projects may cause worker morale to suffer because of a lack of concrete, continuous achievement. At the same time, top management may

TABLE 2.2 Projects Classified by Duration

Name	Estimated Period of Duration	Expectancy
Short term	One to six months	Quick results, usually successful
Intermediate term	Six months to one year	Reasonable assurance of success
Long term	One to several years	If successful they usually bring a large return on the investment
Miscellaneous and service	One to several weeks	Improvements of methods, minor improvements in processes and products

wonder if the technical group is producing anything of value to the company.

Short-term projects hold the promise of quick, virtually assured success. They favorably affect the morale of those associated with their success, and the technical group may soon be able to show top management an imposing list of accomplishments. The danger of an imbalance in the direction of short-term work is concealed in the complacency that may overcome the company by virtue of a favorable competitive position with regard to current products and processes.

Progress results in the appearance of new products and the improvement of old ones. A company whose technical program has been devoted to short-term projects may someday find that although its products are better and less expensive to produce than similar ones of other manufacturers, they are, unfortunately, being replaced by new products that have been developed by their competitors.

Almost all of the pressures are exerted in the direction of selecting short-term projects (the high probability of success, the securing of quick results, the sense of achievement in completing a project, etc.). If the technical manager does not consciously recognize this and take action to assure a balanced program, the group's apparent success may well be short lived.

The director of government technical activities is faced with the identical problem. The problem, however, usually goes under the guise of development projects versus basic and applied research. If efforts are concentrated on today's weapons or spacecraft, the country is exposed to possible future disaster. The government must not only build and improve today's deterrent force or space vehicles but must also lay and expand the scientific base for the weapons or explorations of tomorrow. As in the industrial sphere, quick results can be achieved in short-term, relatively simple projects. It takes a person of courage and strong convictions to insist on a level of long-term effort, even though that technical effort is necessarily denied to or diverted from short-term work.

2.15   Unique Problems of the Government Administrator

There are other factors that make the selection of projects for a director of government R&D more difficult. First, the objectives of government R&D are not as clear and distinct as those of industry. The industrial laboratory is a part of the economic order, and its activities must contribute in some way to the satisfaction of economic wants. Such wants can be foreseen by and large and can even be created in some cases. R&D are directed toward an economic objective in industry. Research in the government, on the other hand, is pursued in the interest of the public welfare. Considerations of cost, time, reliability, performance, national prestige, etc., may be important, but it is discouragingly hard to define the precise terms of the objective.

Second, in the government there seems to be no measure of effectiveness quite as striking as the profit and loss statement of the industrial enterprise. The driving force behind the technical functions in industry is the financial condition of the company, be it reduced costs, higher-quality products, or a new line of products to promote business survival. The profit motive is totally lacking in government, even though the consequences of failure may be more serious than mere bankruptcy.

The spur of competition, which provides a stimulus to good performance in industrial laboratories, is not as effective in government activity. The technical work done in an industrial organization eventually has to meet the test of the marketplace. Although it is difficult to appraise the performance of any technical organization, it is reasonably clear that if competitors frequently introduce better, cheaper products, or if they introduce new products more quickly, then the record of the technical organization is not good. The government technical organization, on the other hand, has neither periodic nor continuous tests of its performance. Although national survival may depend on the results of its work, the *ultimate* test may come too late. The outbreak of war or of an epidemic is a poor time to find out that the research program has been insufficient or ineffective. Hence, the government administrator has no yardstick comparable to the competitive market for appraisal of results.

Lacking the economic or profit motive to aid in planning and evaluating the program, the government technical manager must look for other criteria. Criteria such as the public welfare or the public good are so abstract in nature that they are of little benefit. What is in the public interest: crash programs to develop new weapon systems in the shortest possible time in case war comes tomorrow, or an orderly, lower-cost, normal-priority development that will help keep taxes lower, the budget balanced, but take longer? Tell the military administrator when war will break out and the nature of that war—then a precise decision can be made as to what is in the public interest. But who can give that information?

How can the government administrator in the space exploration field determine the worth of national prestige? What criteria can be used to determine how much additional funds are justified to launch a certain satellite in January versus in July? How much is an increase in reliability from 0.995 to 0.996 of a certain valve, which will be used on a manned vehicle worth? How much is enough? How much is too little?

The only guide is the amount of resources available from the public through their elected officials. But, within this broad guideline, the possibilities are still very nearly infinite. A government technical organization must go to Congress annually for money. The amount of financial support received varies with the economic outlook, the political outlook, the military outlook, the current popularity of technology, and the general attitude of Congress. Thus, the government administrator must expect fluctuating financial support for the technical program. Any decision to begin any long-range project (taking more than a year) must be made without assurance that it can be financially carried to a conclusion. Although this is somewhat true of industrial organizations, there is a marked difference in degree.

Other problems, such as personnel policies, control from Washington, fiscal and accounting policies, and procurement policies also make the government administrator's job more difficult but, again, most of these are matters of degree. None of these preclude the government administrator from doing a good job of conducting a worthwhile technical program, but they certainly do make it more difficult.

References

1. Ayres, R. U., *Technological Forecasting and Long-Range Planning,* McGraw-Hill, New York, 1969.
2. Blackman, A. W., "Forecasting through Dynamic Modeling," *A Guide to Practical Technological Forecasting,* J. Bright, Editor, Prentice-Hall, Englewood, N.J., 1973, pp. 257–275.
3. Box, G.E.P., and G. M. Jenkins, *Time Series Analysis Forecasting and Control,* Holden-Day, San Francisco, 1970.
4. Bright, J. R., *Technological Forecasting for Industry and Government, Methods and Application,* Prentice-Hall, Englewood Cliffs, N.J., 1968.
5. Dalkey, N. C., and O. Helmer, "An Experimental Application of the Delphi Method to the Use of Experts," *Management Science, 9* (3), April 1963, pp. 458–467.
6. Dathe, H. M., "Cybernetic Models as Aids in Normative Forecasting," *Technological Forecasting in Practice,* H. Blohm and E. Steinbuch, Editors, Saxon House, Westmead, England, 1973, pp. 39–53.
7. Enos, J. L., *Petroleum Progress and Profits: A History of Process Innovation,* M.I.T. Press, Cambridge, Mass., 1962.
8. Enzer, S., "A Case Study Using Forecasting as a Decision-Making Aide," *Futures, 3* (6), December 1970, pp. 341–362.
9. Forrester, J. W., *Urban Dynamics,* M.I.T. Press, Cambridge, Mass., 1969.
10. Gerstenfeld, A., "A Study of Successful Projects, Unsuccessful Projects, and Projects in Process in West Germany," *IEEE Transactions on Engineering Management, EM–23* (3), August 1976, pp. 116–123.
11. Gordon, T. J., and H. Hayward, "Initial Experiments with the Cross-Impact Method of Forecasting," *Futures, 1,* (2), December 1968, pp. 100–106.
12. Hollander, S., *The Sources of Increased Efficiency: A Study of Dupont Rayon Plants,* M.I.T. Press, Cambridge, Mass., 1965.
13. Kahn, H., and B. Bruce Briggs, *Things to Come,* Macmillan, New York, 1972.
14. Kovac, F. J., "Technological Forecasting-Tires," *Chemical Technology, 1* (1), January 1971, pp. 18–23.

15. Marquis, D., "The Anatomy of Successful Innovations," *Innovations,* No. 7, 1968, pp. 28–37.

16. Martino, J. P., "Technological Forecasting for the Chemical Process Industries," *Chemical Engineering, 78* (29), December 27, 1971, pp. 54–62.

17. Martino, J. P., *Technological Forecasting for Decision Making,* American Elsevier, New York, 1972.

18. Meadows, D. H., et al., *The Limits of Growth,* Universe Books, New York, 1972.

19. Naylor, T. H., and H. Schauland, "A Survey of Users of Corporate Planning Models," *Management Science, 22* (9), May 1976, pp. 927–937.

20. *Project Hindsight,* Office of the Director of Defense Research and Engineering, Washington, D.C., 1969.

21. Richardson, J., "Tomorrow's Aviation, The Sky Won't Be the Only Limit," *Futurist, X* (3), June 1977, pp. 169–177.

22. Skinner, W., "Manufacturing—Missing Link in Corporate Strategy," *Harvard Business Review, 47* (3), May-June 1969, p. 141.

23. Sullivan, W. G., and W. W. Claycombe, *Fundamentals of Forecasting,* Reston Publishing, Reston, Va., 1977.

24. *Technology in Retrospect and Critical Events in Science* (TRACES), Illinois Institute of Technology Research Institute, Chicago, 1968.

25. Von Hippel, E., "The Dominant Role of Users in the Scientific Instrument Innovation Process," *Research Policy, 5* (3), July 1976, pp. 212–239.

26. Von Hippel, E., "The Dominant Role of the User in Semiconductor and Electronic Subassembly Process Innovation," *IEEE Transactions on Engineering Management, EM–24* (2), May 1977, pp. 61–71.

Discussion Questions

1. Define the logical sequence of steps involved in planning.

2. Since most forecasts are erroneous to varying degrees, what are the benefits of formalized forecasting?

3. How do operational, tactical and strategic planning differ?

4. What are the advantages and disadvantages of formal planning for applied research, development engineering, and plant engineering?

5. In view of the rapid advance of scientific frontiers, it is difficult to know what kinds of skills will be needed 10 years from now. Should an organization seek specialists or more broadly educated generalists? Discuss both the short- and long-range implications.

6. Prepare a technological forecast for private transportation 15 years from now.

7. What impact will microprocessors and minicomputers have on the home by the year 2001?

Case Study II

OFFICE EQUIPMENT CORPORATION

Glen Jordan, the president of the Office Equipment Corporation, knew that today's meeting of the board of directors was a crucial meeting both for himself and for the organization. The problem was that he was not sure of his own feelings. For 40 years the company had made and successfully marketed a line of typewriters, calculating machines, accounting machines, and tabulating equipment. The company had an excellent reputation for quality products and service. Sales had continuously increased, and the rate of return was better than that of comparable companies in the industry. One reason for the high rate of return was that up to this time, engineering research had engaged mainly in improving existing machines so that new models could be introduced every few years. These changes had been incremental or evolutionary in nature. They required only small changes in tooling, and the change over to new models entailed minimal disruption.

Everything had been going smoothly until the last 2 years. Although total sales had still been slowly increasing, it was more and more apparent that this was predominately due to the increase in typewriter volume. The sales of calculators had dropped by better than 50 percent during these 2 years, while sales of accounting and tabulating equipment had been level. Ray Fisk, the vice president for sales, had explained that the drop in calculator sales was due to the influx of low-cost, hand-held calculators into the market. "The only desk calculators we are selling are those with paper tapes," he explained. "No one wants a big calculator sitting on their desk when they can buy one that they can put in their pocket for a fourth the price." It had also become evident that the company's line of accounting and tabulating equipment would soon be in trouble. Fisk had said that his field salespeople were reporting that more and more customers were holding off on new purchases, waiting to see if they should buy minicomputers.

Jordan was somewhat familiar with the revolution that integrated circuits was bringing about. His wife had given him a small pocket calculator for his birthday that he proudly showed his friends. It was about half the size of a package of cigarettes and could add, subtract, multiply, and divide. In addition, it had a clock with an alarm and a calendar. It also could tell you what day of the week a certain date would fall on either 100 years in the future or had fallen on 100 years in the past. Jordan took great delight in telling people on what day their birthday would fall 10 years from now.

The purpose of today's board meeting was to consider the budget for next year and a new 10-year plan. In fact, Jordan was going to present the board with two budgets and two plans. The first plan and budget constituted pretty much of a logical continuation of the present mode of operation. The only thing radically different about this plan was that Fisk was proposing a major national promotion program that would require a 50 percent increase in the advertising budget. In order to balance the overall corporate budget, this would require postponing a plant modernization program that had been planned and a 15 percent cut in the research budget. Fisk believed that this promotion campaign would increase sales to the point where the plant renovation could take place the following year and the research budget could be restored. In the meantime, he hoped to increase the corporation's share of the market by 15 percent.

The other 10-year plan and budget was being pushed by Dr. Fred Hunter, the director of engineering research and Bob Christian, the director of corporate planning. This plan represented a radical departure from the past. It entailed a major commitment by the corporation to enter the minicomputer business. Since the corporation had not been involved in the use or manufacture of integrated circuits, Hunter was proposing that his engineering staff be doubled over the next 2 years. Other than a continuation of the work on upgrading the present line of typewriters, all work on the other product lines would cease. He was proposing the development of a new line of minicomputers based on large-scale, integrated circuit microprocessors that were designed especially for office financial and data processing use in small to medium-size organizations. He was also proposing a new line of typewriters using integrated circuits and internal memory. This plan would entail indefinite postponement of all plant modifications until the future manufacturing needs were clear. It also entailed the necessity of raising a large amount of new capital through a bond issue or a preferred stock issue.

Jordan had listened to both sides. He really did not understand what Hunter and Christian were saying when they started talking about chips, integrated circuits, and microprocessors. He had come to the presidency from the sales group. It scared him when he thought about moving the corporation into a completely unfamiliar area. He felt confident of his intimate knowledge of the details of the present operation. He understood the present business but was not at all confident he understood what was being proposed. How could he manage if he did not understand the business he was in? Would he be able to draw on the resources of his experience in order to trust his own judgments? Would he become completely dependent on the proponents and designers of the new products and processes? He did not feel comfortable with the situation.

On the other hand, Christian had scared him with his charts and projections. The corporate planning group had spent the past year on a major technological forecasting effort. They were convinced that microprocessors were going to revolutionize the industry and that the corporation was already 5 years behind. They had shown him charts of the plummeting costs of integrated circuits and the exponential growth of the use of microprocessors. The frightening part was how closely this growth had matched the decline of the corporation's present products. Christian was projecting that sales on the present calculators and accounting and tabulating equipment would go to zero within 8 years. He was even projecting that typewriter sales would drop 50 percent within 10 years.

Ray Fisk and the sales group did not agree with these projections. They blamed the stagnant sales in accounting and tabulating equipment on the general economic conditions. Fisk also did not believe that the prices for minicomputers being projected by Christian would ever be achieved. He conceded that the corporation might have to reduce its prices and increase its advertising, in order to stay competitive, but he believed that the new computers were too complicated and that customers would prefer to stay with the special-purpose, transistorized equipment with which they were already familiar. He was projecting that calculators would hold about where they were and that overall sales would increase at a rate of 10 percent per year for the next 10 years. He also pointed out that Hunter and Christian's proposal would entail new marketing approaches and a different marketing and service organization. The present equipment was marketed through business supply houses, but it was not clear if this would be true of the new equipment. Salespeople in the field could often repair the present machines on the spot, but this would be doubtful with the new lines. Fisk argued that what was being proposed was an entirely new business.

Terry Buford, the vice president of manufacturing, was siding with sales. He argued that the hard-won established technology and experience would be rendered obsolete. Workers who had built up their skills over years would suddenly find these skills irrelevant to the new problems. The new proposal would require new means of controlling product quality, production scheduling, and inventory. Radically different production equipment and processes would be required at a tremendous capital investment. Buford just could not see rocking the boat when everything was going so well.

Jordan had listened to the conflicting arguments and was confused. He could see both sides. Christian's projection made sense, but then so did Fisk's. One thing Jordan did know was that if Hunter and Christian's plan was adopted, the business and hence the nature of the corporation would no longer be the same. Thus he had decided to present both plans to the board and let the two sides fight it out. He had also decided he better take a tranquilizer before the meeting.

Case Study Discussion Questions

1. Discuss why each of the participants in the board of directors meeting are taking the position they are.
2. What action would you take if you were an outside board member?
3. Do you think Jordan is taking the correct approach?

CHAPTER 3 organization

3.1 Traditional Organization Theory

One of the key mechanisms through which management strives to achieve its goals is the organizational structure itself. The job of the manager is not that of the organization; it is the specialized work of designing the organization, setting its goals, and maintaining its operations. This is accomplished by formulating and defining the purpose and goals, providing the system of communications, and securing the cooperative efforts of the required personnel. The formal organizational structure helps the manager to carry out these functions by:

1. Specializing executive activity.
2. Simplifying the tasks of management.
3. Grouping employees for the purpose of direction and control.
4. Providing the formal channels of communication and coordination.
5. Encouraging the interaction of employees.

Thus, the organizational structure is one of the most important means by which management can bring its limited and precious resources to bear on a problem. Before we look at a new form of organization called the matrix, we consider the traditional hierarchical pyramid structure that has served us so well (Figure 3.1). We will then try to analyze its strengths and weaknesses and why it sometimes does not lend itself to the rapid responses required by a changing environment.

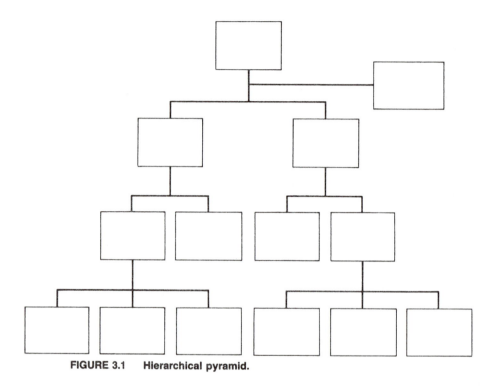

FIGURE 3.1   Hierarchical pyramid.

The pyramidal structure is an old and proven organizational form. For example, in the Old Testament (Exodus 18:25) we find that on the advice of his father-in-law, Moses chose able men from Israel and made them heads over the people, rulers of thousands, of hundreds, of fifties, and of tens. A little later we find that the Roman Army was organized as a strict hierarchical pyramid based on each level of command having 10 people reporting to each officer. As a command structure it enables the commander to give instructions to thousands of troops in just a few easy steps. The commander tells 10 senior officers what he wants done. Within minutes, each of them tells 10 junior officers, each of whom in turn tells 10 noncommissioned officers (NCO). Each NCO tells 10 soldiers what is to be done, and we have given directions to 10,000 troops in four easy stages [2]. The pyramid is at its best when it is squat; this permits rapid communication.

Clearly, such a structure has tremendous power as an instrument of command. As long as each executive can control 10 subordinates (certainly not an unreasonable span of control), an organization of 10,000 people could theoretically consist of only four hierarchical levels. But how many large organizations do you know with such a compact structure? They are more likely to have 10 or more levels and one might wonder why. The answer is that at each level, only half the executives are actually line executives, and the other half are advisors or staff specialists. The distinction is between those who are doing something and those who are commenting on how something should be or is being done. The result is that each executive is directing an average of 5 instead of 10 doers, and the hierarchical levels proliferate. Unfortunately, as the number of managerial levels increases, so do the communications problems. It is well documented that some of the content is lost each time a message is retransmitted. Therefore, as the number of expert advisors rises in proportion to the number of line executives (a trend that is very evident; see reference 9), the number of hierarchical levels will also increase, causing a decrease in the speed and efficiency of executive control.

Looking back at history, it is interesting to note that most organizational forms first appeared in military contexts. The hierarchical pyramid, for example, was the basis of the Imperial Roman Army, with its Centurians (commanders of 100 men), Tribunes (commanders of 1000 men), etc. The formal use of staffs to assist the line managers is generally attributed to the Prussian Army [8]. With the arrival of the Industrial Revolution, there was a need for organizational structures that could cope with the specialization of labor, mechanization of processes, and their requirements for coordination. The framework and policies that had worked so well for the military were adapted to suit the needs of the young, burgeoning enterprises.

The pyramidal form of hierarchical organization fit well with the concepts and ideas of theorists such as Max Weber and Henri Fayol. Weber described his classic, bureaucratic model as the best means to efficiently perform a variety of tasks with precision and reliability and to administer the large, complex organizations developing in his time. A bureaucracy was to be based on [22]:

1. A division of specialized labor.
2. A system of rules.
3. A system of procedures.
4. A well-defined hierarchy of authority.
5. Impersonality of interpersonal relations.
6. Employment and promotion based on technical competence.

Fayol proposed his 14 principles of good administration, which also depended on and reinforced the use of the pyramid. These were [5]:

1. Division of labor.
2. Authority and responsibility.
3. Discipline.

4. Unity of command.
5. Unity of direction.
6. Subordination of individual interests.
7. Remuneration of personnel.
8. Centralization.
9. Scalar chain.
10. Order.
11. Equity
12. Stability of tenure of personnel.
13. Initiative.
14. *Esprit de corps*.

The basis for the hierarchical bureaucracy lies in economic theory and its attendant concepts of authority and responsibility. The organization is viewed as a means of providing goods or services to customers within a particular market. The ultimate power or authority is viewed as deriving from the owners (stockholders) in the private sector or from the citizens through their Congress or appropriate governing body in the public sector. As organizations have grown larger and larger, ownership and the citizens become more and more divorced from the day-to-day operation of the organization. Because of this, the management profession, separate from ownership but responsible to it, developed. Management is responsible to the owners or ultimate source of authority for the profitable or efficient operation of the organization.

Authority is the power to carry out a job; responsibility is the obligation to do so. As organizations become more complex, the danger of inappropriate or delayed action within and by the organization increases. This in turn requires that management exercise greater control in order to meet its responsibilities. Traditional concepts of control have centered on the use of authority to prevent inappropriate or delayed action. This authority is perceived in the bureaucracy as flowing downward in the organization; each level of authority is responsible or accountable to the level immediately above it. Thus the organization is viewed as a pyramidal structure with decreasing decision-making discretion as one proceeds down the levels of the hierarchy. Koontz and O'Donnell [12] express this traditional view as follows.

> The key to the management job is authority, managers must work through people to get things done. The resulting complex of superior-subordinate relationships is therefore founded on the concept of authority, the legal or rightful power to command or act. Authority is the binding force in organizations.

From this concept of managerial authority most of the traditional basic assumptions and principles of organization derive. Most important and crucial decisions are made at the higher levels in the organization, in keeping with the retention of authority at those levels. There is also a basic assumption of greater competency as one proceeds upward through the various levels. This is made explicit in the form of compensation and privileges. It also is recognized in the widespread use of the terms *subordinate* and *superior*. Any conflicts at one level are referred to the next higher level for resolution by a shared superior because of the presumed greater competency of the superior.

We find that the term *chain of command* refers to the chain of direct authority relationships between superiors and subordinates throughout the organization. The logical extension of the concept leads to the principle of unity of command (i.e., a subordinate should report to a single superior; otherwise it is difficult to delegate authority). If superiors do not have total authority to hold their subordinates responsible, they do not have the power to maintain their positions.

In summary, the traditional hierarchical pyramids rest on the legal distribution of power, influence, or authority from the presumed ultimate source down through the hierarchy and, subsequently, a decreasing level of importance of decisions made. Not all theorists agree with these assumptions, and more will be said about this later. Suffice is to say for now that there are serious human costs associated with running a smooth bureaucracy. Kingdon [11] lists these as: (1) hardening of communication arteries to official channels, (2) inflexibility of behavior because of the need for order and predictability, and (3) sublimation of individual initiative and creativity.

Other early theorists such as Gulick [7], or Mooney and Reiley [16] also defended and rationalized the hierarchical pyramid to the point that it became the universal structural form until the middle or late 1950s. The basic form has remained unchanged except for the addition of the staff structure. The only variations were in the bases of specialization used for departmentalization. No matter what structural form we use, the bases of specialization for any organization are one or more of the following.

1. The place where the work is done (geographic).
2. The time at which the work is done (shifts).
3. The persons with whom the work is done (function: engineering, manufacturing, marketing, etc.).
4. The persons for whom the work is done (customer).
5. The things on which work is done (product or project).
6. The method by which the work is done (process).

Very few organizations use only one of these bases. In most cases there will be some mixture. For example, at the first level of the organization the breakdown may be geographic, at the second level it may be project or product, and at the third level it may be functional. The problem that managers continually face is the fact that each of these bases have certain strengths, but also certain weaknesses. When organizing a certain level of the organization in accordance with one of the preceding bases, the manager loses certain other advantages. This is one reason that we often see an organization switching back and forth each time they have a major reorganization.

3.2 The Stage or Phase Structure

Since R&D moves thru a phased life cycle (see Section 1.4), several organizations have tried to organize on the basis of the different phases (Figure 3.2). Under this concept work flows from group to group from left to right on the organization chart. The conclusion of efforts by one group becomes the starting point or baseline for the next.

Although this may at first seem to be a logical structure, it has not worked out too well in practice. The biggest problem has been in getting the work to flow from group to group. If it is an interesting problem, each group is very reluctant to agree that its phase is completed and release it. Strong feelings of possessiveness develop, and there generally is a concern that the next group will foul up the idea or concept.

These possessive feelings are not difficult to understand. To the creative person, ego satisfaction, recognition, and self-fulfillment are all wrapped up in the ideas generated. The ideas are the only tangible results of some very hard work. It is therefore unrealistic to assume that the creative person is going to turn over those ideas willingly and voluntarily to someone else to develop further. As far as the idea generator is concerned, *no one* else can be trusted to nourish, cherish, and further develop something so personally im-

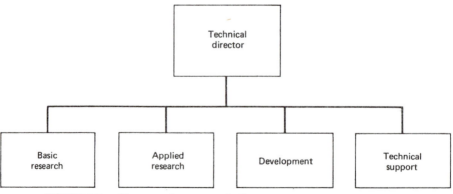

FIGURE 3.2   Stage or phase organization.

portant. When the technical program is organized by stage or phase, getting the work to move from one group to another is the equivalent of ripping a child from its mother's arms to give to someone else to raise.

3.3 The Functional Organization

Major subdivision by function, subject matter, or principal activities is found in many government and private enterprises. It has been found to be particularly effective for manufacturing operations, continuous process industries, and other industries that are characterized by limited product diversity or limited change in operations, where the relative stability of the work flow facilitates the coordination among interdependent, specialized functions. All similar activities are grouped together and identified by some functional title such as manufacturing, marketing, finance, engineering, test, or quality control. Under this concept, responsibility and control throughout the organization and at all locations are usually exercised by one executive for each function (see Figure 3.3). The functional concept assumes that the common bond between individuals and their supervisors (which comes about through their common occupational background) will enhance the cooperation and effectiveness of the individual and the group.

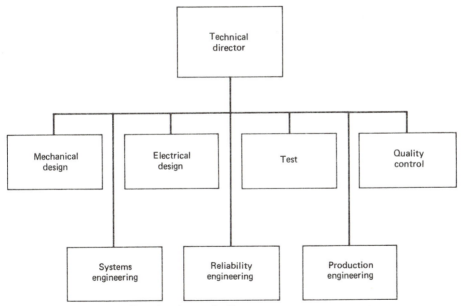

FIGURE 3.3   Functional organization.

The subject or discipline structure (Figure 3.4) is a specialized form of functional organization that groups scientific and engineering personnel by appropriate academic disciplines. This is a carry-over from the traditional university organizational form and is widely used for basic and applied research. Since coordination of activities among groups (interdisciplinary research) is very difficult, it is seldom used for developmental work.

The functional form of organization for technical groups has many advantages. Primary among them is that it facilitates the acquisition of specialized skills and provides a concentration of these specialists for the most efficient use of their collective experience. Since all the personnel from a particular occupation are grouped together, we can hire and train people who possess higher degrees of expertise. For example, we can hire a communication theory expert and a solid device electronics engineer instead of two generalized electrical engineers. It also minimizes the number of people we need in each specialty or skill, since we can pool the manpower resources and time share them across products or projects. The functional organization also provides clearly defined career paths for the people in each skill area. It provides professional identification and growth within a vertically oriented technical specialty. The path to success is up through the hierarchy of the functional area for which the individual has been trained. Therefore, the functional organization can hire, utilize, and retain highly specialized personnel.

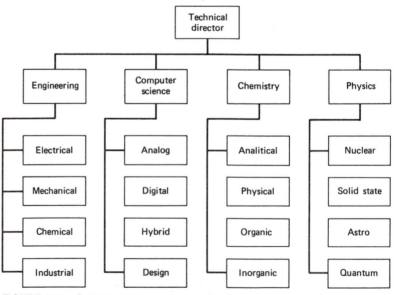

FIGURE 3.4   Subject or discipline organization.

A second advantage of the functional organization is the degree to which expensive equipment and facilities can be pooled and cost shared across projects. It is usually much cheaper to build and equip a few large facilities for the functional divisions instead of a series of smaller, duplicate ones for each product or project division. For example, it is usually more cost effective to have one large, well-equipped test facility instead of five or more smaller, less well-equipped ones. This is mainly because each smaller facility will have to contain certain common, basic equipment, even if it is not fully utilized. In addition, the small laboratories will be unable to justify certain specialized equipment if they only need it 10 percent of the time. However, if several projects need the equipment (even if intermittently), the central laboratory can easily justify its procurement. As with the case of specialized personnel, the functional organization allows us to procure specialized equipment and facilities that no one product or project could justify.

A third advantage of the functional organization is its ability to bring the latest state-of-the-art technology to bear on any particular project. Since all of the particular specialists in a given discipline are gathered together in one group, knowledge gained on one project is immediately and directly accessible to all other projects. The same thing is true of errors. Positive and negative experiences both become part of the group's joint memory and are available for use in all later projects.

A final advantage of the functional organization is closely related to the other three. Because of the presence of specialists, excellent facilities, and rapid transference of experience and knowledge, the group members are able to keep up with and advance the state of the art in their particular disciplines. Thus, the functional organization can exploit the latest knowledge and also hopefully expand and add to it.

In summary, the major advantages of the functional organization are the facilitation of:

■ Hiring, utilizing, and retaining highly specialized personnel.
■ Justifying and obtaining maximum utilization of expensive and specialized equipment and facilities.
■ Rapidly transferring knowledge and experience from project to project.
■ Advancing the state of the art.

Carlisle [4] has pointed out several disadvantages to the functional form of organization. Functional organizations tend to emphasize the separate functional elements at the expense of the whole organization. Each functional manager is most concerned with the success of his or her area of responsibility and will, therefore, make decisions in favor of that function. It is a rare manager who will make decisions detrimental to that functional area because of the needs of the overall or parent group.

Under functional departmentation, no group effectively integrates the various functions of an organization and monitors them from the overall standpoint. This is the function of the general manager; in certain types of operations, the general manager can do this effectively, but in a highly complex, technological operation, this cannot be accomplished. The general manager lacks the knowledge and objectivity to operate effectively as the integrating force. Walker and Lorsch have said that one solution to this problem is to appoint full-time integrators or coordinators for each project [21]. Killian suggests that if an organization needs integrators, they should have formal roles defined by titles and charters. He also says that the more intense the problem of interdepartmental collaboration, the more need there is for integrative roles to be formally identified [10].

Functional organizations do not tend to develop general managers. The path to success in a functional organization is up through a functional area. When individuals are promoted from a functional area to a general management area, they are biased and make decisions based primarily on personal background in the functional area. They will also find it extremely difficult to delegate the decision-making responsibility to someone else in the area in which they have been in charge and successful.

Cooperation between functional areas is difficult to achieve. Functional organizations emphasize functional relationships based on the vertical organization hierarchy. Vertical communication is emphasized at the expense of horizontal communication. This reduces the direct communications between the functions and detracts from the effectiveness of the total organization. Furthermore, functional organizations are closed systems, and they become very parochial. The common bond among members of a functional area builds a wall that encourages internal functional activities. This degrades extrafunctional understanding, coordination, and communication. Functional organizations also develop a strong resistance to change. The emphasis on the function and its objectives emphasizes self-perpetuation. The *not invented here* (NIH) *syndrome* is closely allied to the functional organization.

Many devices have been developed to overcome the weaknesses of functional organizations. In the personnel field, firms have set up training programs, encouraged job rotation, and organized special programs to broaden the perspective of key employees. In some organizations, special task forces have been established to handle interfunctional problems, and staff groups have taken over the integration of management functions such as planning. These steps have all been necessary to integrate activities better in view of increased specialization and complexity.

Galbraith has pointed out several means of integrating the departments of the functional organization to achieve the required coordination. These are rules and procedures, planning processes, hierarchical referral, direct informal contact, and liaison departments [6].

3.4 The Project Organization

The next organizational type to be considered is the project organization. It was first formally used by the Department of Defense in the development of the first nuclear weapon (The Manhattan Project) and was later used in other defense programs. It provides a unity of purpose and a basic simplicity that are hard to match in terms of effectiveness. The project organization brings together, under one organizational roof, all the administrative, technical, and support personnel needed to bring a project from the early stages of development through to operational use.

A project organization (see Figure 3.5) is formed to accomplish a specific objective that requires special management attention and emphasis for a specified period of time (i.e., the design and construction of a specific system). Projects of short duration (a few weeks or months) are usually accomplished by a task team or special task force. The objective of the organization is the completion of a specified task within cost and performance goals and on schedule. It is not intended to be a self-perpetuating organization; it maintains viability only as long as the project is not completed. Under each project organization, all functional entities required for the development and production of each particular project are duplicated. Each project has a complete line organization that is directed by a project manager who has full authority over all people, facilities, and functions required to produce the specified product or system.

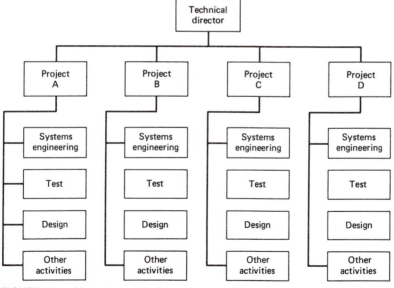

FIGURE 3.5 Project organization.

Closely related to the project form of organization is the product structure (Figure 3.6). This concept groups people of different specialities to work on common problems in order to develop specific products or processes that are of specific interest to the parent organization. The more basic the research done, the less often will it be organized in this particular way. This structure usually resembles the project organization and has about the same advantages and disadvantages.

Generally, the project organization is employed for a onetime activity that is:

1. Definable in terms of a specific, finite objective.
2. Infrequent, unique, or unfamiliar to the existing organization.
3. Complex with respect to organizational interdependence in detailed task accomplishment.
4. Critical to the company in terms of extent of commitment in resources, market potential, or some other aspect that has a significant impact on the company's business position.

There are also several characteristics that distinguish it from the functional organization. Unlike activities of the functional organization, the majority of the business in a project is often conducted laterally instead of vertically

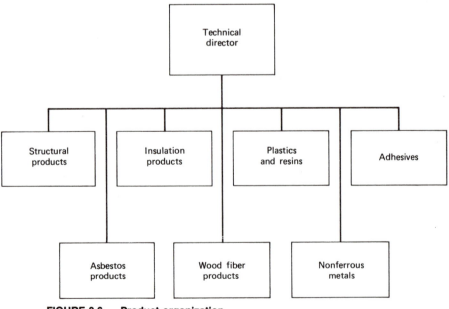

FIGURE 3.6   Product organization.

through the structure. Also, the value of a member to the organization is not necessarily reflected by location in the vertical strata of the organization; instead, it is a function of the ability to perform a role in the total organizational system of which the person is a part. As opposed to a line-staff relationship of work performance in a functional organization, the management relationships in the total project organization are more a "web of relationships."

The project manager also contributes unique characteristics because of his or her position. The manager acts as a focal point for the project by integrating the internal functional support and by acting as a single point of contact for the project to external, or customer, interests. The manager deals vertically, horizontally, and diagonally with peers and associates and with superiors and subordinates; this adds to the concepts of a "web of relationships."

The use of the project form of organization was often "forced" on industrial organizations by government contracting practices. One specification of all government requests for proposals has been the requirement to insure the contracting agency that top management was properly involved in controlling the project. This meant that the organization had to provide the government agency with a copy of the organizational chart for each project showing specific people and how the project organization tied in with top management control. If the organization was engaged in more than one project, it had to develop many different organizational structures (one for each project).

There are several advantages to the project method of organization. First, better control of the overall task is facilitated by the establishment of a single head (the project manager) to direct the entire span of operations for the task. Next, better customer relations are achieved through the appointment of the project manager as the company's point of contact for that project. Product development time can be shortened by the concentration of the necessary skills and resources into a unified group. Finally, program costs can be reduced by the reduction in product development time and by the improved, streamlined coordination of activities to complete the task.

Other reported auxiliary benefits include:

1. Better project visibility and focus on results.
2. Improved product quality and reliability.
3. Higher profit margins.
4. Higher morale and better mission orientation for employees working on the project.
5. An accelerated development of managers because of the breadth of project responsibilities.

To summarize the advantages, the greater the diversity among product lines or project types and the greater the importance of rapid response, the greater are the pressures to move toward a structure based on product or project lines. This form of organization facilitates coordination among the specialties, within the budgetary constraints. It allows quick reaction time to tackle problems that develop, and everyone involved is dedicated to a single goal or purpose.

As with all forms of organization, however, there are some distinct disadvantages associated with the project approach. For one thing, it makes the hiring, utilization, and retention of highly specialized personnel much more difficult. If there are two projects, each requiring a half-time electromechanical engineer and a half-time solid device electronics engineer, the pure project organization must either hire one generalist electrical engineer for each project (thus reducing specialization) or hire four engineers (two in each specialty). This happens because the pyramidal project structure makes it difficult if not impossible to share people between projects. Experience suggests that once specialists are assigned to a particular branch of the pyramid structure, they become reserved by that branch for its sole use. Traditionally, if people are needed in an area where they are not permanently employed, the supervisor will resist even a temporary transfer for fear of losing a good employee.

A second aspect of the specialist personnnel problem is that of technical obsolescence. Everyone today recognizes the extreme difficulty that any specialist has in trying to keep up with the rapid advances and changes in knowledge. In the functional organization the specialist is in daily contact with professional peers and, hopefully, learns a great deal from them in terms of new findings, concepts, etc. However, in the project-type organization, the specialist may be the only representative from a particular discipline and thus may be left to his or her own initiative and devices to combat obsolescence. Most top-notch specialists (particularly in technical areas) recognize this aspect and are very reluctant to go into a project-type organization for fear of becoming obsolete. From the organization's viewpoint, it may find after a few years that its experts are not experts at all.

Closely related to this problem of obsolescence is the fact that it is virtually impossible to transfer experience (both good and bad) and knowledge from project to project. Also, the project organization is completely unequipped to advance the state of the art. This is not surprising, since the organization has the singular goal of completing its project on time and at the least cost. Many organizations that have operated on a project basis for a prolonged time suddenly realize that the whole group has become obsolete.

An additional drawback of the project type of organization derives from the reluctance of personnel to become associated with risky projects. If a certain project seems to be relatively risky, the process of recruiting staff in this area becomes very difficult. People realize that despite assurances to the contrary, in the project-type structure, the success or failure of their project can make or break their careers. They know that they can disappear when the particular job does. In addition, specialists recognize that they are not prepared to advance upward in the hierarchy in the project organization and that generalists are more likely to advance faster.

One other important shortcoming of the project-type structure is the lack of flexibility. Most jobs are staffed for peak workloads. The organization functions very well during that period, but problems arise as the scope of the work changes and an imbalance of skills begins to occur. For example, if you do not have enough engineers in a particular area, the impact is clear—the job does not get done. If you have too many engineers, the impact is not as obvious. What happens is that the engineers begin to "make" work. The excess of engineers in a department that has no work partly accounts for the fact that it is very difficult to move a project out of R&D, and into production. The engineers keep inventing and improving the product. Since they can always present cogent technical reasons for what they are doing, it is almost impossible for managers to know when it is legitimate and when it is merely to protect their jobs.

3.5   From Functional to Project to Matrix

We can now examine the process by which many organizations evolved from one of the hierarchical forms to a new form called the *matrix structure*. Most of the technical organizations that I have studied started from a functional base. Although the functional organization facilitated the acquisition of specialized inputs and the establishment of specialists, it could not cope with the problems of a multiproduct operation that required constant decision making by top management or with subsequent squabbling and confusion at the lower levels. The initial reaction by the functional management to these problems was to add advisory staff offices to coordinate and correct the problems. However, since these staff offices had only the powers that they could generate themselves and lacked delegated authority to direct the functional departments to take action, their performance was very erratic; indeed, they were viewed by the functional supervisors as nuisances.

To alleviate the management problems that were occurring more and more often and with which the staff offices could not cope, the project or program form of organization was established. This concept was instituted in the military after the success of the Navy's Polaris program, a system development project requiring the merging of the missile, the submarine carrier, and the submarine launch system. The project organization was superior to the functional organization in that it provided a quick reaction capability to tackle problems that developed in one specialty and thereby reduced the impact on other specialties. Although the project organization could accomplish the job better, as we have seen, it also had problems, such as duplication of personnel and effort and the lack of an ongoing program to advance the state of the art. In large, complex R&D programs, the project was often completely self-sustaining and actually a functional organization itself.

To avoid some of the problems inherent in both the functional and the full-blown project organizations, the projects were sometimes staffed with only essential personnel, with resources being drawn from the appropriate functional organizational element, thus providing for the best in each concept. There is a definite time span on the life of a project and, after completion of its task, it is disbanded. Because of this short life span, the emphasis within the project is to get it done with minimum regard to precedent or established procedures. To accomplish this goal, the project manager had to interface with the functional organization. This was good for the functional organization, since they had to service the project on their wild ideas, forcing the functional organization to grow and not continue doing things as they had always been done. This interface led into the next organization structure—the matrix.

The evolution to the matrix system in the space industry is typified by the experience of Lockheed Aircraft. Lockheed started out with the aircraft industry's typical functional management pattern. There were engineering, manufacturing, and sales departments; a single product or product line was the core of business. Then the aviation field grew in complexity, cost, and number of product lines. Lockheed found that customer concerns often did not mesh with the corporate structure. The departments worked on a time and budget basis set up by the functional managers; they did not specify customer identity in their project progress reports. Customers would call and ask to speak to the top person assigned to their particular project, but the functional management concept did not allow for such a person. All projects were treated in the same way. This conflict between customers' concerns and management practices sparked the start of evolution to a matrix structure.

First came the creation of a project expediter, who was the customer's contact within Lockheed. If delivery dates were missed or other complaints arose, the expediter was charged with the mission of determining why. However, the expediter was given no authority, so frequently hard feelings were created in the company without helping the customer. As the customer relations gap continued to widen, the project coordinator was created at a higher management level. The coordinator, acting as a catalyst, brought together functional managers to deal with customer problems. But the position still had no authority. Not until the late 1950s when the systems approach began sweeping through industry, did Lockheed establish a project manager who had full authority to deal with the functional managers; this started the transition to the matrix management concept [18].

3.6 The Matrix Organization

The basic concept of matrix management is to try to achieve the advantages of two different bases of organization by setting up an interplay of checks and balances, or "controlled conflict," between a group of managers who have specific product, program, or project responsibilities and another group of executives who have specific functional responsibilities [19]. The concept is essentially a derivative of the well-known task force approach that has been modified, improved, and refined to meet the complex management needs of today. Figure 3.7 illustrates the fundamental structure of the matrix management organization as adapted to, or superimposed on, the conventional functionally oriented organization. Obviously, the titles of the program managers and the functional lines of responsibility will vary from organization to organization. Likewise, the determination of whether the program managers or the functional managers are the vertical or horizontal segments varies. The important aspect is the formal specialization of management responsibilities from the two viewpoints (project and function) and the establishment of built-in checks and balances between the different responsibilities.

The object of this superimposed configuration is to allow projects to be born, mature, and terminate in an orderly manner. Each project manager has

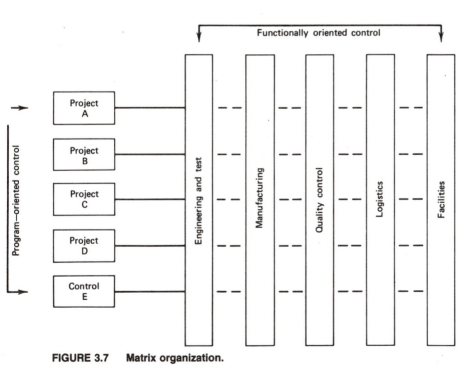

FIGURE 3.7   Matrix organization.

direct access to the specific personnel and expertise required for these projects for a planned time duration and to the rapid release of surplus manpower as project needs decrease. By controlling personnel in this manner, the project manager has a vital cost control weapon; the project organization can expand and contract as dictated by budget and technical needs without the need for layoffs or new hires.

In a company with management that is basically decentralized and organized around product-line responsibilities, the functional executive provides a unifying force that crosses the boundaries of the various product-line organizations to establish and maintain high standards of technical performance; to transfer the latest techniques and practices throughout the company; to insure that certain important technical aspects are not being overlooked; and to assure that experienced personnel are retained and developed.

In the company that is organized primarily along functional lines, the program or project executives provide the unifying coordination to insure that their project or program is getting the appropriate attention and required level of effort from each of the functional areas. In addition, the project manager continuously monitors the status of costs, schedules, and performance; provides the technical integration; defines requirements; and provides the prime contact with the customer for program activities. Regardless of which group of managers was horizontal and which was vertical in the organizations, the program managers clearly have been in charge of the programs. Functional executives have appeal channels, but they can neither ignore nor procrastinate on a decision by a program manager. Although the functional executives implement the decisions of the program managers, they are in the position to (and are expected to) reraise or question any decision with new facts as often as it is felt necessary. The program and functional managers both report directly to top management. Conflicts that cannot be settled by the appropriate program and functional managers are referred to higher management for resolution.

When operating under a matrix management approach, it is obviously extremely important that the responsibilities and authority of each manager be clearly defined, understood, and accepted by both functional and program people. The relationships must be spelled out in writing. It is essential that in the various operating policies, the specific authority of the program manager be clearly defined in terms of program direction [1]. A typical breakdown of the program and of the functional managers' responsibilities and authority is shown in Table 3.1.

In addition to the advantages already mentioned, there are several other noteworthy aspects of this management concept. For one, the project managers can devote their entire efforts to planning, organizing, staffing, directing, and controlling the technical aspects of the project without the hindrance of

TABLE 3.1 Project versus Functional Responsibility

Program Manager	Functional Manager
Program Direction • Directs and controls company program and functional organization and subcontractor activity to achieve program objectives • Develops master program plans • Determines and issues the work breakdown structure and related work statements, budgets, and schedules which define *what* effort will be accomplished, *when* it will be performed, and *who* will have accountability • Assures the attainment of the technical, schedule, and cost objectives of the program	**Operational Direction** • Determines *who* will perform detailed tasks, *where* they will be done, and *how* they are to be accomplished • Provides a stable base for the development of talent and skills to assure the maintenance of technical capability • Provides necessary facilities and services to support program requirements
Program Control • Monitors cost, schedule, and technical results against master program plans • Replans and rebudgets as necessary to assure accomplishment of program objectives • Monitors contractual reporting	**Operational Control** • Responsible for the technical excellence and quality requirements of assigned tasks • Assures that all tasks are accomplished in accordance with technical specifications, on schedule, and within budget
Configuration Management • Controls changes and assures configuration accountability affecting the program	**Administration** • Performs administrative services in support of personnel assigned to a program • Initiates merit increases for all personnel within his organization
Customer Coordination • Provides the prime contact with the customer for program activities	
Administration • Approves the assignment and concurs in merit increases of key functional personnel assigned to the program	

complex administrative responsibilities. The administrative responsibilities are managed by the functional managers, who are not subject to enormous project pressures. The matrix concept also opens direct communication channels from both sets of managers to upper levels of the management hierarchy. Thus, when a serious condition erupts or promises to erupt, either manager can draw on executive authority to expedite situations that would normally proceed through the formal chain of command. Finally, there is a tremendous possibility for work-load balancing. The need for this balancing of manpower can best be demonstrated by Figure 3.8. Note that manpower requirements for each project grow slowly at first, rise rapidly to a peak, and trail off with time. By programming manpower needs and time phasing projects, it is possible to overlay projects so as not to exceed available manpower resources. Residual work provided by low-priority functional tasks handled in the normal organizational fashion may be used to ''absorb'' excess manpower (crossed area under upper manpower resources line) that may remain after the superposition of project manpower load curves. With diligent long-range planning and careful time phasing of projects, the ultimate in manpower work-load balancing may be achieved.

Whenever there is such an ample supply of obvious advantages to any scheme of organization, there are usually some equally obvious drawbacks. A student of the classical management school will immediately detect an apparent serious flaw in the matrix management approach: Fayol's second principle of management, ''unity of command,'' has been violated [5]. The conviction that the very foundation of good management rests on this principle (i.e., that no one can work under two bosses at the same time) is so deeply rooted in popular mythology that many managers will cringe at the very thought of the matrix concept.

On examination, however, this apparent shortcoming may not be as serious as it at first seems. The casual observer may fail to recognize that almost every organization today already contains elements of the matrix philosophy, although they are camouflaged under the guise of line and staff. Ignizio and Shannon [9] suggested that a blurring of line and staff relationships and the concept of unity of command has already taken place, and it is expected that

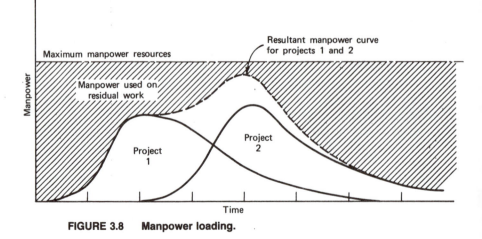

FIGURE 3.8   Manpower loading.

this trend will grow in the future. *Business Week* has also detected this prevailing tendency to violate the unity-of-command principle and the crumbling of other old management maxims [20] and has pointed out that it is not at all uncommon today for midlevel executives and staff personnel to report to half a dozen different bosses during the course of a project. Furthermore, whenever you have a situation in which the quality control department can reject a batch of parts and perhaps shut down a production line, when the scheduling department can tell the plant what to make and when to make it, and when the engineering department tells the plant how to make something and how long it should take to do it, you no longer have unity of command. Traditionalists will argue that all the commands come through the supervisor, but they are confusing semantics with reality. The crucial question is who makes the decisions, not what mechanics are used for transmittal of the information.

The violation of this important unity-of-command principle cannot be disregarded or taken lightly. Because of the psychological and sociological implications, management must be constantly on the alert to head off or solve personnel problems promptly. It is interesting to note, however, that in organizations that have adopted the matrix concept, the major personnel problems have derived from conflicts arising among the managers, not among the workers.

Also note that most of us already have personal experience with this type of dual-authority relationship by virtue of growing up in a family. In the normal family, the father and mother share authority equally. Each has a sphere of influence in which their decisions prevail—they are equal but different. It should be obvious that the dynamics of the family and of the matrix organization are the same. The mother and father will not always see things in the same way or have the same priorities. Disagreements arise and must be negotiated. Feelings are hurt and must be soothed. Good communication between a mother and a father is essential. The same is true of the managers in a matrix organization.

It is also observable that children try to play one parent off against the other in an attempt to get what they want. The same is true of employees in the matrix organization. Again, it is essential that parents (managers) communicate freely in order to preclude such games. Problems begin within the family when communications break down or when one parent dominates the other. We should expect the same within the matrix organization.

Looking at the matrix concept from the nonmanagerial employee's viewpoint, there are several distinct advantages. First, the multiboss situation allows the individual to gain greater visibility. It also means that the individual will be working with a larger number of different people and will be able to establish a more satisfactory array of personal relationships. It provides the chance to avoid the boredom and stagnation that often come from doing the same job, at the same desk, and with the same people for an indefinite period of time. The matrix concept permits employees who are dissatisfied with their jobs to change them more radically with less upheaval than in a typical pyramidal organization. Without forcing a showdown with the boss, employees in the matrix organization can usually explore different job areas. They need not request a formal transfer or make a long-range commitment if they want to try something new. The employee no longer must change companies in order to change activity. The matrix organization requires a greater number of personal transitions, but all of them keep the employees actively involved in their areas of expertise.

In addition, employees will quickly learn to appreciate the fact that they have gained a check and balance type of performance review, one from the project manager and one from the functional manager. Future salary and advancement opportunities will not depend totally on the judgment or whims of a single individual. This dual evaluation will give the competent employee a greater sense of security and a greater assurance of fair treatment. Finally, the quick pace of most project-oriented assignments eliminates the concerns of multi-boss allegiances. Employees engaged as integrated members of a project team become engrossed in their assignments and develop great enthusiasm toward meeting project goals.

A much more fertile area for "people problems" is that of interactions between the managers. Both the strength and weakness of the matrix concept is that we are deliberately setting up a system of checks and balances and controlled conflict; the key word here is controlled. We must carefully guard against a manager developing an attitude or feeling that his or her authority is being usurped by someone else. We need to maintain a balance of power between the project managers and the functional managers so that decisions are made on the merits of the case and not on the basis of power relationships. Although the exact balance of power is an unachievable goal, a reasonable balance can be obtained by careful definition of functions and enforced collaboration on budgets, salaries, reporting systems, and dual-authority relations. The authority and responsibilities of each manager must be carefully detailed in job descriptions and the formal communication paths carefully planned.

In the matrix organization, the problem of communication is more significant than it is in the conventional hierarchial arrangement. Communications are more difficult, more costly, and generate much more paper. Obviously, the problems of keeping tabs on all employees for scheduling purposes and for job and cost control can become an enormous problem. More people have to be continuously apprised of what is going on all of the time. Fortunately, the computer provides us with a powerful tool; by careful design of the management control system, budgeting reports, job cost control reports, and technical progress reports can be prepared in as much detail as necessary.

3.7 The Power Struggle

One of the basic concepts of the matrix is the deliberate setting up of controlled conflict or checks and balances between the two sets of managers. We must, therefore, squarely face the problems of controlling the conflict and not letting it get out of hand. Ideally, we would like to achieve a razor's edge balance between the two groups. Such a fine balance is obviously not possible, but it is the goal we must constantly be seeking.

The managers in the organization hopefully are ambitious, creative, motivated, hard-driving individualists. If this is true, we must acknowledge that each manager will constantly seek to gain the upper hand, to attain a little more power or responsibility. We would not have it otherwise. However, if we allow them to succeed, the matrix will be wrecked. As soon as one group of managers gains a power advantage over the other group, we no longer have a true matrix. For example, if the project managers become more powerful over a period of time, we will find that in effect, we have a project form of organization, regardless of what the organization chart shows. The functional managers will become administrators who handle the paper work and carry out the directives of the project managers. The reverse is equally true if the functional managers usurp power.

The top executive is thus placed in a paradoxical position. Each set of managers must be encouraged to keep striving, be ambitious, and continually try to become more influential in the achievement of the organizations goals. At the same time, the executive must see to it that they do not succeed at the expense of the power and influence of their counterparts. Finding the balance is extremely difficult and requires sensitivity and wisdom. As one of the managers begins to gain the upper hand, the top executive must cut him or her back, but must do so in a way that does not discourage or, even worse, destroy initiative.

A link must be found between the project managers and the functional managers that will accommodate the power struggle but not stifle the leadership characteristics of the project types or the creative characteristics of the functional types. How are we to achieve this delicate balance of power? We must first look to the power bases from which each set of managers must negotiate with the other. The basic source of power for the project manager is the control of the money and top management's interest in the project. The basic source of power for the functional manager is the control of the required manpower, knowledge, and facilities. One of the keys to achieving the desired balance of power is to place both of them in the position where it is in their mutual best interests to be able to negotiate an amicable agreement, but where neither one has absolute veto power over the other.

We can usually achieve this balance by providing each manager with another source of the commodity that the other manager has to offer but making it difficult to obtain. For example, the project manager should possess the potential threat of going outside the organization to get tasks done if the functional manager refuses to provide sufficient support; that is, the project manager should potentially be able to contract with some other group to get a task done. The functional manager, on the other hand, should not be placed in the position of having to release people if the money for operations is not obtained from the project; the functional manager should have some discretionary funds that do not depend on project support to use for payroll, equipment, and facilities.

Unfortunately, if it is too easy for the project manager to go out on contract or if the functional manager does not badly need the project funds for support, neither will be willing to make the necessary accommodations or seriously negotiate when major disagreements arise. As soon as either manager is in too independent a position, the required balance of power is gone and the advantages of the matrix are destroyed. This is the challenge to the top executive. How can each set of managers be forced to negotiate seriously and yet leave each some flexibility and independence?

Based on previous experience, it seems that it is generally the project managers who have the advantage in the power struggle. This is due to top management interest in the project and the ramifications to the parent organization if the project fails. Thus, it is usually the functional units that need some protection. The top executive might, therefore, start with a situation where the project manager is free to contract out 10 percent of the project funds and the functional manager has 30 percent of the needed operating funds in more or less discretionary form. This rule is predicated on the idea that the functional manager is expected to advance the state of the art in the area of responsibility in addition to maintaining project responsibilities. Second, the functional group must assimilate personnel back into the functional pool after their release from the projects, and there may not be an immediate need for that capability on another project. The top executive will have to be very sensitive to how the power struggle is going and move to make adjustments accordingly. It may also be necessary to allocate more discretionary funds to the functional groups in order to push the state of the art at the desired rate.

One of the major difficulties in the negotiations between project and functional managers is the assignment of specific personnel. In the pure matrix, people are assigned by name to the projects. Each project wants the best people, and there are always some people that no one wants. To make matters worse, the functional manager would really like to keep the best people working on favored internal tasks. Past experience would indicate that in the standard functional unit, 20 percent of the personnel are really top notch, 20 percent are not very desirable (but not bad enough to be released), and 60 percent are average. It is therefore imperative that project managers and functional managers realize that each project is going to have to accept a cross section of personnel and that a certain number of top-notch people are going to have to be retained by the functional group to pursue its own interests.

The matter of promotions is also always a source of conflict in the matrix organization. If a person assigned to a particular project is really doing a good job, the project manager is going to want that individual promoted, both as a reward and to provide further motivation. The functional manager, on the other hand, must maintain a specified grade or salary level within the functional organization and must consider the specific individual in relation to others in the group. The promotion of certain personnel often becomes a specific and touchy matter for negotiation. A great deal of mutual concern, fairness, and understanding is required of both managers in these negotiations.

Summing up, an exact balance of power is an unachievable goal, but a reasonable balance can be maintained by careful definition of functions and responsibility and enforced negotiations and collaboration. Conflicts that cannot be settled by the appropriate program and functional managers are referred to higher management for resolution. When this occurs, the top executive must be very careful. If rulings are consistently in favor of one group or the other, the balance of power will soon be destroyed.

3.8 Interactions Between Functional Groups

In addition to the necessity for interaction between project managers and functional managers, there is obviously also a need for close cooperation and interaction among the functional groups working on the same project. In many ways the relationships among the functional groups are even more important, because:

1. Personnel from the functional groups must operate as a team. Poor performance by any one group can greatly reduce the effectiveness of the effort or, in some cases, can jeopardize the results.
2. Actions taken and technical decisions made by one group usually impact the efforts of other groups.
3. Joint planning is necessary to ensure that the knowledge possessed by each group is shared with the others. It is usually difficult for one group to be aware of all the information needed by another group.
4. Engineering specifications for a research and development project should

specify goals and scope. If they are too specific, they become restrictive and eliminate creativity, so the detailed specifications must evolve during the project.

5. Real-time communications between the functional groups of current difficulties are important. If one group is experiencing a problem, it may significantly impact the other groups. If other groups are aware of the problem early enough, they can prepare contingency plans. There is also the possibility that one of the other groups can change something that will alleviate or help solve the problem.

It would be unrealistic to assume that these interface relationships can always be resolved without conflict; the resolution of the conflicts that arise from these interface relationships is one of the most important roles of the managers. The matrix organizational design requires negotiated interaction to take place continuously during the project instead of being specified in advance. Thus, we are faced with the necessity of continuously solving interaction conflicts.

Conflict is any difference between two persons or parties. It is important to realize that the organization and its managers are going to be confronted with having to deal with two different types of conflict—emotional and task. The task conflicts deal with the project and can be further broken down into technical and operational problems. Technical problems deal with the design or interpretation of test results, analyses, etc. They are hopefully subject to rational, objective investigation and resolution, based on some agreed to criteria. Operational problems deal with questions of who is responsible for something or how to do the task. Questions such as "How much reporting is to be required," or "Who will approve overtime?" are operational questions.

The resolution of operational problems is usually a matter of good managerial judgment, not rational, objective analysis. Unless operational conflicts are handled with sensitivity and tact, they can easily lead to emotional conflicts. Emotional conflicts are based on the ego involvements, hurt feelings, etc., of the participants. Of the three types of conflict—technical, operational, and emotional—the emotional conflicts are the most difficult to resolve.

Kingdon [11] proposes that as the interface relationship develops and conflicts arise, the managers will go through the following five distinct attitudinal phases.

1. Deny problems. ("We do not have any problems between us.")
2. Blame problems on the other group. ("If only they would improve, we would not have any problems.")
3. Accept responsibility for problems. ("We create some for them, they create some for us.")

4. Work out problems with the others. (''We jointly determine the appropriate steps to be taken to solve current problems.'')
5. Anticipate critical classes of problems. (''We define mechanisms and procedures for handling recurring types of problems.'')

The passage from one attitudinal phase to the next higher one represents growing sophistication in the handling of conflict resolution and a maturing of the managers involved. It is critical to the health and well being of the overall organization that the matrix managers progress as rapidly as possible through to the higher levels of interface relationships. Older, more mature managers will have to show patience and understanding as their younger, new colleagues pass from phase to phase.

Openness is vital to achieving the desired collaborative relationships within an organization. This requires mutual respect, trust, commitment to the task, and common interest in seeing the project successfully completed. The necessity of openness is obvious from the fact that conflict cannot be resolved until it is acknowledged and brought into the open. Only then can the involved parties analyze the situation and express feelings so that the real issues can be identified and the technical, operational, and emotional conflicts can be separated.

To acknowledge the importance of openness is easy, to achieve it difficult. Each manager is immediately faced with all kinds of doubts and questions: ''What happens to me if I play it fair and open but the other person does not? What do we do when we really cannot agree on a mutual solution to a conflict? How will top management feel about us if we just cannot work things out? What will my people think about me if I give in on this point to the other group?''

3.9 The Resolution of Conflict

Follett [15] has pointed out that conflicts can be resolved by one of three means—domination, compromise, or integration. Alternately, we can say that the outcome of a conflict is capitulation, bargaining, or collaboration. When a conflict is settled on the basis of domination, the disputant who has the greatest amount of power dictates the solution. The most powerful or dominant person wins, and the dominated person loses. The one who dominates may be quite pleased and satisfied with the solution, but the loser will not be; in fact, the dominated person will be very bitter at this demonstration of inferior position and will be motivated to challenge the oppressor at the earliest opportunity.

The exercise of power or dominance need not be direct. For example, if each time there is a conflict between a project manager and a functional manager (that is brought to higher management for resolution), it is resolved in favor of one or the other, we have a solution through dominance. Both groups will quickly perceive that bringing a problem to higher management is a wasted effort, and the dominant party will prevail. The matrix is then no longer a matrix, and we are back to the hierarchical pyramid. When two disputants bring a conflict to a manager for resolution, the manager should always ask if it is *really* cut and dry and must be decided wholly in favor of one party or the other.

The second basis of resolution is compromise through bargaining. There is no decisive victory or defeat in a compromise solution. Each party gives up part of what was wanted in order to obtain or retain a share of the compromise. Compromise agreements usually reflect the relative power or bargaining position of the two disputants. This means is preferable to domination because it diminishes the bitterness by dividing the frustration in some proportion between those who are at odds. However, because each party has had to give up something that was wanted, frustration will still be present and will aggravate future differences. In fact, each participant may resolve to strengthen his or her bargaining position before the next dispute.

Resolution of a conflict through integration (achieved by collaboration) is greatly preferred to dominance or compromise. A conflict is integrated when both parties gain and the actions that are taken result in a better situation for both of the disputants. Neither party dominates the other, and there is no yielding by either in the way of a compromise. The conflict itself is made to work for those who are in dispute to yield a result for both that is better than what existed prior to the dispute.

Obviously, not all disputes can be integrated. Some disagreements do not lend themselves to this kind of resolution. In addition, it takes a special type of manager who even thinks of this type of resolution. If either party to the dispute is determined to dominate the other or if there is no mutual trust, integration and collaboration are not possible. Roy [17] in discussing integration, says:

> "Mistrust between those in conflict often is too deep to permit either disputant to lower his guard to make integration possible. And, above all, the desire to dominate is so very strong in all of us as to put integration beyond our reach. We lack the wisdom and the strength to sacrifice the will to win, the desire for victory, for the larger but less personal gains of integration.

Resolution of conflicts through integration may sound like a utopian, unobtainable goal mainly because we see it in operation so seldom. The matrix adapts extremely well to integration because of the different goals of the two sets of managers. As already stated, the project manager's goals are short range, while the functional manager's are long range. Because of this, it is often possible to resolve a problem so that the short-range goal of the project can be met while contributing to reaching the long-range functional goal. It is much more difficult to achieve integrated solutions when both disputants are concerned with short-range goals. Higher management can play a vital role in helping to achieve the desired collaboration because of a broader viewpoint and perspective. Since the upper manager is not as likely to be emotionally involved, and since personal goals are best served when both managers succeed, the executive is more likely to see the possibility of an integrated solution.

To summarize the preceding discussion, when a manager is asked to settle a conflict, one should first seek an integrated solution (i.e., see if there is some way for both of the disputants to win). Failing this, a compromise solution that minimizes the ill feelings and maintains a balance of power should be sought. Only as a last resort should the manager accept one disputant's position while rejecting the other. Even when this last solution is mandatory, the wise executive will find some way to ease the frustration of the loser by granting some other desire.

3.10 Informal Organizations

Every member of an organization must recognize that there is not just one organizational structure. There are at least *four different organizational structures* within the group. The first is the *formal organization,* based on the relationships among jobs or positions, which we have been discussing up to this point. This is the official structure established by management to provide for delegation of authority and responsibility. It also provides the mechanism for the official channels of communication and resource allocation. The second structure is the *social organization,* based on friendship relationships. The third is the *power structure,* based on control of things that are considered of value to others. Finally, the fourth grouping is the *status or prestige structure,* based on respect and recognition.

The *social organization* arises spontaneously from the social interactions and shared values of people placed in close physical proximity. It fulfills the basic human needs to associate with other people, feel that they belong, and have a sense of importance. The structure of the social organization is determined by the feelings or sentiments that members of a group have for each other. Friendliness and camaraderie are complex sentiments about the like or dislike that one person feels toward another. It is predominately a sense of shared values and beliefs that leads a person to seek association or avoid association with another person. The social organization is like the formal organization in that it attempts to regulate behavior. The customs and codes of behavior of the social organization are based on shared values and beliefs; the rules and regulations of the formal organization are based on the need for efficiency. The social organization may work in support of the formal organization or at cross purposes to it. It also maintains its own communications network, commonly known as the "grapevine" or "rumor mill."

Another strong influence on the behavior of people in the organization is the informal structure based on *power relationships*. Power is a mode of influence that is based on the ability of an individual to induce others to produce a desired result by giving or withholding something of value. It is an interpersonal concept and always refers to a relationship between or among people. It is important to realize that there are sources of power other than those conferred by the formal organization. Thus the power structure is a complex web of relationships composed of officially delegated authority and power derived from other sources. Like the formal and social organizations, the power structure regulates behavior. However, unlike the other two, power is generally wielded for the benefit of the individual holder instead of for the benefit of the group. The power structure does not maintain its own communication network; it relies on the formal and grapevine channels for its communications.

The fourth and final structure that influences behavior within the organization is the *status or prestige structure*. Positions within this structure are held on the basis of technical skills, abilities, acomplishments, and experience. The prestige structure has particular relevance to technical organizations because of the strong desire among engineers and scientists for peer recognition and acceptance. A person holds a high position in the prestige structure by virtue of outstanding technical skill, ability, or accomplishment. Preeminence in one's field carries with it the ability to influence the behavior of others. Such people are looked up to and considered examples to follow. Their advice is sought in technical matters and in relation to career decisions and other personal matters that can impact behavior within the formal organization. Recognition and acceptance by experts in the same field of endeavor are often more important to engineers and scientists than approval and recognition by management.

3.11 The Social Organization

The reasons why a person has feelings of warmth, friendship, and closeness toward one person and not toward another are subtle and complex. Research shows that it is based predominantly on perceived sharing of values and beliefs. Social groups develop codes of behavior and customs based on these shared values and develop enforcement methods called sanctions. The sanctions used may be (1) mild razzing, (2) the "silent treatment," (3) ostracism, (4) withholding information, or (5) refusing help with work assignments. Sanctions of the social group are usually social in nature, while the sanctions of the formal organization tend to be economic. Both can be very effective. The accepted and enforced norms of behavior of the social group and the formal organization may reenforce each other or they may be in conflict. When they are in conflict, the norms of the social group usually prevail. The social group generally determines the workers' attitudes toward the administration, acceptable working habits, and moral codes.

The social structure within a formal organization will consist of interlacing social units or groups. Each group will consist of four to eight people. The members of the group will eat lunch together, take coffee breaks together, and see each other socially outside of the work environment. Some people will belong to only one social group (called a *clique* if you are not a member); others belong to two or more groups. These latter people form links from one group to another and make possible the informal communications network that is known as the grapevine.

The ill informed believe that the grapevine or rumor mill is not well defined, that it is circuitous, and that the information conveyed is false, distorted, and not selective. However, all the research indicates that it operates quickly (in fact, more rapidly than official channels), selectively, and along well-defined paths (or links). The information conveyed has a high degree of accuracy, and (unlike official channels) the system does not noticeably distort the message in the transmission process. Distortion in the system is minimized by excluding from the network persons who are known to distort messages.

The existence of the social organization should not be ignored by the manager. In general, managers take one of three attitudes toward the social organization structure.

1. An entity of whispers and evil intentions that spreads rumors, challenges authority, destroys morale, and is a thorn in the side of management.
2. A positive influence that helps keep people informed, provides informal feedback, and develops *esprit de corps*.
3. A mixed blessing that the manager cannot control but that can be influenced and must be treated with caution and respect.

The social organization will not go away just because the manager wishes it to. It therefore benefits the manager to study and understand the social structure that permeates the formal organization and try to turn it to good use. The grapevine is the quickest and most reliable means to get information rapidly disseminated throughout an organization. It is also an excellent means of floating "trial balloons" of contemplated new policies to obtain reactions prior to committing to them. Finally, it provides a safety valve for relieving tensions and frustrations created by the formal organization and brings sources of irritation to the attention of the manager. Since the grapevine also carries information that is unavailable through official channels, the wise manager will stay firmly tied into the network.

3.12 The Power Structure

Structure in the formal organization is based on the relationships between jobs and the delegation of authority and responsibility. Structure in the social organization is based on friendship choices. Structure in the power organization is based on values controlled by various members of the organization. That is, a person controls things considered valuable by others and is able to influence their behavior in exchange for these things.

There are numerous sources of power within a technical organization; among them are organizational, personal, and group sources. The *organizational sources* derive from (1) delegated authority, (2) location, and (3) job importance. Delegated authority (i.e., that conferred by the formal organization) provides both positive and negative sanctions that can be used to influence behavior. Among the positive sanctions are promotion, commendation, and salary increases. The negative sanctions include demotion, reduction in pay, reprimand, and layoff. The ability to apply or withhold these sanctions derives from administrative authority.

A second organizational source of power derives from the location of the positions within the formal structure. If the nature of the job locates it strategically in the flow of vital information or in the relationships between or among organizational components, the person may have greater power than that allocated by the administration. People who are placed in information-processing positions possess power because others become dependent on them for accurate and timely information. This dependence on people who possess and process information by those who need the information provides the basis for a power relationship. Executive assistants and even secretaries usually possess much more power than is apparent because of their ready access to an executive. Although their official duties may seem clerical and menial, their easy access to the executive, preparation of his or her schedules, and representation of his or her views improve their ability to render things of value to others. A kind word to the executive, a favorable appointment time, or a little "inside information" can be very valuable to a person. The ability to provide these and many other favors sometimes gives secretaries and assistants significant power.

Another source of organizational power is the importance of the job. Some positions are absolutely essential to the performance of the organization, and others are of peripheral importance. The holders of some jobs can be made angry with little repercussion, while others are in a position to exact retribution. Important papers can be expedited, delayed, or lost at the whim of a clerk or junior executive. The drafters can slow up completion of an important drawing. Anyone whose job is important to getting the task done holds potential power over the person who needs the task completed.

Individual sources of power derive from (1) expertise, (2) personal characteristics, (3) interest, and (4) tenure. An engineer, scientist, or technician has expert knowledge about a particular area because of intensive study and experience. If this knowledge or skill is greatly needed, it gives the holder a potential source of power. The degree of power possessed is a function of how readily that expertise can be replaced. All other things being equal, a person who is difficult to replace will have more power than one who is easily replaced. Power deriving from expertise is also conditioned by the importance of the job. An expert on metallurgy who is difficult to replace still has little power if the organization can easily get along for a while without such expertise.

Another personal source of power may derive from certain personal characteristics usually referred to as personality. Some people are so charming, witty, and physically attractive that others seek their approbation, approval, guidance, counsel, and friendsip. To the extent that such a person is able and willing to grant or withhold these gestures, he or she has power over those who value or desire them. We sometimes refer to such attractiveness as charismatic qualities.

Often certain tasks in an organization are essential, but distasteful, to perform to a manager. In such a situation, a subordinate can gain a certain degree of power over a supervisor by being willing to do the "dirty work." The threat of having to do such tasks is often sufficient reason for a manager to give in on certain points that are important to the subordinate.

Finally, tenure in the job can also be a personal source of power. The new supervisor will usually rely on the most senior staff members for guidance and advice while learning the ropes. This dependence gives senior staff members a degree of influence and, hence, power. Likewise, if it is known that the manager's tenure in the job is of limited duration, senior staff members will often have greater power than the manager. This is readily observed in military R&D groups where it is common for the chief executive to be a military officer and the deputy a civilian. Everyone knows that the officer will soon be moving on to the next assignment, but the civilian deputy will remain. In such cases, it is not unusual for the deputy to have more power than the superior. This source of power can also be seen in the relationship between a master sergeant or chief petty officer and a new young lieutenant.

The *group sources of power* derive from the ability to form coalitions. The power that is not available to the individual who stands alone may be available to the group that stands together. A group of engineers or supervisors who band together may be able to exercise great power over a superior. Although each member of a coalition may be readily replaceable, often the entire group is not. In a classroom situation, if one or a few students refuse to do their homework, the professor can fail them. If all of the students decide not to cooperate, there is not much the professor can do.

3.13   The Emergent Organization

The preceding sections have shown that there are at least four different organizational relationships or structures that modify, direct and, to some degree, control the behavior of people in the technical group. These are the formal, social, power, and prestige structures. Each of these structures overlaps, reinforces, or conflicts with the others. The emergent behavior of the individuals is the result of the complex, dynamic interaction of these four structures.

Ideally, of course, we would like to see a situation in which the manager holds a high position in all four structures. Occasionally, we find just such a situation. Wernher von Braun was such a manager. He was renowned for his own personal engineering accomplishments and was held in great professional esteem. He was also Director of the George C. Marshall Space Flight Center and thus held formal authority. He was a charismatic leader who inspired his subordinates to great commitment and enthusiasm. Finally, he was a close personal friend and colleague of many of his subordinate managers, who were with him at Peenemunde and Fort Bliss before coming to Huntsville, Alabama. The von Braun team spirit was very real and paid off in great engineering and scientific accomplishments.

Most of us are not so blessed in personality and abilities. However, every manager must be cognizant of the interplay of these four structural relationships. The manager can, to some extent, influence at least three of them. Certainly the formal organization is under direct control and can be deliberately designed. The manner in which this is done will also influence both the power structure and the social structure.

Physical proximity and enforced working together encourage, but do not guarantee, the formation of friendships. If the manager wishes to encourage collaboration, placing the individuals in close physical proximity will help. Likewise, a careful study of the sources of power and the power relationships as they develop will allow the manager to take corrective action before the power structure distorts or upsets the formal structure. Section 3.8 describes the kind of steps that can be taken.

References

1. "Apollo Program Management," Staff Study of the Committee on Science and Astronautics, U.S. House of Representatives, U.S. Government Printing Office, Washington, D.C., July 1969.
2. Argenti, John, "The Pyramid, The Ladder, and the Matrix," *Management Decision, 2* (3), Autumn 1968.
3. Auerbach, Isaac L., "Remodel the Pyramid Before It Crumbles," *Innovation,* No. 29, 1972.
4. Carlisle, Howard M., "Are Functional Organizations Becoming Obsolete," *Management Review, 58* (1), January 1969.
5. Fayol, Henri, *General and Industrial Management*, translated from the French by C. Stone, Pitman Publishing, New York, 1949.
6. Galbraith, Jay R., "Matrix Organization Designs," *Business Horizons, 14* (1), February 1971.
7. Gulick, Luther, "Notes on the Theory of Organization," *Papers on the Science of Administration*, L. Gulick and L. F. Urich, Editors, Institute of Public Administration, New York, 1937.
8. Hittle, J. D., *The Military Staff*, 3rd ed., Stockpole Co., Harrisburg, Pa., 1961.
9. Ignizio, J. P., and R. E. Shannon, "Organization Structures in the 1980's," *Industrial Engineering, 3* (9), September 1971.
10. Killian, William P., "Project Management as an Organizational Concept," *The Office, 73* (4), April 1971.
11. Kingdon, D. R., *Matrix Organization: Managing Information Technologies,* Tavistock, London, 1973.
12. Koontz, D., and C. O'Donnell, *Principles of Management,* McGraw-Hill, New York, 1964.
13. Ludwig, Steven, "The Move to Matrix Management," *Management Review, 59* (6), June 1970.
14. Mee, John F., "Matrix Organizations," *Business Horizons, 7* (2), Summer 1964.
15. Metcalf, H. C., and L. Urwick, Editors, *Dynamic Administration—The Collected Papers of Mary Parker Follett*, Harper & Bros., New York, 1940.
16. Mooney, James D., and Alan C. Reiley, *Onward Industry,* Harper & Row, New York, 1931.
17. Roy, R. H., *The Administrative Process,* Johns Hopkins Press, Baltimore, 1958.
18. Shannon, Robert E., "Apollo/Saturn Program Management," Source Book of Saturn Benefits, UARI Report, The University of Alabama in Huntsville, Research Institute, December 1970.
19. Shannon, Robert E., "Matrix Management Structures," *Industrial Engineering, 4* (3) March 1972.
20. "Teamwork Through Conflict," *Business Week,* March 20, 1971.
21. Walker, Arthur H., and Jay W. Lorsch, "Organizational Choice and Product vs. Function," *Harvard Business Review, 26* (6), November-December 1968.
22. Weber, Max, *The Theory of Social and Economic Organizations,* 2nd ed., A. M. Henderson and T. Parsons, translators, Free Press, Glencoe, Ill., 1957.

Discussion Questions

1. Should the people be fitted to the organization or the organization to the people?
2. Does the informal organization help or hinder the formal organization?
3. Can the formal organization be designed in such a way as to make advantageous use of the informal organization?
4. Do you think the matrix form of organization will see wider use in the future?
5. Would the matrix form of organization be a good structure for a university?
6. One assumption of the hierarchical pyramid is that of increasing competance for decision making the higher the position. Discuss the validity of this assumption in relationship to technical organizations.
7. Can organizational structure compensate for weak managerial talent?
8. How do the two functions of organizing and staffing differ? In what ways are they similar?
9. Are the two terms "accountability" and "responsibility" synonomous?
10. Discuss the concept of authority and the sources from which it derives.
11. Is there a difference between authority and power?

Case Study III

THE WARDEN COMPANY

Paul Warner, general manager of the Military Products Division of the Warden Company, paced back and forth in front of the window in deep thought. He was awaiting the arrival of Jim Foley, manager of the company's Program Management Office and Roy Blair, the engineering manager. Foley arrived first and seated himself at the small conference table.

WARNER: Well, that session with the Army representatives yesterday was certainly a fiasco. I thought we were going to have a program review meeting—not a knockdown, drag-out fight between our own people. I'd hate to read the reports those guys are going to write when they get home.

FOLEY: How was I to know that the engineering group was going to pick that time and place to set off a bomb? Blair knows better than to air our dirty linen in front of the customer that way.

WARNER: Well, it certainly makes us look stupid when you two guys sit there and argue about how far behind schedule we are and how big an overrun we're going to have on that target tracking system for the M-29 tank. I was appalled to learn we are already a month behind and overspent by $100,000, and the contract is only 6 months old.

FOLEY: I told you we can cut that schedule by 2 weeks and reduce the overrun to $50,000 by the end of the contract.

WARNER: But then Engineering pipes up and says they disagree. They predict a month late and $130,000 overrun.

FOLEY: You know the engineering group always exaggerates. They always want a big cushion so they can act like big heroes when they come in under the estimated schedule and budget. You remember what happened on that Navy gun job.

WARNER: I know, I know. But why can't you guys get together on these figures. Why do I always have to get everyone together and bang heads? I thought when we set your operation up 2 years ago that this would solve all these coordination problems. I'm really having second thoughts about whether this program management scheme is working. I still always seem to end up arbitrating. We can't go on this way, something has got to change.

FOLEY: I agree something has got to be done, but we can't go back to the old way. You remember the chaos we had before, with no one in charge and no central point for the customer to go to.

WARNER: Yes, I remember, but this set up doesn't seem to be working either.

At this point, Roy Blair entered and sat down at the opposite end of the table from Foley.

WARNER: Roy, I think you know why I asked you to come over. After that confrontation yesterday, I'm bound to get a call from the General tomorrow as soon as the army people get back home. We've got to have some firm answers that we can live with. Besides, I'm very concerned with how we got ourselves into such a situation in the first place.

BLAIR: I know. I've reviewed all of the estimates by my department heads and it just wouldn't be realistic to change them. It still looks like a month late and a $130,000 overrun.

FOLEY: That just doesn't make sense. How can you be a month late when we've only been at it for 6 months?

BLAIR: I've looked into that, and I can tell you why. Your office didn't give us permission to proceed until 3 weeks after we should have started and then. . . .

FOLEY: Now wait a minute. Those 3 weeks were spent waiting for you to make up your mind whether or not to accept the schedule and budget we prepared. We got them to you on time; you held them up.

BLAIR: I didn't accept them right away because I knew from the start we couldn't meet your budget. You took our estimates and then cut them 20 percent. That's why we have the overrun.

FOLEY: But you did accept them. I have your signature right here.

BLAIR: Sure I finally accepted them. My back was up against the wall, and you knew it. I have a very limited overhead budget to support people not currently on contracts. It was either give in or lay the people off. I figured they might as well be working on the project while we argued about budgets. When you give me a budget that is 20 percent too low and say "take it or leave it," I have to take it and then face up to the overrun later.

WARNER: Let's come back to that later. You've explained 3 weeks of the slippage. Where did the other week come from?

BLAIR: That's easy to explain. We had barely started when Foley's coordinator started coming in with all kinds of dumb questions. What if we did this instead of that? Can you reduce the weight by 15 pounds? Would the system be compatible with the M-25 tank system? We spend 2 or 3 days every week answering questions.

FOLEY: Those questions aren't dumb, and they're coming from the customer. We've got to keep the Army happy if we want to keep doing business with them.

BLAIR: But it takes time and effort to answer them. We've easily spent more than a week digging up the answers. No place in my budget is there time or money for all this. I thought one of the purposes of the project management scheme was to keep those people off our backs. If all you guys are going to do is be messenger boys relaying their questions to us and our answers to them, why do we need you?

FOLEY: We'd gladly answer the questions ourselves if we could, but we don't have the technical expertise in my shop. You'd be surprised at how many questions we do answer and how many requests we turn away because they are outside the scope of the contract.

BLAIR: Well, I don't have those problems on the projects I run myself.

FOLEY: Maybe that's because all the tough projects are assigned to my office. That brings up another problem. Not every project is run through my office. It seems to me that the top priority for manpower always goes to the programs that are entirely under your responsibility. Last week, for example, all the drafters were pulled off this job to work on the hydraulic control unit for the Navy.

WARNER: Let's consider that a minute. Jim, do you think it would help if all the projects were handled by your office? That way you could set the priorities, etc.

BLAIR: Wait a minute. I don't object to Jim coordinating the projects that cross departmental lines. But I've got to be in a position to run the Engineering group. I have to decide where best to use my people and resources, not Jim. I'm the one who has to decide what areas need strengthening and which should be cut back. I also have to worry about how to support my people, so I have to be free to seek contracts on my own. I'm willing to accept responsibility to meet my budgets and schedules as far as possible, but only one person can run Engineering.

FOLEY: That's really the heart of the problem. I've got the responsibility, but every department head has the authority to run things any damned way they want.

WARNER: Maybe we should go to a project-type organization. In other words, when we get a major contract, we assemble the technical people we need, borrowing them from the different departments, and assign them directly to you, Jim.

BLAIR: What happens after the contract is finished? What do you do with the people, send them back to me? What if my budget won't stand it at that point?

FOLEY: I'm afraid I have to agree with Roy. That would put him in an impossible position. I've been in a line position before, and it's a continuous juggling act trying to balance budgets, overhead, manpower forecasts, and all the other problems. I'd hate to be put in a position where people could be taken and sent back without my say-so.

WARNER: Well, thats a long-range problem we have to be thinking about. Our immediate problem is the Army tank project. You two get together this afternoon and hammer out a budget and schedule you can both live with. I've got to have some firm answers the first thing in the morning when the General calls. If you guys have to work all night, I want one set of figures.

As the two men started to leave, Warner asked Foley to remain for a minute.

WARNER: Jim, we can't go on like this. It's obvious to me, just as it was obvious to the Army yesterday, that we don't have control of our own act. How many people do you have?

FOLEY: I've got six people plus my secretary. Four are coordinators, one is a cost estimator and budget specialist; the other one is an expert on PERT and is used for scheduling and status review.

WARNER: How many projects does each coordinator have?

FOLEY: It varies. This tank project is taking one man full time; the other 12 contracts are divided more or less equally among the other three.

WARNER: What do you think is the real problem?

FOLEY: Part of it is lack of manpower. Sometimes the projects are in trouble before we know it. But part of it is that my coordinators have no line authority. We can negotiate budgets, schedules, and work statements with the line departments and try to follow up to see they live up to their agreements. But if they fall down on the job, there isn't anything we can do except holler. I've threatened several times to take a job away from them and go outside on contract, but they know it's an idle threat. I'm not sure you would let me if I wanted to.

WARNER: Well, I don't know what the answer is, but something has got to be done. I don't know what I'm going to tell the General in the morning. But I'm sick and tired of being put in this embarrassing position. Besides, this playing referee constantly is giving me ulcers. I want you to give this matter serious thought and give me some kind of recommendation next Friday.

Case Study Discussion Questions

1. What would you recommend if you were Foley?
2. What type of organization structure does the Military Products Division presently have?
3. Can the present setup be made workable?
4. Should Warner take any action against Blair for agreeing to a budget and schedule he knew he could not live up to?

CHAPTER 4 staffing and training

4.1 The Importance

No problem facing the technical manager is more important or vexing than that of obtaining and retaining an organization's most critical resource—skilled, creative personnel. The determination of the technical program, organizational structure, and procurement of financial support and facilities are all meaningless if the manager fails in the areas of staffing and motivation. Laboratories, computers, and exotic equipment do not make an engineering or research program. Only people can produce innovative results. An interesting and important point to consider is that if the manager succeeds in this one aspect of the job, most other problems will, to a large extent, take care of themselves or at least be much easier to solve.

The technical program is the people. The technical program is not what the project write-ups or budget state, but what the people are actually doing. Unfortunately, many mangers become fascinated by the paper work. If they have good documentation and project write-ups, they assume that they have a good program. Their attitude is that if it is written down, it must be happening. The fact is that the only technical program in any organization is the one that the people are actually doing, not what the paper work says they should be doing. Therefore, if you have good people in the right jobs and they are properly motivated, the technical program will take care of itself with just a little guidance.

The same can be said of the organizational structure. Any group can be put together on paper in a hundred different ways. However, the people in it, not what is written down in the organization chart, will determine the *true* working organization. Innovative people, properly motivated, can work around and through any organizational structure, no matter how good or how poor. The organizational structure is primarily for expediting communications and other logistical aspects of the job such as time-keeping, vacation scheduling, providing secretarial help, etc. Organizational structure can be an irritant or a help, but it cannot get the job done or prevent it from being done. The people in it will cause an organizational structure to function or fail.

Finally, innovative people can go a long way toward counteracting or getting around the lack of equipment and facilities. The creative, dedicated mind can almost always find a way to improvise, or get around the lack of sophisticated equipment. It is also true that a group of creative, productive people will find and retain financial sponsors.

If an organization is to be a continuing success, it must have access to an adequate supply of qualified people. Recruiting applicants for the available positions within the organization is, therefore, extremely important, because an inadequate supply of qualified manpower will adversely impact an organization's chances for success just as much as insufficient financial resources or materials shortages.

4.2 What Kind of People

Staffing is the management function that deals with acquiring and retaining qualified people. More specifically, it involves keeping jobs filled with the right people; it encompasses the following subfunctions.

1. Specification of job requirements.
2. Transfers and promotions.
3. Recruitment of job applicants.
4. Selection of the best candidates.
5. Training.

Since every manager has limited funds available, serious thought must be given to the type of people needed and how many of each kind. This question obviously cannot be separated from the question of objectives and goals of the organization. Ask any technical manager what kind of people are needed and the immediate answer is, "Creative and self-motivated people." Unfortunately, if you were to look at the jobs and functions actually being staffed, you would probably find that a creative, self-motivated person would be completely wasted and unhappy in most of them.

Very few managers have a clear idea of the types and numbers of people needed. Go into almost any technical organization and you will find graduate engineers doing technician jobs and graduate scientists running routine, repetitive tests. Few organizations utilize their technical personnel well. One major study showed that of the 727 engineers and scientists studied (56 percent with advanced degrees) from representative companies in the aircraft, chemical, drug, electrical, and petroleum industries, 72 percent said that management utilized their talents poorly.

The staffing function necessarily begins with the specification of jobs that must be done in order to achieve organizational objectives. A job description should be prepared for each position to be filled. It should be written in specific terms and should delineate the objectives, duties, relationships, and results expected of a person in that position. To complete the job definition, the job description should be combined with a specification of the characteristics of the individual who could fill such a position. These characteristics encompass the following.

1. Physical requirements of the job (vision, hearing, speech, etc.) if they are really important.
2. Educational and occupational attainments normally needed for entry and subsequent advancement.
3. Degree of creativity and innovation expected. (More will be said about this shortly.)
4. Desirable personality characteristics. These become important if the person will be expected to interact with customers and outside contacts or operate as a part of a team.
5. Any special circumstance of the job such as frequent travel, rotating assignments, etc.

Job requirements will vary with time and should, therefore, be subjected to continuing scrutiny. Specifically, the demands of a changing technology, the introduction of a new process, or new promotional opportunities may each modify the requirements of a particular job. This is an important consideration, since a position that entails innovation and frequent change, as opposed to maintaining stable and consistent work, requires special personality characteristics. In particular, considerable self-confidence is needed by executives when a company is continually implementing changes in order to alleviate the problems fostered by new competition or rapid advances in technology. Additionally, a high degree of emotional stability is also desirable, since a consequence of such major perturbations is increased stress on everyone whose job is impacted by new practices.

The importance of distinguishing mandatory job requirements from those that are merely desirable cannot be overemphasized. For example, the net result of setting educational requirements unnecessarily high will be to rule out applicants who may be well qualified otherwise and who, in fact, are able to perform the required duties satisfactorily. This is particularly true in view of the fact that obtaining the right quality of personnel does not necessarily mean obtaining the most highly trained, experienced, or intelligent individuals. Specifically, excessive hiring of such "overqualified" personnel may precipitate an imbalance of personnel in the organization who desire only to manage, design, or perform selected functions while declining to perform other necessary work that they regard as "demeaning." Actually, a combination of technical skills, mature experience, and youth must be pursued and brought together if the organization is to function effectively.

Most positions in a technical organization do not need and cannot tolerate *highly* creative people. High creativity occurs most often in the unconventional—even eccentric—individual. Such people are self-confident and are likely to be antisocial, antiauthoritarian, and excessive in their personal habits. Their very purpose is to destroy the status quo, the old ways of thinking and doing things. We cannot expect them to be conformists. The organization has a hard time tolerating them. They refuse to acknowledge what they consider petty administrative regulations. They are extremely disruptive and a constant trial to the administrators. They delight in swimming upstream, against the tide. They are, according to management, troublemaking, rabble-rousing prima donnas. Any attempts to rein them in will usually result in their leaving the organization and the administration breathing a sigh of relief to be rid of them.

But the technical manager who has a small handful of such people and the good sense to recognize them is lucky. If you want high creativity in certain positions, you tolerate highly creative people. If you do not need highly creative people, do yourself and them the favor of not trying to harness a racehorse to a plow.

The majority of the engineering and scientific positions in most technical organizations do not require a *high* degree of creativity. Most require only good common sense, sound technical training, and some ability to innovate. Many positions actually require only technicians. Unfortunately, since most technical managers are either engineers or scientists and many of them hold advanced graduate degrees, there is a certain ego satisfaction to be found in telling oneself and others that one has X number of engineers and scientists working under one's supervision, and that Y percent of these hold advanced degrees. Unfortunately, this ego satisfaction costs the organization dearly in salaries, recruiting costs, and morale problems.

Almost every technical organization requires a few highly creative individuals, a larger group of engineers and scientists to perform analysis, troubleshooting, tests, design, etc., and a sufficient number of highly qualified technicians. The ideal balance among these various categories of people will vary somewhat, depending on the mission of the particular group. As a guideline, if the organization is charged with technical activities over a fairly broad portion of the spectrum, for every highly creative individual there should be at least 10 to 15 competent engineers and scientists. For every engineer and scientist there should probably be not less than two technicians. If the ratio in an organization varies greatly from this, it is probably paying a high price for ego satisfaction.

4.3 Internal versus External Recruiting

After the technical manager has honestly and dispassionately looked at the staffing needs and determined the requirements for each position, the next problem is attracting the right people. This problem cannot be separated from that of retaining personnel once they have joined the group. This is true because the greatest recruiting resource for any organization is the people already in the organization, particularly when seeking experienced personnel.

There are two basic approaches to recruiting—internal and external. Unfortunately, internal recruiting is not utilized effectively by management in many cases. When a position becomes open, it is common for management to look outside for someone to fill the job instead of giving consideration to someone already within the organization. This approach is generally based on the premises that (1) it serves to bring in new talent, thereby enhancing the effectiveness and efficiency of the organization, and (2) it precludes the disruption of a smoothly functioning team because of the removal of a competent, conscientious worker. Generally, this management policy is detrimental to the organization in the long run. Although one justification for this approach is that it minimizes disruption and thereby maximizes efficiency, this is not always the case. Actually, in many instances it is the primary impetus for internal disruption. This policy fails to consider that the worker whom management did not wish to disturb by placement in another position may be very disturbed at not being considered for the position. Consequently, the worker may elect to seek a new job elsewhere, and management is faced with a greater problem than the one it wished to avoid.

In addition to alleviating the preceding problems, internal recruiting and promotion have another distinct advantage in that better-qualified applicants are generally obtained for the available positions. This is partially because, even though some jobs in different organizations are quite similar, many positions in a given organization require specialized knowledge that can only be obtained through the individual's contacts and associations within that particular organization. The person recruited or promoted from within will have more familiarity with the people, procedures, policies, and special characteristics of the organization than an applicant recruited from the outside. Another reason that recruiting from within tends to obtain better-qualified personnel is because management, by its observations of an individual's performance over a period of time, can make a more realistic assessment of the person's skills than those of an applicant recruited from outside. Consequently, the margin of error in evaluating the capabilities of the present employee should be much less than that associated with the assessment of an outsider's capabilities.

It is therefore reasonable to anticipate that, since the person recruited from within has a greater degree of familiarity with the duties and responsibilities of a position than an outside applicant, that person will function more effectively in the position, and employee discontent will be minimized. Internal recruitment also helps in motivation; people will generally work harder if they feel that this will lead to advancement, but they will have little incentive to perform if it is management policy to fill the more prestigious positions through outside recruiting.

A transfer is generally a change in position without a change in status or pay. In some instances, a transfer is made to rectify an original mistake in selection and placement. This may be predicated on either the individual's feelings that there will be more opportunity for advancement in another position or the desire to gain wider experience. In other cases, transfers may be precipitated by the existence of a manpower surplus in one department and a shortage in another. For example, technological change may cause the manpower needs of some departments to decline and necessitate expansion of the needs of other departments. In order to safeguard the jobs of long-term employees and to preclude losing the skills of trained personnel, most organizations try to transfer employees to other positions. Furthermore, an organization that utilizes a liberal transfer policy generally has less difficulty in adapting to changing environments.

A promotion is generally a change in position with an associated change in status and pay. It might seem that selecting candidates for promotion is considerably easier than choosing among new applicants, but the tasks are essentially equal in difficulty. One reason is that a higher position is likely to require skills that differ in degree and in kind from the one directly beneath it. For example, an individual may be doing well on the present job but may lack the ability to perform satisfactorily in a higher-ranked position.

The preceding problem is further complicated by the fact that the individual who makes the final decision on promotion is probably not the candidates' immediate supervisor. Consequently, the decision maker is usually not totally familiar with what the various candidates have been doing and how well they have been doing it. In some cases, even the immediate supervisor may base a recommendation on general impressions instead of on specific aspects of the job performances of the various candidates. Under these circumstances, it is extremely difficult to measure individual merit, even though the best-performing employees should be advanced if promotion is to be an incentive.

Certain jobs offer employees the opportunity to move about freely, thereby bringing them into contact with high-level individuals whose opinions are crucial in promotion decisions. These employees learn their way around the organization and are "in the right spot at the right time" when a promotional opportunity materializes, even though their individual merits and abilities may not compare favorably with those of the other candidates.

The promotional process is, therefore, characterized by subjective elements that can create inequalities. Most organizations, however, recognize the need for a concerted effort to measure and reward ability, and they utilize devices such as performance appraisals, executive inventories, etc., to accomplish this objective. This is extremely important, because organizations that fail to reward excellence in service invariably suffer in terms of deteriorating efficiency and morale.

The case for outside recruiting also has some valid points. For example, the policy of recruiting from within may, in its more extreme forms, dictate that every applicant recruited from outside must start at a very low position in the organization, regardless of capabilities. Such a policy tends to discourage the highly ambitious and well-trained individual. The policy of recruiting from outside, on the other hand, alleviates this problem, since it facilitates the assignment of newcomers to initial positions that are compatible with their job competence.

If a technical organization is to continue to be successful, there must be the continuing introduction of new perspectives. In many cases, this can best be accomplished by the infusion of "new blood" from outside sources to keep the organization from growing stagnant and repetitious. The organization is generally most successful if there is an optimum mix of newcomers and old-timers.

4.4 Soliciting Applicants

There are various means to reach job applicants through outside recruiting. Some of the methods commonly utilized are:

1. Advertising.
2. College recruiting.
3. Employment agencies—government and private.
4. Professional contacts.

Advertising in daily newspapers, over local radio stations, and in the magazines of professional associations is a popular method used to attract potential employees. These persons usually apply in great numbers, but they are of highly variable quality. This problem can, however, be partially alleviated by judicious selection of the advertising medium, particularly if recruitment of a particular technical discipline or population segment is the objective. For example, a more homogeneous group will respond to an advertisement in the *Journal of the American Chemical Society* than to one placed in a community newspaper. In a similar fashion, newspapers that cater to a specific minority group will be useful in recruiting members of that group.

Advertising tends to be more effective if the advertisement includes one or two glamour jobs along with the ordinary job offerings. This attracts marginal applicants for the glamour jobs who are also willing to be considered for the other jobs. In any case, the advertisement should address the primary interests of the technical person. For example, a survey of over 2500 engineers and scientists indicated that the five most important considerations in seeking a new position were (1) availability of good schools, (2) community attitudes, (3) availability of outdoor recreation, (4) laboratory or office located in safe, clean area, and (5) moderate climate [10]. One of the surprising results of this survey was the importance of the community. When asked whether they would accept a less attractive job in order to live in a more attractive community, 58 percent said yes, 34 percent said maybe, and only 8 percent said no.

College recruitment is now a recognized function of almost every large organization. The years subsequent to World War II have been characterized by unusually heavy competition in this field, particularly for technical personnel. Many organizations, as a matter of course, send representatives to scores of universities and technical colleges to interview prospective applicants. This technique permits the organization to paint an attractive picture of its employment opportunities and to conduct advanced screening of candidates. The candidates who seem to compare favorably with the organization's standards are then invited to visit its facilities for further consideration.

Employment agencies can also be a useful source of job applicants. Government employment agencies are located in nearly every major city. These agencies charge neither the employer nor the prospective employee for their services. In the past, however, the reputations of these agencies suffered substantially. This was primarily because they also administered unemployment insurance benefits. In many instances, individuals who were receiving benefits and had no interest in employment opportunities would profess an interest in such openings in order to continue their unemployment benefits. Obviously such individuals were unacceptable to the organizations to which they were subsequently sent. Many organizations therefore have turned to government employment agencies only as a last resort. Presently, however, these agencies are trying to alleviate such problems and improve their reputations by judiciously screening applicants for the requirements of specific jobs in particular organizations, especially those that deal with technical occupations.

Private employment agencies specialize in specific occupations and skills (clerical, craft, technical, etc.). Unlike the government employment agencies, these agencies charge for their services. Sometimes the employee pays the fee; in other instances, the employer pays. Whatever the case, the fee may be quite substantial. Private employment agencies that specialize in executive recruiting are commonly utilized to find new managerial talent. These agencies may conduct an intensive nationwide search for an individual with highly specialized experience and prescribed personality traits. Most of the persons contacted in such endeavors will already be employed or will have confidentially indicated a willingness to be considered. Conversely, however, an unemployed executive may experience difficulty in receiving serious consideration, since unemployment is often considered synonymous with failure.

A common problem encountered when employment agencies are utilized as recruiting mechanisms is the selection of the agency. If the organization is not familiar with any suitable employment agencies in the locations to be explored, a good approach is to purchase the weekend newspapers in the cities in question and see which agencies do the best job of advertising and apparently have the most extensive job lists pertaining to the technical areas of interest. Such considerations are usually indicative of the degree of success that can be expected by utilizing the services of a particular agency; a large number of open positions generally suggests an active and successful employment agency. In any case, the results obtained by utilizing an employment agency are contingent on (1) the capability of the agent handling the inquiry, (2) the degree to which the agent is cognizant of the organization's needs, and (3) the number of qualified applicants available.

One of the results of the trend toward specialization of the work force that has become readily apparent in recent years is the increasing effectiveness of professional contacts as a recruiting mechanism. Many individuals who share similar training and work experiences become acquainted with one another and develop wide circles of friends and associates through professional society meetings, executive management groups, day-to-day business dealings, etc. Such relationships are extremely fertile recruitment areas. For example, although the stated purpose of professional society conventions is to exchange learned papers, much time is actually devoted to exchanging job information. When a position becomes open, a manager can telephone an acquaintance who may either be interested in the job or who can recommend another associate. In this way, an adequate supply of qualified applicants can sometimes be readily obtained.

The shortcomings in recruiting activities of many organizations include inept interviewing, a poor schedule, one-sided interviews, slowness in reimbursing travel expenses, and slowness in responding after an interview. Such shortcomings can become critical when trying to recruit creative, competent engineers and scientists, since these individuals are only a small percentage of the total available population.

In locating, recruiting, and selecting these scarce individuals, it should be noted that "it takes a thief to catch a thief." Experienced, well-qualified technical personnel gravitate to well-run organizations. They are attracted by many things, but mostly by word of mouth and visible accomplishments. The best recruiter for any organization is the competent, reasonably contented technical person in the organization who is challenged and utilized by the organization; these people want to bring in their competent friends and professional acquaintances. One of the unique characteristics of the competent technical person is the fact that they seek and desire competent co-workers. They will not, however, try to bring them into a situation with which they are discontented or do not believe to be desirable.

When good engineers or scientists see meaningful technical results in the form of new products or technical reports and articles coming out of an organization, and they know that its employees are enthusiastic about their work, they will seek out the organization. Geographic location, physical facilities, and other fringe benefits may help to rationalize a decision to join the organization, but they will not be decisive. Competent technical organizations have been built up in every part of the country.

4.5 The Selection Process

Attracting qualified job applicants is only one aspect of the overall staffing function. Given two or more candidates for a position, there is no aboslutely sure way of selecting the person who is best fitted for the job. There are, however, various techniques that have been utilized to enhance the effectiveness of the selection process. They include:

1. Examination of each candidate's past record through application forms.
2. Interviews.
3. Personality and achievement tests.

Each technique will now be discussed in detail.

The application form and personal resume are traditional devices for recording information that pertains to the applicant's educational background and past occupational experience. In many cases, application forms are also designed to elicit information that will provide clues to the applicant's personality. Since they are generally completed by the applicants, the application forms and resumes also demonstrate the candidates' ability to write concisely, organize thoughts, and present facts clearly. Specifically, the information recorded provides interviewers with leads and points of departure for a formal job interview. It also provides the organization with data for permanent employee records.

Although references are generally listed as part of the application, they are of little value, because most people named are reluctant to handicap the applicant's chances of finding employment and will be inclined to provide favorable references. This situation is exemplified by the fact that there is little correlation between ratings given by references and observed job performance.

The interview is perhaps the most widely utilized selection technique. It is generally regarded as the crucial part of the selection process, since many people believe that they can get a better idea of the applicant's overall personality, including intelligence and job interest, by face-to-face contact than in any other way. At this point, the organization has probably invested a lot of time and money in the recruitment program, and the interview is perhaps the last step in selecting the final candidate for the job. Three objectives should guide the interviewer.

1. Whether the applicant is eventually selected or not, the interview should create a good feeling toward the organization and its management policies.
2. The interview should be a basis for giving truthful job and company information so that the candidate can make an intelligent decision to accept or reject employment if offered.
3. The interview should provide relevant information about the applicant that is unavailable from other sources.

The interview generally covers the applicant's job record, with particular emphasis on the most recent job. The interviewer must determine the actual responsibilities of the applicant's most recent (or present) job and how well he or she has handled them. This is especially important, since relevant experience and past performance are likely to be good indicators of the applicant's future job performance. The applicant is usually informed as to how the position fits into the overall organization and is given some indication as to the type of people with whom he or she will be expected to work. Any question regarding training facilities, prospects for promotion or transfer, etc., should be dealt with frankly at this stage, because the organization is also being evaluated by the applicant.

If the interviewer is the individual who will be the successful candidate's supervisor, the interview will enable the supervisor to gain some idea as to how well they could work together. This, in turn, is usually one of the primary considerations in actually making the selection.

The interview is not, however, a precise technique and, even at its best, skillful interviewing is extremely difficult. The reactions of applicants are highly dependent on who is interviewing them and how the interview is conducted. The basic problem with the interview as a selection device is that many people tend to have preconceptions and prejudices. Since there are no quantitative criteria for success or failure, it is easy for the interviewer to evaluate the candidate's performance erroneously in accordance with personal stereotypes. For example, the interviewer may believe that people can be evaluated on the basis of the type of tie they select, the length of their hair, their tone of voice, or whether or not they "look you in the eye." Furthermore, a candidate may bear a resemblance to someone who previously performed extremely well or badly in the organization.

In any case, the impression that an applicant makes in a single interview, or even in multiple interviews, can be misleading. A person who makes a good first impression may not turn out as well on further acquaintance. For example, some individuals talk intelligently but do not act intelligently. Additionally, some people who project a decisive image are actually indecisive, whereas others who seem to be very hesitant may act quickly, surely, and wisely in an actual on-the-job situation.

4.6 Academic Achievement

One common method used for screening inexperienced applicants is academic grades and test scores such as IQ or creativity tests. Test scores and grades are thought to provide a stong indication of a student's competencies in the world outside the testing and classroom situations. Unfortunately, this is not the case. The evidence is now overwhelming that tests and grades tell very little about talent and are extremely poor at predicting professional achievement. In fact, the evidence is more convincing that there is an inverse relationship.

Intelligence tests and other academic tests such as the Graduate Record Exam (GRE) and Scholastic Aptitude Test (SAT) do correlate fairly well with academic achievement indices such as grade point averages, but they do not predict later professional achievement. Just a sampling of some of the research reported in this area will suffice. Harmon [6] made a careful study of the professional contributions of a group of physicists and biologists. These were then compared with college-level academic proficiency data such as verbal and mathematical aptitude test scores, advanced achievement tests in the student's field of concentration, and grades obtained in science courses.

How good a professional scientist the person became could not be predicted by any of this academic proficiency information. In fact, nearly half of the correlations computed were negative, not positive.

The same result has emerged in study after study, whether intelligence test scores or course grades were used as predictions. Helson and Crutchfield [7] found, for example, that mathematicians whom knowledgeable peers identified as doing particularly good work had no higher IQ scores than a group of mathematicians chosen at random. Research on chemists done by Bloom [2] and data on research scientists analyzed by MacKinnon [12] yielded the same outcome. No matter what the field—psychologists [13], artists [1], architects [9], engineers [9], or business students [8]—the results were the same, either no significant correlation or else a negative correlation.

One study by Holland [8] showed that the nonintellectual factors most related to academic achievement were persistence, good behavior, and rigidity. When he compared these to the characteristics of the creative person, the two sets of personality traits for academic achievers and for creative types were at odds. Although two of the scales correlated, five were neutral, and five had a negative correlation with one another. The implication is that the college achiever has less potential for creativity than many nonachievers. This can be readily explained by the observation that the more creative and individualistic students are more troublesome to the average teacher than other students. If the teacher's concern is with order and covering the material (which is more or less inevitable in large universities), anyone who diverges from this may get in the way of instruction and is penalized for it when grades are determined.

An interesting aspect of this problem is that the faculty seems to be aware of the discrepancy. Studies done by Davis [4] at Amherst, California Institute of Technology, Cornell, Dartmouth, M.I.T., Rensselar Polytechnic Insitutute, Rutgers, and Stanford showed that faculty evaluations of students for creativity had a low correlation with the grades that the same faculty members gave to the students. In another study done at the University of Michigan by Platz, McClintock, and Katz [15], it was found that the students' grade point average had a 0.08 correlation with faculty predictions of contributions to engineering and science. It seems reasonably clear that the grading system (at all levels, including the graduate one) rewards the conforming plodder and penalizes the imaginative student who is most likely to make a significant contribution to engineering or science.

The preceding discussion is not intended to negate or downgrade the importance of the student obtaining good grades. Good grades are required in order to get into graduate school and to receive a degree. However, grades should not be used as the sole or even main criteria for hiring selection, since they do not measure the traits that are of primary interest. It would seem reasonable not to abandon traditional ability tests and grades but, instead, to limit their use to the screening out of those who score too low. For example, a manager might specify that only students who rank in the upper two-thirds or upper half will be considered. There is nothing absolute about the particular cutoff points, but some such thresholds should be specified and further increments above them ignored in the selection process.

For undergraduate engineers, the manager might specify successful passing of the Engineer-in-Training (E.I.T.) test that is required for professional registration and not grade point or class ranking as adequate proof of minimal qualifications. In the case of students with graduate degrees, the grade point average and Graduate Record Exam are meaningless for selection purposes, since an adequate grade point average is required for graduation.

4.7 Tests for Creativity

As the evidence mounted that intelligence tests and grade point averages were not good predictors of professional performance, extensive attempts have been made to devise special tests to assess creativity and originality. It was suggested by psychologists that since there is now a pretty good understanding of how creativity works and of the personality traits of the creative person, specialized creativity tests and personality assessment tests could be used for screening. Consequently, there was a great deal of activity along these lines during the 1960s. Unfortunately, if academic skills tests and grade point averages tell little about professional competency, creativity tests in the middle- to high-intelligence groups are not about to fill the gap. The two surveys by Wallack [20,21] provide an extensive examination of the evidence resulting in a negative finding.

Some limited evidence can be found to support ideational fluency tests for screening purposes. Typically, these tests ask the respondent to generate possible ways in which specified pairs of objects are similar (such as a cat and a dog) or possible uses for some common object (such as a toothbrush). Very little correlation has been found between idea fluency and standard intelligence tests. In one research project with college students, those scoring in the highest third on idea fluency did show more out-of-school attainments in literature and science than those scoring in the bottom third but, at best, the relationships were tenuous and statistically nonsignificant. All other attempts to prove validity for idea fluency tests have been largely negative in their outcomes.

Despite the overwhelming evidence against the use of creativity tests, intelligence tests, and grade point averages, a surprisingly large number of organizations continue to use them. The same can be said of personality assessment tests. These tests screen out the very people the organization is seeking to identify, because they will generally refuse to take the tests or resent the procedure. The more independent, self-assured, and creative the individual, the more likely he or she is to resent the invasion of privacy and the indignity that such tests represent.

4.8 Assessing Achievements

If we cannot rely on academic grade points, intelligence tests, creativity tests, or personality assessment tests, what criteria can be used? There is no easy answer. We do not want to rely on perceived personality traits such as appearance, glibness, dress, or manners; to do so will almost assure us of precluding the most creative people. Fortunately, the technical manager has several alternatives available. First, candidates should be requested to submit reports on any engineering design or scientific projects they have conducted either in school or outside of school. These should be evaluated by some of the most productive senior members of the organization. We can best recognize talent from the display of excellence at vocational pursuits. These significant accomplishments, where the candidate has had to apply skill and orginality, offer the most legitimate bases (once certain minimal academic skills and qualifications have been met) for the judgment of merit. All engineering and scientific educational programs today require design projects, term projects, etc. If the student is so disinterested in the work or not proud enough of it to have saved copies, you have learned a great deal about professional interests and pride. Likewise, hobbies and nonacademic pursuits can be very indicative of the candidate. Is the candidate interested in intellectually or competitively challenging activities? The bookworm with no outside activities is probably a bad bet.

The second good source of information is the faculty. Faculty members usually recognize creativity in their students, even if they do not always reward it in the classroom. With graduate students this faculty appraisal is even more meaningful. The closer contact and smaller classes in graduate study puts the professors in an excellent position to evaluate potential. This is particularly true of the student's thesis or dissertation director. Their personal appraisal is probably the most valid one available. The manager should think very seriously before hiring a graduate student who has not written a thesis for a research position. Writing a thesis or dissertation develops and demonstrates certain skills that additional course work can never do.

The third important source of information is the fact that creative, innovative people have an uncanny ability to recognize each other. Thus, the technical manager should rely on senior personnel, who are known from experience to be productive, to screen and interview prospective new employees. This has a double advantage; not only will the screening process be more effective, but it will also enhance the chances of getting the people to whom offers are made. The young prospect will be attracted by the technical competence of the interviewer.

Utilizing senior personnel for such tasks dilutes their activity and is considered an unwarranted intrusion on their time by some. However, no other activity is so vital to the continued well-being of the organization. The impact can be minimized by judicious prescreening (talks with faculty, etc.), choosing the senior staff member who stands most to benefit by the new addition, and conducting most of the talks on the scene (at the plant or laboratory). A smoothly efficient personnel department is also of immeasurable help, but the final screening process of candidates should be done by other creative individuals.

Whether recruiting experienced or inexperienced personnel, the best recruiters are the competent, satisfied, productive personnel already associated with the organization. Competent, new people, whether experienced or inexperienced, will be attracted by success. If they see an organization bringing new products and devices out of the laboratory, if they read excellent reports or articles being published by its people, and if they find its people enthusiastic about their work and situation, they will seek to join that organization.

4.9 Follow-up Responsibility

Bringing competent personnel into the organization does not finish the staffing responsibility. The manager must also provide continuous counseling and training to the employee to insure that skills are maintained and motivation sustained.

Some individuals proceed through a technical career with ease. They manage to make the transition from the educational institution to the working world with little difficulty. They readily adapt to a changing environment and manage to keep up-to-date in their technical speciality. As they become more experienced, they consider the ranks of management; if they enter management, they make the transition with few problems and seem to enjoy their work. Growing old gracefully, they lead happy, productive lives. But these individuals are in a minority.

Most people who pursue a technical career are subject to recurring crises of varying degrees of severity throughout their careers. The thing that makes life both interesting and frustrating is that it is always changing. This year is very different from last year, and next year will be different from this one. Life is change, and change presents both opportunities and dangers. Psychologists have been studying humans in a work environment very intensely for a number of years. They have identified certain times and occurrences in our lives that often bring about crises that affect our futures. In the following sections we will discuss a few of these, such as the early career crisis, the middle-age crisis, technical obsolescence, and what management can do to ease the problem.

4.10 Young Engineers and Scientists

In 1975, Cook published an article [3] based on his observations of the lives of young doctoral graduates entering the real world. These observations apply to any student graduating in engineering or science, although possibly to a lesser extent to bachelor's and master's degree students. Cook's experience reveals that ego satisfaction and self-esteem needs are the major driving forces behind the motivation of graduate students. The better the student, the stronger the psychological commitment and the stronger the ego-centered motivation. If the student is married, the spouse usually feeds this motivation by a similiar dedication to ''the cause.'' Often the spouse is making almost as many sacrifices to achieve the goal. This situation foreshadows potential conflict areas in postgraduate life when more basic needs such as love and security become more important in the family life. Relatives are also a source that feeds this ego-centered need of the graduate student. This is especially true if the student is the first in the family to obtain such a degree. Thus a student may enjoy the benefits of a family while neglecting the associated responsibilities that will become a major factor in later life.

What occurs when the individual first leaves the campus and is faced with a typical job environment? Initially, the job assignments require a short time to complete relative to the acquisition of the degree, and this helps to build self-confidence. But then the individual begins to be frustrated by certain observations. Some of the older personnel do not seem to be as interested in technical matters as had been expected. Also, most employees arrive at 8 A.M. and leave at 5 P.M., contrary to the university style. The administrative red tape is recognized as a new obstacle. These frustrations, although annoying, usually do not cause a crisis.

Cook observes that a young graduate student leaves the university with a productivity-creativity measure that is increasing, but that reaches a peak about 6 to 18 months following employment. At this point, productivity-creativity begins to decline and continues to decline for the next 6 to 18 months, until it reaches the point equal to that of graduation; it continues to decline to a point representing a critical period of potential crisis. The first period of productivity-creativity increase is attributed to the impetus provided by the award of the degree. The decline is caused by several factors. With an increase in salary and new family experiences, the responsibilities mentioned earlier begin to pressure the young worker. Financial obligations such as a new home, new car, etc., and family obligations such as children and a career plan for the spouse all lead to a critical period.

If a crisis occurs it is usually due to the frustration caused by company red tape. This frustration may take the form of open criticism or silent "stewing" and may lead to a number of responses from the young worker. He or she may decide to face the situation and live through it, or change employment either to a university (retrenchment) or to another company (flight), which will probably lead to a repeat of the previous experience. Since the 1960s, the mobility options are not viable alternatives, and the young graduate must often "stick it out." They may develop a "tell me what to do, and I'll do it" attitude. Equally bad, the young worker may become disinterested in keeping up-to-date professionally and may gradually join the ranks of oblivion and no longer be a part of the highly productive group.

What can be done about this extremely bleak situation? The manager should step in and provide counseling when danger signals become apparent. The person to provide the counseling should be someone whom the young peson respects from a technical standpoint and someone who understands the pattern just discussed. If the counselor has experienced similar circumstances, this should be shared with the young person in order to establish a frank and honest line of communication.

The basic problem in this crisis period is one of goals and occupational purpose. The counselor should explain the young person's situation and the nature of their difficulty to them. Then two key factors must surface in the discussion.

1. The young person must learn that the goals and objectives at work and in life will change as time passes and that this requires frequent revision of goals.
2. No one else can set these goals; the worker must establish them. When the young person establishes these goals, it may then be determined if these goals are consistent with company goals. This harmony of goals is of utmost importance to motivation. All the job enrichment and enlargement in the world will do little good if personal goals are not in accord with company goals. This reestablishing of goals and motivation replaces the decrease of ego satisfaction that occurs after graduation. This concept is also applicable to older employees.

4.11 Experienced Engineers and Scientists

As the technical or professionally trained person progresses through this post-graduate period, what lies beyond? Many studies have been conducted to study the performance of these people as a function of age. Decker und Van Atta [5], after discussions with the management of more than 20 organizations, gained the following insights.

1. Creativity generally diminishes after age 35 or 40.
2. The total value of the individual to the organization may continue to increase due to experience and judgment.
3. Those with leadership potential move into management positions and are subsequently judged in that role.

Pelz and Andrews [14] conducted an extensive and careful study that revealed that on the average, technical persons show performance age curves that are double-peaked with a late forties sag. They suggest that the first peak (age 25 to 35) represents work of a more divergent or innovative type (great discoveries). The later peak (age 45 to 50) represents work that is more convergent or integrative in character. They suggest midcareer reviews with persons in the 35 to 40-year age bracket prior to the first sag. This review may result in recommendations for transfers, such as from research into development, production, or administration. This 35 to 40-year-old period is the onset of the so-called middle-age crisis. Almost every professional who is or who has been middle aged knows that it is no exaggeration to apply the word "crisis" to this period of transition in life. Reaching a plateau after steady professional progression represents a time of great stress and tension for most employees in our youth-oriented culture.

A survey conducted by the California Institute of Technology of over 1000 middle-aged men in professional and managerial positions revealed that five out of six went through a period of intense frustration and turmoil that began as early as their late thirties. One in six never fully recovered from the emotional upheaval. This midlife crisis affects the individual and those who work and live with them. Just as the middle-aged individual views himself or herself in different terms, so also are others viewed in different ways. The passage through the middle years involves a realization of loss that is difficult to accept but irreversible. The individual is, in fact, beginning to grow old. Equally devastating is the loss of dreams, hopes, and goals—the sense of future. One psychologist estimated that at least half of all middle-aged people suffer from the disappointment of not fulfilling their ambitions and dreams.

Midlifers respond to this crisis in various ways. Some are less affected by this transition than others; nevertheless, sufficient numbers are affected in ways that are detrimental to themselves, their colleagues, and their company that the problem cannot be ignored. For those who are affected, new behaviors are developed and job performance is changed. Some of these behaviors seem to be displayed more consistently: depression, poor health, extramarital affairs, fear and hostility toward subordinates, "retiring" on the job, or leaving the organization to begin a new career. It should be emphasized that not all middle-aged professionals react in one or more of these ways or in any other visible way.

Depression probably results from a deep sense of loss for what has passed. The midlifer may lose interest in almost everything he or she used to enjoy, particularly work. The employee's health can be affected. It has long been known that emotions can affect physical well-being. Some research (still to be verified) has tied the increased incidence of heart attacks directly to lack of satisfaction at work. Fear and hostility toward young subordinates result for some midlifers, who develop depression and insecurity about themselves and their futures. They do not give subordinates, especially the younger ones, a chance to display what they can do, and they do not let others see the subordinate's talents and promise. "Retirement" on the job is too often seen as midlifers surrender to doubts and fears, frustration and unhappiness and, in effect, withdraw from competition. They shelve the drive, persistence, and innovativeness that may have been possessed and concentrate on hanging on to the present position. Starting a new career is a more positive approach for those who are adversely affected by this midlife transition. These second careers may involve totally new directions, challenges, and responsibilities. The individuals who take this approach seem to be people for whom personal challenge and fullfillment are highly important factors.

Faced with this situation, the first action any organization should take is open recognition of the problem. Through company training programs, seminars, or informal communications, midlifers should be informed of the nature of the midlife crises—what it is, how it affects behavior, and how it can be handled. Open recognition and communication about the problem would, in and of itself, provide some solace to those who are currently experiencing the crisis. They too often feel that there is something uniquely wrong with them, that they are alone in suffering these new doubts, fears, and anxieties.

Along with this personal counseling, vocational guidance should be offered. Interests and desires change over the years, and the kind of work that suited the individual 25 years before may now be distasteful. Also, one's choice of career at the age of 21 is often dictated by considerations other than one's interests and aptitudes. By midlife, new interests often develop, or old interests, long kept dormant by the press of daily affairs, are rekindled. This suggestion might seem at first to encourage an employee to leave the job. Even if this is the result, both the company and the employee would be better off than if the employee "retired" on company time for the many remaining years of working life. Fortunately, there is always the possibility that the employee will stay with the company in another division or department that involves new challenges and responsibilities. A new career within the company can mean a resurgence of the keenness and drive that made the professional a valuable employee during the first career.

4.12   Technical Obsolescence

Closely allied to the aging process is the problem of technical obsolescence. In this regard two questions should be considered: (1) is obsolescence inevitable?, and (2) can we reverse or arrest the process of technical obsolescence? A study of the problem over a 9-year period by Price, Thompson, and Dalton [16] lends some interesting insight. This study showed that obsolescence is not inevitable, that high performers remained high performers, low performers remained low performers, and those in the middle were unpredictable.

What is technical obsolescence? Obsolescence is the process of passing out of use or usefulness; therefore, technical obsolescence is technical knowledge that is no longer useful. To combat this obsolescence, it would be wise to know what it is that has passed out of use. This loss is technical vitality. A technically vital engineer or researcher is able to work effectively at the frontier of the field. Personal motivation, understanding, opportunity, and a supportive environment are required to be a technically vital engineer. Technical vitality is, therefore, a shorthand way of referring to a set of activities designed to help engineers and scientifically trained people to become more productive. Enhancing this vitality is the key to the current and future productivity of scientific and engineering professionals.

Persons are obsolescent technically if, when compared to other members of their profession, they are not familiar with, or are otherwise unfitted to apply, the knowledge, methods, and techniques that are generally considered important by members of their profession. However, obsolescence takes many forms: obsolescence caused by simple lack of use of knowledge of a specific skill; functional or organizational obsolescence occurring when the professional has performed a function over a period of time and the function is no longer required; energy or motivational obsolescence when the professional "retires" on the job; and obsolescence induced by management bias of employee capability. Obsolescence means more than obsolescence of formal knowledge. It is related to our culture, our work environment, and to available opportunities to change and grow.

The problem of technical obsolescence was recognized and talked about in the 1950s. The problem then seemed to result from rapidly changing technology and the loss or nonexistence of up-to-date technical knowledge. From this thinking emerged the concept of the half-life of an engineering education. Today this view of the problem seems to be a great simplification. From the viewpoint of the individual, continued formal education has not necessarily made employees technically vital. Education is not a sufficient condition to combat obsolescence. From the viewpoint of the organization, new research findings indicate that the organization more than the individual is becoming outdated (obsolete) and may be a heavy contributor to the obsolescence of the individual, who is really the heart and soul of the technical organization.

Although continued study does not guarantee vitality, educational availability and an environment that encourages learning are positive contributors and a powerful tool for future productivity. Education does help to slow the drift toward obsolescence. Obsolescence is an annoyance and a problem for a company and an inevitable disaster for an individual. Therefore, individuals should be most concerned about the design and implementation of their own professional development program. The person who wants to develop does; the person who wants to be developed rarely is. In establishing their plan for combating obsolescence, employees should draw the distinction between training and education. Each has its place, and an overemphasis on either will probably be detrimental to the ultimate success of the endeavor. Training can be thought of as the acquisition of the skills that are needed for the proper functioning in the present environment. Education is more long range and concept oriented. Failure to design and implement such a program may become a major factor in becoming technically obsolete.

Data generated by Kaufman [11] indicate that three out of four engineers believe that formal instruction in modern technology developments is necessary for keeping up-to-date, but that short courses, as opposed to advanced degree work, are sufficient. Despite this apparent desire for continuing education, almost half of these engineers have never participated in any noncredit course and over two-thirds have not attended graduate school.

This discrepancy between the recognition that continuing education is of great importance for technical updating and relatively limited course participation can be attributed to organizational influences and personal reasons. For engineers who do engage in continuing education, there are indications that their primary objective is to keep from becoming obsolete, and not to obtain an advanced degree, as is often assumed. A further point is that graduate courses (education) are clearly more effective in keeping engineers from becoming obsolete than in-company courses (training). However, the usefulness of graduate courses for retarding obsolescence of all professionals may be limited since, according to Kaufman's findings, they are avoided by those who have the greatest disposition toward obsolescence. He found that the people most prone to obsolescence preferred in-company courses. Therefore, in-company courses have the potential to contribute to the updating of those engineers who are more prone to obsolescence, but their effectiveness may be questioned.

Using this information, it seems obvious that organizations should devote more careful efforts toward planning, implementing, and assessing their continuing education programs. Continuing education is only one of many approaches to prevent engineers and scientists from becoming obsolete. However, the wide acceptance of continuing education requires that company-sponsored training and education programs be analyzed in order to satisfy the development needs of both the employees and their organizations.

4.13 Managerial Obsolescence

The problems of managerial obsolescence have received less attention than technical obsolescence. If a technical person progresses up the technical ladder and then moves to the managerial ladder only to discover that he or she is unhappy or incompetent, that person may theoretically return to the technical ranks without a loss in pay or status. More often, however, once a person enters management, the system is not flexible enough to allow that person to leave gracefully. In addition, a manager will inevitably reach a plateau as a natural consequence of the narrowing organizational funnel. In most organizations there are simply more candidates than promotional opportunities. Upon reaching such a plateau, a manager may enter the midcareer crisis previously discussed or become a "shelf sitter," "retiree on the job," or "ineffective plateauee."

Reecer points out several indicators of obsolescence in managers [17].

1. They avoid hard work but want the benefits thereof.
2. They are resistant to change.
3. They make no attempt to update or upgrade their experience and education.
4. They avoid goal setting.
5. They only hire those perceived to have less ability than themselves.
6. Technical obsolescence.

When managerial obsolescence is indicated, higher-level management has several options.

1. Terminate the obsolescent employee.
2. Move the employee laterally to a position of more challenge and motivation.

3. Demote the obsolescent employee.
4. Provide for early retirement.
5. Move the employee to a position that maintains dignity but is out of the mainstream.

A study by Shearer and Steger [18] gives general suggestions about how to combat managerial obsolescence. For managers, obsolescence is highly correlated with lack of participation in the decision-making process. Participation represents an essential element of experience. As mentioned earlier, education and experience are the most critical factors to obsolescence. But for managers, experience has a more significant correlation than education. Education is necessary and helps the manager to maintain the technical respect of subordinates (an important factor to motivation), but experience is more important to combating managerial obsolescence. Managers, or potential managers, should strive to be involved in the decision-making process. They should seek task assignments that are varied enough to develop and maintain a wide range of capabilities in their fields and that require the use of new knowledge and skills.

Obsolescence is not inevitable. If symptoms appear, steps should be taken that have been effective in the arresting of obsolescence. Although the organization can contribute somewhat, the individuals must have or must develop the ambition, character, and patience to develop themselves. Apparently, obsolescence can best be avoided through the proper blend of education and experience.

4.14 Organizational Obsolescence

Many managers assert that the unwillingness or inability of individuals to change is the major cause of technical obsolescence. However, recent research by Thompson and Dalton [9] questions that assumption. In fact, Thompson and Dalton now believe that organizational obsolescence, not individual obsolescence, is the main culprit. Many of the current problems of technical organizations concern the management of human resources. Several environmental changes in the last few years have contributed to this problem of human resource management: minimal growth; increasing average age of the engineer; new age discrimination laws; accelerating rate of technical information; and increasing disenchantment with the prestige of engineering.

Most technical groups are still organized to solve the problems of the 1950s and 1960s in the environment of the 1970s. This organizational obsolescence is claimed to be a major contributing factor to the obsolescence of individual engineers. Two important reasons why technical organizations have failed to adapt are a lack of understanding of obsolescence, both by the individuals and managers, and a lack of understanding of professional careers. (The only way most people have to think of their career growth is in terms of climbing the corporate ladder.)

Another aspect of organizational obsolescence is the rigidity and formality of the organization itself. Webber, in his book on management, states that the more effective technical organizations demonstrated more ambiguity in policy and structure and more participation in relation to the less effective research organization, which demonstrated formalized and centralized structure, policy, and decision making [22]. Unfortunately, for the organization, the aging process develops the undesirable formality, structure, policy, and decision-making traits of the less effective technical groups. This development is not necessarily dictated by stated organization structure and policy, but it may be a consequence of the informal organization and the passage of time.

The danger of these changes is the disappearance of spontaneity in the organization. Policies and procedures, once established and accepted, limit flexibility and initiative. When controls are first established, management may gain in coordination and flexibility what it loses in initiative. However, it is difficult to keep them up-to-date, since policies, procedures, and controls are based on the past. As time passes, policies may no longer apply to new conditions, controls may come to measure irrelevant factors, and rational plans developed to promote organizational effectiveness may interfere with the accomplishment of objectives. If managers blindly follow established rules (formal or informal), spontaneity is lost and apathy will prevail. Under long-standing restrictive controls, some managers try to avoid mistakes through "going by the book" if they feel that punishment awaits an unsuccessful departure from accepted procedure. When plans and controls become ends to be followed, without thought as to whether they contribute to the objectives of the organization, there is an inversion of means and ends. The result of this inversion is an organization that loses direction and becomes technically obsolete.

Given that the problems of technical obsolescence are strong functions of organization obsolescence, what can the manager do to combat the problems? For the formalized, heavily structured organization, the realization of the possible detrimental effects of such an organization and subsequent reaction by management will go a long way to alleviating the problems of apathy and loss of innovation. Also, there are external forces that should effect the technical organization. A renewed interest in technology from industry is developing; there is increased emphasis on short-term results, with a definite product and market in mind. Long-term research will no longer mean 5 to 8 years, but 3 to 5 years focused on short-term payback. This more dynamic approach should do much to break down the walls of formalized, structured organizations.

Managers have a responsibility to design organizations so that they can remain capable of developing in the future. Thompson and Dalton [9] indicate three broad areas in which managers can make improvements and thus avoid having an obsolete organization: reward technical contributions, reduce barriers to movement, and focus on technical careers. The key to success is excellence in technical work. The effective organization must show that it places a high value on technical contributions by providing meaningful rewards to high-performing technical talent. This can be achieved by developing pay scales that pay for performance, not position, by seeking inputs in making important decisions, and by increasing visibility and public recognition of individual accomplishments.

One of the problems for most organizations in the 1970s and 1980s will probably be less personnel movement in all directions. Slower growth means fewer promotions, fewer transfers, fewer people leaving the organization, and fewer people being hired. If an organization is not careful, a kind of rigor mortis may set in. Limiting tenure in supervisory positions and more effective use of lateral transfers are changes that could help to reduce barriers to movement and increase motivation by providing new assignments and challenges.

Finally, managers can help to reduce the organization's influence on obsolescence through a renewed focus on technical careers. There are always deadlines, budgets, products and profits to worry about. As a result, attention to long-term problems such as individual careers and the technical vitality of the organization tend to be pushed aside. Renewed emphasis on these problems should pay handsome dividends. Obsolete employees are unhappy, frustrated, dissatisfied, inefficient, noneffective, nonproductive, and career deadened. Obsolescence, however, is not inevitable, and age is not a sufficient condition for obsolescence. Professional vitality is crucial to the future success of any technology-based industry, and a shift in management emphasis is necessary to address this goal of vitality. Getting top management to feel responsible for vitality, to make appropriate trade-offs for longer-term gains, and to become intellectually aware of the middle-age crisis are the keys to success. With new management techniques, modified measures, incentives, and more appropriate educational programs, the environment can be modified and the productivity of technical personnel can be extended considerably beyond the historical peak at 35 years of age.

References

1. Barron, F., *Creativity and Psychological Health*, Van Nostrand, Princeton, N.J., 1963.
2. Bloom, B. S., "Report on Creativity Research by Examiners Office of the University of Chicago," *Scientific Creativity: Its Recognition and Development,*

C. W. Taylor and F. Barron, Editors, Wiley, New York, 1963, pp. 251–64.
3. Cook, C. F., "The Troubled Life of the Young Ph.D. in an Industrial Laboratory," *Research Management, 18* (3), May 1975, pp. 28–31.
4. Davis, J. A., "Summary of Major Findings from the College Student Characteristics Study," Educational Testing Service, Princeton, N.J., 1964.
5. Decker, W. D., and C. M. Van Atta, "Controlling Staff Age, and Flexible Retirement Plans," *Research Management, 16* (1), January 1973, pp. 16–21.
6. Harmon, L. R., "The Development of a Criterion of Scientific Competence," *Scientific Creativity: Its Recognition and Development*, C. W. Taylor and F. Barron, Editors, Wiley, New York, 1963, pp. 44–52.
7. Helson, R., and R. S. Crutchfield, "Mathematicians: The Creative Researcher and the Average Ph.D.," *Journal of Consulting and Clinical Psychology, 34* (2), April 1970, pp. 250–57.
8. Holland, J. L., "Creativity and Academic Performance Among Talented Adolescents," *Journal of Educational Psychology, 52,* 1961, pp. 136–47.
9. Hoyt, D. P., "College Grades and Adult Accomplishment: A Review of Research," *Educational Record 47,* (1), Winter 1966, pp. 70–75.
10. Jones, R. R., "Town First, Job Second—Says the Job Hunter," *Industrial Research, 18* (5), May 1976, pp. 73–76.
11. Kaufman, H. G., "Continuing Education for Up-Dating Technical People," *Research Management, 18* (4), July 1975, pp. 20–23.
12. MacKinnon, D. W., "Selecting Students with Creative Potential," *The Creative College Student: An Unmet Challenge,* P. Heist, Editor, Jossey-Bass, San Francisco, 1968, pp. 101–16.
13. Marston, A. R., "It is Time to Reconsider the Graduate Record Examination," *American Psychologist, 26* (7), July 1971, pp. 653–655.
14. Pelz, D. C., and F. M. Andrews, *Scientists and Organizations,* Wiley, New York, 1966.
15. Platz, A., C. McClintock, and D. Katz, "Undergraduate Grades and the Miller Analogies Test as Predictors of Graduate Success," *The American Psychologist, 14,* 1959, pp. 285–289.
16. Price, D. R., P. H. Thompson, and G. W. Dalton, "A Longitudinal Study of Technical Obsolescence," *Research Management, 18* (6), November 1975, pp. 22–28.
17. Reecer, C., "Managerial Obsolescence—An Organizational Dilemma," *Personnel Journal, 56* (1), January 1977, pp. 27–31.
18. Shearer, R. L., and J. A. Steger, "Manpower Obsolescence: A New Definition and Empirical Investigation of Personal Variables," *Academy of Management Journal, 18* (2), June 1975, pp. 263–275.
19. Thompson, P. H., and G. W. Dalton, "Are R&D Organizations Obsolete?" *Harvard Business Review, 54,* November 1976, pp. 105–116.
20. Wallack, M. A., "Creativity," *Carmichael's Manual of Child Psychology,* 3rd ed., P. H. Mussen, Editor, Wiley, New York, 1970, pp. 1211–1272.
21. Wallack, M. A., "Tests Tell Us Little About Talent," *American Scientist, 64* (1), January–February 1976, pp. 57–63.
22. Webber, R. A., *Management: Basic Elements of Managing Organizations,* Richard D. Irwin, Homewood, Ill., 1975.

——————————— **Discussion Questions** ———————————

1. Discuss the use of psychological and personality test for selecting technical personnel and technical managers.
2. Can an organization develop people or must employees take the initiative to develop themselves?
3. In your opinion, which are most beneficial in combatting technical obsolescence, company in-house courses or college courses?
4. If economic conditions required a 50 percent reduction of technical personnel, what criteria do you think should be used to decide who to let go?
5. Should a company require that all of their engineers and managers take at least one educational course per year?
6. In what types of long-range training programs should an organization engage?
7. Discuss the advantages and disadvantages of an organization paying the dues for each professional employee to the professional society of his or her choice.
8. It has been suggested that managers in a technical organization should be elected (say for a period of 4 years) by the people in the group. Discuss the pros and cons.
9. It has been suggested that technical managers should either be forced to retire or step down from their management position after a fixed number of years if they have not been promoted. Discuss the possible effects of such a policy.
10 One way to insure a steady flow of new people and ideas into a technical group would be to release or transfer 10 percent (the lowest performers) of the people each year. Would such a policy be desirable?

——————————— **Case Study IV** ———————————

AMERICAN PRODUCTS, INC.

Don Edwards, director of manufacturing engineering, was sitting in his office looking through three personnel folders when George Capra called. Capra was the personnel representative for hiring professional personnel.

CAPRA: Don, have you had a chance to review the files of the three applicants I sent up to you? Those are the three that appear to me to be the best for your vacant position of group leader.

EDWARDS: I was just doing that now. I'm really not all that impressed with any of them. Is this really the best we can do, George?

CAPRA: Well, you know its strictly a seller's market right now for experienced manufacturing engineers. I counted 29 ads in last Sunday's newspaper for these guys. I placed ads in six major newspapers across the country and in two professional journals, and I contacted three placement agencies that specialize in engineers. I could keep looking, but I really don't think it will do any good.

EDWARDS: Alright, let's go ahead and bring all three in for interviews. Maybe they'll look better after we talk to them.

Edwards turned back to the three folders. American Products was adding a new line of lightweight vertical air conditioners to its products. These new air conditioners would weigh less than 50 pounds each and would discharge the cool air straight down instead of sideways. They were designed for use in recreational vehicles such as vans, pop-top trailers, and sailboats. These would be the first of their kind on the market, and the cost to manufacture was critical. The sales group was projecting first-year sales of 100,000 units, climbing to 1 million units a year by the end of the fifth year if the units could be retailed at under $250. R&D was almost completed, and the project would be moving to the manufacturing engineering group in about 3 months.

Edwards believed that when a new line was to be introduced, one person should be responsible for all of the manufacturing engineering. This included choosing the methods, selecting the equipment, designing and setting up the production lines, establishing the man-loading and production standards, setting up the quality control system, and mothering the product until everything was operating smoothly. This required a very special person who was an excellent engineer and a good planner, and who could get along well with others. The group leader or project engineer would have to work with personnel from research and development, purchasing, plant engineering, quality control, production scheduling, manufacturing, and shipping.

Although Don Edwards had a number of excellent engineers on his staff, he did not feel that any of them had the experience and capability to head up this important project. He had selected three of his engineers to work on the project, but had decided to look outside of the organization for the group leader or project engineer. In the job specification that he sent to personnel, he had requested an industrial or mechanical engineer with a minimum of 15 years experience in manufacturing engineering (preferable in air conditioning), previous supervisory experience, and evidence of an ability to obtain the cooperation of other departments.

Edwards was not particularly pleased by the three applicants George Capra had given him. The first was a woman, Mary Daniels. She had a B.S. and M.S. from Georgia Tech in industrial engineering. For the past 12 years she had worked for a large electronics firm on the East Coast. According to her resume, she had set up a manufacturing line for producing an electronic air filter and dehumidifier. Her present job classification was that of lead engineer. Edwards noted that her current salary was about $5000 lower than his own people with a comparable background. She was 36 years old, divorced, and had one child.

The second applicant was Bill Lions. He was 45 years old, married, and had two children. He had worked 20 years for the same company, a well-known manufacturer of heating and air conditioning equipment. He had a B.S. in mechanical engineering from Purdue. He had started out as a draftsman and had slowly progressed to his present position of senior engineer. Edwards noted that he could not tell from the resume whether Lions had ever been fully responsible for a project or whether he had always worked under someone else.

The third applicant was Harry Perren. Perren was 38, single, and had a B.S. and M.S. in industrial engineering from Penn State. In the past 14 years he had worked for four different companies. The first 2 years he worked in plant layout for an aerospace company in California. The next 4 years he worked for a large farm implement company in the reliability and quality control area. The next 5 years he worked in manufacturing engineering for a Kansas company that manufactured heating and air conditioning equipment for mobile homes. Finally, for the last 3 years, he had been working for a division of one of the nation's largest heating and air conditioning companies, setting up a line to manufacture compressors; his job title was project engineer.

Two weeks later, George Capra had made arrangements for the three applicants to make a plant visit on separate days. Capra took each applicant on a plant tour and discussed personnel policies, fringe benefits, etc., prior to bringing them to Don Edward's office.

The first applicant to visit was Bill Lions. He looked older than his 45 years and seemed very nervous. He was dressed very conservatively in a suit that was about 8 years out of date. He spoke very slowly and deliberately and asked few questions. He responded directly to questions posed to him, but did not elaborate or volunteer information. Part of the interview went as follows:

EDWARDS: You've been with your present company for a long time. Why are you interested in leaving now?

LIONS: I just don't see any future there. I'm not getting any younger, and I'm just not making the kind of progress I think I should.

EDWARDS: It says here you are a senior engineer. Do you supervise any people?

LIONS: I have two or three people on an informal basis. As the senior man in the department, I sort of provide advice and guidance to some of the younger people.

EDWARDS: What are your objectives? What would you ultimately like to do here at American Products if you came?

LIONS: I guess you call it group leader or project engineer. I'd like to be directly responsible for three or four engineers doing some really challenging work.

EDWARDS: Does that mean you're not interested in moving up the managerial ranks?

LIONS: Oh, no. I've always wanted to get into management, but I just never got the chance.

EDWARDS: Well, here a group leader is a working engineer who has a managerial responsibility part of the time.

LIONS: Yes, that's exactly what I want. The kind of job I want is where I can still do engineering but also have some management responsibility.

The second applicant to visit the plant was Mary Daniels. She arrived for the interview dressed in a conservative, stylish pantsuit. She seemed very much at ease and asked many questions. She seemed particularly interested in the idea of one person being fully responsible for all aspects of getting a new product line started and quizzed Edwards about budgets, manpower, etc., that would be available for the project. Part of the interview follows.

EDWARDS: According to your resume, you have been responsible for setting up a manufacturing line for producing an electronic air filter and dehumidifier. With what aspects were you concerned?

DANIELS: Only the tooling and equipment. I had to interface with industrial engineering, manufacturing, and other groups on the other aspects. That's one reason this job appeals to me so much. I found it very frustrating to have to make so many compromises in what I thought should be done.

EDWARDS: Do you supervise any people?

DANIELS: Yes, I have three engineers plus one technician who report directly to me.

EDWARDS: Do you like supervising people?

DANIELS: Very much. It lets me get so much more done than if I had to do everything myself.

EDWARDS: It sounds to me as if you've done very well with your present company. Why do you want to leave?

DANIELS: I think being a woman works against me where I am. Although the company has treated me well in almost every other respect, they have not treated me fairly in salary. They seem to have the idea that a woman doesn't need as much money as a man. I get about 20 percent less than the other lead engineers. My son is ready to start college, and my expenses are going up. Besides, it's just not fair to not pay me what I deserve.

EDWARDS: Do you think being a woman hurts you professionally? Do you have a hard time getting people to accept you as an engineer?

DANIELS: No, I don't think so. For instance, I've been very active in the local chapter of the American Institute of Industrial Engineers. I've been an officer for the last 6 years and have just completed a term as president. No, I've never had any problems with being accepted professionally.

The third applicant was Harry Perren. He was very friendly, outgoing, and self-assured. He was immaculately groomed, with the latest style haircut and suit. Most of his questions dealt with company policies on raises and promotions. He was particularly interested in likely promotion prospects for Mr. Edwards and promotion routes open to engineers. Part of the interview follows.

EDWARDS: I see you went into the aerospace industry right out of school.

PERREN: Yes, I was attracted by the high salaries and living in California. Unfortunately, the cost of living in California was also high, so the big salary didn't mean that much. Besides, I didn't like the job insecurity and the fact that they had two engineers for every one job.

EDWARDS: Then you switched to farm implements. That's quite a change.

PERREN: Yes, it was. I really suffered from culture shock for a while, but I wanted to get into a more traditional industry. The problem was that management was so conservative, you couldn't get anything done.

EDWARDS: Is that why you left?

PERREN: That plus the fact that I just didn't see any future. The company wasn't growing and all the managers were firmly entrenched. I could see that it was going to be 10 or 15 years before I'd get my first promotion.

EDWARDS: Why did you leave the Kansas company?

PERREN: Well, to be very honest about it, girl problems. I got into a very unfortunate situation with a girl who was the daughter of the vice president for manufacturing and I felt like the best thing to do was get out of town.

EDWARDS: Now we come to your present job. Tell me about it.

PERREN: Well, I was very fortunate to find my present position. It gave me a chance to see what I could really do. It was a situation similar to your position in that I had complete responsibility for designing and setting up the new compressor line. I had two really top-notch engineers working for me, and we really enjoyed ourselves. We brought the new line into full production 6 months ahead of schedule and within estimated cost. I don't know when I've ever enjoyed myself so much.

EDWARDS: That sounds great. But why do you want to leave now?

PERREN: The job is done. Its been operational for 6 months now, and all the bugs are worked out. Unfortunately, there's not another line to start up, and they really don't know what to do with me. I'm not willing to set around for 10 years waiting for someone to die or retire so that I can get promoted.

Edwards later talked to the three engineers who would be working in the group. They rated the applicants (1) Lions, (2) Daniels, and (3) Perren. They were particularly impressed by Lions' depth of knowledge and experience. Apparently he had really opened up with the working engineers, and they had carried on a long technical discussion about the problems to be faced. They were also favorably impressed with Daniels, but were not sure how they would get along working for a woman. Perren had struck them as too much of a slam-bang, big-time operator.

George Capra had rated the applicants (1) Daniels, (2) Perren, and (3) Lions. Lions had come across to Capra as a slow plodder who had already reached his peak. "He's a damn good engineer, but not a leader or manager," was Capra's appraisal. Perren worried Capra because of his open ambition and his jumping around so much. "He'd stay just until something looked better." Daniels, on the other hand, had impressed Capra as a level-headed person with a good perspective on things. He also reminded Edwards of the pressure the company was under to hire and promote women and other minorities. "It would be a real feather in your cap to have a woman supervisor," he pointed out. "Besides, you better have a real strong justification for not hiring her if you decide on one of the others."

Edwards was sitting in his office mulling over his own reactions. He tended to rank them (1) Perren, (2) Daniels, and (3) Lions. He had really liked Perren. His easygoing friendliness had made a very good impression. He also liked his self-assuredness and the fact that he had already succeeded in a similar task. Edwards felt that Perren could work with and obtain the cooperation of all the others. Lions, on the other hand, was obviously not so easy to get to know. Edwards wondered how Lions would react if some of the other department heads gave him a hard time. The problem with Daniels was a really sticky one. Edwards felt she had the knowledge and capability, but again he wondered about her ability to obtain cooperation. How would the others feel about working with a woman? He was a little ashamed of his male chauvinist attitude, but the issue had to be faced.

At this moment there was a knock on his door, and Carl Kronig introduced himself.

KRONIG: Mr. Edwards, I'm the R&D engineer who developed and designed the new lightweight air conditioner. Its been my baby from the beginning, and I've ate, slept, and dreamed with it for 4 years. I've met the three people you're considering for putting it into production, and I'm worried. They all three seem nice enough, but I don't think they can get the job done.

What I'd like to propose is that you let me transfer to your department and let me see this project through to completion. I've talked to my boss about this, and he reluctantly agrees.

EDWARDS: Have you ever done any manufacturing engineering?

KRONIG: Yes and no. My master's degree is in mechanical engineering, and I worked for 2 years in manufacturing engineering when I first got out of school. But the biggest thing is no one knows more about the system than I do. I know every nut, bolt, and piece of metal in this thing and why its there. I've also got a vested interest in seeing it succeed. The detailed know-how of what can and can't be done can come from your guys. I'll learn and I'll learn fast. I've worked 24 hours a day, 7 days a week for 4 years on this thing. I'm more than willing to continue the same way for a couple of years more to see it succeed.

EDWARDS: Well, you've caught me cold with your proposal. I'll have to think about it and talk to your supervisor. I'll let you know something later.

KRONIG: Fine. Just one last thought. I've been with the company 12 years now, and I know most of the people I'd have to work with already. A new person won't even know where the bathrooms are.

Case Study Discussion Questions

1. List the pros and cons for each of the candidates.
2. Consider each of the drawbacks expressed about each candidate. Are they valid?
3. Is Kronig likely to be able to get the job done?
4. Which would you choose?

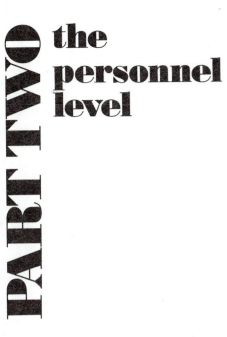

PART TWO the personnel level

CHAPTER 5 creativity and innovation

5.1 Importance of Creativity

The ultimate purpose of the technical group is problem solving. Since the end result of problem solving is primarily ideas, new concepts, new designs, evaluations, and information, the major productive force is the minds of the workers. The ultimate degree of success that a technical organization achieves depends almost totally on the creativity of its personnel. Recognition of this fact has resulted in a great deal of research and discussion regarding which factors influence creativity and led to the creation of some of our modern research and engineering facilities that have picture windows, views, informal dress, pipes, and understanding—but very little increase in creativity.

Creativity is a will-o'-the-wisp whose results can be seen but cannot be accurately defined, measured, or controlled. The investigation of creativity has resulted in its being probed, dissected, and analyzed by some of the finest minds in the world. As an example, in July 1959, Harvard University invited 70 of the world's best known creative people from education, industry, and government to a three-day conference on "creativity in an organizational setting." Although the group reached agreement on certain innate characteristics that contribute to creativity, they did not agree on how to measure it or even on how to define it. They also could not agree as to whether it could be learned or enhanced. Things had not improved 15 years later at a conference of 21 of the world's most prominent engineers, scientists, and philosophers of technology brought together in West Germany.

This latter group explained their failure by pointing out that creativity and innovation are essentially a preverbal process, and it is very difficult to translate this process into words [11].

Creativity is basically the ability to produce new, interesting, and useful results. It is the production and disclosure of a new fact, law, relationship, device, product, material, or process that is based generally on known and available knowledge but does not follow directly, easily, simply, or even by usual logical processes from the information at hand. Creativity can also be defined as a successful step across the borderline of knowledge, a defining of things previously unknown. Creative engineering design usually entails a combination of known components, or principles in a novel and unique way. Creative behavior demonstrates both uniqueness and value in its product.

Because of the immense importance of creativity to so many areas, a great deal of research has been directed toward ascertaining how the creative process works and why some people appear to be more creative than others. If we know what creativity is and how it works, we can hopefully:

1. Discover and recognize creative people.
2. Teach people how to use more of their creative potential on a reliable basis.
3. Create a mode of leadership and operation aimed at encouraging engineers and scientists to be more productive.
4. Rationally explain to management the unique needs of the technical group.
5. Actually produce more technical breakthroughs that utilize the results of creativity for the benefit of the parent organization.

The following sections summarize what is known about the characteristics of creative people, the creative process, some personal barriers to creativity, methods sometimes used to break down these barriers, and some organizational barriers raised by management.

5.2 Characteristics of the Creative Person

Real creativity occurs most often in the unconventional, even eccentric, individual. They have strong faith in themselves, are likely to be antisocial, antiauthoritarian, and perhaps even excessive in their personal habits. Their very purpose is to destroy the status quo; therefore we cannot expect the conformist to come up with unique solutions and ideas. If they are creative, they do not think along conventional lines. If they do not think along conventional lines in their specialty, they should not be expected to think along conventional lines in other matters. Comfortable, conservative, complacent people do not create. Why should they? They like things as they are.

Much of the current body of knowledge about the characteristics of the creative individual are attributable to research by Guilford [5,6], Roe [16,17], and Pelz and Andrews [14]. The following list summarizes the characteristics of highly creative people from these and other studies.

1. High degree of autonomy, self-sufficiency, and self-direction.
2. Inner drive for knowledge that must be continually satisfied.
3. Knowledge and acquaintance with a broad range of different subject matter.
4. Great curiosity about how or why things work.
5. Usually a very good observer with a good memory for everything except practical day-to-day matters.
6. Preference for mental manipulations involving things, not people.
7. High ego strength and emotional stability.
8. Liking for method, precision, and exactness in their work but not necessarily in their everyday social life.
9. Liking for abstract thinking.
10. Broad interest in intellectual activities and games.
11. Marked independence of judgment and rejection of group pressures for conformity.
12. Marked disregard for rules and regulations if their purpose is not clear and agreed to.
13. Liking for pitting oneself against uncertainty where one's own effort can be a deciding factor.
14. Capability for intense concentration on a subject of interest to the exclusion of all other matters.
15. Ability to generate large numbers of ideas, most of which are impractical.
16. Keen sense of humor and often a lover of practical jokes.
17. Many, if not most, love and participate in the arts by playing the piano, violin, or some other instrument and writing poetry or fiction.
18. They are intuitive and imaginative.
19. They have drive and are very busy people.
20. Superior general intelligence, some evidence that they tend to place either in the top or bottom decile of their class in school.
21. Small number of close friends; they are not "joiners" of organizations other than technical ones.
22. Can face ambiguous situations easily without becoming upset or anxious.
23. Largely self-satisfied and not very self-critical.

To illustrate the importance of these traits of individualism and their relationship to freedom of action, two quotations are given. The first is from the vice-president of research and engineering for the Burroughs Corporation [18].

> Each technical man has a certain level of creative talent. If he is creative, he does not think along conventional lines. If he does not think along conventional lines in his specialty, he may be expected not to think along conventional lines in other matters. The more creative he is, the more he thinks he should do his own planning, and the less constraint he is willing to accept from others.

The second is from an extremely successful medical investigator and administrator at Harvard University [1].

> One of the most striking characteristics of an expert investigator is his strong individualism. He has his own personal curiosities, his own plans for work, and his own ways and methods for carrying out his plans. It is difficult for him to engage with other experts as a member of a team. New ideas for research come to mind in the course of his investigation that enticingly lead him away to fresh fields for discovery. He wishes to follow the prospects thus not because he fails to respect or appreciate highly what others are doing but because he is satisfying an eager personal interest. What proves attractive to him, furthermore, may not prove attractive to others. Indeed, it may be difficult for him to justify to others the course he intends to pursue.

These statements should not be construed to mean that technical workers desire complete absence of supervision or planning. Not knowing what is expected of them is almost as frustrating as regimentation. They want to know what is expected of them but not how to do it. They want the freedom to choose the projects that they will work on, but they want to know that the results they come up with will be used by the organization.

5.3 Creative Process

Creative ideas do not come uninvited. They must be sought and pursued. We sometimes read of the inventor who suddenly came up with a completely novel idea, and we get the impression that it came from nowhere, with no effort involved. This impression is unfortunate and rarely true. Creative ideas occur most often to people with a driving curiosity (something all children have, but adults outgrow). Creativity results from attention to troublesome detail (that the ordinary mind discards as trivia) and intense effort.

Since creativity is the process of putting existing ideas, principles, devices etc., together in new and unique combinations, it requires knowledge, imagination, and evaluation. Without knowledge, there obviously can be no creativity. Parnes [13] suggests the analogy to the kaleidoscope: the more pieces we have in the drum, the more patterns we can produce. Likewise, in the creative process, the greater our knowledge, the more patterns, combinations, or ideas we can achieve. Therefore, the best preparation for creative ideas is knowledge, and knowledge is gained by experience. Firsthand experience provides the richest preparation, since it stays with you and is more easily recalled when needed. Thus the creative person spends a lot of time gaining personal experience through observing, tinkering with devices, and investigating all kinds of products to find out how they work. This is *active* experience. Passive experience results from secondhand knowledge gained from sources such as reading, talking, and listening to others. All other things being equal, the more elements in one's experience, the more new relationships can be conceived and the greater the chances of producing a potentially useful one.

But merely having the knowledge does not guarantee the formation of new patterns or combinations. Just having the bits and pieces in the kaleidoscope is not sufficient; one must "revolve the drum" to generate new patterns. Similarly, we must manipulate the knowledge by combining and rearranging facts into new patterns through our imagination. Imagination is abundant and obvious in all small children. Unfortunately, society succeeds in suppressing the imagination in most of us as we grow up. And yet Einstein said, "Imagination is more important than knowledge, for knowledge is limited, whereas imagination embraces the entire world."

Finally, the effectiveness of creativity also depends on the evaluation and development of embryonic ideas into usable ideas. Knowledge and imagination are not enough. Unless ideas are implemented, they are usually not useful. There is often a peculiar underlying assumption that imagination and the generation of ideas automatically lead to innovation. In fact, ideas are relatively abundant, but their implementation is more scarce. Ideas do not implement themselves—people implement ideas. The creative people are those who have the know-how, energy, daring, and staying power to generate imaginative ideas and to implement them. Without knowledge, imagination cannot be productive. Without imagination, abundant knowledge will not lead to useful change. And without the ability to synthesize, evaluate, develop, and sell our ideas, we achieve no effective creativity. Creativity is more likely to occur when one lets the imagination soar and then engineers it back to earth.

There is no nice, neat procedure or formula to follow that will guarantee a creative solution to a problem. Based on a great deal of research we do know, however, that certain steps seem to be present and that they suggest an understanding of the mental processes involved.

STEP 1. IRRITATION AND DECISION

Creativity is triggered when one is confronted with something irritating or disturbing in a situation and decides to do something about it. The creative person characteristically pays attention to troublesome details that the ordinary minds discard as irritating trivia. Curiosity and a desire to understand, coupled with the conviction that an answer can be found, separates the creative from the uncreative. Necessity may be the mother of invention, but action is its father.

STEP 2. PREPARATION

The preparation stage is a period of conscious, direct, mental effort devoted to the accumulation of information pertinent to the problem. This vital second step requires mental discipline of the highest order. Quite often the problem is solved at this stage as one submerges oneself in the problem while trying to:

(a) Structure the problem.
(b) Collect all available information.
(c) Understand relations and effects.
(d) Solve subproblems.
(e) Explore all possible solutions and combinations that may lead to a satisfactory solution.

STEP 3. FRUSTRATION AND INCUBATION

If the problem is not solved at step 2, frustration leads to a decision to discard the task and go on to another assignment. A period of complete or relative inactivity follows, with perhaps a recurrence of ideas or thoughts about the problem, but with no evident progress toward a solution. However, the subconscious mind, now fully prepared with all kinds of information from step 2, continues to work on the problem. During this stage the problem is allowed to ferment, to cook, to incubate over a period of time as the subconscious tries different combinations of the facts and experience fed to it.

STEP 4. ILLUMINATION

Illumination involves sudden inspiration, which consists of spontaneous insight into a possible solution. The creative idea or unique solution occurs in a flash, usually during a period of rest or while engaged in an activity completely foreign to the problem. Some experts believe that the subconscious mind works harder in probing for ideas when the conscious mind is at rest, such as during sleep or relaxation. Dreaming a solution is not unusual; many creative people keep a pencil and pad at their bedsides and carry them at all times.

STEP 5. VERIFICATION

Illumination has occurred and the creative idea is at hand. The idea must now be checked and tested to see if it indeed provides a solution. Not every hunch is sound. Intuition can be wrong and a flash of insight defective. Sound judgment requires solid evidence to prove whether an idea is actually worthwhile, so we must go through a program of critical analysis, testing, and evaluation. If the idea turns out not to be a solution to the problem, we usually return to step 2 and another period of intensive effort to find a solution.

How do we know this process is true? Because thousands of creative people have described exactly this process when discussing their work. Over and over again we see this interplay between the conscious and the subconscious. For creative work we have this wonderously competent coupling where each part (conscious and subconscious) is indispensable in its own way, but each is helpless without the other. When applied to problem solving, the human mind has two aspects: (1) a judicial, logical, conscious mind that analyzes, compares, and chooses; and (2) an imaginative, creative, subconscious mind that visualizes, foresees, and generates ideas from stored knowledge and experience.

Some authors have suggested that the subconscious is actually a servomechanism that strives to achieve the goals set by the conscious mind. This concept was named psychocybernetics by Maltz [10]. We can perhaps gain some insight into the creative process by considering it from this viewpoint.

In steps 1 and 2 we are setting the goals and feeding information into storage. It would seem that we have two basic types of information stored—temporary, short-term storage and permanent, long-term storage. Temporary, short-term storage occurs when we store something in our memory only briefly for the period needed. We receive millions of impressions and stimuli every day. If we automatically stored all this information we would be overwhelmed by remembering trivia. However, we do have to remember things such as telephone numbers we have looked up long enough to dial it (although we do not want to remember every number we call).

To store an item in long-term storage, a person must give it attention, interest, and time. This accounts for the success of tricks that we use for acquiring permanent learning such as repetition, reading it twice, underlining it, and making notes. If an item passes from the attention too soon, it is stored only in a fragmentary form, if at all. Basically, this is what we are doing during steps 1 and 2. We are devoting attention, interest, and time to the problem and to the information that will be potentially useful in the solution.

Authorities now believe that once something is stored in the long-term memory, it stays there and is never forgotten. The fact that you cannot recall the details at will does not mean it is gone. Thus, long-term permanent memory can be subdivided into active storage and inactive storage. Nearly everything stored in long-term memory is stored in an inactive state. It is there, but has been used so little that it cannot be brought out no matter how hard we try. The large amount of learned material that we do keep available and ready for use is kept there by use and reuse. A vastly larger amount is tucked away in inaccessible form because we have not used it recently. Fortunately, we can still gain access to this information by calling on the subconscious.

Intense and hard thought and work during the preparation phase is necessary for two reasons. First, new learning essential to solving the problem is being acquired. Second, all the time the hard work is going on, we are defining the goal and ordering our subconscious to get busy on it. As stated earlier, a creative thought is usually not a completely new thought and does not come out of a vacuum. No one can create something that does not already exist. The creative thinker actually evolves new and untried combinations of ideas that already exist in the mind. It is obvious that the active and curious mind adds more ideas into storage than a passive one and therefore is able to come up with more new combinations.

The period of incubation allows the subconscious to search through the inactive and active memories while we focus on other matters. We know that the conscious mind can attend to only about seven items or ideas at one time. The subconscious, however, does not seem to have this limitation. As the problem "simmers" in the back of the mind, the subconscious searches through the memory, trying different combinations and patterns of ideas and matching them against the goals we have set. When the subconscious believes that it has found a pattern or combination that will solve the problem, it triggers it back into consciousness. The reason that illumination occurs so often during periods of relaxation is twofold. First, lack of conscious effort may allow the subconscious to work harder and more efficiently. Second, those may be the only times and opportunities that the subconscious has to get the conscious mind's attention.

Each of us often experiences a process similar to this. For example, we run into someone at a store who looks very familiar and speaks to us. We recognize the face but cannot connect it with a name or sometimes even with the context in which we know the person. As we exchange pleasantries, the conscious mind frantically looks for clues and searches our active, long-term memory to no avail. As we leave the person, we continue to search our memories for a short time and then put the incident from our mind. Later (perhaps 15 minutes, an hour, or the next day) the name suddenly comes to us. Even though we have forgotten the meeting, the subconscious has continued the search in the inactive memory until it found the answer.

Instead of waiting indefinitely for the subconscious to report back with illumination, it is helpful to put a time limit on it. If nothing seems to be happening, perhaps we should give the subconscious a "booster shot." These booster shots consist of a periodic return to conscious, active effort. In these returns, the work so far is reviewed, new insights are sought, different approaches are tried, etc. Such returns may be necessary because our original preparation was not intense enough or because we are still lacking one key piece of information.

We can summarize the creative process as follows.

Irritation and Decision. The conscious mind is intrigued by a problem.

Preparation. A conscious effort is made to set the goals and provide ammunition.

Incubation. The subconscious takes over, searches the memory storage, and hunts for the answer.

Illumination. The subconscious reports to the conscious.

Verification. The conscious tries to verify the answer.

5.4 Personal Barriers to Creativity

Because of the tremendous importance of creativity, a great deal of research has been directed toward trying to ascertain why some people are more creative than others. One result of this research is the identification of certain personal characteristics that raise barriers that prevent full realization of a truly creative approach to problem solving and design. In this section we will consider several of these personal barriers.

Functional Fixedness.   Familiarity with certain objects or concepts within a fixed usage context prevents us from seeing the possibility of other uses. We think of a brick as only a building material, not as an object with mass, size, color, and other characteristics. We think of a paper clip as something to hold papers together, but not as a pipe cleaner, lock pick, spring, or connecting link. One interesting aspect of this problem is that just naming the object can result in functional fixedness. I have run the following demonstration numerous times in classes with invariant results. We hold up an old frayed toothbrush and give the following instructions. "During the next 3 minutes, write down all the uses you can think of for this used toothbrush." About 80 percent of the class will come up with less than eight uses, *all* of which will involve using it as a brush. The remaining 20 percent will average about 15 to 20 uses; more than half the list involves utilizing the brush as a stick (prop open a window, mark end of rows in a garden, etc.). If I change the procedure and merely hold up the toothbrush and say, "During the next 3 minutes, write down all the uses you can think of for this object" (i.e., I do not name it), the length of the lists will almost double.

As another demonstration of functional fixedness, Dunker [3] conducted a test in which the subjects had to use a thumbtack box as a candle holder in order to solve the problem. Almost all of the group saw the solution when the box was presented empty, but when it was presented full of thumbtacks, 87 percent of the students failed to find a solution. Obviously, presenting the box while it was serving its usual function fixed this purpose in the students' minds, and they were unable to see other uses for it.

Habit Transfer. Past conditioning and fixed methods of thought cause us to approach problems in the same old ways. All engineers and scientists have been trained in certain specific methods of analytical, evaluative, and deductive thinking. By the time they have finished college they have learned the customary or "correct" solution or approach to problems without considering other, perhaps more creative, approaches. They are also taught to rely heavily on textbooks and handbooks for solution methods; however, books relate only to what is known, and the creative approach or solutions will not be found there. Too often the engineer or scientist fits the problem to known solution methods, not the solution to the problem.

We are all creatures of habit, and these habits often keep us from even looking for new approaches or methods. One of my favorite stories showing how habit can lock us into a poor solution is attributed to Charles Kettering [8]. Kettering lived in Dayton and worked at the General Motors plant in Detroit. One day a friend who also made the drive asked Kettering if it was true he could make the drive in 4½ hours. When Kettering said yes, the friend expressed disbelief. The next week the friend rode with Kettering, and they made it in about 4½ hours. The friend expressed indignation by saying, "No wonder you can do it. You don't stay on Route 25."

We like to develop habits because we are basically lazy and want to perform our tasks without much thought. But habits are nothing more than repeating today what we did yesterday. If we only consider solving a problem the way it has always been solved, we will never find a better solution. The use of customary solutions or approaches to problems without considering other, more creative approaches locks us into using yesterday's solutions for today's problems.

Dependency on Authority. Closely allied to the barrier of habit transfer is the problem of overdependence on authority. Often engineers and scientists are so impressed by the judgments and approaches of recognized experts and authorities that they immediately accept them as the whole truth. The fact is that it is easy to demonstrate the erroneous judgments of even the giants of science and engineering. Thomas Edison wrote several papers and letters decrying the research on alternating current. He was positive that alternating current was too dangerous to use in the home and that direct current was the only way to go. Albert Einstein fought a stubborn battle against some of the new theories in physics such as quantum mechanics and the Heisenberg uncertainty principle, even though they developed from his own discoveries. Werner von Braun argued vehemently that the design of the Lunar Excursion Module (LEM) used for landing on the moon could not possibly work (although he later changed his position).

The overreliance on authorities may create barriers to individual creativity in two ways. First, if the individual accepts the judgment of recognized authorities about the ''correct'' way to solve or approach a problem, new and better ways will never be pursued. A well-established concept may prove to be a formidable barrier to the seeking or acceptance of a new one. Second, if the individual places too much reliance on the judgment of the experts, he or she may immediately accept statements that the idea will not work as true. During the depths of the Great Depression, Charles Darrow invented the game of Monopoly to while away the hours while making fun of his poverty and dreaming of better days. All the game manufacturers, including Parker Brothers (who since made a fortune from the game), told him that it would never sell because it was too complicated and people did not want to be reminded of their poverty. But Darrow ignored the experts' opinions; Monopoly has been the largest-selling game since 1935 and continues to be so.

M. W. Rosen *knew* his design for the lunar landing vehicle would work, despite the negative opinion of the engineers at the George C. Marshall Space Flight Center and of Werner von Braun, the world's most renowned and respected space expert. He persisted in his studies and analysis until he convinced the experts that he was right and they were wrong. Every experienced, creative person knows that the world is full of experts and recognized authorities who will gladly point out our errors. Almost any idea can immediately and logically be shown to be wrong. Sometimes that proof is so convincing that one is tempted to discard further thought about the new proposal. But the creative individual must always remember that the recognized authorities are human and have vested interests in their own ideas and concepts.

Premature Judgment. Many people pride themselves on being pragmatic and practical. These individuals insist that we get down to the facts immediately and not roam imaginatively around the problem. As stated earlier, our thinking mind consists of two parts: (1) a judicial mind, and (2) a creative mind. We are at our best when these two work in harmony. But in creative effort, judgment is good only when properly timed. The judicial mind is primarily negative in nature and asks questions such as, ''What's wrong with it?'', ''What will keep it from working?'', and ''What have I overlooked?'' Such an attitude is good when we are trying to choose between alternatives but deadly when we are trying to generate new ideas. Creative success is usually in proportion to the *number* of alternatives thought up. It is a little like the development of a football team; the more people who try out, the more people to choose from and the better the quality of the team. If we conceive of 100 alternatives, our chances of finding a good one are *more* than 10 times greater than if we stop at 10 alternatives. Creative thinking requires a positive attitude. We have to be hopeful and sure that a solution will be found. We need enthusiasm and self-confidence. Unfortunately, when we let judgment throw cold water on our ideas too soon, the ideas stop and the well runs dry. It is almost as if our subconscious mind says, "Well, if you're going to reject my ideas immediately, why should I put myself out any further?"

Numerous experiments [13] have shown that if we can suspend our judgmental minds and delay or postpone making judgments until our imaginations have piled up all possible ideas, our chances of coming up with a unique solution increase tremendously. We should let our imaginations soar and free them from practical considerations. There is strong evidence that during the idea generation phase, the wilder the ideas, the better. There is no need for any decision as to the relative merits of our ideas until we come to the question of which one, if any, is to be used. The truly creative person lets the imagination roam freely, soaring to heights of ridiculousness, and then engineers it back to earth and practicality. Do not commit yourself too early to a course of action or you may find it hard to break from the path if it turns out to be a wrong one. A good slogan might be, "Judge wisely, coldly, and dispassionately, *but* not until the right time."

Overspecialization. Engineers and scientists are trained in one profession, and each one has specialized talents that he or she relies on to solve problems. Most professional people have their own way of viewing the world and attempt to relate problems to this view. Specialization limits our horizons, and we see the world through the blinders of our professional training. There is no question that in this day of exploding knowledge some degree of specialization is necessary and desirable. However, the significant breakthrough in almost every field has come from people outside of the field. The individual must realize that one's own professional field does not contain all the answers or any divine right to be the possessor of all truth. The best and most creative solution may be found in a seemingly unrelated field, but it will not be found unless we look there. The creative person must learn as much as possible about different areas of knowledge—psychology, medicine, the arts, economics, world affairs, etc. If we do not cultivate a curiosity about what others are doing, we may find that in the process of digging deeper into our field, we have dug ourselves into a rut.

Fear of Failure. Most of us have been raised to consider failure as something very shameful. As a result of that attitude, Osborn [12] says, "The mortality of good ideas in infancy is appalling. And most of them are strangled by their own parents before anyone ever hears about them.'' From the time a child enters the first grade, performance is examined each 6 weeks or at least two or three times a year; of course, if the child fails, that is terrible. Mother and father continually stress the importance of success and the embarrassment of failure. By the time of college graduation, the person is so afraid of the word ''failure'' that it is easier to avoid any undertaking unless success is assured. But it is a rare occasion when a new idea does not first meet with failure. The inventor or innovater may fail again and again and, must succeed only once. Edison and his associates reportedly tried 6000 different fibers before they found one suitable as a filament for the light bulb.

Failure is largely a mental attitude, or how we view a situation. After failing 1000 times to find a solution to a problem, a completely discouraged employee came to Charles Kettering, who was then head of the General Motors Research Laboratories [8]. Kettering told him not to look at what he had done as a failure. ''Actually you have progressed wonderfully; you have found 1,000 ways it won't work.'' In a similar vein, Einstein spent most of his later years searching for a unified field theory [2]. Asked one day by his friend Leo Mattersdorf if he felt he was nearing his goal, he replied, ''No, but I have learned a great deal. I know at least 99 ways that won't work.''

Fear of failure usually stems from self-doubts of one's ability to be creative. People do not trust themselves to create and sell ideas. Shakespeare said, ''Doubts are traitors and make us lose the good we oft might win by fearing to attempt.'' Self-confidence is critical to creativity and to the courage and willingness to stick out one's neck. The creative person learns from failure but does not fear it. The person who always wants to be right never creates anything.

Fear of Ridicule. As we have seen, creativity is exhibited by the individual who is free from a way of thinking that is held by friends and associates who may be more intelligent, better educated, and better disciplined, but who have not mastered the art of the fresh, clean look at the old knowledge and ways of doing things. Since the ideas are new and unconventional, almost all of the world's great ideas were laughed at when first suggested. Creative effort will almost always breed discouragement by others as long as there are pessimistic people around. We should recognize that each new discovery or invention occurs under the stress of the attitude that it cannot be done. The more creative an idea, the more unconventional it will appear. The more unconventional it appears, the more likely it is to be met with ridicule and statements such as, ''I've seen it before someplace,'' ''It won't work,'' ''Someone must have thought of it before,'' or ''That's the silliest idea I've ever heard.'' Such statements are obviously discouraging and hard to take, but if the individual is continually evaluating ideas to see if others will consider them acceptable, creativity will be stifled and many excellent ideas will strangle in infancy.

Even if someone does develop a reputation as a crackpot, as soon as one or two ideas pay off, that reputation will soon change to that of a genius.

In addition to trying to guard against the personal barriers that hinder creativity, there are certain things the individual can do to enhance creativity. Researchers have been seeking ways to help people be more creative in their problem solving for a long time. We now know that what we want to do is free the mind from conventional ways of thinking and generate the largest number of alternatives possible. Almost all of the suggested techniques for creativity enhancement are designed to help in one or both of these endeavors (i.e., freeing the imagination or generating a large number of ideas). Since almost every creative idea is selected from among a large number of less significant ones, if enough alternatives are listed, the mathematical likelihood of one of them leading to a really creative idea is increased. In the following five sections we will explore some of the methods that have been suggested to accomplish this.

5.5 Ideation Through Word Association

One of the most fruitful approaches to the generation of large numbers of alternatives is to trigger the power of association. Association occurs when a word or idea causes us to think of another word or idea. This is also called chain-thinking or link-thinking. Idea A comes into my thoughts and reminds me of B, which reminds me of C, etc. Thought A can trigger a whole string of ideas, each of which has some association with its predecessors. The ancient Greeks such as Plato and Aristotle were fascinated with the association of ideas and the chains of thought that they triggered. They suggested the three laws of association: contiguity, similarity, and contrast. By *contiguity* they meant nearness, as when the sight of a friend's favorite flower reminds you of the friend. By *similarity* they meant, for example, that a seesaw reminds you of a lever. By *contrast,* they meant that a midget might remind you of a giant.

Ideation and *imagineering* are two words that have been used to describe the concept of trying to use association directly to generate ideas. One method is to use check lists of questions that have proven useful in the past. Every idea is like the branch of a tree, at the end of which another branch grows, etc. The idea of a check list is that each question represents a branch or direction in which an existing product, material, process, or service might conceivably be improved. When using a check list, one considers the object to be improved and asks a series of questions such as the following ones.

1. *Magnify.* Can it be made larger, longer, thicker, deeper, higher, wider, heavier, stronger, etc.?

2. *Minify*. Can it be made smaller, shorter, thinner, shallower, narrower, lighter, weaker, etc.?
3. *Reorder*. Can we reverse it, interchange parts, change places, change its representation, turn it upside down, place it vertically, horizontally, or slanted, etc.?
4. *Form*. Can we make it curved, straight, irregular, harder, softer, notched, rougher, smoother, change its color, make it hotter, colder, liquified, solidified, vaporized, pulverized, wetter, drier, etc.?
5. *Quantity*. Can we add more, less, join something, subtract something, combine with something else, fractionate, etc.?
6. *Motion Change*. Can it be slowed down, speeded up, stopped, attracted, repelled, lifted, lowered, rotated, oscillated, agitated, synchronized, alternated, stabilized, etc.?
7. *Convenience*. Can it be made easier, less work, easier to reach, disposable, quicker, simpler to use, automatic, etc.?
8. *Combine*. Can something be added to enhance its value, performance, or number of functions; can we combine ideas, principles, methods, groups, components, etc.?
9. *Substitution*. What can take its place (plastic for metal, round instead of square, light instead of dark, etc.); what other process, principle, theory, or method can be used?

When you are searching for a new idea or an improvement on an existing product, process, or service, words often suggest ideas and ideas suggest action. Check lists may touch off a spark that will bring an answer. It is impossible to predict ahead of time what kind of words will suggest ideas. Some people have found a thesaurus or dictionary helpful. For other people, trade journals and technical books are a good source of words for idea stimulation. The preceding check list of words is not complete; its purpose is to show some of the possible ways a product, process, material, or service might be improved.

5.6 Idea Matrix

Another procedure for idea generation is the use of idea matrices. One first analyzes the independent variables related to the problem or task. Each variable is then subdivided into all the possible types, features, or methods and listed separately as one dimension of a matrix grid. For example, suppose we are trying to think up a new and innovative land transportation system. Two of the variables or parameters would be the vehicle itself and the type of power or propulsion. Figure 5.1 shows one possible idea matrix that we might generate. We have listed possible vehicle types along the side and possible power sources along the top. The intersection of each row and column represents alternative ideas or suggestions for a solution to our problem. This small matrix suggests 100 different possibilities. Obviously, not all of them are really viable candidates but, if we let our imaginations run free over each possibility suggested, even the most ludicrous combination may trigger another idea that is a good solution. Again, the purpose of the idea matrix is to help us get a large number of ideas, not necessarily all good ones. The very process of trying to expand this matrix makes us think harder about possibilities. Just one more vehicle type or power source increases the number of ideas by 10. For example, if we add compressed air and a nuclear reactor as possible power sources, we have added 20 new possible ideas, one of which may trigger an idea for a solution.

5.7 Group versus Individual Creativity

The subject of teamwork or group activity work requiring high creativity is quite controversial. Some writers consider teamwork detrimental, while others consider it essential. The arguments against teamwork will be considered first. Team research and the so-called "group ideation techniques" have largely replaced the individual investigator in some organizations. Harmonious team adjustment is put at a premium, and rarely is the person allowed enough freedom and scope to follow individual spontaneity and impulse. A few companies have realized that there is a tremendous social pressure factor in enforced teamwork and that the pull of the lowest common denominator frequently rules. More and more industry representatives are beginning to question whether any real creativity can be expected in collaborative enterprises. There is a feeling that the widely accepted notion of the "group supermind" is a dangerous illusion, and that a really creative idea can originate only in the mind of a single person. It is now also more readily admitted that the group ethos that permeates an industrial organization and the attendant pressure on personnel to become good organization people are contributing to the increasing suffocation of creative individuals; this constitutes one of the greatest hindrances in the development of their talents.

Real creativity is an extremely private and individual affair. It cannot be enforced, scheduled, or programmed through teamwork. By simply reviewing the landmarks of innovation and discovery, it becomes obvious that they have been, almost without exception, one-mind departures. Like the late Albert Einstein, most really creative people readily admit that they are "horses for the single harness and not cut out for tandem or teamwork." Even in industry it has now been discovered that the more creative people are, the more

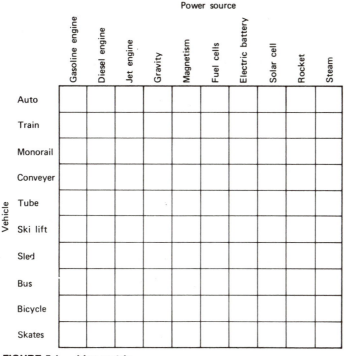

FIGURE 5.1   Idea matrix.

energetically they fight for their individuality and the more they refuse to be sucked in and distracted by endless meetings and the rituals of being part of the group. In an important sense, one of the strong motivations of creativity in a technical organization is the desire to get out of the fetters of herd-existence.

Those who advocate the organized group approach base their recommendation on some of the following considerations. The cross-fertilization of ideas that teamwork provides is imperative for best results. The number of stimuli that can spark a new idea are greater in a group than what an individual can get when working alone. Teamwork stimulates discussions, pooling of knowledge, and exposure to different viewpoints and facets of a situation. It provides each individual with more ideas and more constructive criticism.

5.8 Brainstorming

One type of group collaboration that has been found to be very effective is the so-called "brainstorm sessions." The term and idea go back to 1939 [12], when Osborn described it as a group "using the *brain* to *storm* a creative problem—and doing so in *commando* fashion, with each stormer attacking the same objective.'' The idea is for a group of people to attack a problem from every angle they can think of and come up with all the ideas that occur, no matter how farfetched or ridiculous they may seem. The rules are simple but critical. They are:

1. Criticism of ideas is not permitted. Judgment and evaluation are to be suspended until the next day.
2. Wildness is welcome. The crazier the idea the better. Freewheeling and loose thinking are to be sought and encouraged.
3. Quantity of ideas is wanted. As discussed earlier, the probability of coming up with a good idea is proportional to the number generated.
4. The combination and improvement of ideas are sought. Group members should try to improve or elaborate on the ideas of others, allow one idea to build on another, and join two or more ideas into still another idea.

The spirit of a brainstorm session can make or break it. Brainstorming is not a bull session but a concentrated group effort to produce creative ideas for the solution of a specific problem. The problem should be as specific as possible and limited to a single area so that the group can shoot their ideas at a single target. When a session fails, it is usually due to a failure of leadership that derives from one of two causes. First, if a group leader makes a big display of too much superior knowledge of the problem or in any way intimates his or her omniscience, the more junior group members will be afraid to open their mouths and the attitude of the others will be, ''If you know so much about it, you think up the ideas.'' Second, the leader who allows criticism or judgmental statements to creep into the preceedings will also fail to get useful results. There will always be the incurable critic who will disregard the rule and belittle all suggestions of others. Any transgressor who makes statements such as ''It won't work,'' ''It was tried before,'' or ''That's stupid'' should immediately but gently be warned. If they persist, they must be firmly stopped or asked to leave.

Most conferences, as we know them, are noncreative. They are intended to exchange information or to consider whether this alternative is better than that (i.e., they are either informational or judicial). It is therefore difficult for the group leader to break down prior habits. Osborn quotes a vice-president of a large corporation after a session.

You know, it was hard to get through my head what you were trying to do with us. My 15 years of conference after conference in my company have conditioned me against shooting wild. Almost all of us officers rate each other on the basis of judgment—we are far more apt to look up to the other fellow if he makes few mistakes than if he suggests lots of ideas. So I've kept myself from spouting any suggestions that my associates might sneer at.

Brainstorming sessions work best with 6 to 12 participants. Someone should be designated as recorder and every idea, crackpot or crackerjack, should be written down. Every participant should receive a list the next day. In a surprising number of cases, reviewing the list will trigger new ideas that day or at a later time. Sessions should be conducted to achieve a specific goal, either a specific quantity of ideas or a period of time, for instance 2 hours. During the first hour ideas will appear quickly and easily, but they are the usual ideas that anyone would think of. In the next half hour ideas will evolve progressively more slowly. At the end of 1½ hours everyone will be drained and exhausted but, since you set a goal of 2 hours, you must proceed. Only one or two ideas may come out of the last half hour, but they are likely to be the best ones, because they are not the obvious or common ones. Creativity is stimulated by thinking a little longer than normal, after the obvious has been exhausted. It may also enhance the intense preparation stage of the creative process that was discussed in Section 5.3. In an amazing number of cases, the day after a brainstorming session you will hear someone say: "You remember that nutty idea that Joe had about. . . ? Well, that got me to thinking, and what if we. . . ? "

Group brainstorming can be highly creative for several reasons. For one thing, the power of association is working in two ways. When a member of the group spouts an idea, this almost automatically leads that person toward another idea; at the same time, the idea stimulates the associative power of all the others. Tests have demonstrated that "free associations" on the part of adults are from 65 to 93 percent more numerous in group activity than when working alone [12]. Group brainstorming does away with much of the criticism of the conventional group meetings. For example, the "no-judgment, freewheeling" atmosphere counteracts the tremendous pressure for conformity usually exerted in a group. Brainstorming provides reinforcement for creative behavior and, therefore, provides the psychological safety that is helpful in freeing group members from their conformity complexes.

Another explanation of the productivity of group brainstorming is the stimulative effect of rivalry. Psychologists have proven that competition will increase accomplishment in mental work by 50 percent or more [12]. Rivalry causes us to try harder, and trying harder stimulates creativity. Therefore, the leader should try to create an atmosphere of friendly competition in dreaming up ideas.

5.9 Synectics

The synectic approach to idea generation is similar to brainstorming in that a group effort is used. However, it differs considerably in several significant ways. First, each session has a leader who is the absolute boss. The leader decides which train of thought will be pursued and which will be shut off. A session alternates between intense discussions of the problem at hand and deliberate excursions into analogous and often apparently unrelated spheres. These deliberate departures from the problem into areas of metaphor and fantasy are introduced by the leader when things begin to slow down.

Ideally, a synectics group consists of 5 to 10 members. They should be as diverse in training and background as possible, so that each one will view the problem differently. It is presided over by the leader, who is a member of the group and firmly guides the discussions, but who does not directly contribute ideas. It is also essential that the group contain one or two people who are knowledgeable in the problem area. The technique of synectics was proposed by Gordon [4] and was further developed by Prince [15] and by others.

As a first step, the *problem as given* is stated by the leader. How the problem is defined is extremely important, since it can set up mental blocks that are difficult to break down. For example, instead of defining the problem as "design a unique or novel lawn mower," it should be stated as to function or purpose, such as "design a method or device for shortening grass." Instead of charging the group to "design a novel can opener," define it as "design a method of removing the contents of a container." During the problem-as-given stage, the leader and those knowledgeable about the problem try to tell the group everything that is known about the problem.

The second stage is called the *purge*. When people hear about a problem, they immediately begin to offer suggestions for a solution. The expert responds to these suggestions based on prior experience (often the advice has already been tried or considered). The expert then explains what happened and why it did not work. The purge stage will help to clarify and bring the problem into focus, remove misconceptions, and bring out information on solutions that have been tried. Sometimes promising ideas will emerge during the purge. Such ideas are recorded as *viewpoints,* which is the term for possible solutions to be pursued further. Until a viewpoint is made to work, it is not a solution.

The next stage is called *problems as understood.* In this phase each member is asked to write down one or more versions of the problem as he or she sees it. Each member is encouraged to state as a problem wishful, ideal solutions, such as, "How can we get the grass to stay pretty but stop growing?", or "How can we get a container to discharge its contents on command?" The leader then chooses one of these problems as understood to work with, tells the group, and then requests that they put the problem as given from their minds and simply do as requested.

The leader then requests or proposes an *evocative question that is related to the selected problem as understood. This is a request for analogies in a different world.* The purpose is to direct the minds of the group toward an area that might result in unexpected, interesting responses that seem to be unconnected to the problem. What the leader is trying to do is to precipitate an *excursion* into unfamiliar land that may or may not have an obvious bearing on the problem. For example, if the group was considering a transportation system or materials handling problem, an evocative question might be, "How does a snail get around with no legs?" This would lead to a discussion in the world of zoology.

After some discussion of snails, it would be ascertained that the snail utilizes "ripple power." It does not slide or glide, but uses muscle contractions to send a rippling wave along the singular foot. At this point the leader might bring the group back to the reality of the problem as understood, and an attempt is made to *force fit* (apply) some of the concepts from the excursion. For example, in the snail excursion the leader might say, "If ripple power works for the snail, why not use that transportation system for ourselves? Such a device, or a snailmobile, would have at least 80 percent of its bottom area in contact with the ground; this would spread the weight over a large area, resulting in low ground pressure. It might also be used to transport very delicate cargo over rough terrains. Can this idea of ripple power be used to solve our problem?" If it appears promising after some discussion, it is recorded as a viewpoint to be evaluated later, and a new excursion is started.

Excursions can be analogies of several types, such as personal (role playing), direct (e.g., the snail), or fantasy (blue-sky dreaming). Personal analogies can be pursued by role playing, where one member tries to place himself or herself in the situation and, through self-interrogation or interrogation by the group, asks what he or she would do or feel if that member were the thing, idea, the device, or the issue. For example, consider the situation where we are trying to come up with a new can opener. One member might pretend he or she is the can, and the other members would ask questions. "How do you feel when someone opens you with a can opener?" "How do you think I feel? It hurts. Imagine someone poking a hole in the top of your head and then slicing all around your skull to take the top off." "Does it make you sad?" "Sad? It's the most empty feeling you've ever had. And then, to add insult to injury, they throw me in the trash with all that stinky garbage." This conversation might suggest a switch to the forced fit stage to explore the idea of resealable and reusable containers. The value of personal analogy lies in the direct involvement of the individual and the use of imagination. The role player helps the group to see the problem from another perspective and gives a better feeling for some aspect of the problem.

In direct analogy, members of the group take turns trying to relate the problem as understood to a different but parallel situation. As we have seen, many direct analogies exist in nature. Examples such as the snail problem or consideration of a beehive as an analog to a large office building come readily to mind. Hill [7] discussed an example of designing tools for assembling structures in space. After presenting the problem and discussing the difficulties caused by weightlessness, extreme low temperatures, etc., the leader holds up a piece of styrofoam suspended from a string. The leader then requests suggestions as to how to drill a hole in the foam. Eventually someone might suggest burning a hole in it with a cigarette. This would then lead to an attempt to force fit the idea of burning holes instead of drilling them in space.

Analogy through fantasy is a form of wish fulfillment play. A group member pretends that things can be had the way he or she wants them without regard to facts or practical considerations. The member then describes to the group this ideal solution to the problem as understood. For example, if the problem was one of energy conservation, the member might say, "I have a roof that turns white to reflect heat when it's hot and black to absorb heat when it's cold." The idea, while wishful, is to make others think, "Gee, wouldn't that be great!" The team then tries to support and build on *any* statement, no matter how impractical or seemingly irrelevant. No criticism or judgmental statements are allowed during an excursion. These must wait until the leader brings the group back to the forced fit stage.

During the forced fit stage, if a member comments on a suggestion made by someone else, he or she must first paraphrase the suggestion (to insure that everyone understands it) and then list three good points before turning to its defects. This encourages the group to note the good features while looking for a remedy to the deficiencies. When the group feels that an idea represents a possible solution to a problem as understood, it is listed as a viewpoint. When an apparent dead end is reached, the leader goes back to the lists compiled by the members and picks a different problem as understood to begin a new set of excursions. This process continues until the group feels it has enough viewpoints to potentially solve the problem as given.

5.10 Management Barriers to Creativity

Creativity and the organization are always in conflict. Drawing the first blocks on an organization chart establishes a system that is "inhospitable to a great and constant flow of ideas and creativity [9]." An organization cannot function as an anarchy. It must be organized and routinized, and the actions of its members must be predictable. The whole purpose of an organization is to achieve the degree of order and conformity required to do a job. The organization exists to restrict and channel the behavior and actions of its members. However, as we have seen, creativity is devoted to innovation, change, and thinking in nonroutine ways.

We should not be surprised, therefore, to find that management and the organization inevitably raise certain barriers that stifle creativity. Some of these barriers are both necessary and desirable, since they keep the parent organization on an even keel. Others, however, are not necessary and can be removed by an elightened understanding of both the desirability and requirements of an environment that is hospitable and encouraging to creativity. Among the undesirable barriers are:

1. *Tendency of Management to Tell the Technical Professionals What to Do and How to Do It.* Obviously management must control and direct the activities of its people but, as we saw in Figure 1.7, overcontrol leads to robotlike or zombielike performance.

2. *Rigid Lines of Authority.* Unlike some other departments, technical groups need open and flexible lines of communication. Instead of going through channels, technical people need to communicate directly with all parts of the organization, regardless of lines of authority.

3. *Lack of Long-Range Objectives.* If there is a lack of specified long-range objectives or if there is disagreement in top management as to such objectives, many projects will go down blind alleys. It is frustrating to the professional to have worked long and hard to come up with an innovative solution to a problem only to find that management is not interested.

4. *Frequent Changes of Key Decisions.* This barrier is related to the preceding one in that it leads to lost motion, frustration, and a decline in enthusiasm. It is hard to really immerse oneself in a problem if past experience shows the project may shortly be canceled.

5. *Lack of Effective Communication Between Management and Professional Staff.* The technical staff must know the needs and resource limitations of the organization, and management must understand the problems and frustrations of the technical staff.

6. *Management Emphasis on Immediate Utility of Ideas.* Truly creative solutions to problems often take time to develop. Obstinate persistence in the face of difficulties and frustrations is characteristic of the creative individual. A demand for immediate results will lead to problems being solved in the same old ways.

7. *Failure of Management to Recognize and Reward Creative Ability.* It takes guts and courage to stick one's neck out by proposing new ideas. If the rewards go to the conformist plodders who never rock the boat, creative activity will quickly dry up.

8. *Poor Handling or Ourtright Misappropriation of Credit for New Ideas.* One of the primary joys of a creative accomplishment is pride in the idea and a desire for recognition by its originator. If the supervisor insists that his or her name or those of other co-workers be included on the paper or patent or, even worse, takes full credit for the idea with upper management, all creativity will cease.

9. *Negative Attitude of Management to All New Ideas.* New ideas usually

cause change, and some managers do not like even to think about change. Creativity is so delicate a flower that praise tends to make it blossom while discouragement often nips it in the bud.

10. *Reluctance of Managers to Take Chances.* No manager should accept an idea just because it is new and innovative. On the other hand, there is no such thing as a risk-proof change. The manager should recognize that merely keeping the status quo entails a risk.

5.11 The Creative Environment

Few professionals can produce new ideas and creative solutions to complex problems when they are working in a noncreative environment, so management should try to create an environment that is conducive to creative thoughts for high motivation of the professionals. One should expect to find a climate for creativity in technical organizations but, according to many investigations, this is not the case. Despite the fact that private industry is the largest employer of technical professionals, it does not seem to provide the most favorable auspices for important creative work. Creative engineers and scientists often find little encouragement in industry to make their optimum contribution. Many of them create in spite of the prevailing climate and the lack of external incentives for creativity.

Major factors that affect creativity are autocracy and conformity in organizations. Nothing can be as devastating to uninhibited creative thinking as the social pressure that makes the engineer or scientist feel uncomfortable for exhibiting any orginality. To avoid censure, the technical personnel may arbitrarily constrict the parameters of their work, which concomitantly reduces their potential contribution to the organization. To avoid liability, the individual may reduce the probability of failure by more conservative and stereotyped efforts of a more defensible nature. Thus the pressure for conformity and fear of censure or liability actually foster continuation of the status quo. A conforming atmosphere, as is becoming more and more apparent, is disastrous to vitality and vigorous progress. New solutions to old problems fail to emerge in a restrictive, more rigid and conforming atmosphere, where outmoded routines and obsolete habits and policies hold sway.

Many organizations are beginning to realize that heterogeneity is essential to progress, and constructive variability is one of the most valuable resources they could have. Some technical organizations realize that individuals who are not afraid of their uniqueness bring with them different viewpoints for solving technical problems. In addition, organizations can try to revamp and relax their own system of controls, operations, and procedures so that the influence of conformity is reduced. Organizations must become more flexible, more open to individual freedom and autonomy, and more responsive to the needs that bring forth self-reliance and initiative. They must find means of combining a greater degree of individual initiative with organizational goals. They must lessen the degree of externally imposed discipline and cohesion, which have been mistakenly overrated as necessary factors for a smoothly functioning organization. It has been pointed out that a smoothly functioning, highly cooperative organization can actually weaken organization vitality.

The ability to bring about important results, progress, and creativity can be enhanced in organizations if more power is delegated to individuals and to smaller groups, in which the individual is not overwhelmed by impersonal vastness or mere numbers of people. In addition, management must start fitting systems to people, not people to systems, and must create a new organizational ethos that allows more scope for individuality and individual development. The desirability of encouraging more constructive nonconformity, more individuality, and more autonomy is mandatory for a technical organization. It is also clear that different combinations of approaches can and should be adapted in any one organization, depending on the quality of personnel employed, the degree of creativity desired, and the objectives of each department in the organization.

It is no secret that our most creative professionals are the most dissatisfied employees in industry. They are strongly in conflict with the conformist character of the industrial and business systems, and they lack the passion for anonymity required from an organization person or from a team member. Creative brilliance, until very recently (and even at present) in many technical organizations, was considered secondary to the ability to get along, to be well rounded, and to be a good mixer who adapts easily to the social and formal rules of the group or the organization. The highly creative individuals were either coerced to conform to these rules or subtle pressures were brought to bear on them to leave the employment of the organization. A debate has arisen over the problem of what to do with the brilliant engineer or scientist who simply does not get along with others. Some companies make it their policy not to hire such people. They claim that their technical effort is so oriented to the group approach that the disruptive effect of a person who would not fit well with the team could far outweigh the constructive contribution they might make.

To maximize the contribution of the talented members of our society, organizations need to accommodate the creative individuals differently. Technical personnel want freedom to manage their own work, to use their own approaches in solving problems, and to work on their projects in their own style and at their own pace. They want freedom to complete a job once it is undertaken, and they resent being shifted from one incomplete project to another. They want to follow through and see how their ideas are working out in concrete form. They want to spend a good part of their working hours on problems that interest them. They want freedom to participate in decision making where it involves their own work. They want more flexible working hours and do not want all the rules and regulations of the nonprofessionals imposed on them. Finally, they also need to be convinced that their accomplishments are recognized and appreciated by management.

5.12 Creativity Is Not Enough

Ideas, no matter how unique and new, are useless unless used. The proof of the value of an idea in a technical organization is its implementation. Until the idea is used it is merely an interesting mental exercise. The sad fact of life is that ideas do not implement themselves—people implement ideas. In the first section of this chapter we defined creativity as the ability to produce unique, interesting, and useful results. Until now we may have given the impression that creativity automatically leads to actual implementation. This is not true. Creativity and innovation are not synonymous. Creativity deals with the generation and validation of ideas. Innovation deals with their implementation.

Levitt [9] states that new ideas are relatively abundant in most organizations, but that implementation or innovation is much more rare. He argues that the fact that you can put 10 or 12 people together in a room and conduct a brainstorming or synectics session that produces exciting new ideas shows how little relative importance ideas have by themselves. What is even more important are the scarce individuals who have the know-how, energy, daring, and persistence to see their ideas implemented. Quinn [19] said:

> A new creative idea is like a baby. You can't just bring it into the world and expect it to grow up and be a success. It needs a mother (enthusiasm) to love it and keep it going when things are tough. It needs a pediatrician (expert information and technical skills) to solve the problems the mother can't cope with alone. And it needs a father (authority with resources) to feed it and house it. Without any one of these, the baby may still turn out all right, but its chances of survival are a lot lower.

Too many creative people believe the familiar quotation attributed to Ralph Waldo Emerson: "If a man can write a better book, preach a better sermon, or build a better mousetrap than his neighbor, though he builds his house in the woods, the world will make a beaten path to his door." There is some doubt that Emerson ever said those words; I hope not, because the statement is totally invalid. Ideas do not sell themselves; those who believe they do are in for shock and frustration.

Many technical people complain that management does not listen to their ideas. They complain about the stand-pat senility of management and its refusal to recognize a brilliant idea when presented on a silver platter. They conclude that management does not really want new ideas, because they cause change (which they do), and that management is only interested in having a smooth-running organization (which they are). The reason for such complaints is that the people to whom they address their ideas ignore them and tell them to go away, and for good reason. The explanation of why a manager often rejects new ideas is that he or she is a very busy person whose chief task is to handle a constant stream of problems. The average manager must answer an unending flow of questions and make many decisions. The creative individual must understand that every time a new idea is presented to the manager, another problem, of which there is already no shortage, is being created.

It is important for everyone connected with engineering and research operations to realize that the actual products of the technical organization are only *potentially* new or improved products, processes, materials, or solutions—and nothing more. They must be sold to management before they can be implemented. Selling technical results requires skill, persistence, and courage. When a technical person suggests an idea, the reasonable procedure would be to include at least some indication as to the costs, risks, manpower, time, and perhaps even specific people that would be requested to pursue the idea. By presenting the idea along with such information, it becomes easier and less time consuming for the manager to evaluate the idea.

One has only to scan the literature to realize that almost every new and innovative technical idea that has been implemented had its "champion"— someone who risked a reputation or possibly even a job to put it over. To be a champion for an idea takes courage, because there is always the danger of failure of the idea and subsequent damage to one's reputation. Despite the danger, the truly creative individual will have the motivation to see the idea translated into reality.

References

1. Cannon, W. B., *The Way of the Investigators*, W. W. Norton, New York, 1945, pp. 147–148.
2. Clark, R. W., *Einstein; The Life and Times*, World Publishing, New York, 1971.
3. Dunker, K., "On Problem Solving," *Psychological Monographs, 58* (5) May 1945, p. 270.
4. Gordon, W.J.J., *Synectics*, Harper & Row, New York, 1960.
5. Guilford, J. P., "The Structure of the Intellect," *Psychological Bulletin, 53,* 1956, pp. 267–293.
6. Guilford, J. P., "Basic Problems in Teaching for Creativity," *Instructional Media and Creativity*, C. W. Taylor, Editor, Wiley, New York, 1966.

7. Hill, P. H., *The Science of Engineering Design,* Holt, Rinehart and Winston, New York, 1970.
8. Hueter, J. M., "Creativity—Choice or Chance," *The Journal of Industrial Engineering, XVII* (10), October 1966, pp. 503–510.
9. Levitt, T., "Creativity is Not Enough," *Harvard Business Review, 41* (3), May-June 1963, pp. 72–83.
10. Maltz, M., *Psycho-Cybernetics,* Prentice-Hall, Englewood Cliffs, N.J., 1960.
11. Maugh, Thomas H., II, "Creativity: Can it be Dissected? Can it be Taught?" *Science, 184* (4143), June 1974, pp. 1273–
12. Osborn, A., *Your Creative Power,* Dell, New York, 1948.
13. Parnes, S. J., "Creative Potential and the Educational Experience," *Fields within Fields . . . Within Fields, 2* (1), 1969, pp. 39–50.
14. Pelz, D. C., and F. M. Andrews, *Scientists in Organizations,* Wiley, New York, 1966.
15. Prince, G. M., "Synectics: A Method of Creative Thought," *Engineering Education, 57* (6), March 1968, pp. 805–811.
16. Roe, A., *The Making of a Scientist,* Dodd, Mead, New York, 1953.
17. Roe, A., "The Psychology of Scientists," *Management of Scientists,* K. Hill, Editor, Beacon Press, Boston, 1964.
18. Travis, I., "Technical Management for R&D," *Space/Aeronautics, 31* (5), May 1959, pp. 281–293.
19. Quinn, J. B., and J. A. Mueller, "Transferring Research Results to Operations," *Harvard Business Review, 41* (1), January-February 1963, pp. 49–66.

Discussion Questions

1. Should highly creative people be treated differently (special privileges, such as being exempt from certain rules and regulations) than their less creative colleagues?
2. Should competition or cooperation be encouraged to increase creative output?
3. Should informal communication channels be encouraged or discouraged within the technical organization? How about with outside groups?
4. Is planning detrimental to creativity?
5. Can individual initiative and creativity survive in large engineering organizations? What positive steps can be taken?
6. Are innovation and invention synonymous terms?
7. What are the advantages of a team approach to invention? What disadvantages can you think of?
8. Is it important that the technical manager possess personal creative ability?
9. Are the personality characteristics of creative people compatible with those desired in a manager?
10. Would it be desirable for a technical group to be composed entirely of strongly motivated, self-starting go-getters who were highly creative?
11. Conduct a brainstorming session on private transportation.

---------------------------------- **Case Study V** ----------------------------------

RAYMAR ENGINEERING COMPANY

Dr. Joe Kelly, head of new product development, was deep in thought when Dr. Jeff Rozell appeared at the door. Dr. Kelly had just returned from the president's office, where he had been mildly taken to task for the lack of innovation of his group. The president had been distressed by the fact that the last five new products presented to the board of directors were all obviously imitations of competitor's products. "This company has always been a leader, not a follower," the president had said. "When are we going to begin to see some innovation out of your group?"

Dr. Rozell was one of the senior project engineers who had been with Dr. Kelly for 15 years. Ten years ago they had done some of the pioneering work on the first microprocessors, which had thrust Raymar Engineering into the forefront of mini and microcomputer technology. Kelly was glad to see him just then, because they had always been close personal friends as well as professional colleagues.

ROZELL: Joe, I've got a real problem with your Mike Johnson. He's only been here 3 months and already I'm having problems with him. I can't get him to do anything. All he wants to do is work on that new simulation language.

KELLY: I thought that was what you wanted him to do.

ROZELL: It is, but there are other things that have to get done. I can't get him to write his weekly progress reports, or turn in his 5-year research plan, or any other thing. He missed two staff meetings last week and still hasn't turned in his travel report from that trip he took last month. I'm getting sick and tired of having to hound him every time I need something from him. Besides, he pays no attention to prescribed procedures and doesn't even read the policy statements I put out.

KELLY: What does he say when you ask him about these things?

ROZELL: Oh, he's always very apologetic and promises to get right on it as soon as he finishes the subroutine he is working on, but nothing happens. The next time I check, he is working on another subroutine.

KELLY: Maybe you just haven't gotten across to him the importance of these administrative matters. He certainly is bright enough and seems to do an excellent technical job.

ROZELL: He understands well enough. He is just too self-indulgent and concerned only with enjoying himself doing what he wants to do. He wants everyone else to shoulder the administrative responsibilities while he plays with his computers. I can't get him to understand that everyone has to accept some responsibility and self-sacrifice.

KELLY: Jeff, don't you remember when we used to bridle and scream about all the paper work?

ROZELL: Sure, but you and I made the sacrifice in order to help create and make this organization grow. Everyone would rather limit themselves to research, but all of us have to help carry the load. I just can't have a bunch of prima donnas around here who won't adhere to the rules.

KELLY: What do you want me to do Jeff?

ROZELL: Well, maybe if you talked to him, it would help. He has a great deal of respect for you, because he knows you've done some outstanding research.

A few days later, Kelly walked down the hall to Mike Johnson's office. He found him deeply engrossed in several pages of coding. Kelly stood in the doorway for several moments before Johnson was aware of his presence.

MIKE JOHNSON: Oh, hi. Dr. Kelly, I didn't see you come in. What can I do for you?

KELLY: I just thought I'd drop in and see how you were coming with that new simulation language.

JOHNSON: It's coming great. I'm really excited about the possibilities. Do you realize the impact this will have if we can make it possible to do fairly sophisticated simulations on our minicomputers? I'm convinced the day of the large mainframe computer is almost at an end.

KELLY: You look tired, Mike. Are you feeling all right?

JOHNSON: Oh, I'm feeling great. I am a little tired because I've been working until late at night at home on this thing. It's like being possessed. I get so involved, I even forget meetings sometimes. As soon as I work out one thing, I can see the solution to the next. Poor Dr. Rozell is getting kind of perturbed with me, I'm afraid. I'm a little late with a couple of reports he wants. He just doesn't understand how important it is to follow up on an idea when it's hot.

KELLY: Well, you know, Mike, Dr. Rozell has his problems, too. People are putting the pressure on him to get the paperwork out.

JOHNSON: Yeah, I know that and I really feel guilty sometimes. But I've given him verbal reports, and I really don't see why the written ones can't wait until I'm finished. Would you like to see some of this? It's really great!

Kelly listened for a half hour, as Johnson proudly explained the philosophy of his new language and some of the problems he had solved. He returned to his office and glumly stared out the window. He hadn't understood half of what young Johnson had explained to him.

The next morning, Kelly called a meeting in his office with Rozell and the other two senior project engineers on his staff, Bill Pierce and Joyce Rowe.

KELLY: The reason I've called this meeting is to see what we can do to increase creativity and innovation around here. The top brass says our output is of a trivial nature and too imitative of what is initiated elsewhere. After reviewing our technical project reports carefully, I'm afraid I have to agree. The only new ideas I see are those from the new people, like Mike Johnson. You three have been here a long time. What's wrong? What can we do to get back on top of things?

PIERCE: Well, I don't necessarily agree that what we are doing is trivial, but perhaps if we had each technical person prepare a new 5-year plan, some new ideas would come out.

ROWE: Another thing we could do is have a weekly seminar at which each of the senior engineers could give a report on what they are doing. Maybe this would spark some new ideas in the others.

ROZELL: I think the real problem is public relations. Perhaps we should generate some fancy reports to send to the president and other top executives showing the importance of the projects we are pursuing.

ROWE: Another part of the problem is a lack of manpower and equipment. If we had more people and better facilities, there are a lot of things we could do.

After another hour of similar discussion, Kelly brought the meeting to an end with the request that the three engineers put their ideas into writing and submit them to him by the next Friday.

KELLY: I thank you for your time. I believe we are beginning to make some progress on our problem.

Case study discussion questions

1. Can you identify some of the attitudes, procedures, etc., that might be inhibiting creativity?
2. Should Johnson be reprimanded or perhaps even fired?
3. What specific ideas could you suggest to Dr. Kelly to improve creativity?
4. Does Dr. Kelly understand his problem?

CHAPTER 6 motivation

6.1 Necessity of Benefits

Barnard [4] defined an organization as "a system of consciously coordinated activities of two or more persons." He further stated that one of the essential elements of an organization was the willingness to serve on the part of individuals within the organization. The output and effectiveness of any organization are entirely dependent on the personal efforts of the members. Therefore, the individual is the most important basic strategic factor in the organization. A member of a group will contribute personal effort or exhibit a "willingness to serve" only as long as the beneifts accrued outweigh or exceed the burdens assumed. For this reason, the allocation and dispensing of benefits and incentives occupy (or should occupy) a major portion of the time and creativeness of the technical manager.

Looking at the simple expression (benefits > burdens) immediately indicates that the manager has two methods of attack to secure and hold this willingness to serve: increase benefits, reduce burdens, or do both. The purpose of any management system is to aide in doing this. Most factors clearly fall into the categories of either benefits or burdens, but others are harder to classify. The separation of benefits and burdens into various classifications is a long-standing game of sociologists, psychologists, management consultants, and authors. In any event, the benefits fall into two categories: (1) specific material inducements, which can be quantified (money, floor space, number of direct employees supervised, etc.), and (2) psychological inducements (power, prestige, recognition, reputation, nature of collegues, etc.). Each is important, but they are not equal, and their relative value varies during the career or work life of each individual. The benefits distributed must be consistent with the employee's needs before a "willingness to serve" will be created.

Note that a satisfied need is no longer a motivator of behavior. A benefit is a motivator to a person only as long as it will fulfill some unsatisfied need. As soon as it is awarded, it is no longer a motivator; however, its reduction will constitute a burden.

6.2 Motivation Defined

The question of what makes human beings work productively is a question of obvious and fundamental importance to any manager. The answer to the problem of what a manager can do to increase the performance of employees is vastly complex and only vaguely understood. We can state the problem in the following formula:

Performance = Goals × Ability × Motivation

In other words, performance results from knowing what to do, how to do it and, at the same time, having a reason or motive for doing it. For example, if additional effort on the part of laboratory technicians will provide a shorter turnaround time for a given test, it must be perceived that the shorter turnaround time will lead to some reward before the effort will be expended. From the manager's viewpoint, manipulating the goals and abilities portion of the formula is fairly straightforward. We manipulate the ability portion by our staffing, training, and promotion decisions, and we manipulate the goals portion through planning, project selection, and communicating. Providing and manipulating the motivation portion, however, is a very different matter.

There is only one way to get people to do what you would like them to do, and that is by making them *want* to do it. Motivation flows from within the individual. Motivation is the internal source of energy that tends to activate the behavior of the individual. Because it is internal to the individual, motivation cannot be observed or measured directly and is, therefore, a hypothetical concept that is inferred from observation of behavior and performance. A *motive* is defined as that force or energy within the individual that incites or drives the person to action (i.e., any idea, need, emotion, or organic state that prompts the individual to do something). Because motives prompt individuals into behaving in a certain way, we also refer to them as drives or goals.

Motives can result from natural causes (primary drives) or be learned and acquired (secondary drives). Examples of primary drive motives are pain, hunger, thirst, and probably sex. These motives are the ones that predominantly determine an infant's behavior and continue their influence throughout life. Secondary or learned motives are acquired as we seek to avoid adverse effects and feelings and seek to achieve emotionally positive events and feelings. Secondary drives (or motives) are acquired through conditioning. The person is presented with a stimulus of some sort by another person, thing, or environment. The individual then finds that certain behavior results in pleasant feelings and sensations (positive reinforcement) or unpleasant feelings and sensations (negative reinforcement). Over a period of time, the individual learns from these situations, and the presentation of these stimuli results in acquired motives or drives.

When we say we are trying to motivate a person, we are attempting to provide a motive, to impel or incite the person to do that which we desire and avoid doing that which we do not desire. The words "incentive" and "motivator" are often used to mean the rewards (either positive or negative) that we present as a stimulus to try to induce the desired behavior. Most psychologists today believe that no action, motion, or thought ever occurs spontaneously, that human behavior does not just happen, but is caused. Such a hypothesis proposes that every act that a person performs is the result of antecedent causes that culminate in an interplay of stimuli with primary and secondary motives or drives.

At any given moment, each of us is being bombarded by stimuli in the form of what we see, hear, smell, and feel. We cannot see or hear everything at the same time, and we cannot think of everything or imagine everything at the same moment; therefore there is a focal aspect to what we attend to. Since we can carry on only a very limited pattern of activity at a given time, what we do follows from what we perceive—the way we "size up" the situation. We are not always aware of all of the internal influences that take part in shaping our perception or appraisal of situations. In many circumstances we may not be able to express by words what we see in a situation, how we feel about it, or how we size it up. But when we do react overtly by word, deed, facial expression, or bodily posture, our reaction is always related to our motives and perception.

Secondary motives or drives are closely associated with learned social values. Objects and situations that become prized or prohibited in various social cultures are not defined solely in terms of their practical or biological significance. French champagne is not required to satisfy thirst, nor truffles for hunger, nor a 30-room mansion for shelter. Tastes for such goals are acquired as the individual develops and interacts with other people. Experiences within the family, school, church, and other groups shape the individual's value system and, consequently, the secondary motives and drives.

Since each individual has been exposed to uniquely different experiences, it is not surprising that each person develops a unique set of motives. Some of these motives reinforce each other, while others compete with one another.

An individual is exposed to many stimuli that could motivate the person. Obviously, all motives or needs do not have equal importance to an individual; therefore, if different motives are in conflict in a given situation, some needs will command attention at the expense of others. In a sense, the individual chooses between the many stimuli and reacts accordingly. However, since each individual possesses a unique set of motives and a unique hierarchy of values, each will react differently to the same set of circumstances.

It is the uniqueness of the perception-motivation-action interaction for each individual that presents the manager with the problems and challenges of getting the very best performance from each worker. Even though each person is unique and must be motivated differently, a great deal can be learned by the study of what motivates people in general. In the following sections we will examine some of the more widely accepted behavioral science motivational theories and then try to relate them specifically to technical personnel.

6.3 Behavorial Science Theory on Motivation

The understanding of the employee-employer relationship can be divided into two periods—before Mayo and after Mayo. Elton Mayo [20] (a sociologist at the Harvard Graduate School) was one of the participants who conducted the now famous experiments at the Hawthorne plant of the Western Electric Company between 1927 and 1944. This research started an avalanche of studies of the human relationships between employee and employer. The most significant finding of this research was the conclusion that there were more important things to the workers than physical conditions and monetary gains on a job.

Prior to the Hawthorne experiments, the doctrine of economic self-interest had been the prevailing concept. This self-interest doctrine is stated in one of Adam Smith's basic assumptions: "Every individual is continually exerting himself to discover the most advantageous employment for whatever capital he can command." We also see the same ideas in the work of Frederick W. Taylor, whose basic concept was to design the job scientifically, select the best person for it, and devise an appropriate wage incentive plan to provide motivation. Although the concept of self-interest based on financial reward is important in explaining worker behavior, the Hawthorne experiments demonstrated that it presents an incomplete and inadequate picture of human needs and motivation. Roethlisberger [25] summarized the findings in the following way.

. . . man at work is a social creature as well as an "economic man." He has personal and social as well as economic needs. Work provides him with a way of life as well as a means of livelihood. To understand motivation we must understand the social as well as the physical and economic setting in which the work takes place.

In 1943 Maslow [17] suggested that humans have a basic set of needs that they strive to satisfy that can be ranked or categorized into a hierarchical order based on their relative importance. He further elaborated on this idea in 1954 when he published his classic book, *Motivation and Personality* [18]. In this work he hypothesized that people have a never-ending sequence of needs that motivate them and that these could be categorized into five classes, as follows.

1. *Physiological* needs are the basic factors that maintain life. Food, air, shelter, and rest requirements must be fulfilled before the individual can consider other factors. A hungry person can only think of something to eat. Maslow suggested that people are only partially fulfilled at one level before their needs at the next level begin to emerge.
2. *Safety* needs take over after the physiological needs are basically or minimally satisfied. Safety needs are characterized as needs for protection against danger, threat, and deprivation. Job security falls into this category. Note that money or economic factors can be used to basically satisfy most of the needs contained in these first two categories.
3. *Social needs* come next in the hierarchy and represent the beginning of the psychological categories. These derive from the need for a feeling of belonging, for association, for acceptance by peers, and for giving and receiving friendship and love.
4. *Ego* needs are divided into two groups. The first is related to one's self-esteem (i.e., needs for self-confidence, independence, achievement, competence, and knowledge). The second is related to a person's reputation (i.e., need for status, recognition, and appreciation). These needs are rarely fully satisfied.
5. *Self-fulfillment* needs are the most difficult to obtain and describe. These are the needs for the full realization of one's own potentialities, for continued self-development, for being creative in the broadest sense of the word. Transcendental Meditation practitioners call the fulfillment of these needs the reaching of cosmic consciousness. Maslow referred to it as perfect self-actualization, personal growth, self-awareness, or the peak experience.

Prior to Maslow's work, the most popular theory of individual motivation was based on the economic man concept and Sigmund Freud's pleasure principle. Freud's theory suggested that gratification leads to rest and decreased motivation, but Maslow cited studies that showed that in healthy, fully functioning people, "gratification breeds increased motivation: the appetite for growth is whetted rather than allayed by gratification. Growth is in itself a rewarding and exciting process" [19].

Basically, according to Maslow's theory, people have a never-ending sequence of needs that motivate them. The basic needs in this hierarchy are monetary in orientation (physiological and safety), and the higher needs are physchological in nature. Furthermore, these needs are overlapping and interdependent. Before a lower need is completely satisfied, the higher-level need emerges. Also note that specific incentives often shift from one category to another and are a function of the employee's mental attitude and the particular stage of career fulfillment and development. For example, a pay raise and promotion may fulfill a physiological need at one point in time (particularly early in one's career) and an ego need at another point in time. Cost-of-living pay raises, which are given "across the board" to all employees, fall into the realm of physiological satisfaction, since the individual's ego can hardly share a raise with hundreds or thousands. Similarly, annual raises lose a good deal of effectiveness if there is no real discretion exercised or discrimination used by management in awarding them. If raises are given in equal percentages (or nearly equal) to all employees, whether deserved or not, they are not incentives or motivators. In fact, they can have almost the reverse effect. The average-to-poor performer will not be motivated to do better, and the outstanding performer may take the attitude of "What's the use, I knock myself out and get the same raise as everyone else."

Maslow described motivation as the driving force toward personal growth, which is now recognized as a major aspect in the motivation of technical people. If one talks to highly successful, creative engineers and scientists about what drives them, they invariably describe a desire to reexperience what Maslow called the "peak experience." Generally, occurring spontaneously, a peak experience is:

> . . . an episode, or spurt in which the powers of the person come together in a particularly efficient and intensely enjoyable way, and in which he is more integrated and less split, more open for experience, more idiosyncratic, more perfectly expressive or spontaneous, or fully functioning, more creative, more humorous, more ego-transcending, more independent of his lower needs, etc. He becomes in these episodes more truly himself, more perfectly actualizing his potentialities closer to the core of his being. [19[.

When engineers or scientists describe the joy of a highly creative act, they usually describe the "peak experience." Having once experienced it, they strive throughout their lives to repeat it over and over again. Such people are trying to fulfill the self-actualization needs.

Maslow proposed that this was a strict hierarchy. The most important (or lowest-level) need that is not reasonably well satisfied will demand the attention of the individual and will motivate that person to seek satisfaction of the need. The needs at the higher levels are overlooked, according to Maslow's theory, while the lower-level needs, which are presently reasonably well satisfied are forgotten. Gratified needs are not active as motivators of behavior. Straus and Sayles [27] bring up two main difficulties with this theory. The first is the proposal of a strict hierarchy. Reversals in the ordering of needs for some individuals are readily apparent. For instance, it is reasonably common for a person to apparently need self-esteem more than love. To some, creativeness seems dominant, even though physiological needs such as hunger are unfilled (as evidenced by the starving artist). It is not difficult to recall instances of people who, for the sake of an ideal (even a social ideal), have essentially martyred themselves by giving up eveything else (including their lives) in pursuit of that ideal. An example of more immediate interest is that many studies have indicated that a scientist or engineer may shun social contacts in order to devote more time to research. This would in a sense indicate that self-actualization or the esteem needs rank higher for that individual than the social need. Of course, a counterargument could be that the scientist or engineer has already satisfied the social needs and therefore moved on to the next higher level.

Their second criticism is that the levels overlap so much that the categories are meaningless. For example, when does the physiological need end and the safety need begin? Should additional money be used for physiological need fulfillment in the form of wages or for safety need fulfillment in the form of company paid insurance? How do you determine the point where ego need fulfillment changes to self-actualization? Perhaps the main message to management that can be gained from Maslow's work is that individuals seem to have a needs hierarchy of sorts, and it is somewhat useless to devote resources to satisfy the higher-ordered needs until the lower-ordered needs have been relatively satisfied.

6.4 Job Environment versus Content

In 1959 Fredrick Herzberg published his motivation-hygiene theory [12], which proclaims that humans have two broad categories of needs that govern their behavior. One, which is common to all animals, is the need to adjust to the environment or to avoid pain. The other, unique to humans is oriented toward psychological growth and the desire for self-actualization. The first category is related to the job environment and the second to the job content. Herzberg's concepts are similar to Maslow's except that he does not accept the idea of different levels (a hierarchy of needs). He argues that an individual can and does seek to fulfill physiological, safety, ego, and self-actualization needs at the same time.

Herzberg's study attempted to identify what factors in work situations cause strong sources of satisfaction or dissatisfaction. Perhaps the most important discovery was that, for the most part, these satisfiers and dissatisfiers are unidirectional in effect. The dissatisfiers turned out to be job environment factors such as work conditions, pay, company policies, interpersonal relationships, and the technical competence of supervisors. If these are perceived to be adequate, they do not necessarily produce satisfaction; however, they do eliminate dissatisfaction. The second group of factors is related to job content and includes achievement, advancement, recognition, responsibility, and the work itself. The presence or absence of adequate levels of these factors will yield feelings of satisfaction or no satisfaction, but it does not *create* dissatisfaction. The acceptability of the first group (also called hygienic factors) will not motivate subordinates, yet they must be present or dissatisfaction will arise. The job content factors are the real motivators because they have the potential of yielding a sense of satisfaction. Thus, Herzberg found that maximizing satisfaction and minimizing dissatisfaction are two different processes.

According to Herzberg, the opposite of job dissatisfaction is not job satisfaction, but no job dissatisfaction. The opposite of job satisfaction is not job dissatisfaction, but no job satisfaction. The factors relating to job satisfaction are not the same as those relating to job dissatisfaction. He called the factors that lead to job dissatisfaction "hygienic factors." Hygienic factors are the items around the job that do not relate directly to the work content itself. Examples are wages, fringe benefits, company policies, working conditions, job security, supervision, and interpersonal relationships. It is important to note that these are the very items that managers usually consider as incentives or motivators. Hygienic factors are usually promoted in the hope that the employee will become more satisfied and therefore work harder. But, according to Herzberg's theory, this is an erroneous hope. Adequate provision of these hygienic factors will lead to a lack of job dissatisfaction but not to job satisfaction. Also note that hygienic factors tend to be taken for granted as time passes.

According to Herzberg, the factors that lead to job satisfaction are the real motivators. These are all factors that operate through the job or as a direct result of job content. These motivators are the work itself, achievement, recognition of achievement, responsibility, personal growth, and opportunities for advancement. The fact that the "motivators" are all factors that operate through the job suggests the job improvement technique called "job enrichment." The goal of job enrichment is to introduce as many of the real motivators into a job as possible. Job enrichment differs from job enlargement. Job enlargement entails increasing a job horizontally (i.e., giving the worker more tasks to do at the same level of skills and responsibility). Job enrichment, on the other hand, increases a job vertically (i.e., placing more responsibility and decision making on the worker).

Job enrichment is based on certain assumptions, such as:

1. A job is meaningful and therefore motivating if it involves the worker in the identification and solution of problems of direct interest.
2. A worker is highly motivated to solve the problems that have a direct personal affect.
3. The motivated worker can assume a part in the managerial functions associated with the job (planning, organizing, and controlling) and, if allowed to do so, will experience increased job satisfaction with resulting higher performance.

Herzberg's study was based on the study of 200 engineers and accountants in the Pittsburg area whose pay, job security, etc., were relatively high, so their physiological and safety needs were already satisfied. The Maslow hierarchy of needs might be compared with Herzberg's motivation-hygiene concept, as shown in Table 6.1. This comparison is inexact, but the clear inference that the real motivators deal with the higher level needs is inescapable.

6.5 Money as a Motivator

Older motivation theories assumed that the need and desire to obtain money are the work motives that overshadow all others. The consensus of modern theories strongly disputes this. Money may be considered the intitial motive for obtaining a job, but it is not considered to be the most important incentive either for inspiring job performance or for job satisfaction. Innumerable surveys and research projects have shown that money ranks considerably down the line in terms of influencing worker attitudes and performance. Yet the idea persists among many managers that money is the ultimate incentive.

This issue needs to be faced squarely and must be understood by every manager. Money presents a paradox in that it is simultaneously not important and very important. Money in and of itself is not important as a motivator. It is important, however, as a scorekeeper or indicator for other motivators and dissatisfiers. It becomes symbolic of recognition and of how a person is evaluated by management. For example, consider two engineers working in the same group. Both are making $25,000 per year salary. One receives a

TABLE 6.1   Motivation Factors

Maslow's Hierarchy	Herzberg's Theory
Physiological	Dissatisfiers
	Pay
Safety	Company policies
	Working conditions
Social	Supervisor relations
	Co-worker relations
Ego	Satisfiers
	Advancement
	Recognition
	Responsibility
Self-fulfillment	Achievement

raise of $2500 and the other a raise of $2495. The second engineer will become very upset and disturbed, not because of the $5, but because the relative raises say that management values the contribution of the first engineer more highly than that of the second. The motivator affected is recognition, not money! A second important aspect of money is that in our economy, it may be used to satisfy a wide range of other, nonmaterialistic motives such as philanthropic, artistic, intellectual, and religious motives. In addition, money is widely used as an index of social status, personal development, and success.

A final aspect of money that every manager should understand is its value as a focal point for dissatisfaction. If I am unhappy with the way my supervisor is treating me, I do not feel free to confront the issue by saying, "Look boss, I don't like your attitude toward me. You never smile at me or tell me how great I'm doing. You treat me as if I were a chair or a computer terminal. How about starting to act like you appreciate my efforts?." Such a confrontation would be embarrassing and unprofessional. But I can say, "Company XYZ has just offered me a good job with a significant salary increase. Unless you can come up with a $2000 raise, I don't see how I can turn it down." This statement translates into "Show me you appreciate my efforts."

Every manager should recognize that probably fewer than 5 percent of all resignations are *actually* due to the need for more money, although probably 95 percent of the *reasons* given are salary increase. Money is a symbolic scorecard and a convenient mechanism for registering complaints. If an employee complains about money, you can be sure the employee is unhappy about something. You can also be equally assured it is *not* the money that constitutes the unhappiness.

6.6 Recognition as a Motivator

Recognition also serves both motivation and maintenance needs. In order to understand this dichotomous behavior clearly, we must understand that recognition takes two forms—earned and unearned. Earned recognition is an act of approval that confirms successful achievement and individual worth. It is the manifestation of justice for a job well done and of merit. Merit pay increases, as well as discretionary awards and bonuses, are tangible acts of recognition. Praise, congratulations, and being bragged about are intangible acts of recognition. Unearned recognition, in the form of friendliness, reassurance, small talk, and personal interest, on the other hand, satisfy security, status, and social needs. Certificates of appreciation or achievement issued to all those who participated in a project are also a form of unearned recognition. This type of recognition is not a substitute for earned recognition, but it is essential as a maintenance factor.

How can the manager provide recognition to employees? Recognition is provided by communicating to the individual by word and deed. You must demonstrate by what you say and what you do that you value the person's ideas and contributions. Let us consider several hypothetical situations.

You are walking down the hall alone when you meet Joe, one of your better engineers. Do you:

1. Nod in acknowledgement?
2. Say "Good morning, Joe"?
3. Stop and say something like, "Hi, Joe. Did that experiment work out the way you hoped"?

You are walking down the hall with a visitor; again, you meet Joe. Do you:

1. Nod in acknowledgment?
2. Say "Good morning, Joe"?
3. Stop and say something like, "Mr. Visitor, I'd like you to meet Joe Engineer. He's one of the top test engineers in the country, and we couldn't get along without him. Joe, this is Mr. Visitor, who is here to. . . ."

The results of a series of tests must be presented to higher management. Joe is the engineer who designed and ran the tests. Do you:

1. Present the results yourself, with Joe there to help answer any questions?
2. Have Joe present the results and introduce him by saying "Mr. Joe Engineer from our test group will now present the results of the test program"?

3. Have Joe present the results and introduce him by saying something like, "I've asked Joe Engineer to present the results of the test program. I'm really proud of the way Joe took hold of this problem and ran the program. I'm sure you'll agree with me after you hear the results of this well-planned and well-executed test series"?

These examples portray the differences between poor, acceptable, and top-notch managers. In all three cases, the first response communicates, "I acknowledge your existence, but I really don't think you are too important." The second response says, "I acknowledge your existence and at least consider you important enough to call you by name." The third response communicates, "I really value your opinions, ideas, and work and intend to tell everyone how valuable you are to the organization." Only the third manager is providing motivation, and it costs nothing. Of course, the manager must also show by deeds that the contributions of the individual are highly valued. Care must be taken to see that appropriate raises, promotions, and other rewards are bestowed as warranted. Each individual must believe that the manager will look out for his or her best interests and that good work will be tangibly recognized.

6.7 Effect of Management Philosophy

In the final analysis, the workability of any theory of motivation depends on its integration into the total management process. McGregor [21] has explored the impact of management philosophy on the motivation of workers. In many ways McGregor's work is the clearest expression of the modern view of what management's attitude toward workers supposedly should be. Later theories have often been stated in terms of McGregor's theories or in contrast to them. Management philosophy can be defined as, "all those ideas taken for granted, all those unquestioned attitudes which form the normal operating background for a given organization" [9].

McGregor classified two opposing philosophies of management in his famous Theory X-Theory Y [21]. The assumptions of these two theories can be summarized as follows.

Theory X:

1. The average human being has an inherent dislike of work and will avoid it if possible.
2. Because of this dislike of work, average workers must be coerced, controlled, directed, and threatened with punishment or depredation (e.g., being fired) to get them to put forth adequate effort toward the achievement of organizational objectives.

3. The average worker prefers to be directed, wishes to avoid responsibility, has relatively little ambition, and wants security above all.

Theory Y:

1. The expenditure of physical and mental effort in work is as natural as play or rest.
2. Workers will exercise self-direction and self-control in the service of objectives to which they are committed.
3. Commitment to objectives is a function of the rewards associated with their achievement.
4. The average worker learns not only to accept, but to seek responsibility.
5. Most workers have a relatively high degree of imagination, ingenuity, and creativity.
6. The intellectual potentialities of the average worker are being only partially utilized.

Thus, under Theory X, it is assumed that workers will be most productive if directed and closely controlled in the work environment; under Theory Y, it is assumed workers will be most productive if allowed to participate in the determination of their own work and the determination of organizational objectives. Theory Y is practiced with professional workers much more frequently than with others. McGregor believes that it should be practiced with most workers. Argyris [1, 2] agrees and argues that workers will respond according to management's expectations (i.e., if management believes in Theory X, workers will respond accordingly). Both McGregor and Argyris believe that individuals and the organization exert pressure on each other that causes people to behave as they do. According to this argument, if managers will just assume that Theory Y is correct and act accordingly, they will have self-motivated, creative, self-controlled, highly productive workers.

Argyris has extensively investigated the effect of the organization, its structure, and its controls on the motivation of individual workers. His general conclusion is that the organization stifles individual motivation and creativity. In his view, the organization, with its traditional concepts of structure, power, and management controls, is in effect treating workers as immature beings. Some workers are not fully mature emotionally. For these a repetitious, controlled way of life may be satisfactory. For the others, a growing bitterness or at least a limited utilization of their abilities is inevitable. There are three main mechanisms through which the organization can frustrate the mature employee: the formal organization structure, managerial controls, and authoritarian leadership.

Although there seems to be a great deal of truth in the Theory X-Theory Y argument, experience shows that real life is not so simplistic. For example, Myers [23] conducted a 6-year study of workers at Texas Instruments Incorporated that closely agreed with Herzberg's findings. However, he also concluded that workers could be divided into two categories that sound very much like Theory X people and Theory Y people. He called these two groupings maintenance seekers and motivation seekers. Motivation seekers are primarily motivated by the nature of their work and have a high tolerance for poor environmental conditions. Maintenance seekers are preoccupied and dissatisfied by pay, status, supervision, and working conditions. According to Myers, some maintenance seekers can be influenced to become motivation seekers if no dissatisfying factors (see preceding sections) are present. Conversely, the absence of real motivators can cause motivation seekers to behave like maintenance seekers.

In a similar vein, Likert [15, 16] has extolled the virtues of the "employee-centered" supervisor as opposed to the "production-centered" supervisor. The employee-centered supervisor is characterized as being amenable to a high degree of employee participation, cooperative, and more concerned with the satisfaction and well-being of the employee. The production-oriented supervisor is authoritarian and concerned with productivity at any cost. These two orientations coincide nicely with McGregor's Theory Y and Theory X, respectively.

At first it seemed likely that one could assume that employee-centered supervision is better than production-centered supervision. However, as more research was conducted, it became apparent that this is not necessarily true. The evidence is now strong that not all employees respond to Theory Y and employee-centered supervision [22]. More will be said about this in Chapter 7 but, for now, it is enough to say that the best leadership style is a function of (1) the personality of the manager, (2) the personalities of the employees, and (3) the environment and situation of the moment.

6.8 Profile of Engineers, Scientists, and Technicians

The motivational theories discussed up to now were based on studies whose subjects varied from factory workers to engineers and scientists. In this and the following sections we will concentrate on the unique characteristics of technically trained personnel that must be taken into account.

Technical people are highly individualistic and, as such, defy a single description that is all-inclusive; however, they share common traits that are useful when attempting to motivate the individual. In the following discussion, scientists are considered as individuals with doctoral or master's degrees in physics, chemistry, engineering, and related fields; they are involved in research and development work of a scientific nature. A large portion of the scientist's time has been spent in the university environment, so that much of the perception of self, work, and work association is a product of that environment. Scientists are characterized as people who:

- Are highly individualistic.
  May be revolutionary or a nonconformist.
  Often develop independent of the organization.
- Desire challenging work to do.
  Possess more of a creative nature than the general population, do not like routine or mundane work that management often requires be performed.
- Are found to be more oriented toward scientific and professional goals than the organizational goals.
  Have a dual loyalty toward the company and the profession; seek to contribute to knowledge.
- Are self-directing.
  Desire freedom to do the work their own way with little hindrance from management; expects management to provide the environment and tools to aid the work and to be left alone to do it.
- Seek approval from peers.
  Are more concerned with being judged by their peers, who they feel are more professionally oriented, than by the standards of management.
- Desire to share their knowledge.
  Particularly when they have been successful or have added to present knowledge, prefer to share with those who will recognize the importance of their work.

Engineers are individuals involved in work that requires technical knowledge equivalent to a 4-year college education. Some hold degrees, while others have gained expertise through on-the-job experience and outside study. The engineer shares with the scientist a desire for meaningful and challenging work but, in contrast, identifies more with the organization than with their profession. Engineers are basically described by:

- A desire for challenging work.
  From the viewpoint of scientists, engineers' work may be less challenging, but it is commensurate with engineers' backgrounds. Engineers perceive it as challenging.
- An orientation toward organizational goals.
  Engineers accept organizational goals more readily than scientists do. They have a greater business orientation and relatively less professional orientation.

- Seeking approval from within the organization.
  Engineers value recognition by peers, but to a lesser degree than scientists; they value concrete material rewards as symbols of status and recognition. Advancement is a relatively stronger motivator than work for the sake of increased knowledge.
- Relatively applied work.
  A relatively small percentage of their work requires a *high* level of creativity or innovation; their tasks are more straightforward, demanding a high skill level, common sense, and a knowledge of applications.
- Less time spent on engineering tasks.
  Considerable time is spent on nondirect engineering activities; however, engineers feel that these tasks are necessary to accomplish their overall assignment.
- Pursue less formal education.
  Fewer engineers than scientists update the formal knowledge obtained in college but seek more practical or application skills through experience.

A technician's formal education requirement is less than a college degree. It normally consists of 1 to 2 years of study in a technical school in a particular specialty or equivalent on-the-job training. Technicians include machinists, drafters, model makers, laboratory assistants, electricians, and electronic technicians. In a research laboratory, the technician assists the engineer or scientist perform a specific portion or phase of the research program. In general, technicians place less importance on the work itself, compared to scientists and engineers, and greater emphasis on advancement, pay, and positions of responsibility. In the research laboratory this is understandable because of the relative status position technicians hold. The recognition for products developed or knowledge generated is given to the scientists or engineers whom they assist. Increased economic returns and promotions are the main paths to success that are open to technicians whose traits can be summarized as:

- Striving for advancement and financial rewards.
  Advancement or higher pay is one of the highest motivational factors possible; in a research environment and many others, technicians are on the bottom of the technical status ladder and have limited career opportunities.
- Possess a high level of ingenuity.
  They must take the theoretical concepts of the scientists and engineers and convert them to practical applications.
- Lack a clear-cut sense of occupational and professional identification.
  In many ways they are marginal workers in industry, located somewhere

between manual workers and engineers, but not fully a part of either group.

■ Like to be informed.

They like to be informed in regard to the organizational goals and their individual progress.

■ Desire freedom to control their work.

They would like to have more freedom to use their own judgment and initiative in planning and executing their own work.

6.9 Motivation Studies of Technical Personnel

As a group, scientists, engineers, and technicians are well paid and receive adequate fringe benefits. Therefore their physiological needs have been largely satisfied. These lower-level needs no longer act as primary motivators of behavior, and management must concentrate on the higher-level psychological needs that have not been satisfied. A number of research studies based on the previously discussed theories have been conducted. The results of a few of these studies are shown in Table 6.2.

TABLE 6.2 Perceived Motivational Factors

Author	Landis [14]	Gomersall [10]	
Organization	12 Manufacturing design and research organizations	Texas Instrument	
Subjects	1131 Engineers and scientists	Scientists, engineers, and technicians	
		Scientists	*Engineers*
Order of importance of motivational factors	Achievement (pride, accomplishment, reputation)	Work itself	Work itself
	Recognition (salary, promotions)	Company policy	Advancement
	Recognition (status, respect, prestige)	Advancement	Responsibility
	Challenging work	Recognition	Pay
	Management relationships	Supervisor competence	Company policy
	Nature of work	Achievement	Achievement
	Personal growth	Responsibility	Recognition
	Responsibility		Supervisor competence
	Company image		
	Relationship with associates		
	Working conditions, etc.		

Gomersall [10], reporting on research at Texas Instrument, indicates a definite difference in the factors that impact the motivation of scientists, engineers, and technicians. He found that work itself, followed by company policies, had the greatest impact on scientists. Recognition, considered high on the scientists' list, was not considered one of the high motivators for engineers and technicians. He suggests, therefore, that management concentrate more on the work itself and on company policies that allow the scientists to pursue their work with the least encumbrance. The work itself, followed by advancement and responsibility, also rated high on the engineers' list. The technicians' most important factors were responsibility, with advancement a poor second, followed by pay. The rationale offered was that technicians strive for responsibility because they are generally treated like pawns in the technical environment.

Badawy [3], in his study of scientists involved in both basic and applied research, found that scientists perceive their most important needs to be the opportunity to do meaningful scientific work, freedom to work in their own way, and recognition. The least important factors were salary and other hygiene factors. The scientists' goals were found to be oriented more toward the scientific profession and less toward the organization. Kleingartner [13] directed his study specifically toward engineering technicians in the aerospace

	Badawy [3]	Bogaty [4]		Kleingartner [13]	
	Leading industrial research organization	Report on studies of Hidrich and Herzberg		Aerospace companies	
	100 Research scientists (applied and basic)	Chemists and engineers		199 Engineering technicians	
Technicians	*Most Important Motivators*	*Chemists*	*Engineers*		
Responsibility	Opportunity to do	Opportunity to do	Achievement	Expect wage	
Advancement	meaningful	creative work	Recognition	increases	
Pay	work	Work interest	Work itself	Interest in work	
Company policy	Freedom to work	Chance to apply	Responsibility	Prospect of	
Work itself	in your own way	training	Advancement	promotion	
Achievement	Recognition	Salary	Salary	Responsibility	
Recognition		Knowledge		Recognition	
Supervisor	*Least Important*	Recognition			
competence	*Motivators*	Advancement			
	Good	Salary			
	communications				
	Fringe benefits				
	Authority				

industry. The results indicate that expected wage increases along with interesting work and the prospect of promotion were the main motivators, followed by responsibility and recognition. The studies of Landis [14] and Bogaty [5] follow the same basic pattern.

Although the studies do not all agree as to the exact order of importance of motivational factors perceived by each of the respondent groups, a common thread does exist that provides some general conclusions that could be useful to management. Scientists seem to be motivated more by the work itself, company policies related to the manner in which the work is performed, and the freedom to work in one's own way. Engineers seem to share much of the scientist's desires for interesting work and place work itself as their main motivator. Engineers, on the other hand, place more importance on responsibility, achievement, and advancement than the scientists. Technicians place further emphasis on motivators such as responsibility, advancement, and pay. The trend indicates that scientists lean toward satisfaction derived from the work itself, while technicians are more oriented toward recognition through advancement and wages. Engineers are somewhere in between.

Obviously, the theories and survey studies discussed up to this point apply to today's technical personnel. However, the application of these theories by management is not a clear-cut process. Management must determine the needs and abilities of each individual while taking into account the objectives of the organization in order to optimize the efficiency of the organization. This optimization must take place in a constantly changing environment, both for the individual and the organization. How does the manager optimize efficiency? That is the art of management. Each manager must use his or her experience, knowledge of the individual, and organizational objectives to determine the optimum course of action.

6.10 Source of Benefits

It is obvious that a broad program of incentives is essential to secure and maintain the contribution of individuals to the organization. Furthermore, the difficulties of securing the means of offering incentives and the determination of the precise optimum combination of benefits and incentives that will be effective and feasible are matters of extreme delicacy and require great wisdom and creativity on the part of management. As Barnard [4] points out, the availability and awarding of incentives are probably the most unstable of the elements in the cooperative system since, invariably, external conditions affect the possibilities of material incentives, and human motives and needs are in a constant state of change. People refuse to be satisfied or motivated by the status quo. Thus, a constantly increasing flow of benefits for disbursement must be available to the manager. Unfortunately, all incentives are costly to the organization and, if not disbursed with care, may threaten its survival. Therefore, the distribution of incentives must be proportioned to the value and effectiveness of the contributions sought and received. In other words, the objective of the benefits distribution scheme must be to maximize the relationship between rewards and performance.

There are two available routes of making the continuous flow of expanding benefits available for distribution to employees.

1. *Organizational Growth.* This allows for the creation of added supervisory positions, expanded facilities, more rapid promotions, new and unique endeavors that allow freedom of imagination or creativity, and fewer management constraints to innovation.
2. *Qualitative Growth without Expansion.* This route is available to relatively few organizations but is possible for technical groups. Ths means being able to allow increased personal freedom to members, greater time for personally chosen research, increased emphasis on factors that lead to recognition and achievement in the eyes of persons outside the organization, and more personally satisfying work.

The most direct means and the route pursued by most organizations for maintaining and expanding the benefits available for employees, managers and, hopefully, owners is organizational growth. Parkinson's humorous thesis on organizational growth describes the tendency of all organizations to expand, whether or not there is a genuine need for more of their services. As a matter of fact, all organizations, when not constrained, seek this means of expanding benefits. Galbraith [8]), in his excellent book, *The New Industrial State,* discusses how this universal tendency molds and distorts our value system and very mode of living. Growth through expansion creates an additional benefit, that of reduction of internal conflict, since individuals can increase their personal status without lowering the status of others. It is not surprising, therefore, that almost all organizational leaders encourage and seek expansion to maximize the benefits that are available for distribution and to minimize internal conflict. As Galbraith says, "One would encounter less dispute, on the whole, by questioning the sanctity of the family or religion than the absolute merit of increasing growth."

6.11 The Static Technical Organization

Many readers will hopefully have experienced what a youthful, expanding technical laboratory, institution, or organization is like. It is an exhilarating experience. The organization throbs with life and is electric with ideas, and enthusiasm runs rampant. The staff is generally young, the majority are engaged in meaningful technical work, and the top technical leadership is an example and stimulation to all levels. The few administrators and executives are overworked but are always available to the professional staff. The output per person and the accomplishments and impact on technology of such an organization are hard to believe.

As time passes and the organization grows and matures, the organization ages rapidly, and paralysis, decay, and senility set in. The old organization is unrecognizable. What has happened? Where are the old fire and electricity? More important, where is the productivity?

For those readers who are unfamiliar with the aged technical organization, I quote extensively from Harrison [11].

It has grown in size and the average age of the staff has increased. Nobody is in his dotage and yet the place is bereft of scientific ideas and, apart from out-of-date work of a trivial nature, tends to be imitative of what is initiated elsewhere. The majority of the staff is employed in administrative, executive, and an array of para-scientific duties. More and more organizes less and less. There is a multiplicity of committees; procedures are laid down, routines established, and forms designed and prescribed for every conceivable situation. Printing and duplicating apparatus everywhere abounds, and the minority of active scientists is bombarded with more scrap paper than it can use. Organizational senility can be gauged by the number of filing cabinets in the possession of the administrators and the number and size of the waste-paper containers in the possession of the scientific workers.

Formal and cold relations tend to replace the early informal relations. The widening abyss between the scientific worker and the management intimidates and enervates the former and robs the latter of the excitement and stimulus of contact with scientific work.

Those in the most senior positions were often the brightest and most active scientists in the youthful years of the organization. Each, in his desire to create and serve the organization, has sacrificed a career of active scientific work. Disillusion only follows after they are devoured by the monster of their own creation. Having no time to keep abreast with science in their own field they lack knowledge, energy, and nerve to make original contributions or initiate ideas.

Most of our sympathy, however, must go to the young and active scientist in an aged organization, for he occupies a truly anomalous position. Possibly he has never spoken with or even seen his director. He is in the minority and at the beck and call of every facet of the administration. Multitudinous secretaries and typists are too busy to type scientific papers. The library thrives with executive and clerical activity but is otherwise empty. In the course of his career the young scientist is expected to shoulder an increasing amount of the organizational burden, and the chances of elevation to higher income and status depend on his willingness to give these duties priority over his scientific work. Failure to conform stamps him as eccentric; he will be regarded as self-indulgent, concerned only with enjoying himself doing science, and refusing to sacrifice himself as his seniors have done. Clearly, he cannot have the best of both worlds; either administrative or scientific work, and only the former entailing "responsibility" and "self-sacrifice" is deserving of increased income and status.

The aged organization is a potential well that traps low energy particles with the lure of security and the need for paying only lip-service to science; the high energy dedicated particles come and then go without evoking comment or concern. The problem of the aged scientific organization, with its mis-interpretation of the scientific spirit, its misdirection of scientific effort, and the attendant misuse of fantastic sums of money, is a modern dilemma that only the active scientist sees etched in its starkest form.

Perhaps on the basis of the prior discussions a partial answer is seen to what has just been described. During the young, growing days, the benefits available for distribution were increasing rapidly. Because of this growth, the hygienic and motivating factors were available in sufficient quantity and quality. At this stage of organizational life, the inefficient use, or even squandering, of benefits goes unnoticed. More benefits are always available in a rapidly expanding organization.

However, at some point in the organization's life cycle, it reaches its optimum permissible size. Factors external to it limit its growth, and a leveling-off period sets in. This is a period of retrenchment and, perhaps it is even a slight decline. As mentioned, the factors that cause this leveling off and retrenchment are usually caused by forces that are external to it and beyond its control.

There is one other aspect of this problem that we have not mentioned but of which the technical manager should be aware: the types of people who are attracted during the different life cycles. For purposes of discussion we will use the identification of types of personnel proposed by Downs [6]. He divides personnel into two broad classifications with two subcategories in each.

1. *Purely self-interested persons.* Are motivated almost entirely by goals that benefit themselves. These include:
   (a) Climbers, who pursue power, prestige and money.
   (b) Conservers, who pursue convenience, security and merely seek to maintain the status quo in power, or prestige, rather than improve them.
2. *Mixed-Motives Persons.* Have goals that combine self-interest with some loyalty to some other large value. This group includes:
   (a) Zealots, who pursue very narrow goals and seek to influence organizational policies to further these narrow goals. An example of these narrow goals might be the development of nuclear powered rockets.
   (b) Advocates, who pursue a broader set of goals (such as space flight) and who seek to influence organizational policies to these ends.

With these definitions we can now consider which phase attracts and holds these various types of individuals and which types will dominate. During rapid growth of an organization the added opportunities that are inherent in growth begin to attract the climbers and zealots. Both thrive in the atmosphere of change, uncertainty, and hard work, whereas the conserver is not attracted by it and may even be repelled. Advocates will also be found joining the organization, but not in the same proportion. Furthermore, the increase in the number of climbers and zealots in the upper levels of the organization draws even more climbers and zealots and modifies organizational policy to a more aggressive, innovational position. The era is characterized by segmentation of the organization and branching out into new fields of endeavor.

As the organization expands, it overshoots its mark of importance and usefulness. Added resistance to its growth arises because its gains come at the expense of other organizational segments and functions. Hostility and antagonisms are engendered in competitive segments. Furthermore, it is difficult to continue to show the impressive results so essential to its growth. As the growth rate begins to level off, internal tension develops among thwarted climbers and zealots. The combination of these factors slows growth and may even cause a retrenchment or decline.

If the organization's growth rate declines below that of comparable organizations or if a reduction in force is required, the benefits available for distribution may drop to a level below that prevailing for comparable organizations. This change usually is the sign for the climbers to begin departing. If certain areas of prior activity are curtailed or dropped, the zealots for those areas will also depart. If the skills possessed by the climbers and zealots are highly marketable, their departure is foreordained. However, not *all* climbers and zealots will depart. The passage of time and other factors may convert some of them into conservers and advocates.

Clearly, the dominant type of personnel during each cycle is different. We can summarize the result as follows.

Period	**Dominant Types**
Rapid growth	Climbers, zealots
Leveling	Conservers, advocates
Retrenchment	Conservers

6.12   Motivation in a Stable Organization

Most of us have been nurtured on the growth ethic. Therefore, on first thought about motivating technical performance in a period of no (or little) growth, one can easily presume that there must be something inherently bad about a stable organization. However, a stable organization may not be such a bad motivational situation after all. It may, in fact, present some unique opportunities for motivating performance [26]. From a motivational point of view, difficulties may occur in a stable organization from having an older staff with less current technical information, limited career opportunities, and possibly job security doubts, but other factors (e.g., challenge and expectations concerning work goals and roles in the informal organization) are inherently no worse in a stable organization than in an expanding one.

To foster motivational opportunity and organizational renewal, managerial strategies should involve clarifying and organizing in areas that management may have neglected during times of expansion: career opportunities, informal organizations, and work goals. The effectiveness of most technical organizations depends on the motivation and performance of their technical staffs. In spite of this, many organizations, including stable organizations, have no more than token programs for staff development (career opportunities). This problem is especially critical in stable organizations, since such organizations are apt to employ the same technical people for some time to come. Management can attack this problem on many fronts, such as clarifying the issue of job security and applicable company policy, providing a technical promotion ladder to reduce the problem of promotional opportunities and financial incentives, and having periodic changes in project assignments to satisfy the need for challenging work.

Most technical people do not work alone; they collaborate in varying degrees with their colleagues in technical problem solving. In a stable organization many opportunities occur to enhance technical performance through the informal organization. By its very nature, technical collaboration should be readily encouraged in an organization with a stable technical staff. In addition, there are positive steps that management can take to enhance this technical collaboration, such as (1) regrouping technical teams to overcome the tendency of performance to level off in some technical teams that remain intact too long; (2) developing key people in the informal organization who are much more helpful to their colleagues than other people; and (3) encouraging greater internal and external contacts to decrease the possibilities of technical obsolescence.

Technical performance can also be enhanced through measures taken to clarify or establish work groups. Assigning people to multiple tasks can increase challenge for technical people in a stable organization. Also, good performance should be rewarded with more challenging work. In a stable organization with limited socioeconomic incentives available to it, the challenge in the next assignment may be a good way to recognize the quality of performance in the previous job.

6.13 Effects of Aging

What about motivational drives in engineers and scientists as they grow older? Some interesting things have been said about aging. Gellerman [9] has developed a theory that he calls the "psychological advantage." It says that there is one basic underlying order of logic to human behavior at work. People continually seek to serve their own self-interests, and these self-interests change as they grow older. Thus one is motivated at work to do things, but the things the person is motivated to do are a function of his or her age.

Steinmetz [26] has applied the psychological advantage to three distinct phases of 15 years each in one's working career. These segments are: young people (20 to 35); middle working years (35 to 50); and later working years (50 to 65). Peoples' motivational drives change as they enter into a different age group. Table 6.3 presents a brief summary of what motivates a person as he or she occupies a particular age group.

A study performed by Landis [14] looked at technical personnel and drew some conclusions about what they liked and disliked about their jobs. His survey covered 12 manufacturing, design, and research organizations in various fields of engineering. The results of the most important goals of engineers as a function of age are presented in Table 6.4.

The data presented broadly reinforce the ideas presented earlier. As might be expected, the younger group is not concerned with job security; it wants to be challenged by technical problems. Employment stability is somewhat more important for the 35 to 39-year group than for the 45 to 59-year group, indicating the feeling of insecurity many people in their thirties exhibit. On the other hand, older and established engineers associate fully with their company; they believe that what is good for the company is good for them.

6.14 Management Implications

It is important for the manager to realize that motivation is psychological, not logical. It is primarily an emotional and unconscious process. In most instances the reason for a particular action or lack thereof is unknown even to the person involved. Reality is what the person perceives, not what is actually going on. We can represent this mathematically as

$$B_{it} = f(P_i, E_t)$$

TABLE 6.3 Age Group Motivation [26]

Later working years, 50–65	Motivated by prestige and the pleasure of doing a job well
Middle working years, 35–50	Motivated by titles and what others think of them
Age of youth, 20–35	Motivated by money and pursuit of power

TABLE 6.4   Most Important Goals of Engineers as Function of Age [14]

Under 30	35 to 39	45 to 49
1. Work on projects requiring new technical learning.	1. Live in a desirable location.	1. Help company increase its profit.
2. Live in a desirable location.	2. Have employment stability	2. Live in a desirable location.
3. Become more involved in decision-making process.	3. Work on projects requiring new technical knowledge.	3. Have employment stability.
4. Work on projects that influence business success of company.	4. Work on projects that influence business success of company.	4. Work on projects that influence business success of company.
5. Help company increase its profits.	5. Help company increase its profits.	5. Gain knowledge of company management practices.
6. Become more involved with technical aspect of work.	6. Work for a company with a good reputation.	6. Work for a company with a good reputation.

This can be expressed as follows. The behavior of the individual, i, at moment, t, is a function of the personality of the individual, P_i, and the perceived environment at the moment, E_t. Thus motivation is an individual matter and the key to a person's behavior lies within. The manager can do very little (if anything) with the personality of the individual. It has taken a lifetime of influence from parents, family, friends, church, and school to form this personality. It can be changed (if at all) only slowly and over a period of time. Thus the manager is limited to the manipulation of the perceived environment in attempting to influence the person's behavior. We can also see from this equation that the requirements for motivation will not only differ from person to person, but also from time to time in the same individual. Motivation is inevitably a social process, and the behavior of the individual is influenced and shaped by the people and events surrounding the individual.

The challenge to management is one of providing the individual with satisfaction of basic hygienic needs, creating an atmosphere conducive to self-motivation, and encouraging and rewarding growth and accomplishment. Motivation is not a one-shot cure-all; it is a continuous process. Properly done, motivation leads to the enhancement and growth of the organization and the fulfillment of the employee's needs.

Pelz [24] describes motivation as a spiral (see Figure 6.1) that has three essential qualities: competence, achievement, and recognition. As he describes it, the spiraling cycle works as follows. Management hires the most

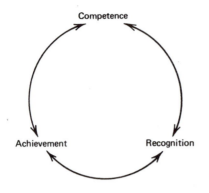

FIGURE 6.1   Spiral to success.

competent personnel it can find. Competence in the individual increases self-confidence which, in turn, sustains a growing curiosity. If the engineer or scientist is working on and probing into areas that are new, this curiosity increases knowledge, which creates greater competence.

Competence and curiosity are, of course, major factors in technical achievement. Technical achievement helps to qualify the individual and his or her laboratory for more resources and equipment, which contributes to still greater technical achievement and, once again, enhances individual competence.

The third major factor, recognition, comes from the dissemination of information generated by the technical achievements of the competent individual. As knowledge about the work spreads (both within and outside the organization), the worker meets with and exchanges ideas with other competent people in the same field. This recognition enhances self-confidence, which contributes to competence and, at the same time, helps to obtain new resources for greater achievement in order to enhance competence still further.

We can see that to start the spiraling cycle, the manager should help competent new scientists or engineers to select jobs that are within reach, see that they achieve, and be sure they get credit for achievements that are disseminated outside as well as within the organization. Many new technical managers do not understand or appreciate the importance of publications and patents to the motivation of scientists and engineers. Pelz sums it up with the question, "How can one feel pride in one's ideas without an output in which one can take pride?" Publications and patents provide tangible form for obtaining recognition for an achievement, so one sees technical competence being measured in universitites and research laboratories by number of patents and publications. For example, to demonstrate his inventive genius, writers and speakers always mention that Thomas Edison held 1093 patents.

Thus, in order to build the individual's pride in his or her work and encourage self-reliance and independence, the manager should:

1. Make sure each scientist and engineer has a chance two or three times a year to tell a gathering of colleagues about accomplishments, work in progress, and future plans. In meetings to review progress on projects, allow the individual, not supervisors, to explain what has been done.
2. Actively encourage the publication of papers and reports and the filing of patents.
3. Let the individual sign design documents produced.
4. Break a big project into meaningful segments so that progress and accomplishment of each segment is visible to its workers.
5. Show intense interest in each project the person is working on.
6. Assign some administrative responsibility as soon as possible so that the individual can deal meaningfully with people and become involved in decision making. This results in a tangible recognition of responsibility.
7. Insofar as possible, allow the scientist or engineer to work on projects of greatest interest. This results in personal commitment and involvement.

In conclusion, remember that efforts to motivate technically trained personnel must be fitted to each individual's needs, abilities, and personality. Motivation is not merely manipulation, but also the knowledge of how best to appeal to the individual's needs and desires so as to stimulate the person for the good of the organization *and* of the individual. If one approach fails to get results, regroup and try another. Every person *can be* motivated, it is a matter of taking the time to understand how.

References

1. Argyris, C., *Personality and Organization,* Harper & Row, New York, 1957.
2. Argyris, C., *Integrating the Individual and the Organization,* Wiley, New York, 1964.
3. Badawy, M. K., "Industrial Scientists and Engineers: Motivational Style Difference," *California Management Review, XIV 11,* Fall 1971, pp. 11–16.
4. Barnard, C. I., *The Functions of the Executive,* Harvard University Press, Cambridge, Mass., 1960.
5. Bogaty, H., "Employees of Technical Organizations Can be Motivated." *Research Management, XII* (1), January 1969, pp. 5–24.
6. Downs, A., "Bureaucratic Structure and Decision Making," RAND Corp., Memorandum RM-4646-IPR, October 1966.
7. Farris, G. F., "Motivating R&D Performance in a Stable Organization," *Research Management, XVI* (5), September 1973.

8. Galbraith, J. K., *The New Industrial State,* Houghton Mifflen, Boston, 1967.
9. Gellerman, S. W., *Motivation and Productivity,* American Management Association, New York, 1963.
10. Gomersall, E. R., "Current and Future Factors Affecting the Motivation of Scientists, Engineers and Technicians," *Research Management, XIV* (3), May 1971, pp. 43−50.
11. Harrison, E. R., "The Problem of the Aged Scientific Organization," NASA Report No. TMS-57084, Accession No. N67-18199, November 30, 1965.
12. Herzberg, F., B. Mausner, and B. Snyderman, *The Motivation to Work,* Wiley, New York, 1959.
13. Kleingartner, A., "The Characteristics and Work Adjustment of Engineering Technicians," *California Management Review, XII* (3), Spring 1969, pp. 88−96.
14. Landis, F., "What Makes Technical Men Happy and Productive?", *Research Management, XIV* (3), May 1971, pp. 25−42.
15. Likert, Rensis, *New Patterns of Management,* McGraw-Hill, New York, 1961.
16. Likert, Rensis, *The Human Organization–Its Management and Value,* McGraw-Hill, New York, 1967.
17. Maslow, A. H., "A Dynamic Theory of Human Motivation," *Psychological Review, 50* (4), 1943, pp. 370−373.
18. Maslow, A. H., *Motivation and Personality,* Harper & Row, New York, 1954.
19. Maslow, A. H., *Toward a Psychology of Being,* Van Nostrand, New York, 1968.
20. Mayo, Elton, *The Social Problems of an Industrial Civilization,* Harvard University Press, Cambridge, Mass., 1945.
21. McGregor, D., *The Human Side of Enterprise,* McGraw-Hill, New York, 1960.
22. Morse, J. J., and J. W. Lorsch, "Beyond Theory Y." *Harvard Business Review, 48* (3), May-June 1970.
23. Myers, M. S., "Conditions for Manager Motivation," *Harvard Business Review, , 44* (1), January-February 1966.
24. Pelz, P. C., "Freedom in Research," *International Science and Technology,* No. 26, February 1964, pp. 54−66.
25. Roethlisberger, F. J., "A New Look for Management," *Worker Morale and Productivity,* General Management Series, No. 141, American Management Association, New York, 1948.
26. Steinmetz, L. L., "Motivation Theory: Toward an Eclectic Synthesis," *Performance, 3* (1), January-February 1973.
27. Strauss, G., and L. Sayles, *Personnel: The Human Problems of Management,* 3rd ed., Prentice-Hall, Englewood Cliffs, N.J., 1972.

Discussion Questions

1. Discuss the relationship between morale and performance.
2. Discuss the relationship of money to motivation and performance.
3. What are the advantages and disadvantages of a policy of promotion from within?

4. Assume that the inflation rate was 8 percent last year and a fixed 8 percent of payroll is available for raises. Should everyone receive a flat 8 percent pay increase, or should the available money be divided on the basis of merit?

5. In order to encourage turnover, one company pays above average for the first 15 years and then allows salaries to fall to the industry lower 10 percent for older employees. Outstanding engineers and managers are retained by paying them a bonus. Is this a good idea?

6. Discuss the implications of hiring engineers at salaries higher than the prevailing rate and then giving lower increases until they are back in line.

7. If one of your top engineers comes to you and says she has an offer for a new job that she will take if you do not exceed the pay offer, what should you do?

8. Discuss the feasibility of group financial incentives for engineers.

9. Discuss the pros and cons of a policy of keeping salaries within the organization secret.

10. Discuss the pros and cons of unionization for technical personnel.

11. Should an organization reward (through pay increases) employees who further their formal education?

―――――――――――――――― **Case Study VI A** ――――――――――――――――

GOVERNMENT STRUCTURES LABORATORY

Bill Prince was reading through his morning mail when his secretary announced over the intercom that Jim Sloan was waiting outside. Prince was the director of the production research branch of a government aerospace laboratory. Sloan was one of his six branch chief's and was in charge of the metals joining branch. Prince sighed audibly as he told his secretary to send him in. Although Sloan was a highly competent engineer and researcher, he took up more of Prince's time than the other five branch chiefs put together. Anytime Prince asked the branch chiefs for anything, he knew that Sloan would have to discuss the matter at great length, questioning every aspect of the request and objecting to almost everything.

SLOAN: Bill, I've been thinking about your request for recommendations for promotions and sustained superior performance awards. It is really difficult to decide who of my people deserve what, but here are my recommendations.

Prince was almost afraid to look as he took the memorandum. Sure enough his worst fears were confirmed. Sloan had eight professionals in his branch, and he had recommended four of them for a grade promotion and the other four for a sustained superior performance award.

PRINCE: Now, Jim, you know this is not reasonable. I'll be lucky if I can get four promotions this year for the entire division. With six branches, there is no way that I can support four promotions in your group. The same is true of the SSP awards. You know that the laboratory does not have a budget that will allow us to promote half the people and give cash SSP awards to everyone else. Besides, what about your non-professional people. Aren't any of them deserving? Your secretary hasn't been promoted in 8 years and is the lowest-grade secretary in the division. Doesn't she deserve some consideration?

SLOAN: Of course, my technicians and secretary deserve promotions. But I knew you wouldn't support everyone. The technicians are easily replaceable and, besides, they can't go anywhere else. I've told Mary that she certainly deserves promotion and that I'll do what I can. But I think it's a lot more important to keep the professionals happy. They are all doing a tremendous job, and I couldn't replace any of them.

PRINCE: I agree that most of them are doing an adequate job, but so are the engineers in the other branches. I really haven't noticed any outstanding stars in your group.

SLOAN: Look its really important to keep these people happy. You and I both know that metals joining is the most important area of production research to this agency. Besides, my group has not gotten its fair share of promotions and awards in the past. Every year I turn in a list of recommendations, and every year you turn them down.

PRINCE: I seriously doubt that the other branch chiefs would agree with you that your area is the most important, and neither do I. Yours is an important area, but so are the others. As to your group not getting its fair share of promotions and awards, you may be right. But every year you do the same thing you did this time. When you recommend everyone and their dog, you put me in the position of having to make the decisions for you. I think I know most of your people and what they are capable of doing, but I don't see their work on a day-to-day basis. All I have is an overall image of each one, and that may not be a fair appraisal.

SLOAN: But if I recommend one and not another, then I've got to explain and defend my decision to them. How can I do that when I think they are all doing a terrific job?

PRINCE: I'm sorry, Jim, but I just can't buy the fact that all of your people are doing an equally good job. How did you decide which ones to recommend for promotion and which ones for the SSP?

SLOAN: On the basis of seniority. I've already discussed this with my people before I made the decision, and they agreed that was the fairest way. I've told the ones I put in for the SSP that I would recommend them for promotion next year. They are all really mad. They keep asking me why Maloy's group always gets at least one promotion and one SSP award every year, and we don't get any. They know I keep putting them in each year because I tell them. I want them to know that I support them and that the problem is higher up. They think you are biased against the metals joining group.

PRINCE: That's a bunch of rubbish. Why should I be biased against your group?

SLOAN: I don't know, but it sure looks suspicious when year after year Maloy's people get promoted and my people don't.

PRINCE: Let me show you why Maloy's people get promoted. Here is his recommendation memo. Notice that he has rank ordered every person in his group along with the strengths and weaknesses of each. He has included both the professional and nonprofessional people. You will also notice that he has strongly recommended only one person for promotion and one for the SSP, along with a justification for each. He also recommends a second person for each if the money is available, again with a justification.

SLOAN: What does he tell the other people, the ones he doesn't recommend?

PRINCE: Nothing. He doesn't discuss it with them until the promotion or award is approved. Some years he doesn't recommend anyone.

SLOAN: Well, I can't do that. I want my people to know that I support them and am trying to get everything for them I can. I want them to know that I appreciate their hard work.

PRINCE: But Jim, don't you see the impossible position you put me in? Supposing that I do pick one of your people for promotion and one for an SSP award. On what basis am I supposed to do it, and how will you explain to the others my choice?

SLOAN: I assume you will tell me your rationale and then I'll tell them.

PRINCE: In other words, you want me to be the villain?

SLOAN: It's better for them to be mad at you rather than at me. I've got to live with them every day. Besides, I don't see why you can't just go along with my recommendations and send them on with your recommendation to the laboratory. Who knows? They might approve them. If not, at least we can both say we tried.

PRINCE: I can't do that, Jim. That would just be abdicating my managerial responsibilities. The laboratory has already told me that I shouldn't expect more than four promotions and four SSP awards. I've got to rank order my recommendations for each one and provide a strong justification.

SLOAN: Well, then, why not just make my people the first four?

PRINCE: You know I can't recommend every professional person in your group for a promotion or SSP award and no one from the other branches. The laboratory director would think I'd lost my mind. Besides, it wouldn't be fair to the deserving people in the other branches.

SLOAN: Well, it's not fair for my people to be shafted year after year, either.

PRINCE: Then why don't you take this memo back and rank order them for me?

SLOAN: I can't do that. I've already told you what I think. Now it's up to you.

Case study discussion questions

1. What do you think the relative result of Sloan's versus Maloy's approach to promotions and awards is? Whose group will be more motivated?
2. Is Prince being fair to Sloan's people? What should Prince do?
3. Is Sloan being fair to his people?
4. Who do you think is probably the better supervisor, Sloan or Maloy?

--- **Case Study VI B** ---

SOUTHEASTERN RESEARCH INSTITUTE

The Southeastern Research Institute is a nonprofit research and testing laboratory. It was established to provide research and testing support for regional governments and industry. All contracts were on a cost plus fixed fee basis. The institute employs about 700 persons, including managerial, professional, technical, and clerical personnel.

The organization was widely known for its excellent technical work and its progressive and intelligent personnel policies. The turnover of employees has been very low.

John Riley had been head of mechanical testing for 5 years. All mechanical testing activities were conducted in this department, including the designing, building, procuring, and running of test equipment. These activities were conducted both for outside clients and for other departments of the institute. Trained as a mechanical engineer Riley had been with the institute for 15 years.

One morning his immediate supervisor, Bill Pickens, manager of the institute test division, asked Riley if he was interested in a newly created position in product development. This position was of a new nature in product development, and they wanted someone who was thoroughly experienced in institute policies and procedures to fill the position temporarily for 1 year. After that time, the position would either be made permanent or eliminated. Pickens told Riley that he was reluctant to lose him even on a temporary basis, but that acting in accordance with institute policy of promoting from within wherever possible, he wanted Riley to make the decision Pickens also informed him that the new product division had specifically suggested Riley because of his widespread institute reputation as a highly skilled engineer and manager. The new position would constitute an advancement to the next managerial level with a commensurate increase in pay. After discussing the position with the director of the new product division and thinking the proposal over for several days Riley decided to accept it.

On the following Friday, Pickens called Riley into his office to discuss his replacement as head of mechanical testing. In discussing his three section chiefs, Riley was uncertain in his own mind which, if any, would make the best successor.

Dodd, head of Section A, had the longest tenure and was the most experienced Riley felt, however, that he was rather quiet and did not communicate well with outsiders. Both Riley and Pickens were concerned with Dodd's ability to sell the services of the department to others. Yeager, head of Section B, was a competent leader, but prone to make hasty judgments. He sometimes committed to an expensive course of action without thinking through all of the alternatives. This had on occasion led to costly mistakes that were hard to rectify. Bennett, head of Section C, was an ambitious and aggressive leader, but he often created hard feelings with his colleagues On several occasions, Riley had been required to step in and smooth out ruffled feelings.

After considerable discussion, Riley suggested that since there was a possibility that he would want to return in a year and since there was no clear-cut choice, each of the men should take turns as acting head. Each would hold the position for 4 months in an acting capacity. At the end of a year, if Riley did not return to the position, the choice could be made from among the three on the basis of their performance. Pickens agreed to this proposal and put the plan into operation.

Ten months later, while Yeager was the acting department head, Pickens was promoted to associate director of the institute. Dick Terry, who had been head of electrical testing, was immediately appointed to replace Pickens. Pickens briefed Terry on the leadership situation in mechanical testing. When Terry asked Pickens about his evaluation of the performance of the three men in the position, Pickens replied that although Yeager had not finished his 4-month period, he seemed to be the best man for the job. ''In fact,'' Pickens said, ''I more or less told him last week that he would probably get the job.''

Toward the end of the year, Riley was informed that his new position was being made permanent. Since he was enjoying this new position and found it very challenging, he informed Terry that he would not be returning to the test division. Upon receiving this notice, Terry knew that he must now decide on a permanent department head for mechanical testing. He carefully reviewed their personnel records, including all past performance appraisals by former supervisors. He also made it a point to sound out informally the engineers and technicians in all three sections. Terry also held lengthy interviews with each of the three men.

In the course of the investigation he discovered that a great deal of ill feeling and jealousy had developed among the three men. During the past year, the three men had competed rather viciously for the department head's job. Each had tried to sabotage the others and frustrate any innovations or changes instituted. All three had campaigned throughout the year for the support of the engineers and technicians in the department. This had taken the form of granting special favors and making derogatory remarks about the other two. All three men had participated in such activities, and the end result was a year of poor morale and low productivity within the department. During the personal interviews, each of the three asserted that the assignment should be given to him.

Terry was appalled at the animosity that had developed. He was not at all convinced that any of the three could pull the department back together. Therefore, after lengthy discussions with Pickens, Terry announced that Dennis Brown, a section head in experimental research, had been named head of mechanical testing.

Case Study Discussion Questions

1. Did Terry make the right decision?
2. What will be the likely result?
3. Did Pickens make the right decision in deciding to rotate the job?
4. Could the results have been anticipated?

CHAPTER 7 leadership

7.1 Nature of Leadership

In any discussion of management the topic of leadership eventually arises. We hear or read statements like, "The manager must exert leadership in . . ." or "Selection of the natural leaders for management positions will. . . ." Such statements assume that we know what is meant by terms such as leader and leadership. Unfortunately, although each person probably does have a fairly firm idea of what these terms mean, they usually have a difficult time articulating a definition. This is not too surprising, because leadership is subjective and ethereal; it can be observed, but not measured or isolated. There are at least two different meanings of the verb "to lead." One of these is "to excel, to be in advance, to be preeminent"; and the other is "to guide others, to govern their activities, to be head of an organization, to command." The distinction between these two uses should be clear. People like Einstein, Spinoza, and Beethoven are leaders under the first concept. Personalities such as Henry Ford, Franklin D. Roosevelt, and Adolph Hitler qualify under the second. We will ignore leadership through accomplishment or preeminence here and concentrate on leadership as it relates to the guidance and governance of the behavior of others.

Such a distinction still leaves us with a problem for several reasons. First is the tendency of many writers to use leader and manager as synonymous terms. There are distinct differences between the two. A person becomes a manager through a formal appointment by some appropriate legal authority. A person becomes a leader when someone else does something you wish them to do. A leadership position is conferred by the followers. The confusion arises because we would like the manager and leader to be the same (i.e., for the power to be conferred from both above and below). We can also distinguish management and leadership as the difference of *authority of position* and the *authority of influence*.

Influence is an interpersonal concept. It refers to a relation or relationship between or among people. *Influence* is defined as the ability of an individual to induce others to produce an intended result. There is only one way to get a person to do your bidding, and that is by making the person want to do it. There are, of course, many ways to make the person want to produce the intended result. We are interested in two ways: persuasion and power. *Persuasion* involves an effort to influence by argument, reasoning, or a presentation of ideas. *Power* involves an effort to influence, either through coercion or the offering of something valued.

The person who is the object of persuasive efforts may refuse to produce without fear of reprisal. But the person who refuses to respond to the application of a power relationship must suffer the consequences. Influence through the use of power is affected by the application (or threat of application) of sanctions. Sanctions may take two forms: withholding something of value or imposing conditions that are not desired. Thus, power derives from the ability of a person to grant or withhold things of value such as promotions, pay increases, praise, or friendship, or to impose negative sanctions such as demotion, layoff, reprimand, expulsion from the group, or physical harm.

Leadership, therefore, is exercised either through the use of persuasion or the threatened use of power. It is important to emphasize that the effective leader does not go around constantly threatening to use sanctions. It is usually sufficient for the person who is the object of influence by power to realize that the leader can and will use sanctions when necessary. Power does not attach to those who are unable or unwilling to use sanctions. A manager who has the right to use sanctions but is unwilling to employ them when necessary has authority, but not power. By our definitions, therefore, leadership through the exercise of power means the power holder has a predisposition or capacity to use available sanctions, and this is recognized by "others" in the relationship.

One of the difficulties that researchers have had in studying leadership has been the impossibility of determining the true motives of participants in the relationship. Leaders almost always seem to exert influence through persuasion. Even the most autocratic of leaders seldom display raw threats of the use of power. Attempts to influence almost invariably are presented as arguments, ideas, and reasoning. However, it is much easier to be persuaded by a person with power than by one without power. The question then is whether the person followed because of the persuasion or was the persuasion effective because of the perceived power? In most cases even the participants cannot answer that question.

Actually, both parties (leader and follower) possess something of value. The leader in the relationship is trying to achieve an intended result and therefore values the response of the other party (the follower). To obtain the desired response, the leader must either persuade or possess and be in a position to provide or withhold something of value to the other party. In effect, leadership involves *mutually dependent relations*, with each party to the relation dependent on the other for gratification. Therefore, as we will see later, leadership depends on three things, the characteristics of (1) the leader, (2) the followers, and (3) the situation or conditions.

7.2 Theories of Leadership

Leadership pervades all management activity. It is the implementing force behind all of the other management functions. None of the other things we have talked about can take place if leadership cannot be exerted. Because of its importance, leadership has received a great deal of attention from theorists. We can presently identify at least four distinct theories of leadership: (1) natural leader, (2) scientific management, (3) human relations approach, and (4) context approach.

The *natural leader* theory states that leaders are born, not made. This school of thought believes that there are certain critical personal, innate characteristics of leaders that make them different from nonleaders. These characteristics are usually classified as (1) physical qualities, (2) psychological qualities, (3) attributes of personality, (4) attributes of character, and (5) intellectual qualities.

Adherents of the natural leader theory, although specifying what may be considered essential personal qualities of leaders, do concede that these attributes are not all indispensible to the extent that the absence of any one of them would disqualify an individual from leadership. The discussion by Peterson and Plowman is typical of such an approach [14]. They list the following as desirable attributes or characteristics in the leader.

1. Physical qualities.
    (a) Health.
    (b) Vitality.
    (c) Endurance.
2. Personality attributes.
    (a) Personal magnetism.
    (b) Cooperativeness.

    (c) Enthusiasm.
    (d) Ability to inspire.
    (e) Persuasiveness.
    (f) Forcefulness.
    (g) Tact.
3. Character attributes.
    (a) Integrity.
    (b) Humanism.
    (c) Self-discipline.
    (d) Stability.
    (e) Industry.
4. Intellectual qualities.
    (a) Mental capacity.
    (b) Ability to teach others.
    (c) Scientific approach to problems.

The natural leader approach proposed that these traits were essential for effective leadership and were transferable from one situation to another. Since all individuals did not have these traits, only those who did should be considered for management positions. Under this theory, if we could discover how to identify and measure these leadership traits, we could screen the leaders from the nonleaders. This would allow us to concentrate on training and developing those with inherent leadership qualities.

Unfortunately (or fortunately) reviews of the research literature using this trait approach reveal few significant or consistent findings [5, 15]. Jennings [7] concluded after a careful examination of the evidence that ''Fifty years of study have failed to produce one personality trait or set of qualities that can be used to discriminate leaders from non-leaders.'' It seems that if any pattern of leadership traits exists, it exists only in a given leadership setting.

Beginning in the late 1890s and continuing through about 1935, another school of thought on leadership was advanced. We can use the generic term *scientific management* to characterize this general theory; people are viewed as a passive, inert instrument, performing the tasks assigned to them. The idea was to set up an abstract, depersonalized system that would rationally make decisions without the friction of subjective judgment and human error. Typical of this approach is the theory of bureaucracy developed by Max Weber, the German sociologist [2] and Frederick W. Taylor [18], who stressed the impersonal rationality of measurement.

The scientific management approach can be described as a ''technique approach'' to leadership. Its principle purpose is to discover what particular management procedure is applicable to a given situation. The scientific management approach can be condensed to four principles.

1. The development of each person's work into a true science.
2. The scientific selection and training of workers.
3. Friendly cooperation between managers and workers.
4. Equal division of work and responsibility between management and workers.

Thus, the idea of the scientific management school is to define the purpose, discover the "one best way" to accomplish it, and set up the policies and procedures to carry out the work. Leadership is transferred to the "system," and the frailities of people are neatly sidestepped. Inherent in this approach are certain assumptions about people, such as people want to be dependent, are incapable of taking responsibility, need a strong leader, etc. Such assumptions lead naturally to the conclusion that what is needed is a "benevolent autocracy," as called for by people like MacMurray [12].

From 1938 to 1950 a new theory of leadership arose that is usually called the *human relations* approach. Whereas the scientific management approach treats organizations as if they existed without people, this school regards people as if they exist without organizations. Starting with the Western Electric Hawthorne Plant experiments, this school places primary emphasis on workers' feelings, attitudes, beliefs, perceptions, ideas, and sentiments— exactly the elements that the scientific management school tries to ignore and avoid. The basic concept is that workers can be induced to behave the way we wish on the basis of fulfilling certain social and psychological needs.

Some of the names associated with the development of this theory are Elton Mayo, Kurt Lewin, and Chris Argyris. This approach to leadership assumes there is no essential conflict between satisfaction of the needs and wants of the worker and those of the organization. The leader is seen as a facilitator, as an agent who helps smooth the pathway toward goal achievement. If high morale and job satisfaction for the worker are attained, goal achievement will surely follow. Unfortunately, research has shown that the idea that productivity is strongly correlated with morale or job satisfaction turns out to be more of a wish than a reality; there seems to be little or no interdependency between morale and productivity.

In essence, the natural leader movement emphasizes the characteristics of the leader, the scientific management movement emphasizes a concern for task, and the human relations approach stresses a concern for relationships (people). The *context* school of thought on leadership is that all three aspects are important. This approach takes the attitude that each of the other three schools of thought are correct, but insufficient by themselves. Certain characteristics or traits of leaders such as honesty, consistency, and enthusiasm are deemed mandatory, although concern for both the task and human relationships cannot be ignored. The relative importance of each will vary from situation to situation and must be considered in a specific context. The remainder of this chapter is about the context approach to leadership.

7.3 Use of Authority

Tannenbaum and Schmidt [17] have suggested that one dimension of leadership style can be depicted as a continuum that goes from authoritarian-oriented behavior to democratic-oriented behavior (see Figure 7.1). This continuum refers to leadership style as it relates to the degree of authority (i.e., power) utilized by the leader. It can also be considered a continuum of the willingness of the leader to delegate. The positions on the extreme left characterize the manager who maintains a high degree of control and decision-making authority; those on the extreme right characterize the manager who exercises little control and decision-making power. Neither extreme is absolute, in that neither authority nor freedom are ever without their limitations.

We will now look more closely at several of the behavior points that occur along this continuum. The letters of the following list correspond to the letters in Figure 7.1.

a. *The Manager Makes the Decision and Announces It.* In this case the manager identifies the problem, considers alternative solutions, chooses one of them, and turns it over to subordinates for implementation. The manager may or may not consider the feelings of subordinates in this matter and may or may not specify how the decision is to be implemented.

b. *The Manager Sells the Decision.* Here the manager, as before, makes the decision. However, instead of merely announcing it and ordering its implementation, he or she tries to persuade subordinates to accept it. If they are not persuaded, the implementation will still be ordered.

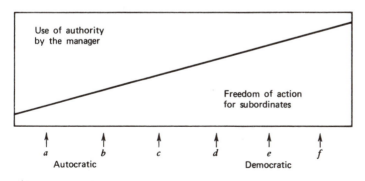

FIGURE 7.1   Delegation of authority continuum.

c. *The Manager Presents a Tentative Decision, Subject to Change.* In this case, the manager diagnoses the problem and comes up with a tentative decision but, before finalizing it, seeks the ideas and reactions of subordinates.

d. *The Manager Presents the Problem, Gets Suggestions, and Makes a Decision.* Up to this point the manager has come to subordinates with a preconceived solution. Here, subordinates are asked to suggest solutions from which the manager will select the most promising.

e. *The Manager Defines the Problem and Its Limits and Requests Subordinates to Make the Decision.* In this case, the manager has delegated decision making to the group, or subordinates.

f. *The Manager Permits the Group or Subordinates to Define the Problem and Make the Decision within Prescribed Limits.* This form of complete freedom is found rarely, except in basic research groups.

Each position represents a valid point of view about "good leadership." Considerable practical experience, research data, and theoretical arguments can be cited to support each of them, even though they seem very inconsistent when placed together. Such a broad spectrum of attitudes presents a real dilemma for the technical manager. Should "strong" or "permissive" leadership be exerted? Should I make the decision, since I understand the problem better, or should I get the group to help make it so they will accept it better?

The perceptive reader will have noticed that we could call the extreme left side of the continuum Theory X and the extreme right side Theory Y (see Section 6.7). We could also refer to the left side as the scientific management approach and the right side as the human relations approach. Which is correct? Which is most successful? It all depends on the context. Barnard [1] said that leadership depends on the characteristics of three things: (1) the individual leader, (2) the followers, and (3) the current conditions. To select the best leadership style, we must examine and evaluate all three dimensions.

7.4 Other Leadership Dimensions

A number of studies have been conducted over the years to identify characteristic styles of leadership that were most effective. Studies at the Survey Research Center at the University of Michigan identified two concepts or leadership dimensions that they called employee orientation and production orientation [8, 9]. An employee-oriented leader stresses the human relationships aspects of the job. Such a leader takes an interest in each person and accepts their individuality and personal needs. The production-oriented leader emphasizes the production and technical aspects of the job and views the employees as tools to accomplish the goals of the organization. These two orientations closely parallel the human relations and scientific management approaches.

Another series of leadership studies was conducted by the Bureau of Business Research at Ohio State University to identify various dimensions of leader behavior [16]. They also eventually narrowed their description of leadership behavior to the dimensions that they called *consideration* and *initiating structure*. The leader whose behavior was indicative of friendship, mutual trust, respect, and warmth toward staff members was said to be high in consideration. If there was a strong endeavor to establish well-defined channels of communications, methods of procedure, and patterns of organization, the leader was classified as high in initiating structure. In studying leader behavior, the Ohio State staff found that these were separate and distinct dimensions. High scores on one dimension do not necessitate being low on the other. The behavior of a leader could be described as any mix of both dimensions.

Blake and Mouton have popularized these concepts in their *managerial grid,* which they have used in management development programs [3]. In their managerial grid, concern for production is represented on the horizontal axis and a concern for people is illustrated on the vertical axis. The higher the concern for a particular dimension, the higher the numerical score. They also identify five different types of leadership located in the four quadrants and give them names, however, any point in the grid represents a possible leadership behavior.

The implication of the managerial grid is that there is one most desirable leadership behavior or management style (i.e., maximum concern for both production and people). Unfortunately, this is easier said than done. The idealized leader would have to have all of the personal characteristics listed for the natural leader in Section 7.2 plus the wisdom of Solomon.

There is ample research evidence to suggest that the desire to have a single ideal type of leader behavior is unrealistic. Using the Michigan and Ohio State studies as a starting place, Likert did some research on the leadership style used by managers of both high-producing and low-producing groups [10], as did Halpin and Winer [6]. Although both studies showed greater success for the employee-centered, democratic leader, they also found a significant number of production-centered, authoritarian leaders who were highly successful. For example, in Likert's studies, in 30 percent of the low-producing groups, the suggested ideal type of leadership produced undesirable results, and 15 percent of the high-producing leaders used the undesirable style. Similar results showed up in the Halpin-Winer study. No explanation of these discrepancies is offered by the authors.

This desire to have an ideal type of leader is very common. Most managers seem to want to be told how to act, and there is no shortage of writers who are willing to do just that (i.e., prescribe the ideal leadership style). Most of these writers have supported either a utopian style of high concern for both task and people or a permissive, democratic, human relations approach. Interestingly, most of these writers have never been managers, and they dispense their wisdom safely ensconced in academia. Experienced managers are usually not so dogmatic.

The evidence continues to mount that there is no one ideal leadership style for all groups and all situations. Appropriate leadership results when a manager adopts a style that is comfortable, compatible with the prevailing situation, and meets the needs of the followers.

7.5 Personality of the Leader

As we have seen, there are at least three separate and distinct dimensions to leadership style, and each can be considered as a continuum from low to high. These are (1) willingness to delegate authority, (2) concern for the task or production, and (3) concern for people or personal relationships. The problem of choosing a leadership style might be considered as one of choosing a point in the three-dimensional space depicted in Figure 7.2. There are an infinite number of points in this three-dimensional space; therefore an infinite number of leadership styles are possible.

There is strong evidence to suggest that it is extremely important that a good leader be *consistent, predictable,* and *reliable*. Such behavior is mandatory if the followers are going to be able to understand what is expected of them and the rules of the game. If a leader is very friendly one moment and surly the next, delegates authority and for no apparent reason suddenly withdraws it, or if a particular project is of extreme importance one day and of no concern the next, the members of the group soon become frustrated and unable to anticipate how they should act. Such behavior destroys the confidence of the followers, and they will quickly withdraw and try to isolate themselves from the manager. The truth is that even if a person is difficult, if he or she is consistently difficult, we can learn to accept such behavior and adjust to it. It is unpredictable, inconsistency that we cannot tolerate.

If a manager is going to be consistent, predictable, and reliable, the leadership style used must be compatible with his or her personality, beliefs, and value system. Leadership problems will be perceived by each manager in a unique way, based on past background, knowledge, and experience, and the manager's behavior in any instance will be influenced by complex, internal, personal forces, including:

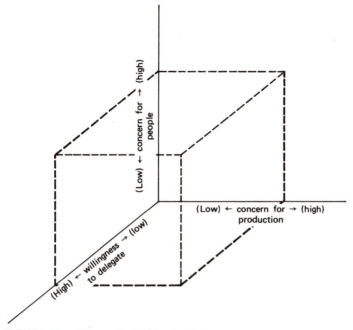

FIGURE 7.2   Dimensions of leadership.

1. *Attitude toward People.* There are two aspects to the importance of the manager's basic attitude toward people. The first is where on the Theory X-Theory Y spectrum the manager's beliefs lie (See Section 6.7). If the manager basically believes in Theory X, to try to operate in a highly democratic fashion will lead to frustration and inconsistency. The second aspect deals with basic sociability and concern for people. Some individuals have a genuine love and concern for people. They have a natural trust, respect, and interest in each person and enjoy camaraderie and friendship. Other individuals do not feel comfortable in close, friendly relationships. They prefer to maintain courteous, polite, formal relationships with no personal involvement.

2. *Confidence in Subordinates.* Managers differ greatly in the amount of trust or confidence that they have in other people, both generally and specifically. When considering particular employees, the manager will likely consider their perceived knowledge and competence with respect to a particular problem. Justifiably or not, the manager may have more confidence in his or her own capabilities than in those of the subordinate.

3. *Leadership Inclinations.* Some managers function most comfortably and

naturally as highly directive leaders. They thrive on resolving problems and issuing orders. Most leaders of this type are convinced that the person who is paid to assume responsibility should personally carry the burden of decision making. Others are more comfortable operating as a member of a team, sharing their functions with subordinates. The manager's behavior will also be affected by the perceived relative importance of organizational efficiency (perhaps believing that meetings are a waste of time) and the need to develop subordinates.

4. *Feelings of Security in Uncertain Situations.* When a manager delegates decision-making authority, the predictability of the outcome becomes more uncertain. The leader remains responsible, but loses some control when authority is delegated. Some managers have a low tolerance for ambiguous situations and require predictability and stability in their environment.

A person's leadership style does and should reflect the individual's basic personality. It has taken the individual a lifetime to develop that particular personality structure and, at best, it takes 1, 2, or 3 years of intensive psychotherapy to effect any lasting changes. It is not surprising, therefore, to find that most management training courses do not change managerial behavior. A 40-hour short course cannot change what has taken so long to develop. What it can do is lead to inconsistent behavior if the manager tries to adopt a leadership style foreign to his or her nature. There will be no problem as long as things run smoothly but, as soon as an important issue or crisis arises, the manager will revert to the old, comfortable style that has the force of habit behind it. This will be viewed as inconsistent behavior by subordinates. In summary, the manager's personality and leadership style must be compatible. Otherwise, inconsistent, unpredictable, and unreliable behavior will result, accompanied by a failure of leadership. Consistency is probably more important than style.

7.6 Attitudes of the Followers

The second part of our leadership equation is the followers. Here we are concerned with both the personality and expectations of subordinates. The individuals whom the manager is trying to lead are of critical importance in choosing a leadership style. Followers in any situation are vital, not only because they will individually accept or reject a leader, but also because as a group they actually determine how much power a manager will have. The individual employee decides whether to accept the leadership of the manager. Each person has the freedom to choose whether or not to cooperate. This is true even in a strictly authoritarian organization such as the military. In fact, an army is in one sense pure democracy in action. When a commander gives an order to advance, each individual soldier votes with his feet. If a majority votes "yea," the army moves forward; if a majority votes "nay," the army stays put or retreats. Even though the consequences of not obeying an order may be dire (such as execution), the fact remains that each individual decides whether to cooperate or not.

Both the personalities and expectations of the workers are important. As previously discussed, personality is defined as the behavior patterns of an individual as shaped by personal values, morales, and past experiences. Expectations are the perceptions of appropriate behavior for one's own role or position and one's perception of the roles of others. In other words, the expectations of individuals define what they think they should do under various circumstances and how they think others should behave. It is actually the interaction of personality and expectations that determine the behavior of an individual in the organization.

First, we should recognize that people vary greatly in the amount of direction they desire. Some individuals want freedom of choice and responsibility for decision making, while others want to be told what to do. Some want to be told exactly and precisely what is expected of them in terms of clear-cut directions, while others prefer a wider area of freedom. One individual will see delegated responsibility as an opportunity and a tribute to his or her ability, while another will see it as "passing the buck."

If the personalities and expectations of leader and follower vary too much, conflict is probable. Vroom [19] gives the following example.

> Place a group of strong independence drives under a supervisor who needs to keep his men under his thumb, and the result is very likely to be trouble. Similarly, if you take docile men who are accustomed to obedience and respect for their supervisors and place them under a supervisor who tries to make them manage their work, they are likely to wonder uneasily whether he really knows what he is doing.

So it is not only the expectations and desires of the manager that are important, but also those of the workers. If an incompatibility exists, the manager must either change the personalities and expectations of the followers or adapt, at least temporarily, to their present behavior. Authority and responsibility can only be delegated if the recipient is willing to accept them. As we have already discussed, personality changes are hard to bring about and take long periods of time. It may be more effective, therefore, if the manager concentrates on changing the expectations of the followers. In other words, the manager should convince them that his or her style, even though not what they normally expect, will still be adequate and effective if accepted.

Perhaps this is the appropriate place to suggest the applicability of "Pareto's principle" to leadership. Pareto's principle says that in every group or collection, a vital few and a trivial many exist. He further postulates that 80 percent of the action, effect, or achievement is caused by only 20 percent of the group, while the remaining 80 percent of the group contribute only 20 percent to the total productivity. Pareto was an economist and postulated his principle in relation to marketing (e.g., if a firm sells 1000 items, 80 percent of the profit will be derived from only 200 of them). Based on personal experience, plus the experience and research of others, I believe the same principle applies to technical organizations (i.e., 80 percent of the productivity will come from 20 percent of the people). This assertion is somewhat backed up by the research of Schockley (see Section 1.10), and Myers (see Section 6.7). I further propose that in any organization, Theory X accurately describes 20 percent of the people, Theory Y another 20 percent, with the rest falling somewhere in between (see Section 6.7). I am suggesting that the Theory Y people are Pareto's vital few and that true Theory Y people constitute only about 20 percent of a group. These are the self-motivated self-starters.

If this assertion is true, it is implied that the same leadership style will not be effective with everyone in the group. Obviously, the manager cannot simultaneously adopt 16 different and distinct leadership behaviors. What is suggested, however, is that within a general, overall leadership pattern, adjustments should be made for dealing with each individual in the group. For the 20 percent who are self-motivated self-starters, the manager need only step aside and serve as an expeditor and facilitator. For the remaining group, closer control and greater structure will be required.

I also believe that Pareto's principle partially explains the mixed research results on leadership style. The more permissive, democratic leader is unleashing the highly productive 20 percent, while the autocratic, task-oriented leader is perhaps getting greater productivity out of the less productive 80 percent.

7.7 The Leadership Environment

In addition to the personalities and expectations of the manager and subordinates, we must also consider the work environment or context and its effects on leadership behavior. Among the environmental factors that affect behavior are (1) superiors' personalities and expectations, (2) associates' personalities and expectations, (3) type of organization, (4) job demands or problems, and (5) time pressures.

Everyone has a superior of one kind or another (even the chairperson of the board has to answer to the majority stockholders). A manager very quickly finds that meeting the superior's expectations is often an important factor affecting one's style. If one's superior is very authoritarian or task oriented, for example, it will usually be very difficult to operate in a democratic, human relations-oriented manner. Suppose, for example, that an authoritarian, task-oriented executive often asks the manager about the plans or status of particular projects. If the manager always answers that it will be necessary to check with the engineer in charge, the executive will soon ask, "Don't you know what is going on in your group?" A lecture to the executive on the desirability of freedom of action and planning for technical personnel will not be well received. Likewise, if the authoritarian executive asks the manager for a decision related to a project, a response that "I'll have to get a decision from the group" will get a chilly reaction. It is not surprising that several research studies have shown that the leadership style of a manager does not deviate very far from that of the superior. A certain style permeates each organization and is usually a reflection of the personality and expectations of the top executive.

A manager's leadership behavior is also strongly influenced by associates and peers (i.e., those individuals who hold similar positions within the organization). Leadership transpires within a social and technical environment. The manager often finds that he or she must negotiate and cooperate with other managers in order to get the job done. As with all the others in the leadership environment, these associates have certain expectations of how a manager should behave. Not all associates are significant to a manager, only those who require frequent interaction. One interesting aspect of this influence is the effect of the manager's personal ambitions. If a person desires to advance through the management ranks, he or she will tend to adopt the leadership behavior of the immediate superior. However, for those who are satisfied with their present positions, the expectations of their associates may be more important in influencing their behavior than those of their superiors. This is particularly true of technical managers, who may be more concerned with their peer group in their area of expertise than they are with being promoted.

A third environmental factor influencing leadership behavior is the type of organization. Over a period of time an organization, much like an individual, develops certain modes of operating that become its personality, or "corporate image." For example, certain corporations pride themselves on the fact that the environment of certain technical groups is like that of a university. Hence the leadership style of managers in such groups must conform to the image. It is also true that people will have certain expectations for certain types of technical organizations. For example, one would be surprised to find a highly authoritarian leader in a basic research group (although they exist) or a laissez-faire leader in a maintenance engineering group.

My military time was spent as an enlisted man in a scientific and professional detachment assigned at a U.S. Army Ordnance Arsenal. All of the enlisted men in the group had degrees in engineering or science, and many of them held graduate degrees through the Ph.D. The working hours were spent working alongside civilian engineers and scientists on high-priority army R&D projects. Many of the enlisted men held highly responsible technical positions. The officers of the group were regular army and often came from combat groups. Needless to say, this was not a spit and polish group. Each new officer assigned to the group swore he would shape up the outfit. Each failed miserably and quickly requested a transfer. Even though the detachment was an army ordnance group, its true image and value system was that of a R&D group. Any leadership style incompatible with that image and value system was bound to fail.

Another important element of a leadership situation is the type of problems or demands of the job that the group has been assigned. A highly structured task will require different behavior than an unstructured one. For example, the leadership style will depend to some extent where the project occurs in the product or system life cycle (see Section 1.4). As one moves from the conceptualization stage through definition, design, development, production and, finally, operational support, the tasks become more structured. This will require the manager to become more and more task oriented. The leadership style that is effective at the research end of the spectrum (see Figure 1.3) may be ineffective at the development end.

A final important element in the environment of a manager is the time duration available for decision making. If the manager's work area is on fire or if a space vehicle develops problems just as it is ready for launch, the manager does not have the time to call a meeting to discuss the situation. Therefore, short time demands (such as in an emergency) demand task-oriented, authoritarian behavior. On the other hand, if time is not a major factor, the manager has a wider range of behavioral choice, depending on the other environmental factors.

One could probably enumerate other environmental factors that impinge on the manager's behavior and leadership style. Specific organizations may have additional factors that are unique to them and that play an important role. Organizations are infused with a system of values and modes of behavior that reflect their history and the people who have played vital roles in their formation and growth. Such values and modes of behavior will limit the range of behavior within which the manager can vary his or her style. Managers differ in their ability to vary their leadership styles to fit the situation. The more adaptable the manager is, the more likely is it that he or she will be an effective leader in a wider number of situations.

7.8 Leadership in the Matrix

One of the most important problems facing managers in the matrix (or any other) organization is how to obtain and hold the support and cooperation of personnel. This problem is somewhat more difficult for the project manager, since he or she is usually not able to command formally the support of project personnel from the functional areas. Very little research has been done to try to identify the types of influence that a manager in a matrix organization can most effectively use in eliciting the necessary support from project personnel.

One very interesting field study was conducted by Gemmill and Thamhain within the General Electric Company [4]. They investigated five basic forms of influence that can exist among project managers, functional managers, and project personnel. These were:

1. *Formal Authority*. Project personnel perceive the manager as being officially empowered to issue orders.
2. *Reward Power*. Project personnel perceive the manager as capable of directly or indirectly dispensing valued rewards such as salary increases, promotions, desirable future work assignments, etc.
3. *Penalty Power*. The manager is perceived as capable of directly or indirectly causing penalties that the project personnel wish to avoid.
4. *Expertise*. The ability to gain support because of possession of special knowledge or expertise.
5. *Referent Power*. The ability to gain support because project pesonnel feel personally attracted to the manager or to the project.

In this study both project personnel and managers were asked to rank order the importance of nine forms of influence. For example, the project personnel were asked to rank order the following nine statements as they apply to why they usually responded to requests from functional managers or project managers for whom they worked.

1. Has the formal authority.
2. Can influence my salary.
3. Can influence my promotion.
4. Can influence future work assignments.
5. Can influence the allocation of funds to my unit.
6. Can penalize me in some way.

7. Has special expertise.
8. Has established a personal friendship with me.
9. Can provide interesting and professionally challenging work.

Let us first look at the comparative rankings of project personnel and those managers who exercise functional authority over them and act as supervisors. The rank order of the four most important items were:

Supervisors Ranking	Employee Ranking
Work challenge	Work challenge
Expertise	Authority
Authority	Salary adjustment
Salary adjustment	Expertise

For both groups the two least important basis of influence were punishment and friendship. It is interesting that the managers perceive the basis of influence in almost the same order as their subordinates. The one exception is that managers consider their own expertise as of much greater importance than do their subordinates. Managers considered it the second most important reason for gaining support, whereas their subordinates considered it as only the fourth most important reason.

Next let us look at the ranking for project managers and those project personnel whose services they use but over whom they lack functional authority. The four most important items were:

Project Manager	Project Personnel
Expertise	Expertise
Work challenge	Work challenge
Authority	Future work assignments
Fund allocation	Friendship

It is evident that there is some disagreement between the project managers and project personnel. First, project managers consider authority and fund allocation more important sources of power than the project personnel do. The project personnel, on the other hand, consider friendship and future work assignments more important than the project managers do.

A comparison of the ratings reveals some interesting similarities as well as differences.

1. Both the project managers and functional managers saw the same factors as their base of power.

2. None of the three groups perceived penalty power as significant in gaining support.

3. Project personnel consider work challenge and expertise to be important factors in supporting both types of managers. However, expertise was ranked first as a reason to support project managers and fourth in relationship to functional managers.

4. Another major difference is that authority and salary are important reasons to support the functional manager, while future work assignments and friendship were considered among the four most important reasons to support project managers.

This study suggests that project managers should not rely on their formal authority or control of resources when trying to lead project personnel. They should pay closer attention to developing strong personal relationships and the potential for future interesting work assignments. The study confirms that coercion or fear of penalties is a poor and often ineffective basis for power. It also points out that different leadership styles are required in different contexts or situations.

7.9 Leadership Roles

As discussed in Section 1.7, sociologists often use the concept of roles and role playing to study and explain inter- and intrapersonal activities. A role is the expectation by oneself or others of how a person should behave and perform under a certain set of circumstances. Mintzberg [13] has suggested that these roles for the manager can be divided into three groups: (1) interpersonal roles, (2) informational roles, and (3) decisional roles.

The interpersonal roles relate to the manager's behavior when dealing with members of the group, peers, and other people outside the group. We have already discussed these roles extensively insofar as internal relationships are concerned, so will now mention a few aspects of external relationships. One important role that the manager must play is that of *figurehead*. As the legal authority of the organization, the manager is a symbol of the group. As such, the manager presides at ceremonial events such as awards, retirements, group dinners, etc. The manager also receives visitors and represents the group with outsiders. It is important that the manager recognize the critical nature of this role. Pride of group membership is important to motivation and a willingness to follow a leader. It is important that the manager play the role of figurehead in a manner in which each member can take pride. A mumbling, tongue-tied, foot-in-mouth performance by the manager will cause embarrassment and shame to the members. Likewise, a confident, self-assured manager who says exactly the right thing at the right time causes pride in being a member of the group.

It should be obvious that the effective manager also serves a *liaison role* by maintaining a complex web of lateral or horizontal relationships with other managers at all levels. The manager establishes this network of contacts primarily to bring information and favors to the group. The manager provides time, information, and favors to others in return for the same. Many of these relationships must be established and nurtured on the basis of friendship, trust, and mutual respect. The fact that the manager has the trust and respect of outsiders will help to build like feelings within the group.

The *informational roles* of the leader relate primarily to the gathering and dissemination of information that is important to the group. Control of information that is needed by others is a tremendous source of power. Decision makers at all levels of an organization depend on others for the gathering, analysis, interpretation, and transmission of information. If this information is not accurate and timely, decision makers cannot function. The manager is, therefore, the nerve center of a complex information network for both internal and external information that is critically important to each member of the group. This network carries information about objectives, environmental conditions, who is doing what to whom and the availability of resources. A leader who is obviously "in the know" is easier to respect and follow than one who is always "in the dark." The leader must take in all of this information (including gossip and hearsay), integrate it, interpret it, and disseminate it.

In addition to the gathering and internal dissemination of information, the leader must also serve as a *representative*. In this role the manager must transmit to people outside the organization information about the plans, policies, performance, and needs of the group. The followers must be confident that the leader is effective and will make their accomplishments known and see that they are properly rewarded and their needs met.

The decision-making roles of the leader are predominantly those of *resource allocator, disturbance handler,* and *negotiator*. In the next chapter we will discuss extensively the role of resource allocator, so we will limit our comments to the roles of disturbance handler and negotiator. The role of disturbance handler arises when a situation occurs that is either new or cannot be handled routinely by the group. Disturbances can take the form of internal conflicts between group members or disagreements with people outside the group. These disturbances often involve a great deal of emotion among the participants and require careful, skillful handling. Because of this, the leader must move cautiously and be sure of all the facts before taking action.

The role of negotiator describes the manager's role as a politician and arranger of agreements. Most managers do not like to consider themselves as politicians, but an effective leader must also be an effective politician. We use the term politician in the sense of one who negotiates and promotes a policy or plan based on self-interest. Managers must negotiate with higher executives and other groups who are providing the needed resources, performing support activity, and setting standards of performance and to whom they wish to "sell" their services. In this process, the manager will use all available resources of influence, argument, and power to gain the best possible deal for the group. This, then, is essentially a political process. Horse trading, bluffs, and threats as well as logic and reasonableness are all part of the negotiating process.

7.10 Effective Leadership

I will now summarize what is meant by effective leadership and the characteristics of a successful leader. I have defined leadership as the ability to get people to do and behave in some desired manner and made a distinction between the authority conferred by virtue of a position and that conferred by personal influence. Leadership deals with authority of the latter type (i.e., personal influence). Influence, or the ability to induce an individual to produce an intended result, derives from either persuasion or power. It is conferred not by the organization, but by the followers.

The authority of influence (or leadership) can exist without the formal or legal confirmation by the organization. Likewise, conferring the authority of position does not automatically bestow leadership. Sometimes the leader and manager of a group are two separate persons. The ideal situation occurs when the leader and manager are the same person. Then the individual possesses both the authority of position and the authority of influence. Leadership is a relationship between persons in a particular situation. Persons who are leaders in one situation may not be leaders in other situations. Since you cannot have a leader without followers, the ideal situation is one in which the manager adopts a leadership style that is comfortable, compatible with the prevailing situation, and meets the needs of the followers. The diversity of personalities and environmental contexts within which leadership occurs is probably responsible for the fact that there is no one recognizable pattern of ideal leadership style.

Leadership, then, is an interpersonal relationship in which the leader must first win the confidence of the followers. The followers must be convinced that their needs and desires will be fulfilled by supporting the leader. This requires a measure of self-confidence on the part of the leader. If the leader is secure in his or her own position and capabilities, this will instill confidence in others. Indeed, it has been shown that the more secure a supervisor feels with his or her superiors, the more effective will be the leadership exerted [11].

Success also instills confidence. In leadership, as in any other activity, "nothing succeeds like success." The successful manager, whether in engineering, business, or baseball, will find it easier to be a leader. No one wants to follow a failure. No one wants to place their fate in the hands of the unsuccessful.

The leader must also generate enthusiasm and commitment in the followers. This is not achieved by exhortations of inspiration or threats of punishment. It is more likely to be achieved by setting a personal example. If the leader does not exhibit great enthusiasm and commitment toward the goals, the followers are unlikely to display them. All successful leaders are characterized by personal enthusiasm, commitment, and confidence. Furthermore, they take great care to see that commitment and enthusiasm are acknowledged. The follower who exerts extra effort is commended and rewarded.

Finally, the leader must be consistent, predictable, reliable, and fair. Consistency and fairness are the cornerstones of any leader-follower relationship.

─────────────────── **References** ───────────────────

1. Barnard, C. I., *Organization and Management,* Harvard University Press, Cambridge, Mass., 1956, p. 84.
2. Bendix, R., *Max Weber: An Intellectual Portrait,* Doubleday, Garden City, N.Y., 1960.
3. Blake, R. R., and J. S. Mouton, *The Managerial Grid,* Gulf Publishing, Houston, 1964.
4. Gemmill, G. R., and H. J. Thamhain, "The Effectiveness of Different Power Styles of Project Managers in Gaining Project Support," *IEEE Transactions on Engineering Management, EM-20* (2), May 1971, pp. 38-44.
5. Gibb, C. A., "Leadership," *Handbook of Social Psychology,* G. Lindzey, Editor, Addison-Wesley, Cambridge, Mass., 1954.
6. Halpin, A. W., and B. J. Winer, *The Leadership Behavior of Airplane Commanders,* Ohio State University Research Foundation, Columbus, 1952.
7. Jennings, E. E., "The Anatomy of Leadership," *Management of Personnel Quarterly, I* (1), Autumn 1961.
8. Katz, D., N. Maccoby, and N. C. Morse, *Productivity, Supervision and Morale in an Office Situation,* Survey Research Center, University of Michigan, Ann Arbor, 1950.
9. Katz, D., N. Maccoby, G. Gwin, and L. G. Floor, *Productivity, Supervision and Morale Among Railroad Workers,* Survey Research Center, University of Michigan, Ann Arbor, 1951.
10. Likert, R., *New Patterns of Management,* McGraw-Hill, New York, 1961.
11. Maccoby, N. A., A Quantitative Comparison of Certain Psychological Conditions Related to Group Productivity in Two Widely Different Industrial Situations, Unpublished Ph.D. dissertation, University of Michigan, 1950.
12. McMurry, R. W., "The Case for Benevolent Autocracy," *Harvard Business Review, 36* (1), January-February 1958, pp. 82—90.

13. Mintzberg, H., ''Managerial Work: Analysis from Observation,'' *Management Science, 18* (2) October 1971, pp. B97−B100.
14. Peterson, E., and E. G. Plowman, *Business Organization and Management,* Richard D. Irwin, Homewood, Ill., 1957, pp. 50−62.
15. Stogdill, R. M., ''Personal Factors Associated with Leadership: A Survey of the Literature,'' *Journal of Psychology, 25,* 1948, pp. 35−71.
16. Stogdill, R. M., and A. E. Coons, Editors, *Leader Behavior: Its Description and Measurement,* Research Monograph No. 88, Bureau of Business Research, Ohio State University, Columbus, 1957.
17. Tannenbaum, R., and W. H. Schmidt, ''How to Choose a Leadership Pattern,'' *Harvard Business Review, 36* (2), March-April 1958, pp. 95−101.
18. Taylor, F. W., *Scientific Management,* Harper & Bros., New York, 1948.
19. Vroom, V. H., *Some Personality Determinants of the Effects of Participation,* Prentice-Hall, Englewood Cliffs, N.J., 1960.

─────────────── **Discussion Questions** ───────────────

1. Machiavelli raises the question, ''Is it better for a leader to be loved or feared?'' Discuss this question.
2. How important is it for a manager to be well liked by his or her employees?
3. A manager is subjected to conflicting pressures (external, downward, upward, and lateral) to behave in certain ways. Discuss each of these and how a manager might adjust to them.
4. Are managing and leading the same thing?
5. How important is technical competence versus personality traits in selecting technical managers?
6. Can good managers be developed through formal training programs?
7. How important is it for a technical manager to be able to speak and write well? Why?
8. In managing technical people, which theory of leadership (natural leader, scientific management, or human relations) is more important or most pertinent?
9. Why is power necessary to the functioning of an organization?
10. Give examples where a person might have power without any formal authority.
11. How does leadership influence motivation?

───────────────── **Case Study VII** ─────────────────

CAPITOL AEROSPACE CORPORATION

Dr. Jerry Lucas closed the door to his office and slowly sank into his chair. The four section chiefs from Bob Sanford's department had just left after a 2-hour meeting set up at their request. Lucas was the director of the propulsion division, and Sanford was one of his six branch chiefs.

Lucas had known for some time that there were problems in Sanford's organization, but he hadn't been able to put his finger on the cause. The work was getting done pretty much on schedule, but there were obvious morale problems. Anytime that Lucas spoke to any of the people in Sanford's group, their responses were always very guarded. He had also noticed that if he asked anyone a question about a project or requested any information, he got an evasive answer. Later Sanford would come to his office with the answer or data.

The four section heads had requested the private meeting with Lucas without specifying the purpose. However, they had been very specific in asking that Sanford not be present. The reason for the meeting had immediately become clear as the section heads brought out their grievances. Their basic complaint was lack of authority. On numerous occasions Sanford had reversed their decisions without consulting them. Several of the section heads said this had resulted in their subordinates going directly to Sanford whenever they had a question or needed a decision. They complained that matters had reached the point where very few decisions, even routine ones, could be made without his approval. He also had made it very clear that no information or data was to be given to anyone outside of the branch without his knowledge and concurrence. This policy had made it almost impossible for the section heads or other engineers to work cooperatively with engineers from other parts of the organization.

Finally, they had complained that Sanford's encouragement of engineers and even technicians to go around the section heads directly to him with their problems and complaints had led to an atmosphere of fear and suspicion. Everyone in the organization felt that everything they said or did was likely to be reported to Sanford. One of the section heads said that it was widely believed that Sanford had spies or informants in every section. Whether true or not, this had a chilling effect on interpersonal relations, and everyone tended to pull back into their shells and play everything very conservatively.

Each of the section heads stated that they had great respect for Sanford as an engineer and in his technical judgment. However, they could not tolerate the lack of authority and the oppressive atmosphere. The threat was clear (although not stated explicitly) that each of the section heads felt that if something was not done, they would soon be leaving.

As Lucas sat at his desk after the men left, he realized that the problem was more serious than he had guessed. Sanford was by far the best solid rocket expert in the branch. That was the reason Lucas had made him branch chief 2 years ago. Sanford was totally dedicated to his job, and Lucas knew that he arrived at his office every morning at 7 A.M. and rarely left before 6 P.M. He often came to the office on weekends, never took a vacation, and rarely took even a day off. On the other hand, it was also now obvious that Sanford had not been completely candid in his relationship with Lucas. Many of the projects were not as far along as he had reported, and many difficulties were being covered up. Also, the very fact that the section heads had felt the situation was serious enough to come to him as a group convinced Lucas that something had to be done. He finally decided that he would face the situation squarely and candidly by discussing the meeting with Sanford.

The next day, Lucas asked Sanford to come to his office and reported the meeting to him exactly as it had transpired. He did not, however, tell Sanford who had said what. Sanford became very angry and vehemently denied all of the allegations. Part of the conversation went as follows.

SANFORD: As long as I'm responsible for the solid propellant projects, I've got to know what's going on. The only way I can be sure the section heads are not covering up problems is occasionally to go directly to the people doing the work. If they see that as snooping or spying, that's just too bad. What they are really concerned with is that I sometimes find out about their stupid decisions. They are right about one thing. I do sometimes overrule their decisions when I think they are wrong. But when I do, I always tell them about it. What am I supposed to do when I see a mistake? I can't just let it go and let the project fail just so as not to hurt their precious image with the engineers. Their problem is they just don't want to admit they ever make mistakes.

LUCAS: Perhaps you're not very diplomatic when you find what you think is a mistake.

SANFORD: How can you be diplomatic and at the same time tell a person they've made a stupid decision? An error in judgment is an error in judgment, and there is no way you can make it into anything else. Do you want me to ignore something when I know it is wrong?

LUCAS: No, of course not, but are you sure that you are always right and they are wrong?

SANFORD: Look, I have more experience and knowledge about solid propellant rockets than all four of those guys put together. I know what works and what doesn't. I can't just stand by idly and let the projects get screwed up when I see them doing something I know won't work. As long as I'm head of this branch, I'm going to do everything I can to see that the projects are done on time, within budget, and that the systems work. I thought that was what I was supposed to do as a manager. If that isn't what you want, then you better get another branch chief.

Case study discussion questions

1. Discuss Sanford's leadership style.
2. What are the chances that Dr. Lucas can get Sanford to change?
3. Should Lucas have met with the section heads without Sanford being present?
4. What would you do if you were Dr. Lucas?

PART THREE the tactical level

CHAPTER 8 project selection

8.1 Project Planning Assumptions

Ultimately, the technical manager is faced with the necessity of planning the specific projects that will be pursued in order to achieve the established goals. Planning for specific projects entails evaluation, selection, and allocation of resources. The degree of formality and detail used in the planning of projects varies widely among technical organizations. These differences are partly due to the type of technical programs being pursued (i.e., basic, applied, or developmental). Perhaps more important, however, is the viewpoint or perception by management of the invention-innovation process. Schon [19] asserts that there are two very different viewpoints held by technical managers, which he calls the rational and nonrational.

According to Schon, the rational viewpoint assumes that the invention-innovation process:

1. Is goal directed (i.e., one knows in advance the objectives that are being sought).
2. Occurs within an established discipline or technology framework (i.e., the discipline or technology areas from which the solution is to be found are known in advance).
3. Is essentially an intellectual process (i.e., a logical approach can be laid out ahead of time to achieve the goals).
4. Progresses through an orderly series of steps or stages. For example, ideas are generated in one phase, feasibility is demonstrated in a second, development occurs in a third, etc.

5. Can be planned and managed similarly to that of other organizational functions (i.e., established management principles and practices can be adapted to insure success).

Many technical managers are not particularly comfortable with the viewpoint that the invention-innovation process is as rational as all that. Such a view does not mesh well with their personal experience, and they perceive a more nonrational process. According to this view, the invention-innovation process:

1. Is surrounded with uncertainty (i.e., it requires investigation of the unknown rather than application of the known).
2. Often progresses by turning up answers in surprising places (i.e., the discipline or technology area, where an answer might be found is unknown ahead of time).
3. Is both an intellectual and intuitive process that requires creativity and luck.
4. Does not necessarily progress through an orderly series of stages (i.e., instead of working forward from well-defined objectives in a well-defined manner, it often works backward from observation of an interesting phenomena to exploration of possible uses for it).
5. Does not thrive under the application of traditional management principles and techniques (i.e., they will inhibit or even destroy creativity).

Obviously, how the manager views the invention-innovation process is closely tied to the methods and degree of detail employed in the planning of individual projects. The two substantially different planning approaches dictated by these views can be called the quantitative and qualitative approaches. The assumptions can be summarized as follows.

Quantitative Planning Approach:

1. Assumes that the invention-innovation process approximates the rational view.
2. Responsibility for planning should be organizationally focused.
3. Assumes that a relatively small number of decision criteria can be defined that, when properly related, can be used to specify the desirability of allocating resources to each alternative project.
4. Assumes that well-informed individuals can provide meaningful inputs, such as cost, manpower needs, and probability of technical success, regarding the characteristics of projects.
5. Assumes that the potential benefit contribution of projects can be assessed ahead of time.

Qualitative Planning Approach:

1. Assumes the invention-innovation process approximates the nonrational view.
2. Responsibility for planning should be organizationally diffused.
3. Planning is viewed as principally a function of the individual professional.
4. Views goal setting and planning as a bottom-up process (i.e., the result of putting together the individual project planning of the professionals).
5. Assumes that subjective guesses about project characteristics and benefits are not really meaningful for decision-making purposes.

Each approach has its major advocates who champion their merits. Each has supporters among progressive and successful technical managers. In the following discussions of different approaches, remember that the purpose of the process is to:

1. Aid in making decisions more logically consistent.
2. Allow managers to identify more clearly the projects worth investing time and effort in and eliminating the less useful.
3. Allow managers to terminate unsuccessful projects at the earliest possible time.
4. Serve as a communications link between management and the professional staff.

The purpose of a decision model is not to make decisions for the manager. The manager is still the decision maker. The models supply information that will hopefully enable the manager to make better (more profitable) decisions.

8.2 Quantitative Methods

In an excellent survey article, Clarke [2] noted that by 1973 well over 100 different quantitative models for the evaluation and selection of technical projects had been proposed. Furthermore, new ones have been appearing at a rate of about 15 per year. It is therefore obviously not possible to discuss all or even most of the models proposed.

The quantitative models typically seek to evaluate a technical project through the use of mathematical formulas. Formulas in use often include terms for factors such as:

1. Profits from products created or improved through the project.
2. Savings from processes, methods, or raw materials improved or discovered through the project.

3. Income from research—derived royalties.
4. Royalty payments to other organizations, eliminated by the project.
5. Profits attributable to the project—created goodwill.
6. Investments in R&D programs.
7. Investments required to bring research to commercial fruition.

The technical manager works within a frame of reference defined by organizational policy. The parent organization's field of interest obviously limits the scope of the activity. Within the boundaries established by organizational objectives, the most significant criterion for selecting a project is what it will do for the parent organization. Indeed, no technical project would be undertaken if it were known in advance that the parent organization would not benefit. Therefore, a major objective of technical management policy is profit and benefits derived, and quantitative systems are attempts to obtain better appraisals of the profit and benefit potential of projects.

Although most executives and technical managers have had little success in applying mathematical formulas to the evaluation of technical projects, many researchers continue efforts to develop valid quantitative yardsticks. Moore and Baker [13] have suggested that the quantitative methods (based on the method of analysis) can be classified into four categories.

1. *Scoring Models.* Compute an overall project score based on the ratings of the project against preselected criteria. The ratings are assigned by individuals or groups against each relevant criterion, weighted, and amalgamated into one final score for each project.
2. *Economic Models.* Employ calculations such as net present value of expenditures and returns, internal rate of return, or payback period. Utilize some form of profitability index.
3. *Risk Analysis Models.* In recognition that decision parameters such as cost, revenue, etc., are random variables, these models seek to establish the probability distribution of selected decision parameters such as rate of return or market share.
4. *Constrained Optimization Models.* Seek to optimize some economic objective function, subject to a set of specified resource constraints.

Clearly the lines of distinction between these groupings are vague. In reality, a particular model may combine features associated with more than one category. However, the categorization will be useful in organizing the following description of some typical models reported in the literature. This discussion does not exhaust the wide variety of methods proposed; it is merely illustrative, not comprehensive.

8.3 Scoring Models

This method involves the identification of a small number of criteria or factors that are critical to the success of a project. Such factors might include total cost, time to completion, probability of technical success, probability of commercial success, and size of potential market. Competing projects are then evaluated as to how well they meet each of the criteria and are assigned a number indicative of this degree of compliance. The numbers assigned are then combined to form a project score. The individual criteria numbers are usually combined into this overall score by use of either an additive or multiplicative rule. The higher the overall score, the more desirable the project.

Typical in many respects of a great many scoring models is that reported by Dean and Nishry [6]. The two primary decision criteria considered by the model are technical desirability and market desirability. Sets of factors are defined that express the salient features of the candidate projects regarding these two decision criteria. The total score (Z_i) for project i is taken as a weighted average of its technical and market scores. Thus the total score is given by

$$Z_i = a \sum_{j=1}^{J} V_j W_{ij} + b \sum_{k=1}^{K} X_k Y_{ik}$$

where

V_j = weight for the jth technical factor
W_{ij} = value for project i in technical factor j
X_k = weight for the kth market factor
Y_{ik} = value for project i in market factor k
a,b = decision variables, $a,b \geqslant 0, a + b = 1$

Obviously, this model generalizes readily to any number of decision criteria. Dean and Nishry describe the phases and steps of an application of their model in a company that uses a review board for project evaluation and selection. Of particular interest is the method used to derive the factor weights. Basically, review board rank orders were amalgamated and converted into numerical values, assuming equal intervals between adjacent ranks and assuming a one-person, one-vote rule. The review board was also involved in the evaluation of the projects by collectively assigning values to each project for each factor. The result of the evaluation is a rank ordering of the projects, each with an associated total score Z_i. It remains to select the subset of the candidate projects that provides maximum payoff subject to some resource constraint (such as manpower); that is, we want to find binary decision variables s_i such that we

$$\text{Maximize} \quad G = \sum_{i=1}^{I} s_i Z_i$$

$$\text{subject to} \quad \sum_{i=1}^{I} m_i s_i \leq M$$

where:
$$s_i = \begin{cases} 1 & \text{if selected} \\ 0 & \text{otherwise} \end{cases}$$
$$M = \text{Manhour limit}$$
$$m_i = \text{Manhours for project i}$$

No solution method is suggested for the optimization problem, but note that it is nothing more than a simple 0-1, single-dimension, knapsack formulation.

Moore and Baker [13] argue that although more rigorous analyses might be warranted in the engineering or marketing phases of the product cycle, because of data unavailability and the relatively low economic risk in the R&D phases, scoring models are particularly appropriate for R&D project selection. They present a detailed, step-by-step procedure for systematically constructing a general scoring model. In addition, a method for validating the model design features is discussed generally.

The primary advantage associated with scoring models is their ability to contend with multiple decision criteria. Another advantage is that scoring models typically operate on data that can be developed with low-cost methods. There are, however, disadvantages encountered in the use of scoring models. Both the models and their data are thought to be normally less accurate than their counterparts in economic, risk analysis, and constrained optimization categories. Furthermore, composite project scores are usually dimensionless numbers not tied to a well-defined structure and lacking a well-defined meaning. Since they possess no physical significance, the quantifiers are frequently regarded with suspicion.

8.4 Economic Models

Economic models generally attempt to quantify for each candidate project the expected or the most probable value of a selected decision parameter, which is economic in nature. There are many possible decision parameters from which to choose, including:

1. Return on original investment [average yearly return ÷ (original investment + working capital)].
2. Payout time [original investment ÷ (profit + average yearly depreciation)].
3. Present worth (income − outgo, discounted to present).

Most of the formulas suggested for project selection are simple and include terms for anticipated costs and returns and generally, but not always, a term for risk or probability of success. For example, one of the earliest formulas reported in the literature [16] used the index of return (IR).

$$\text{Value of a new project} = \frac{\text{Estimated IR} \times \text{Probability of success}}{\text{Estimated cost of research}}$$

where the IR is computed as:

IR = the value of the process savings for
1 year + 3 percent of the sales
value of new products each year for
5 years + 2 percent of the sales
value of improved products each year
for 2 years

Disman [7] reports a scheme in which expenditure for a technical project is thought of as an investment. Over a certain period of time, the income stream from the investment should return the original investment plus a profit. Thus:

$$\text{Investment} + \frac{\text{Rate of return on the}}{\text{technical expenditure}} \times \text{Investment} = \text{Income}$$

For 1 year, this expression becomes

$$\text{Investment } (1 + r) = \text{Income in 1 year}$$

$$\text{Investment} = \frac{\text{Income for 1 year}}{1 + r}$$

where r = rate of return on R&D expenditure.

This equation is then used to determine the maximum expenditure justified (MEJ) for a technical project, given a rate of return expected from the technical effort and estimated net income from the product developed. This scheme further utilizes two risk factors, risk of technical success (R_t) and risk of commercial or utilization success (R_c). Thus, the MEJ calculation for a project payoff over n years becomes:

$$\text{MEJ} = R_c R_t \sum_{i=1}^{n} \frac{\text{Estimated net income in } i\text{th year}}{(1+r)^i}$$

where

$\qquad$ MEJ = maximum expense justified

$\qquad$ R_c = risk of commercial or utilization success

$\qquad$ R_t = risk of technical success

$\qquad$ r = rate of return on technical effort expenditure

Rubenstein suggests evaluating results by comparing the 5-year estimated revenue with the total estimated development expense [17]. Results are evaluated by these formulas:

$$\text{Return on investment} = \frac{\text{New earnings (after taxes)}}{\text{Total investment involved}}$$

$$\text{Payout period} = \frac{\text{Capital outlay on projects}}{\text{New average annual revenue (after taxes)}}$$

The estimated return value of the technical results are sometimes evaluated in terms of the present worth or discounted net value (DNV) of the anticipated results. The determination of the present worth of a proposed project involves calculation of any tangible earnings or savings computed in terms of the net return on capital investment, current interest rates, and capital recovery periods. Because the results are expressed as estimates, this refinement is usually eliminated, except where the projects are expected to run over several budget periods. One formula widely used for this calculation is

$$P = R + \frac{\dfrac{D}{R!}}{(1+R!)^n - 1}$$

where

$\qquad$ P = present worth of net income

$\qquad$ D = net income

$\qquad$ $R!$ = average net return on capital investment in the enterprise

$\qquad$ R = current rate of interest

$\qquad$ n = capital recovery period in years

Others have proposed a different type of evaluation that establishes a measure of "venture profit" that is distinguished from the normal profit generally realized in the business. The profit on a given investment in research and plant after taxes is compared with the same investment in going operations. Various research projects can then be compared on the basis of their anticipated extra return.

Dean and Sengupta [4] proposed a variation of the IR formula. Assuming that a project succeeds technically in that a usable result will be derived and that the results are exploited or commercialized, a measure of relative performance of any two projects is furnished by the ratio

$$\pi = \frac{\text{Present value of future returns from the project}}{\text{Present value of future efforts required for the project}} = \frac{S}{R}$$

The ratio of π is referred to as the payoff function of a project. The returns and efforts are measured in dollars. If the rates of return and spending are continuous functions of time, this ratio can be expressed as

$$\pi = \frac{\int_0^\alpha s(t)e^{-\rho t}\, dt}{\int_0^\alpha r(t)e^{-\rho t}\, dt} = \frac{S}{R}$$

where

t = time in years since the inception of the project

$s(t)$ = rate of return (either sales, or cost savings or incremental sales) at time t

$r(t)$ = rate of spending on the project at time t

ρ = a discount factor, which the firm can choose at will

An index π_i for the ith project in a set indicates the expected dollar worth of future sales per dollar of future expenditure on R&D. Dean and Sengupta suggest that the uncertainty about the future status of competition and customer acceptability can be introduced by choosing an appropriate level of the discounting factor ρ.

In a later paper Dean and Sengupta [5] approached the overall problem in two phases.

1. Establish the corporate technical budget.
2. Distribute this budget among the competing projects.

The approach taken in phase 1 was to adopt the technical budget, which would maximize for the following year the expected value of the ratio

$$\frac{SR - PC - OH - RDC}{GVP}$$

where

SR = sales revenue
PC = production cost
OH = overhead costs (sales, administration, etc.)
RDC = R&D costs
GVP = gross value of the plant

For three firms under consideration, estimates of the following relationships were developed from historical data for successive year pairs.

1. Decrease in production cost due to process research expenditures.
2. Increase in ratio of total sales to old product sales resulting from increased product research expenditures and from decreased production cost.
3. Increase in capital expenditures required by increasing ratio of total sales to old product sales and decreasing production cost.
4. Impact of R&D expenditures on an average share of the market and subsequently on overhead costs.

These functions were then used to relate R&D budget value to the constituent elements of the objective ratio. Thus, in maximizing the ratio, we actually maximize expected net return on plant investment. A 31-step iterative algorithm is given for solving the phase 1 problem.

The method proposed by Dean and Sengupta for the phase 2 problem assumes that "no significant changes in the business environment and competitive behavior will take place in the foreseeable future"; therefore pricing and selling policies are well known. The first step for phase 2 is to compute for each candidate project i a payoff index P_i as

$$P_i = P(ts) \cdot P(c{:}ts) \cdot E(pv)$$

where

$P(ts)$ = probability of technical success
$P(c{:}ts)$ = probability of commercialization given technical success
$E(pv)$ = expectation of project present value function

A heuristic method for selecting projects is proposed that consists of ranking them by payoff and selecting those with the largest payoff until the budget is depleted. Projects not selected would be either terminated or not initiated.

The overall two-phase approach of Dean and Sengupta is simple and would be readily understood by most managers. There would be some effort involved in establishing the functional relationships required by phase 1, but this would be no real problem given sufficient historical data. The principal limitation of the method is its shortsightedness. Since budgeting is essentially done year by year, the potential exists to overlook opportunities with long-term payoff. The "optimization" procedure outlined is, of course, very crude by today's standards and should be replaced by a 0-1, branch and bound, single-dimension, knapsack algorithm to obtain an exact solution.

Dean and Nishry [6] proposed a discounted profitability or economic model aimed at three types of product research projects.

Type 1.

Project will lead to a new product line having no significant effect on profitability of existing products.

Type 2.

Project will lead to new product within existing line possibly effecting profitability of others.

Type 3.

Project will lead to changes in exisiting product or process.

The profit P^*_i for each project i is computed as follows.

$$P^*_i = \begin{cases} P_i & \text{for project Type 1} \\ P_i \sum_{j=1}^{J} P_{ij} & \text{for project Type 2} \\ P_i + P_{ij} & \text{for project Type 3} \end{cases}$$

where

$$P_i = [\sum_{n=1}^{N_i} S_i(n)(p_i - m_i - k_i) \, d^n - T_i]q_i - D_i$$

$$P_{ij} = [\sum_{n=1}^{N_{ij}} S_{ij}(n)(p_{ij} - m_{ij} - k_{ij}) \, d^n]q_i$$

N_i = sales life (years) of new product
N_{ij} = loss in sales life of product j resulting from new product
$S_i(n)$ = units sold in year n due to project i
$S_{ij}(n)$ = change in sales of product j in year n due to project i
P_i = unit sales price of new product resulting from project i
P_{ij} = unit sales price of improved product j
m_i = unit manufacturing cost of new product from project i

m_{ij} = unit manufacturing cost of improved products
k_i = unit marketing and general cost for new product
k_{ij} = unit marketing and general cost
d = $1/(1 + r)$
r = annual rate of return on investment.
T_i = tooling cost for new product
q_i = probability that project i leads to a new product
D_i = development cost to complete project i

Dean and Nishry present this economic model in the context of a single-dimension, knapsack, optimization formulation.

The economic model was tested on a sample of six projects (three of type 1, one of type 2, and two of type 3). It was conjectured that the most uncertain input parameter was forecast sales, $S_i(n)$. A sensitivity analysis to this parameter was conducted assuming a management decision criterion of selecting project i if $P_i^* \geq C$, the minimum acceptable profit. It was concluded that at the ± 25 percent level, with profit uniformly distributed, essentially the same ranking of the projects resulted for profit maximization as risk minimization.

8.5   Risk Analysis Models

In this section the features of risk analysis models that are peculiar to that category will be discussed. Risk analysis models basically represent an extension to economic models; however, risk analyses have been performed over a domain of optimized subproblems [10]. The fundamental objective of risk analysis is to quantify the probability distribution of some selected decision parameter, recognizing that it is a function of random variables. Subsequently, it is desired that this information be input to the decision process in some fashion. In an article written to sell this notion to managers, Hertz [9] supports the use of simulation to generate the desired probability distribution. The article indicates the types of data that can be generated by simulation techniques. An example is presented that claims that simulation produced a different "expected return" from "the one best estimate approach." Since Hertz is really addressing the maximum likelihood estimate of return, this result is to be expected. Note additionally that with the traditional definition of expectation, simulation will produce a similar result when interactions between random variables are permitted. Thus simulation can produce more accurate estimates of real expected values than a deterministic expected value analysis, which involves independence.

The central issue in risk analysis is how the distribution information can be used once it is generated. Hertz states that ''the courage to act boldly in the face of apparent uncertainty can be greatly bolstered by the clarity of portrayal of the risks and possible rewards.'' Hertz presents an example of the use of a plot comparing the cumulative distribution functions for the percents of return on two investments. For a small number of alternatives this is probably a good approach to communicating the risk analyses results. Merely presenting the decision maker with three sigma parameter values is certainly not adequate. The implications of these data should at least be explained in terms of decision criteria such as maximax, maximin, expected value maximization, and maximum likelihood maximization.

Lockett and Freeman [10] offer an example of the use of risk analysis in conjunction with optimized economic submodels. They view projects not as discrete entities, but as activities in which one might engage ''partway.'' The optimization subproblem is solved by maximizing a linear payoff objective function subject to $m \cdot t$ constraints, where m = the number of resources involved and t = the number of time periods. In addition, the decision variables are restricted such that $0 \leq x_i \leq 1$ for each project i. The tacit assumption is that the payoff from project i will represent the same proportion of the total possible as do the resources committed to their respective totals. In the terminology of microeconomics, constant returns to scale have been assumed within each project. Lockett and Freeman propose that each project be represented as a branching probabilistic network of its constituent elemental activities. The resources required for each activity are allowed to depend on the particular path taken through the network. For a particular random sample (path) a set of resource requirements is developed for each project. Linear programming is employed to solve the optimization subproblem. The optimal result is then recorded as a random sample outcome. This process is repeated many times and generates probabilistic information regarding the probability of each project being an optimal selection. The results of this simulation analysis were presented in comparison to other solution methods. Lockett and Freeman demonstrated that their method is feasible in practice and that it supports sensitivity analyses, but they proposed no direct method for using their quantitative results in a decision situation. Again, the fundamental problem of relating risk analysis results to a viable decision criterion is seen.

8.6 Constrained Optimization Models

The category of constrained optimization models also represents an extension to basic economic models. Souder [20], in a study performed at the Monsanto Co., employed dynamic programming to solve the following formulation.

$$\text{Maximize} \quad Z = \sum_{j=1}^{J} [G_j \cdot P_j(x_j) - x_j]$$

$$\text{subject to} \quad \sum_{j=1}^{J} x_j \leq B$$

$$L_j \leq x_j \leq U_j$$

where

      $G_j =$ present value of gross profit from successful project j

   $P_j(x_j) =$ general nondecreasing function giving probability of success from resource expended on project j

      $L_j =$ lower bound on resource permitted for project j

      $U_j =$ upper bound on resource permitted for project j

The use of dynamic programming allowed for generality in the form of $P_j(x_j)$. The problem was decomposed over time using time periods as stages.

Lockett and Gear [11] defined a number of versions N_j for each project j. The versions of a given project reflected different start dates and rates of planned resource usage. The objective was to

$$\text{Maximize} \quad Z = \sum_{j=1}^{J} \sum_{n=1}^{N_j} R_{jn} x_{jn}$$

$$\text{subject to} \quad \sum_{n=1}^{N_j} x_{jn} \leq 1, \quad \text{for } j = 1, 2, \ldots, J$$

where $R_{jn} =$ return from version n of project j.

The interesting feature of this formulation is that it allows noninteger solutions. The assumption is that for each project j an implementable and at least near-optimal project structure can be defined as a weighted linear combination of the characteristics of its N_j versions, using x_{jn} (for $n = 1, 2, \ldots, N_j$) as the weights.

Weingartner [24] explores some interesting notions in the application of mathematical programming to problems with dependencies among the candidate projects. Constraints are suggested that accommodate the dependency. Restricting ourselves to binary variables, if project a may be attempted only if project b is selected and project b is independent of all other alternatives, this relationship may be expressed by

$$X_a \leqslant X_b \qquad \text{or} \qquad X_a(1 - X_b) = 0$$

This dependency may be generalized to any number of projects. If projects a and b are mutually exclusive, the following would be appropriate.

$$X_a + X_b \leqslant 1 \qquad \text{or} \qquad X_a \cdot X_b = 0$$

If projects b and c are mutually exclusive and project a is contingent on selection of b or c, we may use

$$X_a \leqslant X_b + X_c \leqslant 1$$

Similarly, if a and b are mutually exclusive and contingent on selection of one of three other mutually exclusive projects c, d, and e, we may use

$$X_a + X_b \leqslant X_c + X_d + X_e \leqslant 1$$

These approaches are merely a sample of the work that has been done in mathematical programming and that may be brought to bear on problems of technical project selection. Weingartner [24] also reviews methods for introducing probabilistic considerations and nonlinear utility functions.

8.7 Comparison of Methods

Several studies in the literature compare different approaches to the problem of project selection. Dean and Nishry [6] report on the results of their comparison of a scoring model with the economic model attributed to them. When tested on a sample case with six candidate projects, the two methods produced exactly the same rank ordering of the projects. This is as much a statement about the projects as one about the methods used to evaluate them, since different decision criteria were considered. The essence of their qualitative comparison of the two methods is that the scoring model is simple to use, requires minimum data, and accounts for intangible factors; but it does not produce a utility measure and, through its use of ordinal data, involves a linearity assumption. The economic model produces a well-defined utility measure and accounts for nonlinear factors, but it requires extensive data and is limited to consideration of economic factors.

Moore and Baker [14], recognizing that technical portfolio composition represents a sequence of time phased decisions and that different models may be appropriate at different times, address a different issue. In determining if a scoring model can be made to be consistent with economic models and constrained optimization models, they compare the three models on their treatment of economic data only. On the basis of steady-state rank-correlation coefficients, the conclusion is reached that by using nine or more scoring intervals and an additive scoring model index, considerable intermodel consistency can be achieved, particularly between the scoring model and the economic model. This would indicate that one could expect to make early phase decisions with a properly designed scoring model and later switch to an economic model with minimal perturbation of results because of model differences. It was also noted in the study that intermodel rank correlations were more sensitive to error in mean estimates than error in dispersion estimates.

Lockett and Freeman [10] compared their risk analysis model to the expected value economic model on a sample case of nine projects and four time periods. Their simulation analysis revealed a most probable solution exhibiting a 0.8 percent improvement in objective function value over the expected value solution. They were also able to generate resource usage variability data and project-portfolio outcome variability data that could not be obtained from the expected value analysis.

Finally, Souder [22] found that economic models and scoring models had higher ease of use and lower cost, while constrained optimization models had higher realism and flexibility. Souder [21] also suggested that the choice of which project selection model to use may depend on the manager's objectives and the life-cycle of the set of available projects.

Scoring models hold great promise for problem solutions that involve a multiplicity of decision criteria. Although they are primarily descriptive, they may be used in a prescriptive fashion if the decision maker so desires. A primary difficulty with scoring models in the past has been the techniques employed for interperson and intercriterion score amalgamation. The full range of applications in this area of the theory developed by Arrow, Kendall, and others is only now being investigated. Another problem faced by scoring model advocates is the criticism regarding the "softness" of much of their input data.

Economic models offer the advantage of a well-defined, single-utility measure. Their results are in a form that can be most readily understood by managers, particularly for situations in which the managers intend to incorporate subjectively considerations of other criteria into the decision process. In such a situation descriptive data of the expected value type are probably all the decision maker could effectively assimilate. However, when the intent is to make project selections on a primarily economic basis, there seems to be no reason not to extend the economic analysis to include considerations of risk and, if prescriptive results are desired, constrained optimization would also be appropriate. This level of analytical sophistication is sometimes regarded as excessive in view of the limited confidence in many of the data elements used.

8.8   Limitations of Current Methods

It is clear from a number of surveys [8, 23] that formal mathematical models are rarely used in industry or government despite the voluminous literature on the subject. The reasons are:

1. Lack of reliable cost, time, performance, and utility estimates.
2. Inadequate handling of risk and uncertainty.
3. Need for multiple criteria for evaluation.
4. Lack of recognition of the interrelationships between and among projects.
5. Ignoring the relationship between effort applied to a project and the chance for success.
6. Continuous nature of project selection and review.

No matter how sophisticated and mathematically correct the proposed formulas and ratios may be, the answers derived will be no better than the input data. Unfortunately, studies have shown how unreliable the estimates of cost, time, performance, and utility actually are. The findings of a group at the RAND Corporation studying military R&D projects bring this into clear focus [12]. Cost estimates based on paper design studies have tended to be highly unreliable. For example, estimates of the production cost of missiles erred by factors ranging from 1.3 to 57.6, with a mean of 17.1. Slippage in availability-of-aircraft estimates ranged up to 5 years, with a mean of 2 years. Cost estimates of R&D costs for all systems studied missed by factors of five or more. More recent studies by Thomas [23] and Norris [15] shows that 12 years later, nothing had changed.

Uncertainties are great even after a project had progressed to a point where investment in plant and equipment is necessary. Carter and Williams [1], studying British companies, found that even with an attempt to estimate project return *after the development stage,* the correlation between actual return and estimated return was an extremely low factor of 0.13. Again almost 12 years later, Thomas [23] found no improvement.

In addition to the inaccuracies of cost and time estimates, there is another problem with obtaining the probability of technical success and probability of successful usage or commercialization. The only source of such probability estimates is the subjective judgment of technical and marketing personnel. Unfortunately, such subjective judgments have been shown again and again to be highly biased. For example, Rubenstein and Schroder [18] showed that if the person giving the estimate was either the idea originator or was prospectively responsible for carrying out the project, the resulting assessment would be high. On the other hand, if the assessment was being made by higher management levels, the higher the rank of the assessor, the lower the assigned probability. Rubenstein and Schroder explained the first finding on the basis of the assessor wanting to see the project approved. The second finding they attributed to attempts to replace personal gaps in knowledge with conservatism and an increased awareness of organizational constraints.

There is also evidence that if the assessor knows that top management is keenly interested in a project, this also causes the probability given to be biased. Souder [21] reports on two cases with differing results. In the first, the perception of top management's specific interest resulted in the reduction of the believed subjective probability before its upward communication. This allowed the assessor to look good if the project is successful and to refer to the low prospects for success if it fails. In the second case, the probability assessment was raised before being communicated ". . . to detract management's attention from problem areas while buying time to work out these problem areas." Thus, although it is evident that top-management interest can distort the probability estimates, it is not clear what direction that bias will take.

Besides problems of getting valid estimates of pertinent parameters, no sound method exists for apportioning credit for a project's return between a company's technical department and its other functional groups. If we attempt to evaluate a technical project in terms of its ultimate effect on sales or profit contributions, we are really evaluating the effectiveness of the whole company. Finally, costs usually cannot be allocated among various projects, except subjectively and imprecisely. However impressively mathematical they may look, formulas based on such figures provide answers no sounder and no more trustworthy than the personal judgments that underlie these figures.

In the realm of government or university research, one is confronted with all of the preceding problems, plus several not faced by industry. As discussed earlier, the technical manager in government cannot as easily tie decisions to dollars and profits. In many (in fact, in most) cases, it is impossible to attach a dollar figure to the value of successful completion of a project. Dollar values ascribed to factors such as national prestige, human life, psychological impact, and others that government executives must deal with are meaningless or, at best, of a highly questionable nature. For example, how would one assign a dollar value to a universal cure for cancer? What is the quantitative value of a major advance in knowledge or understanding? Methods proposed at present do not offer adequate tools for handling these problems.

On the other hand, the strictly qualitative approach is not entirely satisfactory either. Although it may help to spread the blame for poor decisions, it really does not appreciably help the decision maker. It does not provide the analytical structure so sorely needed.

True, formulas do not provide precise answers, but some aspects of technology are fairly well suited to quantification. Moreover, the mere calculation of quantitative values—where they are appropriate—forces managers to think about the project's contribution in a concrete and orderly way. In other words, although evaluation of any technical program requires many qualitative judgments, appropriate numerical data *can* still be useful in appraising some of its aspects and in formalizing the entire evaluation process.

8.9 Current Practice

Surveys show fairly conclusively that formal, mathematical methods for selecting technical projects are seldom used [8]. On the other hand, it is equally clear that all organizations do use both quantitative and qualitative criteria in their selection process. For example, Dean [3] found that 100 percent of the companies surveyed used some sort of quantitative criteria and that 80 percent used one or more economic criteria.

Another interesting survey of techniques actually used was conducted by a task force appointed by the Industrial Research Institute [8]. They found that the selection process used was a function of the nature and cost of the project. This should not be surprising; as we have already seen, the degree of control that we wish to exercise is inversely proportional to the degree of creativity required to carry out a project. Furthermore, as shown in Figure 8.1, the cost

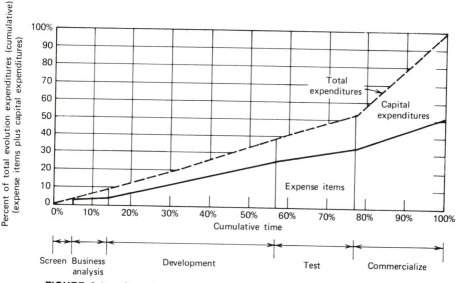

FIGURE 8.1   Cumulative expenditures vs time for new product by state of evolution—all industry average. (Source: Booz-Allen & Hamilton Inc.)

of a project increases as it moves up the technology spectrum (Figure 1.3) from research through development. The IRI task force categorized all technical projects studied in the three classifications of (1) exploratory, (2) high-risk business development, and (3) support of existing business.

For projects of an exploratory nature, they found that the selection process was characterized as follows.

1. Responsibility for approval was usually within the technical group. Generally all that was required was approval of the immediate supervisor.
2. The selection process is generally simple, unsophisticated, and informal. At most a one- or two-page proposal is all that is required.
3. The selection process was based primarily on qualitative judgments that considered criteria such as:
   (a) Consistency with corporate objectives.
   (b) Technical soundness.
   (c) Availability of the type personnel required.
   (d) Availability of special facilities or equipment.
   (e) Reputation and interest of originator.
   (f) Seriousness and importance of the problem addressed.
4. The selection process is influenced most by the views and background of one person or a small group of people.

The project that entailed expansion into a new business area, such as new products, or a significant change in processes used were classified as high-risk business development. For these projects, the selection process was characterized as follows.

1. Responsibility for project selection resided with a corporate-level management committee often headed by the firm's president or another high corporate officer.
2. Quantitative data such as economic projections were likely to be generated (often by other technical function groups) and compared to other opportunities.
3. There was very limited use of quantitative methods for considering risk and uncertainty of projections.
4. Formal proposals with quantitative backup of projected costs, schedules, and results were generally prepared.
5. Proposals that would result in significant changes in the way of doing business were strongly advocated and pushed by one or more of the top executives.

The projects that entailed process improvement or cost reduction proposals were categorized as support of existing business. The selection process for this type of project was characterized as follows.

1. The selection process was strongly influenced by nontechnical function profit center managers in addition to the technical manager.
2. Project selection was based on standard cost effectiveness criteria and urgency of need.
3. Economic feasibility studies usually preceded implementation.
4. There was relatively low uncertainty as to probability of success or results.

In summary, surveys show that project selection becomes more rigorous and sophisticated as the expenditure level increases and the uncertainty of technical success decreases. Exploratory projects are selected on a more or less intuitive or subjective basis, while more costly projects are selected using more rigorous methods. For example, we find that in exploratory projects, the work is decided on by the idea originator and the first-line supervisor with a short informal write-up of activities and costs. But, as a project requires more of the parent organization's resources, the selection process becomes more formal and more information is required, such as:

1. More detailed and accurate description of the technical objective.
2. Estimation of technical success.
3. Projected capital requirements.
4. Schedule for completion.
5. Probability of commercialization or utilization success.
6. Estimation of return on investment.
7. Risk analysis and discounted cash flow analysis.

8.10 Other Factors Influencing Project Selection

Unquestionably, an important factor influencing project selection is the number and type of personnel available that can be assigned to a particular project or activity. If certain capabilities or skills are lacking, time will be required to find and hire the necessary specialists. Alternative sources of capability should also be considered, such as contracting the project out to another company, hiring consultants, or purchasing the technology from outside (i.e., purchasing the rights to a product or process). Suppliers of instrumentation, equipment, and materials will sometimes take on a project at their own expense if the potential market is great enough.

Project selection is also highly influenced by environmental pressures and considerations. For example, a competitor may introduce a new or improved product or process that creates a flurry of activity to create equal or superior ones. Governmental agencies can provide extreme pressure to conduct certain projects in pollution control, product safety, or consumer and worker health safety. Political pressures such as expressed keen interest of higher executives can also exert strong influences on project selection. General economic conditions play a strong part by influencing (1) the amount of funds made available for the technical functions, (2) the psychological attitudes of top management, and (3) the marketing opportunities.

Numerous factors relating to the organizational and managerial climate in which the technical group must function also have an impact on project selection. The management style of the top technical administrator and his or her attitude toward technical work will be reflected in the decision-making process. An executive having a prolonged exposure to, or philosophical affinity toward, an academic environment may resist pressures from other functional areas and also oppose the institution of quantitative business analysis techniques in project planning and selection methodology. On the other hand, the director may feel that technical work must have clearly defined objectives and be closely aligned to economic concepts and, therefore, must be carefully programmed, controlled, and constantly reexamined, using the most modern decision-making techniques.

Efficient and open communication networks within an organization are prime factors in promoting good project selection. A free flow of information and open decision making encourage examination of all alternatives and making the best decisions with regard to desired activities. However, the technical organization, which consists of isolated pockets of people, will find it difficult to identify the most pressing or beneficial projects. An organization that encourages unencumbered channels of communication both within the technical group and between it and other functional areas will be much more likely to select the most meaningful projects.

Finally, the flexibility to start or stop projects at any time is critically important to good project selection. Rigid adherence to previous plans can have a stifling effect on any technical group. As work progresses on approved projects, new possibilities may open up or previously attractive projects be found not feasible or too costly. The technical staff should have considerable opportunity to start projects on a limited or exploratory basis without concern for bookkeeping or budgetary considerations. The group should have a reasonable amount of discretionary funds and time available for such purposes.

8.11   Proposed Project Selection Approach

After carefully considering the literature regarding proposals of how the selection process should be conducted and how it is actually conducted, I offer the following guidelines for developing a procedure.

1. Develop a complete definition of the group's goals, objectives, and the bounds within which it is to function.
2. Develop a checklist of criteria that should be considered in the evaluation. Table 8.1 presents some possibilities.
3. As project opportunities are presented for consideration, prepare a simple written proposal and determine whether each project meets the qualitative criteria of acceptability. A simple scoring model might be used for this purpose.
4. Those that pass the first screening should then be subjected to a more vigorous analysis (perhaps after some further exploratory work) commensurate with their cost. The more costly in terms of money and manpower, the closer the project should be scrutinized.
5. Each project should then be classified as mandatory, acceptable, deferred for further analysis, or rejected.
6. Those deemed mandatory or acceptable should then be compared to ongoing projects and a decision made as to relative priority and allocation of resources.
7. The entire portfolio of projects should be rigorously reviewed on a regular, periodic basis.

TABLE 8.1   Possible Project Criteria

Technical Aspects	Utilization Aspects
Availability of qualified technical personnel	Requirements for results
Availability of technical know-how	Availability of funding for implementation of results
Chances of technical success	Risk of early obsolescence of results
Alternatives to project	Effect on present operations
Adequacy of support personnel	Compatibility with present operations
Adequacy of facilities and equipment	Compatibility with corporate goals
Compatibility with existing projects	Value-to-cost ratio
Completion time relative to need	Impact on safety, reliability, and pollution problems

──────────────────────────── **References** ────────────────────────────

1. Carter, C. F., and B. R. Williams, *Innovation in Industry,* Oxford University Press, London, 1958.
2. Clarke, T. E., "Decision-Making in Technologically Based Organizations: A Literature Survey of Present Practice," *IEEE Transactions on Engineering Management, EM-21* (1), February 1974, pp. 9−23.
3. Dean, B. V., "Evaluating, Selecting and Controlling R&D Projects," American Management Association Research Study 89, New York, 1968.
4. Dean, B. V., and S. S. Sengupta, "A Dynamic Model for R&D Selection," Final Report, National Science Foundation contract NSF-C68, Case Institute of Technology, Operations Research Group, Cleveland, December 1959.
5. Dean, B. V., and S. S. Sengupta, "Research Budgeting and Project Selection," *IRE Transactions on Engineering Management, EM-9,* December 1962, pp. 158−169.
6. Dean, B. V., and N, J, Nishry, "Scoring and Profitability Models for Evaluating and Selecting Engineering Projects," *Operations Research, 13* (4), July-August 1965, pp. 550−570.
7. Dismon, S., "Selecting R and D Projects for Profit," *Chemical Engineering, 69* (26), December 24, 1962, pp. 87−90.
8. Gee, R. E., "A Survey of Current Project Selection Practices," *Research Management, 14* (5), September 1971, pp. 38−45.
9. Hertz, D. B., "Risk Analysis in Capital Investment," *Harvard Business Review, 42* (1), January-February 1964, pp. 95−106.
10. Lockett, A. G., and P. Freeman, "Probabilistic Networks and R and D Portfolio Selection," *Operational Research Quarterly, 21* (3), September 1970, pp. 353−359.
11. Lockett, A. G., and A. E. Gear, "Program Selection in R&D," *Management Science, 18* (10), June 1972, pp. B575-B590.
12. Marshall, A. W., and W. H. Meakling, "Predictability of the Costs, Time and Success of Development," RAND Corporation Report No. P-1821, revised December 11, 1959.
13. Moore, J. R., and N. R. Baker, "An Analytical Approach to Scoring Model Design-Application to R&D Project Selection," *IEEE Transactions on Engineering Management, EM-16* (3), August 1969, pp. 90−98.
14. Moore, J. R., and N. R. Baker, "Computational Analysis of Scoring Models for R and D Project Selection," *Management Science, 16* (4), December 1969, pp. B212-B232.
15. Norris, K. P., "The Accuracy of Project Cost and Duration Estimates in Industrial R&D," *R&D Management, 2* (1), October 1971, pp. 25−26.
16. Olsen, F., "The Control of Research Funds," *Coordination and Financing of Industrial Research,* A. H. Rubenstein, Editor, Kings Crown Press, New York, 1955.
17. Rubenstein, A. H. "Setting Criteria of R and D," *Harvard Business Review, 35* (1), January-February 1957.
18. Rubenstein, A. H., and H. H. Schroder, "Managerial Differences in Assessing

Probabilities of Technical Success for R&D Projects,'' *Management Science, 24* (2), October 1977, pp. 137−148.

19. Schon, D. A., *Technology and Change,* Dell, New York, 1967.
20. Souder, W. E., "Selecting and Staffing R and D Projects via Operations Research," *Chemical Engineering Progress, 63* (11), November 1967, pp. 27−37.
21. Souder, W. E., "The Validity of Subjective Probability of Success Forecasts by R&D Project Managers," *IEEE Transactions on Engineering Management, EM-16* (1), February 1969, pp. 35−49.
22. Souder, W. E., "Comparative Analysis of R&D Investment Models," *AIIE Transactions, 4* (1), March 1972, pp. 57−64.
23. Thomas, H., "Some Evidence on the Accuracy of Forecasts in R&D Projects, " *R&D Management, 1* (2), February 1971, pp. 55−69.
24. Weingartner, H. M., "Capital Budgeting of Interrelated Projects, Survey and Synthesis," *Management Science, 12* (7), March 1966, pp. 485−516.

––––––––––––––––––––––– **Discussion Questions** –––––––––––––––––––

1. Should the interests and qualifications of the project initiator play a part in project selection?
2. How can internal political considerations impact the project selection process?
3. Can project desirability considerations be separated from resource allocation decisions?
4. Should factors such as potential revenues, probability of successful utilization and justification of need be provided by the technical groups or by others?
5. Discuss the pros and cons of quantitative versus qualitative criteria for project selection.
6. Do quantitative selection techniques threaten the technical executives decision-making authority?
7. Should the initiator or advocate of a project be allowed to present and defend the project before the decision maker?
8, Who should have the major responsibility in selecting new product development projects—marketing or the technical group?
9. Projects appear in applied research laboratories and development engineering organizations. How should the selections planning and control schemes differ?
10. Is previous experience in a technical area essential to good project selection decision making?

––––––––––––––––––––––––– **Case Study VIII** –––––––––––––––––––

MELCOM INDUSTRIES

Paul Lutz was sitting at his desk going over his slides for the presentation he was to give that afternoon at the budget review meeting. Lutz had come to Melcom 6 months ago, directly from school after obtaining his master's degree. He had spent the entire period working on a new material handling system for the automatic leveling and stabilizing jacks the company made. These jacks were sold to travel trailer manufacturers and recreation vehicle (RV) dealers. The automatic jack system took all of the work out of setting up a travel trailer. Upon arrival at a destination, the owner simply disconnects the trailer hitch from the towing vehicle and punches a button on the control box. The heart of the system is a simple microprocessor that controls four individually motor-driven jacks. Each jack also contains pressure sensitive switches to inform the controller when contact is made with the ground. A mercury switch tells the controller when the trailer is level in all directions.

The rapid growth of the RV industry had placed severe pressure on the manufacturing facility to increase the production rate and reduce manufacturing costs. Lutz had been hired to look at the material handling aspects, because he had written his master's thesis under a professor who was widely known for his theoretical work in the area of material handling. He had eagerly accepted the job offer, because it would allow him to apply the techniques he had been studying.

Lutz had spent the past 6 months planning the system, drawing layouts, constructing models, and checking out computer simulations of the proposed system. He was confident that he had come up with a good design. Bill Klausner, the chief of industrial engineering, had been very lavish in his praise of Lutz's technical work. The project had now reached the point where a capital investment proposal for implementation had been prepared and was ready to go before the budget review committee for approval.

The budget review committee was a corporate group composed of the major officers. All capital investments requiring an expenditure of $150,000 or more had to be approved by this board. Lutz's system was projected to cost $275,000 to implement. He had calculated the rate of return on present investment to be 25 percent, which was above the firm's minimum standard rate of return for capital investments. He felt confident of his data and was very pleased when Klausner had asked him to make the presentation of the proposal to the board. After running through his presentation slides one more time, he went off to lunch.

That afternoon, Lutz was the third person to present a proposal to the board. Each of the previous proposals had taken 30 minutes for presentation and discussion. This had surprised Lutz, since his technical presentation alone had taken 45 minutes during the dry runs. Klausner had told him to keep the presentation as short and concise as possible, and he had cut it back from the 1-hour presentation he had originally prepared.

Lutz had grown very nervous while he waited outside the conference room, but he had been greatly put at ease by the friendly greeting he had received and the obvious informality of the board members as he was introduced to each one. The board members were John Daniels, the president; Ronald Walls, the vice president for sales; Curtis Holman, the vice president for manufacturing; Jim Hubbard, the director for new product development; and Helen Day, the comptroller.

Lutz began his presentation with a series of slides showing the present material handling system. As he went through them, he pointed out the inefficiencies and bottle necks. After about the fourth slide, Daniels turned toward Holman with a broad smile and said, "Curtis, if I'd have known you did such a lousy job as chief industrial engineer, I would never have promoted you to vice president." Everyone laughed except Holman, who looked rather glum.

Next, Lutz started through a series of slides that detailed how he had arrived at the proposed system. He had just started into a discussion of the assumptions of his computer simulation of the proposed system when the president interrupted him.

DANIELS: Mr. Lutz, I'm sure all of these technical details are of interest to Curtis and perhaps Jim, but perhaps we should get directly into the economic impact of the proposal. Curtis and Jim can get together with you later if they wish to go into the technical details.

Paul was taken by surprise that Daniels didn't want to see all of the background that had led to the recommendations, but he reluctantly went to the last two slides, which showed the rate-of-return calculations. Daniels then asked the board members if they had any questions.

DAY: What do you project the payback period to be?

LUTZ: I haven't calculated it because I believe that the rate of return on present worth is a more meaningful figure of merit.

DAY: Well, I believe that with the present economic uncertainties, inflation, etc., that the shorter the payback period the better, I'd really like to see how this proposal stacks up in this regard when compared to some of our other opportunities.

WALLS: What economic assumptions have you used in forecasting costs and savings in your analyses?

LUTZ: I assumed that sales for this product would increase at a rate of 10 percent per year and that labor and materials costs would increase at an annual rate of 6 percent.

WALLS: Did you check that sales figure with any of my people?

LUTZ: No, sir. I just assumed that with the sale of RV vehicles going up each year that a 10 percent annual increase was a reasonable assumption.

WALL: I'm also curious about your inflation factor of 6 percent. Don't you think that might be a little low, since the inflation rate was 10 percent last quarter?

LUTZ: I chose 6 percent because that was the figure the federal government projected last January. I guess that might be a little low in view of what is really happening,

HUBBARD: My people have been looking at an improved design for the jacks themselves. How would this new design impact your system if we change over?

LUTZ: I don't know, sir, because I wasn't aware that they were working on a new design.

DAY: This sort of thing is the very reason I think the payback period is more important than the rate of return for such projects.

DANIELS: Mr. Lutz, what risks are associated with this proposal?

LUTZ: I was going to cover that in my presentation of how I arrived at my recommendations, but basically I don't see any reason why the system shouldn't work as designed.

DANIELS: No, no. I don't mean technical risks, I mean financial risks.

LUTZ: Well, I showed in my presentation, if my assumptions are correct, I don't see any reason why the system s ouln't pay for itself with a good return.

DANIELS: And if your assumptions are off?

LUTZ: I don't know, sir.

DANIELS: Bill, I think the Industrial Engineering Department needs to look into this matter more deeply. It seems to me there are an awful lot of unanswered questions. We've just heard presentations from sales for a new marketing campaign and from R&D for a new product development project, and we still have two more to go today from the manufacturing people on a new pollution control program. We obviously don't have the money to go into all of these things, and we've got to get them on a comparable basis before we can make a decision. Why don't you and Paul see if you can get some answers to some of the questions and come back next Thursday? Thank you for coming.

As Lutz walked out of the room and down the hall with Klausner, he was crushed.

LUTZ: Bill, they weren't even interested in how the system would work or all the innovations that I put into it. All they seemed to care about was money, money, money.

KLAUSNER: This is my fault, Paul. I should have had you dry run the presentation for me ahead of time. You've got to realize that they are only interested in the end result. They assume that we know what we are doing technically. They count on the proposal being technically sound and are concerned with the impact of the proposed investment on the overall performance of the company. We've got to realize that although you and I are interested in the technical details, their interest is much broader and mostly economic. Try to forget it for the rest of the day, and we'll start tomorrow on a new presentation.

Case study discussion questions

1.   Lutz obviously hadn't done his homework. How could this have been precluded?
2.   Will this first presentation affect the ultimate acceptance or rejection of the project?
3.   Who should Lutz have contacted before the presentation?
4.   What do you think of Klausner as a manager?

CHAPTER 9 control

9.1 Control Defined

Control as a function of management has both positive and negative characteristics. In its positive aspects, it is the purpose of control to secure and maintain the maximum productivity from all of the resources of the organization. In a negative sense, it is the purpose of control to prevent or reduce unacceptable performance. Control techniques and actions are intended to insure, as far as possible, that the organization does what management wants it to do.

Common meanings of the term "control" are to direct, to influence, and to restrain. In administration and management, the concept of control includes all of these common meanings and more. It consists of:

1. Defining the objective or setting the standard.
2. Comparing actual performance with the standards set.
3. Analyzing the difference or determining the cause of variance.
4. Applying corrective action where needed.

The basic purpose of management controls is to insure that the organization is working toward the fulfillment of the goals set by management. Without these controls there is no way of ascertaining whether persons in the group are working toward the objectives of the organization or if they are even aware of these objectives. The effective control of the technical function also entails securing maximum results from minimum dollar expenditures.

As pointed out earlier, since the major product of the technical group is primarily ideas, new concepts, or evaluations, our major productive force is the mind of the worker. The salary of the technical professional constitutes better than 75 percent of the cost of doing technical work. It is therefore obvious that the primary factor that we must control is the utilization of the staff's time.

Most organizations strive to effect this control through either an annual budget, current approval of individual projects, or both. It is literally impossible to control *costs*. One can only control the actions of persons who incur costs. On the other hand, control of projects without relationship to the costs being incurred provides no method of evaluating the profitability of the effort. For these reasons, the only adequate approach seems to be a control system oriented from both a budget and manpower utilization approach. In order to insure maximum profitable achievement, the control system must provide the means of continually evaluating the progress and value of projects that are being pursued against costs that are being incurred.

The essence of the control process can be broken down into the mechanisms for transmitting information and the judgment process of making decisions based on this information. Thus, one important aspect of the control system is the process of providing management with the necessary information and data needed to:

1. Indicate work progress.
2. Properly relate technical performance, cost, and schedule.
3. Supply managers with a practical level of summarization.

To control any process, one must start with an objective. The customer and the organization doing the work on a technical project must agree on the common objectives of the end product. During the project life the technical objective may change, especially early in the program, but further along both the task content and the specific requirements must stabilize for effective project completion. Initially, both the customer and the group base their estimates of the required task effort on considerations of the perceived size of the job and on assessments of the technological effectiveness of the personnel assigned to it.

Project managers continuously try to state what progress has been made, but no particularly relevant measurements are available to verify or deny such statements. Even a system of detailed project milestones that show the subtasks required to complete a task has potential failings because of the uncertainties inherent in the invention-innovation process. Nevertheless, companies do and should go ahead in their planning efforts to map out such a set of project linkages or milestones that must be met before the job has been completed. The technical managers can use this approach effectively by accounting for three indices of project performance: technical accomplishment, elapsed time, and accumulated expenditures. The managers must also include human factors, because technical progress, measurement, and control all depend on the people factor and are subject to motivational influences.

Too many organizations ignore the motivational factor in the design of control systems. The management control system that is being designed should be predicated on minimizing motivation problems by avoiding excessive control techniques that adversely influence these problems. The organizational environment must encourage openness, initiative, and innovation in the individual scientists and engineers, because they will then more likely supply the real progress needed by management. Also, it must be made clear that information transmitted upward to management about problems and troubles is desired so that higher management can help to identify and solve problems. Such action in an organization results from an organizational penalty and reward structure that encourages this openness and allays any fears that exist in most organizations about this matter. Management must demonstrate that they do not want just "sales presentations" that emphasize how successfully the technical people are functioning, because negative results are also important to further the technical control needed.

As a control technique, the budget for a particular project, coupled with milestone charts, offers management one of the most basic and simple controls. Milestone charts have an inherent disadvantage; even if the engineer objectively reports the accomplishement or lack of accomplishment of a particular milestone, the achievement of one or any number of milestones is no indicator of the extent of the project work that has been done or of the extent of project work remaining to be done, since separate milestones may require vastly different levels of effort. Thus, even with milestones, one has to estimate how much work remains, how many months it will require, and how many more dollars are to be spent before the project is completed. Furthermore, milestones do not consist of just the two-phase state of either being accomplished or not being accomplished; at any given time, many tasks are partially complete. It is impossible to separate the concept of project milestone achievement from the concept of percentage completion.

Despite the biases that may be present as a result of evaluating their own work, the engineers or scientists closest to the scene know the difficulties that have been encountered and have at least some feeling for the kinds of problems they expect to encounter before completing their own job. The engineer or scientist decides whether there is a finding or failure to report and whether the job is adequately completed or unfinished. Organizations that push control down to the lowest possible level (to those people closest to the work) have obtained good results, because the professionals are concerned with their work and want to accomplish their technical mission. Thus the process of controlling must take into account the real source of control—the individual engineer or scientist.

To close the control loop, the actions that organizations take as a result of their measurements of progress must now be considered. Problems arise in trying to decide what kind and how much action should be taken in response to deviations in the project progress. Should the program be revised? Should certain technical activities be increased or decreased to restore balance to the resource utilization on the project? The answers to these questions are almost impossible to determine categorically, since it is very difficult to compare with any real meaning the cumulative dollar cost with the scheduled project expenditures to date, or the effort allocation with the expected effort to date, or the anticipated technical achievement with the sensed achievement. For example, assessing performance based solely on a comparison of a planned expenditure curve and a budget curve does not allow an intelligent decision to be made because of the following questions: Are the two curves compatible? Do segments of both curves represent the same work? Is there acceleration or deceleration of performance? A finance department, observing that the expenditure curve is higher than the budget curve would immediately conclude an overrun condition whereas, based on the preceding questions, any of three possibilities could be occurring—overrun, underrun, or on-budget. Therefore, the way in which management responds to indications of errors in job estimates is very critical to the advancement of technical projects.

There are basically two extreme response policies regarding off-target projects—optimistic response and panic response. Assume that management conducts periodic project reviews every 3 months. At the first review, only half the anticipated progress was made. How does management respond to this? Under the optimistic response, management suggests that this error only indicates some of the problems of getting the project underway and that there is no real reason to change the overall original estimate of project progress. They assume, "We always have problems when we're just starting up." This same response is present at the next review, and the next, until finally maybe a year or two downstream, management must admit the problems and radically revise the requirements for the project. This managerial policy for responding to progress measurements, ignoring the error indications, could doom the project to failure or at least serious difficulties. However, the panic response approach dictates immediate response to any apparent error in the estimates as they show up in the project review sessions. At the first quarterly review, management changes radically its initial estimates and begins to take action, such as acquiring more people and facilities for the project. Once this approach is taken, momentum keeps it going and, if the project difficulties were really "due to difficulties of starting the project," ineffective utilization of resources results. This managerial policy forces overexpansion and wasteful haste in the job performance.

Of course, these responses are at opposite ends of the spectrum, and the actual management response can and should be somewhere between them. Without advocating either extreme, it is important to recognize the contrasts in the results produced by each approach. A technical organization's response will be based on its own previous experience, its attitudes, and the ability of its management to understand the underlying project situation. Management should realize that its type of response tends to endure and contributes to successes or failures repeatedly experienced by the group; therefore, examination of the history of past projects enables management to compensate where necessary.

9.2   Criteria for Good Control

Having defined and considered some of the aspects of the control problem, we now set up our design criteria. An effective control system, in addition to certain general characteristics, should also provide a means of accomplishing certain objectives for both the worker and management (i.e., it should be beneficial to both). We will therefore first consider the general characteristics of an effective control system and then consider the benefits that should be derived from the viewpoint of both management and the worker.

1. *Flexibility*. The first and probably most important characteristic of a good control system is flexibility. Flexibility is required by the very nature of technical functions. As a project proceeds from planning, through design of the work, through the gathering of data, etc., an event called *serendipity* may occur at any point. Serendipity means accidental discovery, or getting something out of the project that was not expected. A startling number of breakthroughs in human knowledge have resulted from accidental events, such as the discovery of radioactivity when a sample of pitchblende was accidentally left on top of an unexposed photographic plate or the discovery of penicillin when Alexander Fleming noticed a clear spot in the bacteria on his culture plates where a mold spore had accidentally landed. Such events are not rarities, but they become important only if someone appreciates their significance and is allowed to follow up on them.

    Flexibility is also required, because the normal state of affairs in a technical organization is one of change. A paper may be published in the literature that shows the work has already been done or suggests that a different approach should be taken. A significant breakthrough in the state of the art may occur that makes the project or development obsolete. The test apparatus may contain basic flaws in concept that were not anticipated. Desired test specimens may not be available. The parent organization may decide to drop a certain area of endeavor. These or many other reasons may make a change in the project mandatory. In fact, it is a rare technical project that is carried out from beginning to end exactly as originally conceived and planned. We must recognize this constancy of change and provide the necessary flexibility in our control system to accommodate it.

2. *Coordination.* A second general characteristic of a good control system is that it should provide the information and mechanism for the coordination of effort within the organization. Most technical projects require support that crosses organizational lines. In order for all the organizational elements to plan for and provide this support adequately, they must be kept aware of what support is required, the approximate magnitude of this support, and when it will be required. An effective control system should allow for this coordination.

3. *Difficulty of Prediction.* A third general characteristic that the control sytem should recognize is the difficulty of predicting results and the effort required for a project. In a well-managed production operation of any type (including a job shop operation), an order for a certain quantity, quality, and type of product can be placed and the delivery time and cost can be accurately predicted, plus or minus a few percent. This is not the case with a technical project. An often repeated but true statement that is continuously heard from technical personnel is that if you can predict the results and costs of a project, it is a trivial one. This does not mean that planning and cost estimating cannot be done, but that we must recognize the limitations and probability of their accuracy in the design of our control system.

9.3 Management Criteria

Having considered the general characteristics of an effective control system, we can now consider what the system should accomplish for management.

1. The control system should help management to determine whether personnel of the organization are working on projects that are within the interests and mission of the organization. Because of the high costs, an organization cannot afford to expend money and effort on projects that will not be of value to the sponsor even if they are successfully completed.

2. The system should assure management that a project is as well planned in advance as possible. This will eliminate as much wasted effort and as many false starts as possible. I have seen instances where projects have resulted in the accumulation of great masses of test data at great cost that were of no value because of the lack of a planned approach.

3. The control system should keep management informed as to the progress, major breakthroughs, etc. The results or lack of results in a technical organization will almost always have an effect on the plans and operations of those sponsoring the activity. As an example, in an industrial organization, the sales activity must have a good idea of when or if they will have a new product that is being developed. Or if the technical group is working on the correction of some deficiency in a current product, the sales and manufacturing organizations must be kept informed as to when a solution might be expected.

4. The control system should provide the information to allow management to determine that the costs of a project are kept reasonable in light of the importance of the project, progress being made, etc. Many excellent projects can become unprofitable/because their costs begin to outweigh the possible benefits that can be derived. It is important that management be in a position to cancel such projects at the earliest possible date even, though it means losing what has already been invested.

5. The system should help provide the information that will allow management to decide when to commercialize or put to use the results of the project. One of the characteristics of good technical workers is that they become personally involved in the project. Because the project actually becomes a part of the ego, they are reluctant to release the project until it is perfected. Many projects require a management decision in order to take them out of the technical group so they can be utilized. The control system should help to provide the necessary information on which to base this decision.

6. The control system should provide the mechanism for disseminating throughout the organization the relative importance or priority of current projects. In any organization, certain projects are of much greater importance than others. Some method of relative ranking should be provided by the system so that all organizational elements can be sure they are doing the most important jobs first.

7. The control system should provide the information that will allow the manager to determine the current and committed work load of the organization. This information will allow the determination of when new projects can be undertaken and which other projects, if any, must be dropped in order to begin contemplated projects. If the manager has this information about the current utilization of manpower, a proper balance between

troubleshooting assignments, service functions, long-range projects, and short-range projects can be maintained. Unless extreme vigilance is exercised, there is a tendency for a technical organization to become bogged down in day-to-day service problems for other organizational segments. There is also the very real danger of concentrating too much effort on the short-range projects in order to show a continuous outflow of results. Any major unbalance in the overall program will work to the detriment of securing maximum value from the technical group.

9.4 Investigator Criteria

Any effective control system must be a two-way affair. It must be beneficial to the worker and to management if it is to be optimized and accepted. We will now consider what professional workers should expect from the control system.

1. The control system should allow, as much as possible, for investigators to devote the major portion of time to projects that are of personal interest. Although this is not always entirely possible, the system should at least provide a method for workers to initiate projects for which they see a need or that are of particular interest.

2. The control system should assure investigators that the results of the project will be utilized or at least of interest to management if successful. Nothing is as frustrating to an investigator as to spend considerable time and effort in conducting a project only to find out when finished that no one cares.

3. The control system should make certain that management is aware of the investigators' efforts, including both the successes and problems. This is particularly important to investigators whose major efforts are being devoted to long-term projects where tangible results may be a long time in coming.

4. The control system should allow the investigators to determine what is expected of them. This includes the relative priorities of projects on which they are working, the end result expected, the amount of time that should be devoted to each project, etc.

5. The control system should allow investigators to do their own planning. This relates directly to technical workers' desire for freedom of action. Being (at least in their eyes) professionals, they do not necessarily mind being told what to do, but will rebel at being told how to do it.

6. The control system should help to assure that technical workers are provided with sufficient time and freedom for exploratory investigations of their own choosing and for keeping abreast of the state of the art.

9.5 Overall Control Process

The discussion up to this point has attempted to define the problem and ascertain the factors relevant to it. Any system for the management of technical projects must somehow provide for project initiation, selection, evaluation, determination of resource allocation, and periodic review. If the system is effective, it should result in a smooth flow of well-chosen projects whose statuses are updated and reviewed periodically. The system should help to insure that projects that promise the best expected payoff to the organization are identified and selected for support. The process for accomplishing the preceding objective is essentially the same for all projects. A diagram of the key steps is shown in Figure 9.1.

The first step is *conception of the idea* and *exploratory investigations*. Ideas for fruitful projects can originate from any source. Although many ideas do come from outside of the technical organization (sales, manufacturing, or service personnel, etc.), many do not. Experience in most organizations shows that many ideas originate with the technical staff.

When an idea is conceived, some preliminary, exploratory investigation must be pursued to determine feasibility. This may take the form of a literature search, a few simple experiments, or a theoretical analysis. Since the cost of such exploratory investigations is usually quite small (consisting mostly of the investigator's time) it is usually not desirable to impose management controls on this effort. Moreover, there is no way to apply controls to it, since this is the phase in which the information needed later for evaluation is generated.

Most organizations allow or set aside a certain percentage of each investigator's time to perform exploratory investigations of their own choosing. It is a common practice in technical organizations to set aside approximately 10 percent of each person's time for this purpose. This is probably the most valuable allocation of effort that an organization can make, since it is from this effort that ideas originate and germinate.

The second step in the process is the initiation and *development of a project proposal*. At some point after the origination of an idea and an exploratory investigation, it becomes necessary to devote more resources of time, material, and equipment in order to pursue the project further. At this point, it is necessary to get something in writing. The project proposal comprises a definition of the project and pertinent information such as specific objectives, resource requirements, schedules, state of the art, markets, etc.

The third step is *project selection*. At this point, management's role begins. This step results in accepting, deferring, or rejecting a proposal. The proposed outcome is compared to the organization's objectives and long-range goals. Accepting the proposal means that the organization has a current interest in this kind of project; deferral means the organization may have a future inter-

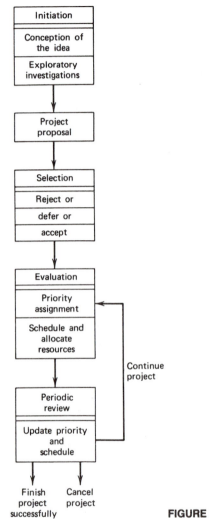

FIGURE 9.1   Project control system.

est; rejection means that it is of no interest. This selection will be handled differently by various organizations (depending on the nature of the project) but, typically, it is done by the group manager, a committee of senior advisers, a new product committee, a research council, or some high management level.

It is important here to add a word of warning. If the project is deferred, rejected or, at a later stage, canceled, curtailed, or put into a lower priority, it is extremely important to explain why to the originator. Generally, a great deal of preliminary work will have preceded the submission of the proposal.

The originator thinks it is practical and feasible, or it would not have been submitted. Disapproval or cancellation *without providing the reasons* will convince the originator that management is very shortsighted. Many managers indicate by their actions that they do not have the time, or do not need, to explain their decisions to subordinates. In dealing with professional people (as the technical manager must), nothing is more important; time spent in explaining adverse actions pays great dividends in high morale, better future proposals, and greater enthusiasm on the part of the investigators.

The fourth step is *evaluation*. This is the point at which management must determine the current relative importance (priority) of a selected project and a proposed schedule for its accomplishment and decide what level of resources to devote to it. New projects that have adequate priority are intended to be put into work shortly after priority assignment, with some perhaps replacing lower-priority, in-work projects. The remaining new projects are deferred.

The fifth step, once a project is in work, is *control,* which is exercised by periodic review. As a result of reevaluation, management may decide to add manpower or capital to the project, extend the schedule, cancel, etc.

Throughout this process, each project must be considered on its own merits and then in relation to all others. With a given capacity of manpower and facilities, it is evident that adding a new project must be coupled with removing some other project (because of successful completion or cancellation) or a lowering of importance, with a resulting extension of schedules. Each of these steps will now be discussed in greater detail.

9.6   The Project Proposal

Formal written proposals should only be prepared for projects that will exceed one man-month in effort. The format used should be tailored to the needs of the individual organization. The proposal should be as short and complete as possible. A suggested, or typical, format for such a written proposal is shown in Figure 9.2. The form on which a project proposal is presented should show the subject, specific objectives, technical backup, utilization information, budget, and schedule of the proposed project.

The *subject* should be descriptive of the content of the proposed project. The *objectives* describe the ultimate results sought and any interim results that the project seeks to achieve. Project evaluation will center first around the objective instead of the technical aspects. In most cases, as a project progresses, the technical approach may change, but the objective should remain the same. The project objective must be tangible, pragmatic, explicit, and end-use or results oriented. The *technical information* is a description of the required technology and materials, what is needed to obtain them, and what is

---

PROJECT PROPOSAL FORMAT

Project Title: _____

Submitted By: _____ Date: _____

Proposal No.: _____

OBJECTIVES

Primary Objective(s):
Interim and/or Spin-off Objective(s):

UTILIZATION INFORMATION

Need or Justification:
When Required:

TECHNICAL INFORMATION

Current State of the Art:
Proposed Approach:
Special Unavailable Resources Required (Personnel Skills, Materials, Equipment):

BUDGET AND SCHEDULE INFORMATION

Estimated Cost of Unavailable Resources: _____

Total Manpower (in Man-Months) Required by Labor
  Skill Category: Professional   _____

                        Technician   _____

Number of Persons Required per Month:
                        Maximum   _____

                        Minimum   _____

Number of Months to Completion:
                        Maximum   _____

                        Minimum   _____

Attach Bar Graph Showing Proposed Schedule by Milestones Assuming Maximum
  Manpower is Available.

FIGURE 9.2   **Typical project proposal format.**

available (i.e., the current state of the art). The utilization *information* outlines why the project is needed, when it is needed, and what the payoff is. The *budget* is an estimate of the capital, facilities, and amount and kind of manpower needed and when they are needed. The *schedule* is a statement of the expected times of completion of the interim and final objectives. The schedule is tied in closely with the budget.

This kind of information is needed on every proposal. In some cases, information will be required on patent and other legal problems, government regulations, etc. Under some circumstances, crash schedules and extended schedules also should be prepared for examination and evaluation.

The information shown is essentially the entire basis for selection decisions. For many applied projects, the data will be complete in almost all areas, particularly in technical and utilization information. Conversely, for many research projects, the data will be incomplete almost everywhere, with only the technical information, an estimate of utilization potential for the area considered, and a short-term budget available. In all cases it will probably be necessary to update the budgets and schedules prior to each review.

9.7 Selection of Projects

On the basis of the information in the project proposal, the appropriate management personnel can select the desired projects. A typical selection work sheet for a project incorporating the factors considered most important and relevant to the organization's environment is shown in Figure 9.3; this is a simple scoring model, as discussed in Section 8.3. Three sets of factors are shown: technical, utilization, and timing. Subjectively, each of these is important in looking ahead to the ultimate payoff of a project. At this stage, the evaluation is still subjective; notations for a specific project are simply that a factor is favorable, unfavorable, or that the evaluator has no meaningful opinion.

Each project should be graded by more than one qualified person. The scorers must understand the technical aspects of the project and must have a broad, intimate understanding of the organization, its objectives, and its environment. The scoring form must be tailored to the individual organization's area of endeavor and particular technological problems. It should be developed through careful analysis and modified with experience.

As *one* guide to provide assistance in the decision of whether to accept or reject a proposal, the scores can be weighted. A numerical weighting factor might be assigned for each of the three sets of factors. For instance, if it was decided that each should contribute equally and independently to the subjective judgment of the project, a score of 10 might be assigned to each set of factors. The scores for the three factors would be added, since they each contribute equally and independently. The unfavorable score should be subtracted from the favorable score. The best possible score would comprise checks of "favorable" for all items. In this case, the best possible score would yield +30. The worst possible score would comprise checks of "unfa-

---

PROJECT PROPOSAL WORKSHEET

Project Title: Development of Superinsulation

Evaluator: John S. Doe

Proposal No.: M-2   Date Evaluated: 2-4-65

Technical Factors	Favorable	No Opinion	Unfavorable
Long-term objectives	X		
Interim objectives	X		
Technical approach	X		
Availability of technology within organization			X
Availability of technology outside organization	X		
Availability of scientific skills	X		
Adequacy of facilities			X
Adequacy of support manpower			X
Tie-in with existing projects			X
Compared to alternative approaches	X		
Estimated chance of technical success	X		
Totals	7	0	4
Utilization Factors			
Requirement for results	X		
Funding for implementation of results			X
Reduction of costs of operation		X	
Increase in reliability		X	
Value-to-cost ratio	X		
Effect on operations	X		
Totals	3	2	1
Timing Factors			
Completion time relative to need	X		
Reduction in time of operations schedules	X		
Timing compared to alternatives	X		
Totals	3	0	0

FIGURE 9.3   Project proposal worksheet.

vorable'' for all items and would yield a weighted score of -30. The ''no opinion'' checks should not affect the scores of either.

The calculation of the weighted score for the example given in Figure 9.3 is shown in Table 9.1.

Thus, after grading each new proposed project, one has a ranking of projects with scores ranging between $+30$ and -30. This scoring and ranking are

TABLE 9.1   Weighting Calculations

	Favorable	Unfavorable
Technical factors	7/11 × 10 = 6.3	4/11 × 10 = 3.6
Utilization factors	3/4 × 10 = 7.5	1/4 × 10 = 2.5
Timing factors	3/3 × 10 = 10	0/3 × 10 = 0
Subtotals	23.8	6.1

Project value = Favorable − Unfavorable
= 23.8 − 6.1 = 17.7

intended to *aid the decision maker,* not make the decision. Therefore, it would be unwise to set arbitrary limits for acceptance or rejection.

The actual selection of projects must depend on management's evaluation of the following questions.

1. Does the proposed result match or meet the long-range goals and plans of the organization?
2. Is the proposed result the type of product, or information, that the organization needs?
3. Does the possible ultimate payoff justify embarking on the project?

There are, of course, other considerations, but they are secondary.

When management has completed the selection phase, each project should have been placed in one of four categories.

1. *Mandatory.* These projects are essential for the well-being of the organization or to the completion of some other high-priority project.
2. *Acceptable.* These are projects that management is interested in pursuing. They will be worked into the work schedule at the earliest possible time in accordance with their priorities.
3. *Deferred.* These projects look interesting and feasible, but are not of immediate interest. Reasons for placing projects in this category might be (*a*) high capital investment required, (*b*) would require penetrating new markets, (*c*) would involve getting into overcrowded markets, and (*d*) unavailability of suitable personnel.
4. *Rejected.* These projects are of no interest to management now or later. Either they do not fit in with the long-range goals and plans of the organization, or the potential payoff does not justify the risk and expense of further pursuit.

9.8 Evaluation of Projects

Once a project has been selected, it is further evaluated and a priority is assigned. In this phase, the project must move into competition with existing projects. It is therefore necessary to evaluate current and new projects. For all projects, this evaluation consists of: (1) determining the status of the project, and (2) deciding whether and how to continue.

The status of a new project is based on the data in the proposal and selection work sheet. The status of a project in process is based on the original information and the amount accomplished and learned since the last review. Figure 9.4 shows a form that may be useful for recording the current status to aid in

```
┌─────────────────────────────────────────────────────────────────────────┐
│                        PROJECT STATUS REPORT                              │
│                                                                           │
│  Project Title: _____ │
│                                                                           │
│  Project No.: _____  Chief Investigator:   │
│                                                                           │
│                                                     _____   │
│                                                                           │
│  Start Date*: _____  Estimated Completion Date*: _____   │
│                                                                           │
│  Initial Priority: _____  Budget: 19__ $ _____   │
│                                                                           │
│                                                       19__ $ _____    │
│                                                                           │
│  (*As covered by project            To Complete   $ _____            │
│  proposal _____)                                                     │
│                                                                           │
├─────────────────────────────────────────────────────────────────────────┤
│  Review Date: _____  Budget Man-Hours _____    │
│                                                                           │
│                                                       $     _____     │
│                                                                           │
│                                             Actual Man-Hours _____    │
│                                                                           │
│                                                       $     _____     │
│                                                                           │
│  Accomplished to Date:                                                    │
│                                                                           │
│                                                                           │
│  Problems Encountered:                                                    │
│                                                                           │
│                                                                           │
│  Action Taken:                                                            │
│                                                                           │
│                                                                           │
│  Current Priority:                                                        │
└─────────────────────────────────────────────────────────────────────────┘
```

FIGURE 9.4   Project status report.

assigning suitable priorities for projects already underway. A brief status report on all ongoing projects should be made once a month.

As previously discussed, management must insure a balance between long-range and short-range projects and a mix of projects over the technology spectrum. If research projects are forced to compete with development or technical support projects for priorities, the priorities will go to the development or technical support project. This would work to the long-range detriment of the organization. It is therefore proposed that the research-type programs should be evaluated separately and not be forced to compete with more immediate and pressing projects.

It is difficult, if not impossible, to separate projects cleanly and unequivocally. The ones at either end of the technology spectrum are easy to identify but, as one approaches the center from either direction, it becomes more difficult. It is proposed that management subjectively (even arbitrarily) divide the projects into two groups for separate evaluation. For one group one would use the definitions of basic research and applied research as given in Section 1.4. For the other group, the definitions of development and technical support would be used.

It would be nice if somehow these projects could be programmed into a magical computer that would automatically assign the correct priorities. Unfortunately, such a program does not yet exist, and educated, experienced, subjective judgment must still be used. If the projects are relatively independent of each other, a procedure familiar to all experienced operations research personnel for weighting objectives might be used. Both the underlying logic and the procedure are simple. The procedure consists fundamentally of a systematic check on relative judgments by a process of successive comparisons [1].

The basic assumptions of the system are:

1. A person's subjective judgment of the *relative* value between and among projects is more accurate than judgment of an *absolute* value of any one project.
2. A person's relative judgment among a few projects is more accurate than evaluation of a large number.

The evaluator is asked to make a series of judgments among a relatively few projects. Each judgment contributes information concerning the relative importance of the projected outcomes to the evaluator, and each iteration should improve the decision.

One method of assigning priorities will now be described [1]. Although the procedure may seem cumbersome at first, it is really simple in practice.

The procedure consists of the following steps.

1. Rank the entire set of projects being evaluated in terms of preference or perceived value of the projected outcomes without assigning quantitative values.
2. Select at random one project from the set. Let P_S represent the desired outcome of this project.
3. Subdivide the remaining set of projects by random assignment into groups of no more than five, and preferably into groups of approximately equal size. Each project (other than P_S) should be included in one and only one group.
4. Add P_S to each group and assign to it a priority value of 1.00 (i.e., priority of P_S = 1.00).
5. For each group, tentatively assign to each project a value that initially seems to reflect the relative value of their proposed outcomes to that of P_S. For example, if the evaluator thought that the value of a successful outcome for project P_A would be twice that of P_S, a tentative priority of 2.00 would be assigned to it. Thus, a group of projects, P_A, P_B, P_C, and P_S, might have tentatively assigned to them priorities of 2.00, 1.25, 0.80, and 1.00, respectively.
6. Make subjective comparisons of combinations such as P_A versus P_C and P_S. Thus, if the evaluator had the choice of having a successful outcome of P_A or the combination of P_C and P_S, which would be chosen? Suppose the evaluator would rather have P_C and P_S. Then the values of P_A and P_C must be adjusted so that $P_A < P_C + P_S$. In making adjustments, the value of P_S must not be changed. Continue these comparisons of combinations until the values for each project in the group are consistent for all evaluations.
7. Compare the rankings obtained for the entire set of projects as obtained by steps 2 to 6 when the groups are recombined with that obtained in step 1. If the rank orders differ, reconsider the ranking from step 1 and, if necessary, proceed again from steps 2 to 6 of this procedure.
8. Once consistent results are obtained, normalize the priorities by dividing the priority assigned to each project by the sum of the priorities assigned to all the projects.

The result is a relative priority assigned to each project in the set and the sum of the priorities equal to one. The procedure just described may be clarified by a simple example. Suppose there are 10 projects.

1. Suppose these are ranked as follows: $P_1, P_2, \ldots, P_{10}$.
2. Suppose P_5 is selected at random as the standard.
3. The remaining projects are assigned at random to three groups.

I	II	III
P_3	P_2	P_6
P_{10}	P_9	P_1
P_7	P_4	P_8

4. P_5 is added to each group and assigned a priority equal to 1.00.
5. Suppose relative priorities are assigned to each project and combination comparisons are made until consistent evaluations are obtained with the following results.

I	II	III
P_3 = 3.00	P_2 = 3.25	P_6 = 1.35
P_{10} = 0.30	P_9 = 0.50	P_1 = 3.60
P_7 = 0.90	P_4 = 2.50	P_8 = 0.80
P_5 = 1.00	P_5 = 1.00	P_5 = 1.00

6. Note that in the computed rankings of step 5, P_5 and P_6 are reversed from those assigned in step 1. The evaluator would then reconsider the initial rankings. If the evaluator decided that P_5 was indeed more important than P_6, it would be necessary to reiterate steps 2 to 6 again and make the necessary adjustments to the calculated priorities. If, after reconsideration, the evaluator decided that P_6 was, after all, more needed than P_5, the priorities stand as adjusted.
7. Finally, the priorities would be normalized by dividing each by 17.20 (the sum of all the priorities) to obtain:

$$P_1 = 0.209 \qquad P_6 = 0.078$$
$$P_2 = 0.189 \qquad P_7 = 0.052$$
$$P_3 = 0.175 \qquad P_8 = 0.047$$
$$P_4 = 0.145 \qquad P_9 = 0.029$$
$$P_5 = 0.058 \qquad P_{10} = 0.017$$

As stated earlier, although this procedure at first seems to be cumbersome and complex, it is really simple in practice. It reduces the problem of relative value judgments to proportions that can be handled more easily. Perhaps even more important, the multiple-combination comparisons force the evaluator to consider decisions from different directions and against multiple criteria.

Most organizations find it neither necessary nor desirable to break the priorities down to such a fine point. The only purpose in doing so would be if some form of mathematical programming was going to be used for resource allocation. Since very few organizations use formal mathematical models for resource allocation, a much simpler priority system is usually used.

Under most circumstances, a three-category system is sufficient, such as: A projects are urgent and take precedence over any other projects; B projects are highly desirable and should be rapidly pursued; and C projects are "rainy-day" projects to be pursued as time and resources permit. The priority classification of a project should be moved up or down as circumstances warrant, and the priorities should be reviewed for appropriateness each time a project is reviewed.

Who should assign the priorities will vary from organization to organization. Priorities could be assigned by the immediate supervisor or some higher managerial rank. They could also be assigned by a group or committee. Someone other than the idea originator should make the assignment, and the highest priority should require the approval of a top executive. Otherwise all projects will end up ranked in the urgent category, and the priority system will be meaningless. The important thing is that the person assigning priorities should be someone who understands the technical implications of the projects and has a general, in-depth understanding of the organization, its objectives, its needs, and its environment.

9.9 Pressures for Continuation of Submarginal Projects

Perhaps no other phase of evaluation is more important and, at the same time, more neglected than the evaluation of ongoing projects. And surely no problem is more vexing than that of deciding when to abandon a project. It is not enough for management to decide to start a project; they must also decide whether to continue it. Clearly, elimination of a submarginal project is of little importance if resources are unlimited, but such conditions seldom, if ever, exist. It is therefore important to screen project ideas prior to committing them to the program and to eliminate submarginal projects at the earliest possible date. Only by doing so can maximum results be obtained from the limited resources.

Very simply, submarginal projects are those that should be removed from the active technical program. Such projects include:

1. Those that are technically not feasible. They obviously seemed feasible once or they would not have been started. Subsequent investigation has since demonstrated their unfeasibility.

2. Those that are technically feasible, but will cost more than they are worth, and the need is not vital. Early estimates of resource requirements or potential payoff were much in error.
3. Those that are technically feasible and would be worth more than their cost, but they are consuming critically needed resources that promise a much higher payoff if applied elsewhere.

Most of the literature does not consider this particular problem or else gives very cursory treatment of it. It is apparently generally assumed that if projects are carefully chosen, the problem of eliminating the submarginal ones is automatically solved. As long as management is dependent on estimates and crystal balls, however, it will be faced with the problem of identifying and eliminating submarginal projects. The reaction of project personnel to the deletion of ''their'' project must be predicted and considered. ''Pressures'' that tend to influence decisions must be clearly recognized and action taken to eliminate those that might result in biased decisions. Therefore, it is important to identify and plan for as many of these pressures as possible.

1. Cancellation of a project is frequently thought by higher authority to be evidence of poor original planning and initial preliminary study. The technical manager recognizes this and reacts to it, so that unless projects are obviously doomed to failure, there is a tendency to retain them in the hope that original plans can be fulfilled.
2. There are some pressures that originate within the group itself. It is not unusual for project engineers to become so interested in their projects that they fail to recognize their deficiencies. In addition, they usually feel a proprietary interest in the work. Any attempt by management to eliminate ''their'' project is likely to be taken personally and resisted. Sometimes this feeling can be so strong that it becomes a valid argument for retention of the project. If the project personnel are high caliber and are involved in other important work, retention of the project may be a better alternative than the consequences of cancellation. It is also well known that a project engineer's driving interest in the project can sometimes result in success despite apparently overwhelming odds.
3. In addition to the sincere project leader, there may also be the not-so-sincere ''empire builder'' who resists any attempt to reduce the scope of his or her work. In such a case, management may find it necessary and desirable to eliminate the project *and* the empire builder.
4. Pressure to keep the project can come from individuals of higher authority. This pressure is generally not the result of action to further personal gain, but because the office or individual has so strongly supported the project that there is a strong desire to see it completed. When a technical

group recognizes that there is such strong feeling for a project at higher levels in the organization, it will hesitate to recommend elimination. This is especially true, since any evaluation of the project's worth must be subjective and thus hard to defend in the face of strong opposition from higher authorities.

5. Pressure is exerted on the manager because of a crowded and busy schedule. In almost any group, there are always "hot projects" that demand immediate attention and keep the manager busy. Matters that require immediate attention are worked on, while project reviews and elimination of submarginal projects are postponed. Because of other pressures, the manager wants to be doubly sure before canceling a project; the manager wants to probe the problem in depth, but does not feel that the time is available and keeps thinking perhaps next week will be better.

6. The most important factor that causes the manager to hesitate in deleting a project is the inherent difficulty of deciding just *which* projects are submarginal. Unfortunately, no one has yet been able to devise a test that will positively indicate submarginality. Therefore, the decision must be made by subjective judgment, and such decisions cannot always be right. In addition, because such judgments are opinion, they can always be challenged by any source that favors continuation of the project. There is also the recognition that mistakes in judgment can have far-reaching effects that may not be apparent until it is too late.

All this makes the task of screening and eliminating projects very unattractive. It is much easier to let the projects continue to completion so that the worth of the project can be more firmly determined, but to do so may be disastrously wasteful of precious resources in the long run.

9.10 Allocation of Manpower

In Chapter 5 we discussed creativity and the creative process and noted the importance of intense application of hard effort toward finding a solution and incubation (or putting the problem aside) when no progress is being made. These factors, in addition to experience and research, indicate that each professional worker in the group should be assigned to at least three, but not more than four, active projects at a time. In any kind of technical work, you invariably find progress delayed because you are waiting for a part, information, materials, a computer run, tests to be coordinated, etc. By having three projects, the worker can be waiting on one project, actively pursuing another, and incubating the third.

It has also been shown that if the worker has more than four active projects at one time, none of them receive the intense interest and effort so vitally needed to achieve a creative solution. No one can give attention to too many different problems at once. Being spread too thin leads to frustration and to a lack of a sense of accomplishment, which is vital to motivation.

A second important factor in the allocation of manpower to projects is the personal interests of the workers. There is little doubt that we will each devote our best efforts to projects and ideas that interest us most. Studies have shown the motivational importance of letting people work on jobs that they considered interesting and challenging. Some authors have gone so far as to propose that professional personnel be allowed to choose their own tasks. Such a utopian solution is obviously not practical for most organizations (with the exception of those engaged in basic research). Certain tasks have to be done, whether or not anyone wants to do them.

Thus one of the major management tasks is the difficult one of establishing areas of mutual interest between the individual and the needs of the organization. Surprisingly, most creative people are very tractable, and you can lead them into almost any field or type of activity. The trick is to show them the intriguing aspects and challenge of the new problem. In fact, a manager must be careful about casually remarking on how interesting it would be to know what would happen if we did this or that; a worker may become as intrigued as the manager with the idea and drop everything else to look into it!

Along these same lines, if the manager wishes the worker to drop one project before it is finished and switch to another, the worker should not be told that the money has run out or that management is no longer interested. Instead, the manager should spend a little time thinking up all the interesting and intriguing aspects of the new work and then have an idea-generating session with the worker on the new project. If this is successfully done, the worker will eagerly drop the unpromising project and pursue the new one. One of the interesting findings of a study by Pelz and Andrews [4] was that technical personnnel were most productive when the projects were mutually selected by the immediate supervisor and the worker.

The problem still remains of the projects that must be done but that by their nature are not very interesting. Here, the manager must rely on the fact that a person will eat a lot of cake to get a little icing. Most professionals will readily see that such projects must be done. If they are also convinced that such projects will be shared by everyone and that they will be counterbalanced by challenging projects, most workers will accept their fair share of such projects.

Another aspect of manpower allocation must be firmly faced. Landis [2] found in a survey of 1311 engineers that nearly 31 percent of the overall time of respondents was spent on nonengineering tasks. Some of this nonengineering time is an integral part of the job and cannot be avoided. However, a significant part of it could undoubtedly be done by clerical or semiprofessional personnel who are lower paid. When Landis asked the engineers in his survey what percentage of the nonengineering work could be done by others, the replies were as follows.

Clerical personnel—12.3 percent.

Engineering aide—39.5 percent.

Technicians and drafters—27.1 percent.

Cannot be delegated—21.1 percent.

The significant implication of this study is that managers should (1) assign sufficient clerical and semiprofessional help to each project, and (2) allow for some amount of administrative and nonprofessional time use.

To summarize, when allocating manpower to projects, management should:

1. See that each professional employee is assigned three to four projects.
2. As far as possible these should be projects that are of personal interest to the employee.
3. The projects for each employee should be a mix of short-range and long-range duration.
4. Approximately 10 to 15 percent of a professional employee's time should be set aside for exploratory studies.
5. Approximately 10 percent of each professional employee's time should be set aside for administrative and nonprofessional activities.
6. A sufficient number of clerical and semiprofessional personnel should be made available to perform as much of the nonprofessional work as possible.

9.11   Management by Objectives

By this point the necessity and desirability of a high degree of participation of the professional worker in the planning of projects should be obvious. It is then only logical to involve the worker in the control process also. One participative approach to the planning and control process is called *management by objectives (MBO)* [3]. MBO is basically a process whereby a manager and the individual worker jointly identify a set of goals, define the individual area of responsibility in terms of the results expected, and use these measures as guides for evaluating the progress and contributions of the individual.

The concept of MBO has been a important tool of top management for some time. It is more than a set of rules, procedures, or methods of managing. It is a particular way of thinking about managing, one that can bring about more vitality and personal involvement in any organization. It stresses individual ability and results. Among the advantages of MBO are the following.

1. Develops a sense of responsibility in subordinates.
2. Insures that the task is understood.
3. Allows the responsible manager to make sound and timely decisions.
4. Places the decision-making responsibility at the most appropriate level.
5. Frees the creative abilities of those responsible for devising solutions.
6. Makes it easier to evaluate and reward good performance by the individual.

Basically, MBO is a method by which the various levels of management identify common organizational goals and define performance objectives so that everyone knows exactly what is expected of them. These goals and objectives are then used to control the organization and assess the individual worker's contributions. The cornerstone of every management control system is the concept of *responsibility accounting*. The basic idea is simple. Each individual is responsible for a part of a total activity that is carefully and explicity defined; each is then evaluated on the basis of how well those specific objectives are met.

Although highly desirable in any type of organization, MBO should be a critical and indispensible component of technical management. The key to the successful use of MBO and decentralization of accountability is the involvement and personal belief and acceptance of these objectives by each manager. MBO requires interaction between the supervisor and the individual worker to the degree that both know what the other is doing, why it needs doing, and how it is getting done.

Involvement and interaction sound like normal features of any management environment. Surprisingly, management research indicates that most subordinates are not tuned in to their supervisor; they are not always sure about what their bosses expect of them. The results are often misplaced priorities, make-work, job dissatisfaction, and management by crisis. For example, a supervisor has certain notions of how subordinates should perform. If they fall short of these expectations, the reason may not be their lack of ability, but their misunderstanding of what was expected of them. In other words, unless the manager makes the expectations clear, they can be easily misconstrued or even ignored. The problem can obviously be corrected or improved if individual workers are allowed to have a role in setting the goals and objectives. This idea of the manager and workers operating under mutual objectives is fundamental to the management process.

It should be obvious that it is much easier to evaluate and reward people when the objectives of each job are made clear. Most managers do not like to talk over employee merit ratings, or appraisals with their people because most of the current rating systems compel them to evaluate people subjectively in terms of personality traits. It is difficult to tell workers that they do not have enough "tact," "initiative," or "motivation"—all terms that appear on appraisal forms. Other common traits used are how well the individual "gets along with others," "accepts responsibility," or "demonstrates loyalty to the organization." To criticize a person on such subjective grounds amounts to a personal attack that is difficult for anyone to accept with good grace.

Moreover, it implies that the person has inherent failings that are an embedded part of the personality, and there really is not much that can be done about them. When a person is judged by the results that he or she achieves and by success in reaching definite objectives, they are encouraged to use their abilities to the full and do not sulk over the shortcomings that the manager alleges. Shortcomings of intellect or personality are immaterial as far as the job is concerned if the desired results are achieved.

Mutual participation with clearly established responsibilities between management levels is the framework on which the MBO system is built. There are, however, several steps inherent to the system. They are characterized by a common denominator of agreement between the manager and each subordinate that can be achieved in various ways, such as joint meetings, person-to-person conferences, and group problem-solving sessions. The steps are:

1. Identifying, selecting, and setting common organizational goals.
2. Determining measures of acceptable results for each goal.
3. Defining areas of responsibility.
4. Determining individual performance objectives.
5. Reviewing performance.

The MBO process first requires organizational goals that are realistic, specific, and attainable. The goals will be useless if they are too easily reached; the organization and the individuals should have to do a little stretching to reach the goals. Formal mission statements, established priorities, internal problems, and headquarter requirements may be helpful in identifying, selecting, and setting common organizational goals.

In order to identify progress (whether success or failure) in achieving a goal, the goal must be explicit and lend itself to measurement. The manager and subordinate must come to an agreement as to how these goals will be measured by identifying specific criteria for each goal. Achievement factors normally can be easily measured if there are quantitative elements to the goals. For example, the goal could be measured by "reducing the completion date of a project by 15 percent." However, some goals, such as improving unit morale, can only be measured qualitatively. MBO requires clear communication, understanding, and acceptance of performance standards. It does not demand that all goals and objectives be relegated to "numbers." Past performance is a good indicator of how results may be measured, and this factor should be considered before an agreement is reached.

The next step involves assigning areas of responsibility to insure that each individual worker has a role in contributing to or achieving a goal. This enables each level of management and each worker to know exactly what is expected, because each has participated in assigning the responsibilities. Organization and function manuals may be used as guides in determining "who is assigned what." Factors to be considered include requirements, work loads, relation to existing responsibilities, and the initiative and talents of the individual.

The performance objectives step of the MBO system is critical to achieving acceptable results. Basically, performance objectives are formal statements of certain results that an individual manager hopes to achieve in trying to attain an organizational goal. Mutually determining individual performance objectives can also assist in developing job descriptions. This step in the MBO system should focus attention on setting the individual performance objectives instead of trying to determine all the details of how the objective will be reached. In other words, the individual worker should be delegated the authority to develop his or her plan of action within the framework of the performance objective. MBO emphasizes developing a several *objectives* for each worker in place of a laundry list of *tasks*.

Performance review enables a comparison of objectives and results. It involves feedback between the manager and the individual that ultimately maintains high motivation. Performance review is a continuing requirement, although there may be specific review periods within the time frame for reaching the objective(s). The basic purpose of this review is to determine progress in meeting an objective. Success naturally deserves reward, since it reinforces the objective and increases positive motivation. Failure requires joint examination to determine why the performance objectives have not or cannot be met. Failure should not be examined in terms of fault finding, but in terms of correcting and improving the situation. It may be that the objective was unrealistic or that the resources available to accomplish it simply were not available or adequate.

In order for MBO to work, very careful attention must be given to the selection of measures of performance. To be successful, the manager must have a thorough knowledge of the parent organization's strategy and goals and a keen understanding of the individuals under his or her supervision. The manager must draw on this knowledge to apply two criteria for deciding which measures to use. These criteria are:

1. *Fairness*. Each individual employee must believe that the measurement used to evaluate his or her performance is appropriate. This means that the employee must see that all of the requirements placed on the job are consistent with each other. Moreover, the worker must believe that the measurements encompass all the factors he or she can control and excludes those over which there is no control.
2. *Goal Concurrence*. The manager designing a management control system with an overall perspective must ensure that subordinates are not working at cross purposes and must select objectives and measurements in a way that insures that they all blend with one another and contribute to the achievement of the overall goals and objectives of the parent organization.

9.12   Planning Individual Projects

There are managers who say that a technical project cannot be planned. They point out that reliable estimates of the time and cost of a project cannot be given. They argue that the technical functions are filled with intangibles that cannot be measured or foreseen. Although this is true, some planning can and must be done. Any student who has done a master's thesis or a doctoral dissertation can attest to the fact that a great deal of planning went into the investigation in order to complete the work within a prescribed schedule. Planning is used in many operations where a precise estimate cannot be made. The military commander cannot predict what the enemy will do or the results of a battle, but must plan ahead on the basis that a rough estimate is better than none at all. The question is not whether a project can or cannot be planned, but whether or not the planning should be formalized.

Professional personnel resist formalized planning mainly because of fears that individuals higher in the organization will not recognize the degree of approximation inherent in the plan. They fear that management will treat the plan as a precise timetable and will criticize them if they do not adhere to it. These fears are, in reality well justified. Roy [5] has analyzed this phenomena and calls it the *deification of numbers*. He points out that numbers and schedules have a tendency to acquire an aura of accuracy. This aura leads the decision maker to forget that schedules sometimes have dubious validity and to give to them a dogmatic and sacred quality they do not deserve. Because of this tendency on the part of humans to deify numbers and schedules, it is mandatory that formalized plans not be shown to or discussed with persons outside the technical organization.

The formalization of plans for long-range projects is desirable to (1) force the investigator to plan the work in as much detail as possible, (2) assure management that this has been done, (3) allow necessary support from other organizational groups to be anticipated and planned, (4) give the investigator a target to shoot at, (5) help managers to keep abreast of progress, and (6) allow both the investigator and management to recognize when deviations from the original scope or concept of the project are being made.

It is suggested that all long-range projects of 6 months or longer should be subjected to formalized planning. Although planning is required on projects of less than 6 months, I believe that a formalized plan is unnecessary and unprofitable. This formalized planning on long-range projects can be done by the research project leader utilizing a modified Gantt chart, such as the left portion of Figure 9.5. The use of the Gantt chart is dictated by several reasons: it makes it necessary to have a plan; it shows the facts in relation to time; it compares what is done with what was planned; it shows what has happened in the past and what is planned for the future; and it is easily understood and simple to use.

In planning the project, it is broken into its component parts. The degree to which the project is broken down will depend on the nature of the project. Each part must be clearly identifiable and have a more or less definite ending point. An estimate of the time required for each component is made, and the components are arranged in their proper sequence. In Figure 9.5 the plan is indicated by the solid stripes on the left portion of the chart. The plan may be revised when it is deemed necessary by stapling a new Gantt chart over the old one. Thus the original plan plus all revisions are available at all times. The plan should not be modified each time a slippage is indicated, but only when the plan has been changed or an estimate of time for some component was obviously wrong. The right side of the control chart represents the financial portion. The dashed lines are the estimated spending rate and are determined by the project leader in conjunction with the administrative staff. These graphs can be expressed either in man-hours or in dollars, depending on which the technical manager feels has the most meaning. Usually the charts are most useful when expressed in dollars. In this way the cost of equipment, materials, supplies, overhead charges, and man-hours can be included.

This aspect of the control system is the one most likely to meet resistance on the part of the individual workers. However, if the investigators are allowed to do the planning and modify the plan as they see the need and if they are assured that the plan will not be used to criticize or evaluate them, no

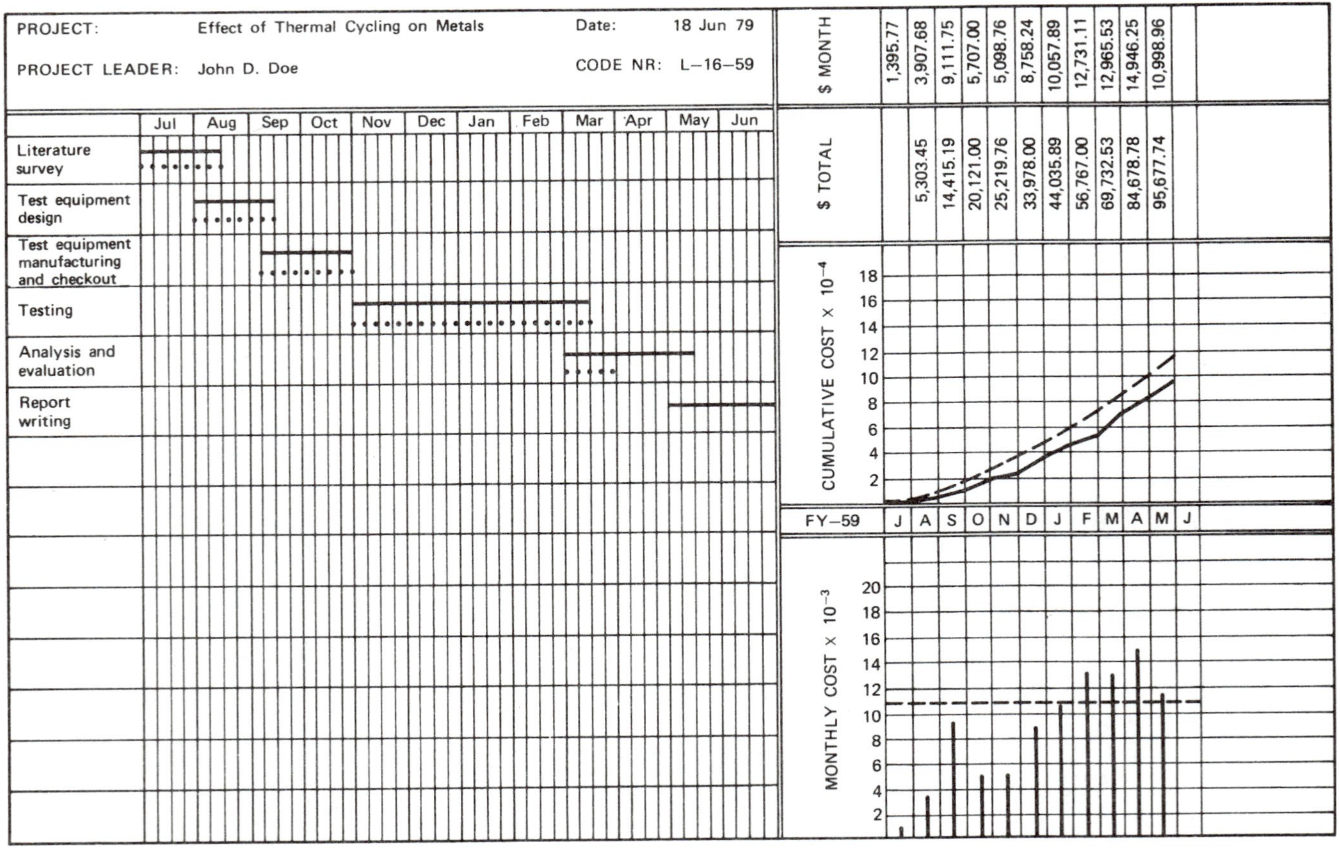

PROJECT: Effect of Thermal Cycling on Metals
Date: 18 Jun 79
PROJECT LEADER: John D. Doe
CODE NR: L–16–59
Jul Aug Sep Oct Nov Dec Jan Feb Mar Apr May Jun
Literature survey
Test equipment design
Test equipment manufacturing and checkout
Testing
Analysis and evaluation
Report writing
$ MONTH
1,395.77
3,907.68
9,111.75
5,707.00
5,098.76
8,758.24
10,057.89
12,731.11
12,965.53
14,946.25
10,998.96
$ TOTAL
5,303.45
14,415.19
20,121.00
25,219.76
33,978.00
44,035.89
56,767.00
69,732.53
84,678.78
95,677.74
CUMULATIVE COST × 10⁻⁴
18 16 14 12 10 8 6 4 2
FY–59
J A S O N D J F M A M J
MONTHLY COST × 10⁻³
20 18 16 14 12 10 8 6 4 2

FIGURE 9.5 **Planning and control chart.**

problem will be encountered. If it is recognized and used for what it is—a tool to aid in the conducting of long-range projects—the benefits to be derived will be readily realized by the investigator and management.

9.13 Reporting

After the project is approved and the necessary planning accomplished, the project becomes active and acquires official status. After a project has been approved, assigned a priority, and allocated manpower, a project cost account number should be assigned by the administrative office. All records and correspondence relating to the project bear the assigned number, and all man-hours and expenditures are reported against this number. The exact form of the numbering system is unimportant as long as it is logical and simple. Management must be kept informed as to the status of each active project in regard to progress, problems, major breakthroughs or accomplishments, costs, etc. The reasons for this requirement were given in Section 9.3.

One mechanism that can be used is the logbook. Every experienced investigator is familiar with the requirement for a technical logbook, both from the viewpoint of patent law requirements and as an instrument for the permanent recording of happenings and findings of the investigation; however, few have considered it as a control device. Upon the approval of the project, a permanently bound, serially numbered logbook, with each page consecutively numbered, should be issued to the chief investigator by the administrative office. The first entry for each project should be a complete statement of the project, the source of the project, when it was authorized, and any other related data. This will be signed by the immediate supervisor and the chief investigator, and does two things: (1) it assures that both the chief investigator and the supervisor have a mutual understanding of the project, and (2) it satisfies the patent law requirements for establishing when the project was initiated. A complete daily record of the project should be kept in the logbook by the chief investigator. Each day's entry must be in ink, dated, and signed by the investigator. Each page should be completely filled, and errors must be crossed out and initialed, not erased. Actual test data can be kept in a cross-referenced data logbook if necessary, but it is preferable to keep the test data and comments in one book.

This project notebook can be reviewed and signed weekly by the immediate supervisor to indicate that he or she has read and understood the preceding entries. Patent lawyers prefer that it be countersigned daily; however, a weekly countersigning will stand up in court. In light of the time demands on everyone concerned, it is believed that a weekly review and signing are sufficient. This weekly review of the notebook by the immediate supervisor does two things from a control standpoint. It keeps the supervisor fully aware of the progress and status of each project and reduces the chances of a significant event being overlooked.

Although keeping and reviewing technical notebooks is a time-consuming task, the benefits to be derived both by the investigator and management make it a profitable expenditure. Few competent investigators will argue with this requirement, since most of them keep a logbook even when it is not required by organizational policy. Therefore, each professional investigator should also be issued a technical notebook in which to keep *private, unofficial* investigations. This is necessary to establish the date an idea is conceived. When the project is completed, the logbook or logbooks are returned to the administrative office for review by the patent lawyers and permanent filing. If a book has not been completely filled, it may be reissued for another project.

The second mechanism utilized in the reporting process is the daily time sheet as shown in Figure 9.6. Every employee in the organization should keep a time sheet, which is turned in to the administrative office weekly. Every project on which the employee is working is listed on the time sheet. There is

Name:		Supervisor:						Week Beginning:		
		Sun.	Mon.	Tues.	Wed.	Thurs.	Fri.	Sat.	Total	
Project Title	No.	RT ¦ OT	RT ¦ OT	RT ¦ OT	RT ¦ OT	RT ¦ OT	RT ¦ OT	RT ¦ OT	RT ¦ OT	
Unofficial										
Unclassified										
Leave										
Total										

FIGURE 9.6   Timekeeping form.

an unofficial category to which to charge time spent on exploratory investigations of the investigator's own choosing. The unclassified category is used for the time that is not connected to any particular project, such as meetings, administration, etc. Time spent on each project should not be broken down below half-hour increments. Although some objections might be voiced when this procedure is first introduced, it is usually found that only several minutes at the end of the day is required for filling out the form. The administrative office then compiles the data from these forms. A monthly breakdown of the time utilization of the organization by categories should be furnished to the top technical executive, who then determines whether a balanced program is being maintained.

The third mechanism utilized in the reporting process is the planning and control chart (Figure 9.5). The right side, or financial side, of the chart is posted monthly by the administrative office based on the reported time expenditures and feedback information from the supply and procurement organizations. The man-hours reported can be multiplied by a weighting factor that includes the average salary, overhead, etc., before being posted to the chart. The weighting factor would be determined once a year in conjunction with the accounting department.

The progress (dotted lines) is posted monthly to the left side of the chart by the project leader. The end points of each component or event can be fairly accurately determined. Progress posted from the initiation of the event until the end must be a best estimate by the project leader. Each month is divided into four equal segments. These do not represent weeks; they merely aid the project leader in posting progress. As an example, if an event was planned to take 2½ months, or 10 segments, and the project leader estimated that the event was half finished, a dotted line would be drawn under the solid one through the first five segments.

The fourth mechanism utilized in reporting is the monthly progress report. Of all the mechanisms, this is probably the most beneficial one if it is properly used. The project leader of each project that lasts over a month should prepare a monthly progress report. This report should not be over one page in length and should give (1) technical status, (2) major accomplishments during the report period, (3) problems, and (4) management action required.

9.14 Appraisal

One of the most important functions of the technical manager is an appraisal of active projects and the functioning of the organization. An experienced manager could cite cases that show (1) the importance of stopping unfruitful or useless projects as soon as possible, and (2) the mistakes made in stopping a project too soon.

The control mechanisms discussed up to now provide the manager with the necessary information, but will not make the decisions.

In the evaluation of technical activities, it is impossible to reduce the work done on a project to a quantitative basis. However, the same purpose can be partially achieved by looking at two things: (1) the progress made, as stated in the progress report and shown on the left side of the planning and control chart, and (2) the money spent, as shown on the right side of the planning and control chart. The progress report and the control chart for each project should be reviewed jointly each month by the top technical executive and each manager. At this time, the priority classification of each project should also be reviewed for appropriateness. Because of familiarity with the project through the weekly review of the logbook and daily contact with the investigator, the immediate supervisor should be in a position to answer most questions that might arise about a particular project. If more details are desired or if an adverse decision with regard to any project is considered, the chief investigator for that project should be brought into the discussion.

Prior to the review meeting the appropriate members of the technical staff (if there is one) should look over the control charts and progress reports. This will allow them to offer their expert opinions where appropriate and call to the attention of the top executive the projects that seem to require a critical review.

At least semiannually a review of the entire docket of projects should be held by the top technical executive and the other managers to be sure that a balanced program is being pursued and that some areas of interest are not overemphasized while other equally important areas are overlooked.

9.15 Summary of a Typical Control System

1. A one-page proposal is prepared for all projects that require more than one man-month of effort (Figure 9.2). The chief investigator is determined by the immediate supervisor.
2. The project is approved by the immediate supervisor or higher level of management, depending on the magnitude of the proposed work. Typically, projects that require over three man-months or the expenditure of $1000 or more for equipment and material require the approval of a higher level of management.
3. The project is assigned priority classification by the approving authority. A projects are urgent and take precedence; B projects rate as active and are given current status; C projects are "rainy-day" projects. Projects may be moved up or down in classification by the approving authority as circumstances warrant.

4. An implementation plan is prepared by the chief investigator on all projects that last 6 months or longer. This is prepared on the planning and control chart (Figure 9.5).

5. Each employee keeps a record of time spent on each project (Figure 9.6) that is turned in weekly to the administrative office.

6. A project number is assigned to all approved projects. All records and correspondence relating to any project bear the assigned number.

7. A complete record of each project is kept in a separate, serially numbered technical logbook. The entry for each project will begin with a complete statement of the project, the source of the project, when it was authorized, and any other related data. This will be signed by the chief investigator and the immediate supervisor. This notebook will be reviewed and signed by the supervisor weekly. Each day's entry will be dated.

8. Current progress and man-hour expenditures are posted monthly to appropriate control charts.

9. A short monthly progress report is written on each active project (Figure 9.4).

10. A monthly check as to progress and cost of each project is held by the top technical executive in conjunction with the responsible manager. Priority classification of each project is reviewed at this time.

11. A semiannual review of the entire docket of projects is held by the managers and top technical executive; at this time projects that lack promise are dropped.

─────────────────────── **References** ───────────────────────

1. Churchman, C. W., R. L. Ackoff, and E. L. Arnoff, *Introduction to Operations Research,* Wiley, New York 1957, pp. 136–153.
2. Landis, F., "What Makes Technical Men Happy and Productive?" *Research Management, XIV* (3), May 1971, pp. 24–42.
3. Odiorne, G. S., *Management by Objectives,* Pitman, New York, 1965.
4. Pelz, D. C., and F. M. Andrews, *Scientists in Organizations,* Wiley, New York, 1966.
5. Roy, R. H., *The Administrative Process,* John Hopkins Press, Baltimore, 1958, pp. 83–97.

─────────────────────── **Discussion Questions** ───────────────────────

1. What is the difference between policies, procedures, and plans?
2. In what ways are planning and control similar?
3. Can a manager receive too much information about what is going on?
4. Why is budgetary control insufficient?

5. Is a budget a technique of planning or control?
6. Is return on investment a good criteria for planning in a technical function?
7. Discuss the impact of a budget on creativity and innovation.
8. It is sometimes said that planning is looking forward and controlling is looking backward. Do you agree?
9. How does the informal organization exert control?
10. "Parkinson's law" states that the size of the administrative staff will grow at the rate of 6 percent per year even if the work load diminishes. What organizational characteristic causes this? What can be done to preclude it?

—————————————— Case Study IX ——————————————

ELROD MANUFACTURING COMPANY

The Elrod Manufacturing Company had been started about 50 years ago as a precision tool and die machine shop. John Elrod, the founder, had quickly expanded the company into general manufacturing through the acquisition of a number of smaller companies, such as foundaries and sheet metal shops in the Chicago area. The company prospered and eventually was engaged in the manufacture of various automotive parts such as gears, axles, transmissions, metal stampings, and various sheet metal subassemblies. The company ended up with six plants in the Chicago-Detroit area that employed a total of 12,000 people. Each plant was operated as a distinct profit center with its own plant manager, who had a complete staff including sales, engineering, manufacturing, warehousing, etc.

The central corporate office, in Chicago, exercised control over the six plants through central planning, budgets, and the control of capital expenditures. All capital expenditures of $5000 or more had to be approved by the vice president for plant engineering. All capital expenditures of $50,000 or more were approved by the executive committee which consists of the president, vice president for sales, vice president for plant engineering, director of planning, and the comptroller.

Vernon Scott, the vice president for plant engineering, had been a long-time friend of the founder and was going to complete his fortieth year with the company in April. Scott was 64 and George Elrod, the son of the founder and president of the corporation, had been worrying about whether he should force the retirement of Scott at 65. Scott had become very conservative as he had gotten older, and several of the plant managers had complained to the president about Scott. The major problem was in the area of approval of capital expenditures, which were between $5000 and $50,000. Scott would readily approve expenditures for machinery and equipment used directly in manufacturing, but he was reluctant to spend anything on building maintenance, expansion, or modifications that were not directly manufacturing related.

The plant managers were all aware of Scott's peculiarities and, therefore, they had begun approving projects piecemeal. For instance, if a project cost $20,000, they would break it up into four or five smaller segments each costing less than $5000 a piece. Since they were authorized to approve anything up to $5000, they were within the letter of the regulations, but not the spirit.

One morning Scott came storming into Elrod's office without even stopping at the secretary's desk to see if Elrod was busy. He was livid with rage and waving a set of papers.

SCOTT: Paul Nelson has really done it this time. I want him fired right now, and I mean right now.

ELROD: Whoa, Vernon, calm down. What in the world are you talking about?

SCOTT: I'll tell you what I'm talking about. Insubordination, cheating, and dishonesty. I want him fired now.

ELROD: Those are strong words and accusations, Vernon. Would you mind slowing down long enough to tell me why I should fire my best plant manager?

SCOTT: Six months ago Paul came to me with a request for $27,000 to buy a computer for his engineering department. I told him they didn't need it, that they could use the corporate computer like everyone else. I thought it was all settled, but now I find out he deliberately ignored my decision.

ELROD: That doesn't sound like Nelson. Why do you think he ignored your decision?

SCOTT: The chief cost accountant was doing an audit of Nelson's plant to set the overhead rate. He casually mentioned to me at lunch that he was surprised at the high usage rate of Nelson's computer and how much easier it was to perform the audit with everything computerized. I thought at first he was kidding, but he wasn't. Nelson does have his own computer.

ELROD: How did he manage that if you turned it down?

SCOTT: That's what I wondered, too. I checked into it and found out he had bought it component by component. Each purchase order was under $5000, so his signature was all that purchasing needed. None of the purchase orders say anything about a computer. They just say C.P.U. logic system or disk drive, etc. Purchasing doesn't know what those things are, so they just go out and buy it. Then all the parts come in, and Nelson has a $30,000 computer setting there without my approval.

Elrod had a hard time keeping from laughing. Nelson was by far the best of the six plant managers. In fact, Elrod had been thinking seriously about bringing Nelson up to the corporate office and making him a vice president. The only reason he had hesitated was the lack of a suitable replacement for him as plant manager. One of the characteristics about Nelson that Elrod had always admired was his ability to get the job done. It was true that he sometimes stepped on some people's toes in the process, but he always got the job done.

ELROD: Vernon, you've got to admit that Paul didn't violate the rules. He does have the authority to approve purchase orders up to $5000 as long as he stays within his budget.

SCOTT: But he was specifically told he couln't buy the computer when he sent the request to me. Hell, he could build a new plant $5000 at a time. Is that what you want?

ELROD: No, no, of course not. I'll get Paul up here and talk to him about it.

SCOTT: Talk to him about it? I don't want you to talk to him, I want you to fire him.

We can't have these plant managers acting like they are God. Either corporate head-quarters runs things or we don't. If I'm not in charge, then I want out. If you don't make an example of Nelson, the others will decide they don't have to pay attention to us either.

ELROD: Just calm down, Vernon. I'll talk to him and then we'll see.

The next day, Paul Nelson came to Elrod's office as requested. He was 35 years old, very self-confident, with an easygoing, friendly manner. He had joined the corporation right out of school and had a master's degree in industrial engineering. He had tremendous drive and had risen through the ranks rapidly. When he was made plant manager at age 30, he was the youngest by far of the plant managers. The others had not reached that position until they were about 50. Elrod had always admired the determination and no-nonsense attitude of Nelson, who had increased the profitability of his plant by 50 percent during his 5-year tenure.

ELROD: Paul, Vernon tells me you bought a computer despite his telling you not to.

NELSON: Yeah, I'm afraid I did. I tried to do it through him to relieve my budget. But he is such an old fuddy-duddy he doesn't know the difference between an abacus and a computer.

ELROD: Why couldn't you use the corporate computer, as he suggested?

NELSON: I tried to explain to him that the corporate computer was tied up all the time on payroll and financial data processing. The turnaround time for engineering jobs was 5 to 7 days, and we just can't operate that way. Besides, I wanted to set up an in-process inventory control system. I tried to explain all this to Scott, but he couldn't understand what I was saying. He's at least 20 years out of date.

ELROD: But this is his area of responsibility.

NELSON: I know, but if we let Scott have his way we'd never be able to get anything done. For example, he'll never approve a plant maintenance project. The whole plant would fall down around my head if I didn't have a way of getting around him. I'm not the only one. If you'll talk to the other plant managers you'll find out we all have to conduct building projects piecemeal.

ELROD: But, Paul, if everyone ignores or finds a way to get around the control systems I set up, we don't really have a control system, do we?

NELSON: No, but on the other hand, we have to get the job done, don't we? Do you want us to worry about the feelings of people like Vernon Scott or do you want us to make a profit?

Case study discussion questions

1.   Should Elrod fire Nelson?
2.   Do you suppose this is a common practice in all organizations?
3.   How can a manager avoid submanagers getting around the control system in a similar manner?
4.   What would you do if you were Elrod?

CHAPTER 10 systems management

10.1 Complex Systems

In Chapter 9 we discussed the management and control of relatively small technical projects. Small projects can be pursued by 1 to 10 professional personnel. Many technical managers are faced, however, with the problem of managing much larger and more complex technical projects. As the problems of our society have become larger in scope and complexity, so have the technical systems designed to cope with them. The planning and control tasks of technical management become more difficult as the person-organized and designed systems of our society become more complex.

As the scope and complexity of a technical project increase, it must inevitably involve a larger number of people and organizations with widely differing backgrounds and skills. This leads to real problems of communication, coordination, and integration of efforts. A complex project of the type we will be concerned with in this chapter involves a series of parallel activities with a significant interplay of human skills, resources, and facilities. Some of these projects are large, of long duration, and of great technical complexity (e.g., designing, building, and opening a new refinery or bringing a new airplane into being and service). Others are of medium size and duration (e.g., constructing a building or designing and starting up a new assembly line). We will call such complex projects *systems projects;* they are characterized as follows.

1. The solution of the problem involves the commitment of large quantities of resources—money, manpower, materials, and facilities.
2. The interrelationships among the parts of the system under development and its interface with the environment are complex.
3. Management of a complex systems development will entail interaction between technical, economic, cultural, psychological and political factors.

A *system* is defined to be a group or set of elements, united by some form of regular interaction, that performs a set of designated functions in order to achieve desired results. Successful planning, design, and implementation of large, complex systems requires the use of the so-called systems approach. The initial impetus in the development of the systems approach to complex projects came from the military and was greatly accelerated by the space program. Since the advent of the space program in the United States, there has been great interest in possible technological spin-off and the application of the knowledge and experience gained to other sectors. It may turn out that the most valuable spin-off will be our improved knowledge of how to plan, coordinate, monitor, and control multitudinous disciplines and organizational segments that are working to accomplish complex undertakings.

The systems approach to the management of complex projects recognizes the interrelationships that tie a system together and the environment in which it must operate. The system is embedded in a set of complex environments—physical, social, political, economic, and technological. These environments comprise a supersystem with which there are strong, complex interrelationships. These environments are a source of constraints concerning the use of the system and of the technology that must be considered in the design, development, and operation of the desired system.

10.2 The Systems Approach

It is important to note that the way in which a problem is conceptualized will dictate the approach taken and will impose strong constraints on the ways in which the individual, group, or organization can seek solutions to it. In the following discussion I borrow heavily from some of the ideas expressed by Russell L. Ackoff in an address to a joint meeting of the Operations Research Society of America, The Institute of Management Sciences, and The American Institute of Industrial Engineers [1].

In his address Ackoff discussed two fundamentally different approaches to problem solving that he said derived from (1) the machine age, and (2) the systems age. The *machine age* approach is based on the concept of reductionism. It is predicated on the belief that everything in the world and every problem can be reduced, decomposed or disassembled to ultimately simple parts. Each part can then be studied and analyzed separately so as to be able to understand and explain it. Finally, this understanding or explanation of the parts can then be reaggregated or reassembled to provide explanations or solutions to the whole. Thus, the analysis or solution of a problem consists of breaking it down into as simple a set of subproblems as possible, solving each, and then assembling their solutions into a solution of the overall problem. If the analyst can succeed in breaking the overall problem into simpler subproblems that are independent of each other, the aggregation of the partial solutions is not required, because the solution to the whole is the sum of the solution of the parts.

This approach to problem solving derives from analytical thinking. It is based on a mechanistic view of the world and is predicated on a study of cause and effect relationships. All phenomena are believed to be explainable in terms of these simple relationships. One thing or event is taken to be the cause of another (its effect) if it can be shown to be necessary and sufficient for the other. Thus nothing else is required to explain the effects other than the cause, and the problem is environment free. Since the effects are completely determined by the causes, this provides a *deterministic* viewpoint of the world. Einstein's comment, ''I cannot accept that God plays dice with the world,'' is an expression of this view of science [4].

This approach to problem solving leads directly to the concept of division of labor. If the solution to a problem consists of dividing it into simple, independent parts, it is desirable to divide the labor of seeking to solve the parts into a number of virtually independent disciplines or groups. What is needed is a highly specialized group for solving each of the independent subproblems and a higher level of management to divide the problem up and aggregate or reassemble the partial answers into the solution of the whole. This approach has been very successful; it gave us the Industrial Revolution and most of the technological advances we saw through the 1940s and 1950s. We might also refer to this as a *multidiscipline* approach (i.e., the problem is decomposed into unidiscipline or uniprofessional problems that can be solved independently of each other).

Unfortunately, there have been some side effects of the machine age approach. The Industrial Revolution brought about the mechanization of work and the substitution of machines for people as a source of physical work. Each machine was designed to perform a specialized task and changed the nature of the work left for people to do. Workers and machines each performed one or a small number of elementary tasks that were organized into processing networks such as assembly lines. Division of labor and specialization was carried to the point where a worker might put on only five bolts on the rear wheel of a car as it was pulled past. As machines began to do the work of people, people began to work more and more like machines. The dehumanization of work became one unforeseen result of the Industrial Revolution.

A second unforeseen result of the machine age approach was the lack of concern or consideration for side effects. With functional specialization and division of labor into smaller and smaller spheres, no one was concerned with the overall picture. Concern for the cost effectiveness of a particular design or approach was the major decision criterion. The cheapest way to get rid of wastes was to dump them into the river or into the atmosphere. What happens to them after that was someone else's concern. Most of the problems resulting from the side effects of technology that concern our society today can be traced back directly to the tunnel vision spawned by the specialization and division of labor required by the machine age approach. The result is an attitude of, "if that's not my job, it's not my concern."

Beginning in the 1940s we began to see a new mode of thinking and a new approach to problem solving. As the systems and problems became more and more complex, managers began to realize that the summation of the partial solutions did not always add up to the best solution of the whole. The era of the *systems age* approach was dawning. The machine age was based on reductionism, but the systems age is based on a concept of expansionism. Expansionism is the concept that all objects, events, etc., are part of larger wholes, that each system is really a subsystem of some other system. The systems age and the concept of expansionism provided another way of viewing things that was different from and yet compatible with the machine age and reductionism.

Analytical thinking leads to the study of cause and effect relationships and a mechanistic view of the world; systems thinking leads to the study of teleology (the study of goal seeking and purposeful behavior) and a holistic view of the world. This way of thinking is based on the observation that when each part of a system performs as well as possible, it does not necessarily mean that the system as a whole will perform in an optimal manner. The holistic viewpoint emphasizes the organic or functional relationship between the parts and the whole. It is based on the theory that the determining factors are an irreducible whole that cannot be studied separately.

The systems approach was originally developed in the aerospace industry. As airplanes, missiles and spacecraft became more and more sophisticated and complex, the need to look at the system as a whole became unavoidable. The old hierarchical form of organization based on functions and the multidiscipline approach was inadequate and could not respond in a timely fashion. What was needed was an organizational form and management approach that would allow an *interdisciplinary* approach to problem solving. The old, familiar, hierarchical form was redesigned into the project form of organization. Under this form of organization the problem was not disassembled into disciplinary parts, but was treated as a whole by representatives of different disciplines working together.

Unfortunately, neither approach to problem solving is capable of handling all problems. Both the machine age and the systems age approaches have strengths and glaring weaknesses. The machine age approach is ideal for providing detailed study and analysis of system components and processes, but it is incapable of looking at the big picture and interrelationships. The systems age approach does an excellent job of examining the overall situation and the interaction of subsystems and keeping focused on the overall end result. Unfortunately, it is ill prepared for providing the in-depth penetration that is often required to fully understand and solve the problem.

As we saw in Chapter 3, the matrix organization provides for a possible compromise and marriage of the two approaches. By putting the systems-oriented people into the project groups and the machine-oriented people into the functional groups and combining the two groups into the matrix, we can provide both viewpoints and capabilities.

10.3 Closed-Loop Systems Control

The systems approach to complex project management assumes that the system is to be planned, designed, and implemented in order to satisfy the needs of a user or customer. This user or customer may be the parent organization or an outside group such as a government agency that has contracted for the work. Thus, in order to be useful, the system must ultimately satisfy the needs of the customer, and consideration of these needs must be paramount in design of the management control system.

Project management awareness and control require a continuous monitoring and evaluation of all program aspects in terms of cost, schedule, and technical performance. Each of these domains present risks to management that must be averted or overcome if the system development is to be successful. These risks are cost overruns, schedule delays, and inadequate system performance. It cannot be stressed too strongly that success depends upon averting all three types of risks. If we are developing a system and the final performance meets our initial specifications and goals, it may still be a dismal failure if the development costs far exceeded our initial estimates. Likewise, it may be a failure from an overall viewpoint, if the time for development was so long that the end product has been made obsolete or the market has been taken over by a competitor. Considering only the three dimensions of cost, performance, and schedule, there are eight possible outcomes of a development project, only one of which constitutes success (see Table 10.1). Thus, if we assume equal probabilities for each of the outcomes, the odds are 7 to 1 against success without even considering whether management made the correct decisions in the beginning. The problem to be addressed in this chapter is how we might change those odds.

Usually, cost overruns, schedule slippages, and inadequate performance can be traced directly to the fact that we overlooked certain technical aspects until they suddenly created or presented serious problems in product or system performance. We are then forced into crash programs of redesign, additional testing, and retrofits. This in turn leads to cost overruns, schedule delays and, frequently, compromise tradeoffs of performance. Since hindsight is always perfect, we find that when we look back at projects that were less than total successes, almost without exception, these failures can be traced to one of three causes.

1. Failure to seek the help of appropriate specialists.
2. Failure to ask the specialists the right questions at the right times.
3. Failure to heed the advice of the specialist after it is given.

Thus, we can see that one of the most significant aspects of management risk aversion is that of trying to insure that the proper specialists are asked the right questions at the right time and that their advice is heeded when given. Over the years, a number of specialist disciplines have developed and have produced powerful tools to aid management in risk aversion. Several of these are shown in Table 10.2. The difficulty is that too often these disciplines and specialists are ignored until a problem is already out of hand and the project is in trouble. Their proper input should be in avoiding the problems before they arise, not in solving or fixing them after the damage has been done. The question is how best to help insure that these specialists are properly used to aid management in risk aversion.

TABLE 10.1   Possible Outcomes of a Project

Cost	Performance	Schedule	Result
Controlled	Adequate	On time	Success
Overrun	Adequate	On time	Failure
Controlled	Inadequate	On time	Failure
Overrun	Inadequate	On time	Failure
Controlled	Adequate	Too late	Failure
Overrun	Adequate	Too late	Failure
Controlled	Inadequate	Too late	Failure
Overrun	Inadequate	Too late	Failure

TABLE 10.2   Aspects of Risk Aversion

Discipline	Goals
Program control	Management visibility into what is really happening regarding costs and schedules and what to do about it
Design engineering	Designing of hardware and equipment that will meet the mission or system requirements
System engineering	Assurance that everything is being done technically that needs to be done
Interface control	Assurance that hardware designed and built by different groups will fit and work together
Configuration management	Knowing what the hardware looks like and when and how to introduce changes
Logistics	Getting the right thing to the right place at the right time
Production and value engineering	Assurance that the designs are converted to hardware at the lowest cost
Reliability and safety	Knowing it is built right, will work right, and will be safe

In order to achieve success, we need to consider the management control process from a feedback control viewpoint. In a very interesting paper, Bartee [2] discusses the process of solution synthesis and control as a closed-loop system (see Figure 10.1). He argues very cogently that we must consider the user of the system as an integral part of the process if we are to succeed. We might translate this general systems concept into a more specific closed-loop

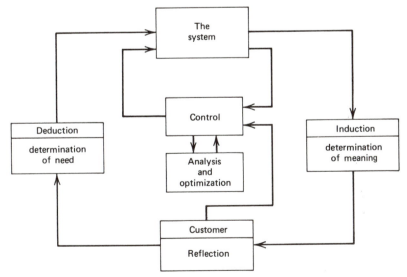

FIGURE 10.1   Closed-loop systems control.

management control system such as that in Figure 10.2. As mentioned earlier, the customer might be a government representative or in an industrial situation the marketing, manufacturing, or operations people of the company might serve in the same capacity.

It is very important when you wish to develop and deploy complex technical systems that there be early and continuous inputs from the operational people or users in the design phases. Toward the beginning of the planning and design process, you must impose certain constraints to ensure proper operational and system efficiency characteristics of the end product. This can best be done by the operational people or users.

10.4 Organizing for the Project

In order for such a closed-loop, feedback control system to operate efficiently, the organizational system must be capable of rapidly responding to the changes required, As I have tried to show, the traditional pyramid is incapable of this rapid response. Too many people have too many vested interests, and the organization is designed for static, not dynamic, operation. The matrix organization, on the other hand, is designed specifically to provide for rapid change without disruption or lengthy delays.

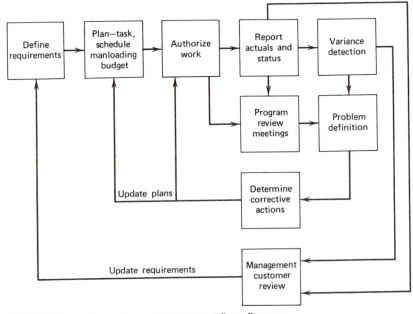

FIGURE 10.2   Closed-loop management flow diagram.

Closely tied into the matrix concept of organization has been the use of the "work package" management control system. The underlying philosophy of the work package system is the concept of MBO and decentralization of accountability. Implementation of the system requires that a work breakdown structure or tree be constructed. This is done by dividing the overall task by project or product subsystems (hardware, software, and services) and then further breaking down the product-oriented elements into functional work packages. Each work package is basically a performance control element that is negotiated with and assigned to a specific manager. This work package manager agrees to a specific objective (which is measurable), detailed task descriptions, specifications, schedule task milestones, and a time phased budget in both dollars and manpower for his or her work package. The work package manager is then held fully and personally responsible for that work package in terms of technical, schedule, and cost performance by both the program and functional managers. All program tracking and accounting for control purposes is done by work packages, utilizing some appropriate scheduling system such as the Critical Path Method (CPM) or the Program Evaluative and Review Technique (PERT). Summary reports are furnished to both the program and functional management structure, as appropriate.

The combination of the use of the matrix concept of organization and the work package control system provides several vital benefits for risk aversion. First, the very process of establishing the work breakdown structure or tree provides an orderly procedure to insure that all of the needed specialist skills are brought to bear on the problem. Since each of the functional managers participates in establishing this breakdown, he or she has an opportunity to see that the project manager recognizes and provides for the input of each of the specialist areas. In addition, when the work packages are negotiated and scheduled, each functional manager can insure that the specialists under his or her control will have their input at the appropriate points in time and not as an afterthought when the project is already in trouble. The matrix organization structure allows the necessary skilled manpower to be deployed and retracted as needed for each work package. If this was not possible without hiring and firing, cost overruns would be almost sure to occur due to people "making work." The matrix concept makes it possible to bring each specialist's skill to bear on the problem at precisely the time it is needed and only for as long as required.

Earlier I said that another cause of problems in system development was the ignoring of expert advice after it was given. A second advantage to the matrix concept is that it helps to preclude this possibility. If a specialist's advice is to be ignored, that decision must be concurred to by at least two different managers (the project manager and the appropriate functional manager). This is the built-in check and balance of the matrix concept. If a specialist raises a question about some aspect of the project and the two managers concerned cannot agree as to what should be done about it, the conflict must be resolved by a higher level of management. This still will not insure that a correct decision will be made, but at least the issue will have been thoroughly aired and everyone will be aware of a potential problem area.

10.5 Work Breakdown Structure

The purpose of any management control system (MCS) is to provide useful data for the assessment of program progress and as a basis for requisite management decisions. As a minimum, this MCS should:

1. Indicate work progress.
2. Properly relate technical performance, cost, and schedule.
3. Supply managers with a practical level of summarization.

A good MCS should provide an effective and efficient technique to organize, plan, schedule, budget, cost, analyze, and review programs. The proper selection of projects, allocation of resources, and evaluation of projects in an ever changing environment requires artful managers and an MCS capable of fast, accurate, and meaningful response.

As a first step in planning, organizational objectives must be broken down into meaningful work packages or tasks to be conducted. When added together, the successful tasks will mean that the overall organizational objectives will be achieved. This breakdown of organization objectives to subobjectives to work packages to tasks will be called the work breakdown structure (WBS). A WBS to display subdivisions of work provides a basis for clearly defining all work to be accomplished [3.].

The overall program manager should be responsible for the development and maintenance of the WBS. The WBS should schematically display the product (objective) and work to be accomplished and reflect the interrelationships of each element of work (see Figure 10.3). The purpose is to divide the work to the level where specific segments of work can be defined and assigned to a single, responsible organization element. This structure identifies the program elements where cost accounts can be established, budgets and schedules assigned, actual costs accumulated, and performance evaluated.

The WBS should have the following characteristics.

1. A single WBS is developed and maintained for the life of the program.
2. The summation of all elements from the lowest to the highest level must represent the total of all program work effort.

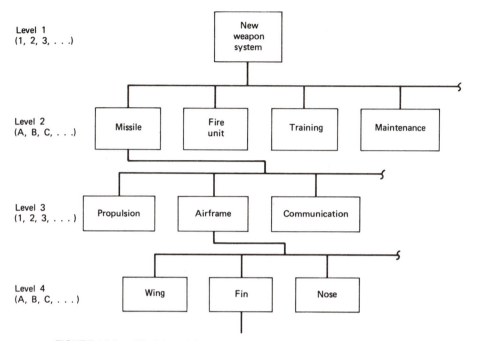

Level 1
(1, 2, 3, . . .)

New
weapon
system

Level 2
(A, B, C, . . .)

Missile | Fire unit | Training | Maintenance

Level 3
(1, 2, 3, . . .)

Propulsion | Airframe | Communication

Level 4
(A, B, C, . . .)

Wing | Fin | Nose

FIGURE 10.3   Work breakdown structure (WBS).

3. Each WBS element must be assigned to a specific functional area and work package (W/P) manager to be responsible for coordinating and managing the work effort.

4. The WBS should be alphanumerically coded to identify the appropriate element in the WBS. Each character identifies a position in the level corresponding to the character position. For example, from Figure 10.3, 1A2A is the wing design work element.

The program manager should assure that the total work of the program life cycle is planned and scheduled and that resources are budgeted. The scheduling will include all milestones (major and minor) that identify significant constraints and achievements of technical performance requirements. Budgets assigned to authorized and scheduled work provide a way to measure performance. Use of the WBS provides a basis for clearly defining all work to be accomplished. To plan properly, a master program schedule is necessary. This schedule is a time phased schedule of WBS elements that portrays the required program development events from inception to completion. It is used by planners to identify and define the program in terms of objectives and support functions necessary to accomplish established goals. A work package network chart indicating interrelationships of all work on the program can be used as part of the master program schedule (MPS) (see Figure 10.4). Once the work to be performed is described and scheduled, the program manager must authorize the funding for the work and provide the funding to the organizational element that will perform the tasks.

The appropriate functional manager will then assign a work package (W/P) manager for each WBS element assigned to his or her functional group by the program manager. The W/P manager will, with the appropriate team members, describe the work to be done, identify tasks and milestones, and estimate the cost and schedule for performing the work. This information will be submitted to both the program and functional managers. The work package will have the following characteristics.

1. Related to a specific job assignment.
2. Assigned to a single functional group.
3. Include clearly defined start and stop dates.
4. Include clear and concise description of work.
5. Include budgets in terms of labor hours, labor dollars, material dollars, and other direct charges.
6. Include technical objectives and milestones.

When the program manager authorizes the work, an expenditure order form is sent to the cost account manager (finance and accounting section, administrative staff), who establish a cost account for work packages. The cost account is opened by initiation of the first work package under that

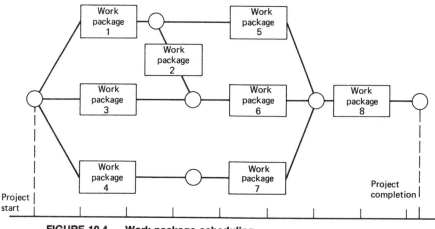

FIGURE 10.4   Work package scheduling.

cost account (identified by the WBS alphanumeric code). A cost account is closed at completion of the last work package.

The organization's budget is fixed and based on the organization's plans and justifications submitted to the sponsor. To maintain flexibility, the budget should be divided into three portions.

1. *Distributed Budget.* The portion of the authorized budget that has been distributed to cost accounts.
2. *Undistributed Budget.* The portion of the authorized budget set aside for work anticipated, but not yet authorized.
3. *Management Reserve.* The portion of the authorized budget for unforeseen and unbudgeted work that management feels is within the scope of the program but is not known at the time of the creation of the original budget.

Budgets assigned to scheduled cost accounts provide a time phased budget baseline for the measurement of task and organizational performance. Each work package will contain a budget that represents the planned value of that unit of work. The sum of the work package values will equal the cost account value.

The cost account is the basic component for cost planning and control. The cost account integrates the program WBS with the functional organization. The WBS identifies what must be accomplished to meet organizational objectives, and the cost account identifies the manager responsible for the accomplishment. Budgets are established, costs are collected, and performance is measured at the cost account level. The accounting system should be capable of accumulating all direct costs in cost accounts and summarizing them to the top WBS level. Cost accumulation should be possible by both WBS and organizational element. Some sort of program budget control (PBC) numbering system should be utilized to control and accumulate costs. Figure 10.5 indicates the breakdown of a typical PBC number.

Controls should be maintained by the administrative staff for safeguarding assets, checking the accuracy and reliability of accounting data, promoting operational efficiency, and encouraging adherence to prescribed managerial policies. The status of all cost accounts should be reported periodically (such as every 4 weeks) by the cost account manager to the appropriate managers and should show funds authorized, costs to date, commitments, and balances.

Written expenditure orders authorized by the program manager should be used to redistribute work from one functional branch to another within the organization. These orders are authority to the receiving functional manager to proceed with the work requested. Acceptance by the performing functional manager constitutes agreement to all terms of that expenditure order.

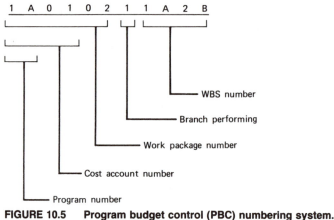

FIGURE 10.5   Program budget control (PBC) numbering system.

10.6   Network Planning Methods

In 1957 the Integrated Engineering Control Group of E. I. duPont de Nemours and Company decided that they were dissatisfied with existing methods of project control and set out to develop a new method. The successful effort resulted in a new technique called the Critical Path Method (CPM). At about the same time, the U.S. Navy Special Projects Office (under Admiral Raborn), in conjunction with Booz-Allen and Hamilton (the management consultants), and the Lockheed Missile Systems Division was developing a similar system for the control of the Polaris project. This system was named the Program Evaluation and Review Technique (PERT).

Both groups, working independently of each other, developed methods based on the same fundamental principles and differing only in minor details. Since then over 50 different titles and code names have been given to variations of this technique for planning and controlling complex, multistage projects that necessitate the coordination of many activities and organizational groups. The basis of all of these techniques is to portray pictorially all the steps and tasks that must be accomplished to complete a project in the form of a network of events and activities [3, 5]. For this reason we will refer to all of these network analysis techniques as PERT/CPM methods. The only real difference between PERT and CPM is that PERT uses the concept of deriving a probability distribution for the accomplishment of each task from three time estimates, while CPM utilizes a single time estimate for each task.

The purpose of PERT/CPM is to help the manager plan a complex project so that the entire project can be visualized and controlled. Each job or task that must be done is examined to determine:

1. What other work must be completed before the job can start.
2. What other work can be started as soon as the task is completed.
3. What other work can be going on while the job is in progress.

This information is put into the form of a network, where the branches, or arcs, are tasks to be done and the nodes represent events or milestones. The tasks or activities require manpower and resources, while the events represent specific accomplishments that are the result of the work. Therefore an event requires no resources and takes no time.

Events and activities are sequenced on a network diagram. Activities may include design, analysis, fabrication, etc., and are represented by arrows connecting two event nodes. The length of the arrow has no significance. Its direction shows which event must precede the other. The network is constructed by starting with the end objective of the program and then working backward until the node representing the project initiation point is reached. First, the arrows representing the final activities that must be completed are connected to the node representing the end objective. The nodes depicting the events that must occur before these final activities can begin are then attached to the other ends of the appropriate arrows. The entire network is obtained by proceeding in this fashion until the starting point of the project is reached. A sample PERT network is provided in Figure 10.6.

The network must be constructed in accordance with a precise set of sequencing rules. These rules are as follows.

1. There must be only one beginning event. This event is represented by a node labeled zero, and the remaining nodes are numbered in such a way that if there is an arrow directed from node i to node j, then $i < j$. Event numbers must not be duplicated in a network.
2. There must be only one ending event (node 12 in Figure 10.6).
3. No event can be considered complete until all of its predecessor activities and events have been completed. For example, in Figure 10.6, events 1

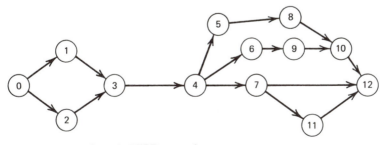

FIGURE 10.6   Sample PERT network.

and 2 both precede event 3; events 5, 6, 8, and 9 must precede event 10; and events 7, 10, and 11 must precede event 12.

4. Two or more activities that are performed concurrently after a single event and have the same concluding event cannot be represented by the same arrow. In this case, a dummy event must be added (node 4), as shown in Figure 10.7, with a dummy activity (dashed arrow) requiring zero time to complete. The concurrent activities are "*a*" and "*b*." This is necessary in order for each activity to be addressed in terms of the nodes at which it starts and ends without ambiguity.

After the network has been constructed, time estimates are required for each activity. Since these time estimates deal with the future and are, therefore, uncertain, PERT utilizes three time estimates: the most pessimistic (i.e., the longest time), the most optimistic (i.e., the shortest time), and the most likely. These three times are usually designated *b*, *m*, and *a*, respectively, and are made for each activity in order to ensure that the time sets will be as accurate as possible.

The expected completion time for each activity and the variance of the expected time can be calculated from the three time estimates for that particular activity by means of probability theory. Specifically, it is assumed that (1) the optimistic time estimate, *a*, and the pessimistic estimate, *b*, are such that the probability of the task time falling outside the range *a* to *b* is very small, and (2) the most likely time, *m*, which moves between the two extremes, represents the peak, or modal value, of a probability distribution. These characteristics are usually described by the beta distribution. Two conceivable conditions are shown in Figure 10.8.

It may be shown that t_e, the expected, mean, or average completion time for the activity, is given by

$$t_e = \frac{a + 4m + b}{6}$$

The standard deviation, σ_t, is assumed to be equal to one-sixth of the range between the pessimistic and optimistic completion time estimates. Therefore

$$\sigma_t = \frac{b - a}{6}$$

and

$$\sigma^2_t = \left(\frac{b - a}{6} \right)^2$$

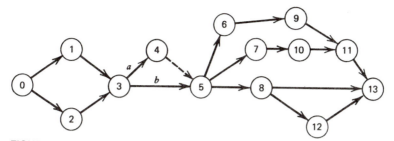

FIGURE 10.7   Introduction of dummy activity into PERT network.

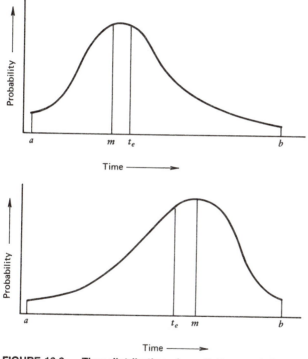

FIGURE 10.8   Time distributions for activity completion.

10.7   Constructing the Network

As already discussed, PERT/CPM employs a network as a logic diagram or
plan chart. Each arrow or activity in this network represents one of the
various planned tasks or jobs leading to the end objective and requires expenditure of resources such as time, labor, and material. The circles or nodes at

the beginning and end of the activity arrows are events or milestones in the PERT/CPM network. They represent specific accomplishments that are the result of work. Each event is a definable point in time and signifies a decision to start or terminate an activity or job. An event, unlike an activity, does not require the expenditure of resources. An event is used, for example, to identify the point in time at which funds are released, a contract awarded, specifications and drawings released, or an item delivered.

The basic steps involved in constructing the network are as follows.

1. Develop a WBS for the project to be done. This WBS serves as the framework for the development of the planning network and cost estimating.

2. Determine the events that must occur and the activities that must be accomplished in order for them to take place.

3. With the time dimension going from left to right on the paper, place the circles or nodes in their proper time relationship to each other and join them by arrows as appropriate.

4. For each activity (arrow) obtain an estimate of the expected time t_e needed to accomplish that activity. Note these estimates on the network.

5. Starting at the left with the starting event and proceeding to the right through the network, calculate the expected completion time T_E for each event. This is the expected time to reach a particular event and is obtained by adding up the t_es for the activities necessary to reach that event.

6. Starting at the extreme right with the end or completion event, work backward through the network calculating the latest allowable date T_L for each event. This is the latest allowable time to reach an event without slipping the end date. Thus the T_L for any event is both the latest allowable completion date for all preceding activities and the latest allowable starting date for the most critical task that follows it. It is calculated by subtracting the t_es from the succeeding T_L.

7. Calculate the slack or float for each event in the network. Slack represents the difference between the total expected time T_E and the latest allowable time T_L for each event. It represents extra time allowable for noncritical events.

8. Determine the critical path through the network. The critical path is the longest one through the network. It is found by connecting the events that show zero or the largest negative slacks. These events or path represent the sequence of activities that is pacing the end date. Any slippage of an event on this path will result in a one-for-one slippage of the end date unless it can somehow be made up.

In order to demonstrate this let us consider a very simple project of seven tasks as follows.

Activity	Predecessor Activities	Time Required in Weeks
A	Start	4
B	Start	6
C	Start	3
D	A	5
E	A	3
F	B, E	4
G	C	5

The network would look like Figure 10.9. Note that the nodes have been divided into three segments. The bottom half of the node contains the event number. The upper left half will be used to record T_E for each event and the upper right half to record T_L. The expected time for each activity t_e is written below the arrow and the activity code appears above it.

In order to calculate the earliest or expected date (T_E), we sum up the activity expected times. For example, activity A is expected to take 4 weeks, therefore event 1 could be accomplished in 4 weeks. In the case of event 2, both tasks B and E must be accomplished before this event can occur. When two or more activities feed into the same event, we must select the longest path. In this case we are looking at 6 weeks by task B versus 7 weeks by task

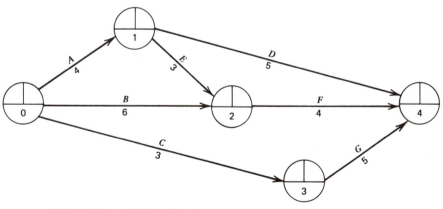

FIGURE 10.9   PERT/CPM network.

E. Therefore the T_E for event 2 is 7 weeks. Since event 3 depends only on activity C the expected time is 3 weeks. Looking at end event 4, we see it has three arrows coming in and, again, we must choose the longest path. The three paths give 9 weeks by task D, 11 weeks by task F, and 8 weeks by task G. We therefore set T_E for event 4 at 11 weeks. These values are shown in the upper left segments of the nodes in Figure 10.10.

Once the expected event times have been determined, the latest allowable time, T_L, by which each event must be accomplished can be calculated. If 11 weeks constitute an acceptable schedule, we use this date for T_L for event 4. If some other date is the desired completion date, we use it. For demonstration purposes we will assume that the 11 weeks is acceptable and assign this as the latest allowable time for the end event. We now start at the end objective where $T_L = 11$ and successively subtract the activity time estimates (t_e) in reverse sequence to get the latest allowable time for each of the other events. For example, if it takes 5 weeks to accomplish activity G, then event 3 needs to be completed by the end of the sixth week (i.e., $T_L = 11 - 5 = 6$). The previous T_E calculation for event 3 indicated that this event was expected to be completed in 3 weeks from the start of the project. Consequently, the accomplishment of event 3 could be delayed by 3 weeks without jeopardizing meeting the expected date for the end objective. The difference, or cushion, is called slack or float and is equal to T_L minus T_E.

The latest allowable time for event 2 is given as $T_L = 11 - 4 = 7$ weeks. When we look to event 1 we see that two activities (D and E) emanate from it. Therefore we must choose the smallest T_L given by the multiple paths. Coming by way of activity D we would get 6 weeks or, by activity E, we get 3 weeks. Thus the T_L for event 2 is 3 weeks. The values calculated for T_L at

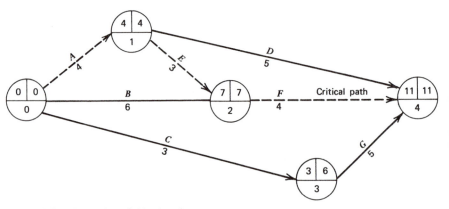

FIGURE 10.10   Critical path.

each event are recorded in the upper right segment of each node in Figure 10.10.

If we now examine T_E and T_L for each node or event, we find they are the same for events 0, 1, 2, and 4 (i.e., there is no slack). The activities connecting these nodes (shown as dotted lines in Figure 10.10) constitute the longest or critical path through the network. The activities and events on this path effectively establish and control the time to reach the end objective. There is no cushion or slack on this path, and slippage of any of these events will result in an equal slip in the achievement of the end objective. Note that there can be more than one critical path through a network.

We said earlier that instead of the calculated T_E for the end event we could use a scheduled target date for the last node's T_L. For example, suppose that the scheduled target completion date is 9, not 11 weeks away. Using this as the latest allowable end date, we would find that events 0, 1, 2, and 4 have a minus slack of 2 weeks. When negative slack is present in a network, the critical path consists of the events with the most negative slacks. Negative slack, of course, tells the manager that the scheduled target date cannot be met unless that time is made up somehow.

In the event that the calculations show negative slack, the manager has several different courses of action that can be taken. These include:

1. Considering the effects of using additional resources on the tasks in the critical path.
2. Considering alternative approaches such as parallel efforts (which may involve greater risk).
3. Considering the effects of relaxing performance requirements.
4. Acknowledging a probable slip in meeting the end objective.

Conversely, if large amounts of positive slack are indicated, consideration should be given to decreasing the planned level of effort in those activities or diverting effort to more critical areas.

10.8 Advantages of PERT/CPM

Network planning and control methods such as PERT/CPM are widely used by almost all industries for large and small projects. They are widely used in the construction industry to plan, coordinate, and control all types of projects with great success. Government agencies and industrial groups have long used them in R&D projects. It is claimed, for example, that the use of PERT succeeded in reducing the development time for the Polaris missile by over 2 years, a reduction of 45 percent. But they have also been used for many other purposes. E. I. duPont, for example, had a periodic overhaul of a particular item in its plants that had taken an average of 125 hours in previous years. Using CPM they reduced this to 93 hours, a 25 percent reduction [3]. I also had one student who used PERT/CPM to plan her very elaborate wedding with great success and minimum emotional strain.

With such widespread use, one would suspect that there are many advantages to their use. This is the case, and among the advantages that come readily to mind are:

1. Provides organization from the outset.
    (a) Forces definition of goals.
    (b) Promotes detailed planning from the very beginning.
    (c) Provides a ready-made framework for reporting, documentation and presentation.
2. Provides a powerful planning tool.
    (a) Segments planning problems to an easily handled size.
    (b) Forces detailed planning.
    (c) Requires definition of all the necessary work.
    (d) Displays relationship of each work effort to the entire plan.
    (e) Promotes consideration of alternate methods.
    (f) Makes resource deficiencies readily apparent.
    (g) Aids in delegating and fixing responsibility.
    (h) Allows planning for time phased financing.
3. Provides a communication tool.
    (a) Standardizes vocabulary and use of precise terms.
    (b) Pictorially displays relationships for ready understanding.
    (c) Explains status and proposed changes quickly.
    (d) Helps everyone concerned understand how their position fits into the big picture.
4. Provides a control mechanism.
    (a) Brings a high degree of visibility and objectivity to bear on analyzing problems.
    (b) Provides the mechanism for reporting and comparing progress versus plans.
    (c) It allows management to identify and concentrate on the critical areas.
    (d) Provides a ready-made framework for management by exception or management by objective.
    (e) Allows the impact of planned changes to be tested for effect before implementation.

(f) Allows each level of management to exercise control at the level of detail desired.

The only real disadvantage of PERT/CPM as a planning and control tool is that it is a tedious and exacting task if attempted manually. Small networks can be constructed and analyzed by hand but, for projects of any complexity at all, computer implementation is desirable. Numerous commercial computer program codes are available under various names that will handle projects of 5000 or more activities. However, the computer only assists in providing calculations and reports at various levels of detail; the manager must still be responsible for the planning and make the necessary required decisions. Equally as important is the fact that computer output is only as good and as accurate as its input. If necessary activities are left out of the network or if time estimates are grossly wrong, the computer will merely grind out the wrong answers to any number of desired decimal places.

10.9 Operational Use

The use of PERT/CPM techniques for planning purposes has tremendous advantage over traditional planning techniques. In fact, if the network charts were thrown away immediately after their completion, the effort would still be justified. Most PERT/CPM networks are not thrown away, but are used for reporting and control purposes. Note that several versions, such as PERT/COST, incorporate cost of each activity as well as time. Thus many network analysis systems incorporate all three dimensions of concern: time-cost-performance.

PERT/CPM methods provide a natural framework for reporting and control purposes. By asking each work package manager to report periodically milestones achieved, estimated date of accomplishing remaining milestones (events), and costs incurred since last report, all of the ingredients needed for control are available. These data can then be fed into the computer, compared to the PERT/CPM network plans, and deviations highlighted for deeper investigation. If desired, the reporting from the computer can be on an exception basis (i.e., only the events that will exceed the latest allowable time are printed out). Such reports can be generated weekly, biweekly, or monthly, depending on the criticality of the project schedule.

In general, project management is interested in information that answers the following kinds of questions.

1. Is the project meeting the committed schedule and cost estimates and, if not, the extent of the difference?

2. Is the outlook for meeting the committed schedule, cost, and performance estimates improving or getting worse, and why?
3. What problems are being encountered? What corrective action has been initiated, and what is the anticipated effect of this action?
4. Can manpower and other resources be shifted to expedite critical activities?

PERT/CPM can help to provide answers to all these questions. Two things should be noted, however. First, not every level of management is interested in the same degree of detail. PERT/CPM lends itself nicely to information compression. Figure 10.11 shows how the PERT/CPM network can be compressed to correspond to the levels of the work breakdown structure, which will generally correspond to the different levels of project management. Second, the computerized output format of the network analysis is generally not the best presentation format to management. The data must be converted into a format that is easily understood and communicates the information to be presented. A considerable variety of presentation formats can be developed.

The use of PERT/CPM does not guarantee infallible planning nor make management decisions. Management alone must decide when to change the schedules, reallocate resources, or change the performance requirements. PERT/CPM methods do, however, highlight the problem areas and allow management to explore the impact of decisions before implementing them. Hypothetical data such as revised schedules, reallocated resources, etc., can be fed into the computer program, and many alternative courses of action can

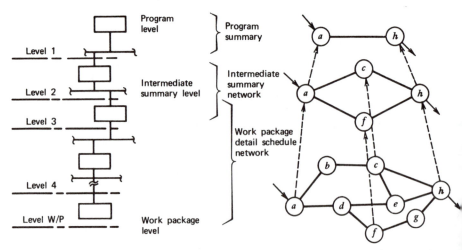

FIGURE 10.11 Relationship between network levels resulting from event compression.

be computed, evaluated, and analyzed before any specific decision is made. In other words, it can be used as a research tool to test various hypothesis.

Activity time and cost estimates should not be arbitrarily changed unless there is a corresponding change in work content or rate of application of resources. Reestimating should be done only under the following conditions.

1. An obvious error has been made.
2. Plans are revised.
3. New resources are introduced.
4. Personnel are added or reduced.
5. Technical difficulties arise.
6. Technical breakthroughs are experienced.
7. Overtime is authorized.

When changes in the time or cost estimates are made, they should be done in writing signed by the project manager, and the reasons for the reestimates should be listed on the authorizing form.

10.10 Audits and Reviews

The principles of visibility, flexibility, and communications are central to successful systems management. Effective visibility and communications systems help give maximum confidence that all program elements (technical, schedule, and cost) are progressing in accordance with established plans. Furthermore, they insure that problem areas surface in a timely manner, thus giving management sufficient time to find solutions with minimum, or no, program impact. The ability of management to anticipate and correct problems and deficiencies in the program prior to their assuming large proportions is a condition that should be sought by all managers.

The management visibility of the status of all aspects of the program must be developed at all levels of the organization. It must be based on detailed monitoring and auditing systems that allow the free flow of information both vertically and horizontally throughout the program. Periodic technical and management reviews are a critical feature. The timing and nature of these technical and management reviews will vary with the characteristics of the particular project. It is, however, critical that the user or customer participate in these reviews. Typical of these periodic reviews are:

1. *Preliminary Design Reviews.* Scheduled periodically as soon as the program begins to take shape in order to establish a relative level of agreement between the user or customer and the project group; culminates in the approval of the basic design approach.

2. *Critical Design Reviews.* Scheduled as the point of detailed drawing and specification release is approached. These reviews represent a last chance to discover problems prior to the building of hardware.
3. *Customer Acceptance Reviews.* Often held in conjunction with first article inspections. These reviews are generally held as the hardware is beginning to be manufactured but prior to release and deployment (i.e., during test and checkout).
4. *Final Design Certification Review.* The final checkout and audit of the system prior to its release for use. This review should include hardware, software, support, and operational elements required for success.

One of the difficulties with conducting such reviews in a complex systems development is the multitudinous disciplines involved. This is sometimes further complicated by the fact that various subsystems are being designed and built by different organizations. NASA solved this problem during the Apollo-Saturn program by establishing joint contractor-government panels or working groups. These technical working groups were organized according to technical disciplines and subsystems to manage technical interfaces and to provide in-depth visibility support to the program manager. All of these working groups had one thing in common—they were real-time, decision-making boards. Problems were identified and solutions decided on. People were stuck with the decisions they made at those meetings. The decisions were recorded and they became binding on the parties involved in the meeting.

These working groups were most useful in identifying problems and making decisions of a technical and hardware nature during the R&D phases. As the designs were hardened and the manufacturing and operational aspects came into the forefront, most of the technical working groups, having served their purpose, were discontinued. These technical working groups played an important role from several viewpoints. First, they exposed the problems at the various interfaces for everyone to see. Second, they forced face-to-face communication of the various organizational segments, thus reinforcing the team concept. Third, visibility and flexibility require a knowledgeable decision point close to the work, and most of the various group members were working level engineers or managers. Fourth, they provided an interchange of technical information and allowed the different organizations to learn from each other and to profit from each other's mistakes. Finally, it forced each organization to defend its decisions before a group of technical peers who were knowledgeable in the discipline under discussion. I believe that the same concept would prove very beneficial in an industrial situation where the working group team members are drawn from the different functional groups and the role of customer is played by manufacturing, marketing, etc.

In addition to the working groups, periodic program management reviews were held with top management in which program managers and functional managers presented progress reports and problem analysis regarding technical performance, costs, and schedule. Significant problems were often exposed in these management review meetings, when the project manager and a functional manager gave conflicting reports of a situation. Neither set of managers could hide their problems because they would most likely be exposed by the other, again demonstrating the desirability of built-in checks and balances.

Two other aspects of management visibility, flexibility, and communications must be mentioned: configuration control and engineering change order control. By their very nature, various parts, components, and subsystems are being designed and manufactured by different people, groups, and organizations. This means that after the baseline configuration and design are frozen, *any* changes must be carefully analyzed to be sure they do not have an undesired impact. Even seemingly harmless changes for manufacturing convenience or to correct a deficiency may cause parts not to fit or components to malfunction. Any changes in design or configuration, no matter how simple, must be reviewed by all parties concerned for possible impacts. This is particularly critical at the interfaces between subsystems or components designed or manufactured by different groups. This is usually implemented through the creation of a *configuration control board* and an *engineering change control board* on which all interested parties are represented. Such boards must be organized and set up, however, for rapid analysis and decisions. Otherwise, they may become bottlenecks that prevent desirable and even mandatory changes from occurring.

In summary, in addition to control through the work package breakdown and some form of PERT/CPM planning and control, other mechanisms must be devised. These should provide for:

1. Early problem detection.
2. A process for problem solving.
3. A process for recovery from anomalies and failures.
4. Rapid communication and visibility of everything that is occurring to all parties concerned.

This is usually accomplished through some combination of periodic technical and management reviews, technical working groups, and formal control boards.

References

1. Ackoff, R. L., "Science in the Systems Age: Beyond I.E, O.R. and M.S.," *Operations Research, 21* (3), May-June 1973, pp. 661–671.
2. Bartee, E. M. "On the Methodology of Solution Synthesis," *Management Science, 17* (6), February 1971, pp. B312-B323.

3. Burman, P. J., *Precedence Networks for Project Planning and Control,* McGraw-Hill (U.K.) Limited, England, 1972.
4. Clark, R. W., *Einstein: The Life and Times,* World Publishing, New York, 1971, p. 340.
5. Whithouse, G. E., *Systems Analysis and Design Using Network Techniques,* Prentice-Hall, Englewood Cliffs, N.J., 1973.

——————————— **Discussion Questions** ———————————

1. Are PERT/CPM methods planning or control techniques?
2. Is it better to make three estimates (pessimistic, probable, optimistic) of an activity time or one?
3. Are the concepts of the systems approach useful to managers?
4. Discuss the effect of geographic separation of cooperating groups on the management control system.
5. Discuss how the work breakdown structure and work package control can aide or hinder motivation.
6. Are the control methods discussed in this chapter compatible with encouraging creativity?
7. Discuss whether the methods discussed in this chapter meet the criteria for a good control system given in Sections 8.2, 8.3, and 8.4 of the previous chapter.
8. How do the methods discussed help preclude:
   (a) Failure to seek the help of appropriate experts?
   (b) Failure to ask the right specialists the right questions at the right time?
   (c) Failure to heed the advice of the specialist after it is given?

——————————— **Case Study X** ———————————

MONROE AIRCRAFT

The Eagle was a ground-to-air missile system designed for use by infantry against attack helicopters. The U.S. Army had contracted with Monroe Aircraft for both the development and manufacture of the system. The system was designed as a lightweight, hand-held weapon that could be carried by a single soldier. It was to be launched from a tube with an integral sight. The missile had a heat seeker guidance control system.

Roger Gurley, the Eagle project manager, was on his way to the management review meeting. This was a meeting held by Dr. Steve Vinson, the vice president for engineering, on each major project on a regular quarterly basis. At this meeting the project manager and each of the responsible functional managers gave a progress report to top management. The purpose was for each manager to report problems and progress on the particular project under review. Gurley felt very confident as he entered the conference room. He had carefully gone over the schedule and budget with his staff, and everything was under control. All of the scheduled milestones had been met on time, and the expenditures were actually 5 percent below budget.

Gurley's presentation went very well. His staff had prepared a series of slides that showed the highlights of the past quarter. He discussed the expenditures versus budget history and bragged that this was probably the first time in history that a project had actually been under budget at the midpoint and right exactly on schedule. One slide showed the current section of the PERT chart with a vertical line designating the current date and the milestones that had been accomplished colored bright green to designate go. Gurley completed his presentation with the statement that the project was in excellent shape and had no current problems. He sat down feeling very pleased with himself. Vinson said it certainly was a relief to see a project in good shape for a change.

The next speaker up was Dr. Vivian Walker, head of aerodynamics. She opened her presentation by saying that she was certainly surprised to see during Gurley's presentation that the drawings and specifications for the guidance control system had been released 2 weeks ago. As of this morning, she said, her group had not received the first bit of documentation from the guidance and control group. In fact, she went on, when she had talked to John Ringer, head of the group, this morning she had been told it would be at least 2 weeks more. Gurley quickly looked at Ringer, who shrugged his shoulders and studiously looked at the table top. Gurley glared at Ringer throughout the rest of Walker's presentation, but Ringer avoided looking at him. Walker proceeded to discuss the ramifications of the delay. If they, in fact, received the drawings and specifications in 2 weeks, she said her people believed that they could make up 2 weeks of the slippage by working overtime.

Vinson asked Gurley if the aerodynamic analysis was currently on the critical path. Gurley told him it was because of the critical design review with the Army people scheduled in 1½ months. Vinson then asked Ringer if the drawings and specifications would be released in 2 weeks. Ringer said that he was going to talk about that during his presentation.

VINSON: Perhaps then we should get right into Ringer's presentation.

WALKER: Before we go on I would like to call your attention to the fact that this delay will require that the budget on our work package be increased by $10,000 if no overtime is scheduled and $18,000 if overtime is used.

GURLEY: Why in the world is that?

WALKER: I've had four engineers assigned to this project sitting around idle for 2 weeks already, and it looks like it's going to be 4 weeks. At $15 an hour, you figure it out.

GURLEY: Why should the project pay for those people when they're not working on it?

WALKER: When I signed your work package, I scheduled the people for when you said. Did you want me to reschedule them to some other project and then not have anyone to do your job? I don't have enough overhead money to carry people indefinitely. When you contract for the people, you pay. It's not my fault you don't have anything for them to do. We can't do anything until Ringer's people release the information.

VINSON: Well, Roger, it looks like maybe your budget isn't in as good a shape as you thought. I think we better hear what Ringer has to say.

RINGER: First of all, it's true that we haven't released the drawings and specs yet.

GURLEY: But you reported a week ago on your PERT report that you had released them a week before that. I can show you the report.

RINGER: I know, but you always raise so much hell everytime we miss a milestone, demanding written justification, make-up plans, etc. Besides, we thought the simulated flight test scheduled for the next day was going to work out, and we could release the documentation. I really only thought I was fibbing by a week.

GURLEY: My God, don't tell me the simulated flight test wasn't completed yet. You reported that milestone was completed 1½ months ago, at least.

RINGER: Well, I didn't think the exact date of accomplishing that milestone was that important. As far as I was concerned, the important thing was to release the documentation on time. We were working on the documentation already, anyway. Besides, we thought then that the run failures were due to faulty instrumentation and that the design was good. Unfortunately, that hasn't turned out to be the case.

GURLEY: You mean you still don't have a successful test?

RINGER: Right, but we now think we know what the trouble is. If the missile tried to yaw to hard to the right, the system went unstable and. . . .

GURLEY: But you assured me that new concept was going to work.

RINGER: I know, and we thought it would. From a theoretical viewpoint it looked great. I told you it had never been done before, but that it was the only way to get a system that light. Besides, now we think we know how to put in a fix and, it will only increase the weight by 4 pounds.

GURLEY: Four pounds, only 4 pounds! We're 9 pounds overweight now. Some poor soul has to lug this thing around, you know!

VINSON: Roger, you haven't said anything about being 9 pounds overweight before.

GURLEY: I know. I didn't want you to get upset unnecessarily. Structures thinks they know a way to get the weight back down. They're running an analysis on it right now and are supposed to let me know by the end of the week.

WALKER: If they change the structure, that would change our aerodynamic analysis.

RINGER: It might change the response of our control system, also.

GURLEY: I know that. I was going to cross that bridge when we got to it. Structures doesn't know yet if it can be done.

RINGER: Before we end up the complete villians in this bit, I want to remind you that I asked for 3 months more when we were first negotiating the work packages. I told you then that this was something new and that things might not go as smoothly as planned.

GURLEY: Everyone always asks for twice as long as they really think they need. If I gave everyone all the time they asked for, we wouldn't be flying this bird for 10 years.

VINSON: The way things sound, it may be that long anyway. It looks to me, Roger, like you better get your heads together and find out what is really going on. I want a factual and complete account of the true status and a plan to get us out of this mess by a week from tomorrow. This meeting is adjourned.

Roger Gurley sat alone at the conference table long after everyone else had left. He was still trying to figure out what had gone wrong. What had started as such a lovely day had certainly turned into a disaster.

Case study discussion questions

1. What can Gurley do about Ringer's inaccurate reporting?
2. Is Gurley guilty of the same thing?
3. Is Dr. Walker correct in charging time to the project when no work is being done?
4. What changes if any would you make if you were Dr. Vinson?

PART FOUR summary

CHAPTER 11

unwritten laws of engineering

W. J. King
Engineering Professor Emeritus
University of California

I can think of no better way to end this book than to republish the series of articles by William Julian King that were published by The American Society of Mechanical Engineers in the May, June, and July 1944 issues of *Mechanical Engineering*. This work is unsurpassed for its wisdom, guidance, and insight for the pursuit of a successful technical career.

11.1   What the Beginner Needs to Learn at Once

Some years ago the author became very much impressed with the fact, which can be observed in any engineering organization, that the chief obstacles to the success of individual engineers or of the group comprising a unit were of a personal and administrative rather than a technical nature. It was apparent that both the author and his associates were getting into much more trouble by violating the unwritten laws of professional conduct than by committing technical sins against the well-documented laws of science. Since the former appeared to be indeed unwritten at that time, as regards any adequate and convenient text, the following ''laws'' were originally formulated and collected into a sort of scrapbook, to provide a set of ''house rules,'' or a professional code, for a design-engineering section of a large manufacturing organization. Although they are admittedly fragmentary and incomplete, they are offered here for whatever they may be worth to younger men just starting their careers, and to older men who know these things perfectly well but who all to often fail to apply them in practice.

Just a few points should be emphasized: None of these ''laws'' is theoretical or imaginary, and however obvious and trite they may appear, their repeated violation is responsible for much of the frustration and embarrassment to which engineers everywhere are liable. In fact this paper is primarily a record, derived from direct observation over a period of seventeen years, of the experience of four engineering departments, three of them newly organized and struggling to establish themselves by the trial-and-error method. It

333

has, however, been supplemented and confirmed by the experience of others as gathered from numerous discussions, lectures, and the literature, so that it most emphatically does not reflect the unique experience or characteristics of any one organization.

Furthermore, many of these rules are generalizations to which exceptions will occur in special circumstances. There is no thought of urging a slavish adherence to rules and red tape, for there is no substitute for judgment, and at times vigorous individual initiative is needed to cut through formalities in an emergency. But in many respects these laws are like the basic laws of society; they cannot be violated too often with impunity, notwithstanding striking exceptions in individual cases.

In Relation to His Work. *However menial and trivial your early assignments may appear give them your best efforts.* Many young engineers feel that the minor chores of a technical project are beneath their dignity and unworthy of their college training. They expect to prove their true worth in some major enterprise. Actually, the spirit and effectiveness with which you tackle your first humble tasks will very likely be carefully watched and may affect your entire career.

Occasionally a man will worry unduly about where his job is going to get him—whether it is sufficiently strategic or significant. Of course these are pertinent considerations and you would do well to take some stock of them, but by and large it is fundamentally true that if you take care of your present job well, the future will take care of itself. This is particularly so in the case of a large corporation, where executives are constantly searching for competent men to move up into more responsible positions. Success depends so largely upon personality, native ability, and vigorous, intelligent prosecution of any job that it is no exaggeration to say that your ultimate chances are much better if you do a good job on some minor detail than if you do a mediocre job as section head. Furthermore, it is also true that if you do not first make a good showing on your present job you are not likely to be given the opportunity of trying something else more to your liking.

There is always a premium upon the ability to get things done. This is a quality which may be achieved by various means under different circumstances. Specific aspects will be elaborated in some of the succeeding items. It can probably be reduced, however, to a combination of three basic characteristics, as follows:

(a) Energy, which is expressed in initiative to start things and aggressiveness to keep them moving briskly.

(b) Resourcefulness or ingenuity, i.e., the faculty for finding ways to accomplish the desired result, and

(c) Persistence (tenacity), which is the disposition to persevere in spite of difficulties, discouragement, or indifference.

This last quality is sometimes lacking in the makeup of brilliant engineers, to such an extent that their effectiveness is greatly reduced. Such dilettantes are known as "good starters but poor finishers." Or else it will be said of a man: "You can't take him too seriously; he'll be all steamed up over an idea today but tomorrow he will have dropped it and started chasing some other rainbow." Bear in mind, therefore, that it may be worth while finishing a job, if it has any merit, just for the sake of finishing it.

In carrying out a project do not wait for foremen, vendors, and others to deliver the goods; go after them and keep everlastingly after them. This is one of the first things a new man has to learn in entering a manufacturing organization. Many novices assume that it is sufficient to place the order and sit back and wait until the goods are delivered. The fact is that most jobs move in direct proportion to the amount of follow-up and *expediting* that is applied to them. Expediting means planning, investigating, promoting, and facilitating every step in the process. Cultivate the habit of looking immediately for some way around each obstacle encountered, some other recourse or expedient to keep the job rolling without losing momentum. There are ten-to-one differences between individuals in respect to what it takes to stop their drive when they set out to get something done.

On the other hand, the matter is occasionally overdone by overzealous individuals who make themselves obnoxious and antagonize everyone by their offensive browbeating tactics. Be careful about demanding action from another department. Too much insistence and agitation may result in more damage to a man's personal interests than could ever result from the miscarriage of the technical point involved.

Confirm your instructions and the other fellow's commitments in writing. Do not assume that the job will be done or the bargain kept just because the other fellow agreed to do it. Many people have poor memories, others are too busy, and almost everyone will take the matter a great deal more seriously if he sees it in writing. Of course there are exceptions, but at times it pays to mark a third party for a copy of the memo, as a witness.

When sent out on any complaint or other assignment stick with it and see it through to a successful finish. All too often a young engineer from the home office will leave a job half done or poorly done in order to catch a train or keep some other engagement. Wire the boss that you've got to stay over to clean up the job. Neither he nor the customer will like it if another man has to be sent out later to finish it up.

Avoid the very appearance of vacillation. One of the gravest indictments of an engineer is to say: "His opinion at any time depends merely upon the last man with whom he has talked.'' Refrain from stating an opinion or promoting an undertaking until you have had a reasonable opportunity to obtain and study the facts. Thereafter see it through if at all possible, unless fresh evidence makes it folly to persist. Obviously the extremes of bullheadedness and dogmatism should be avoided, but remember that reversed decisions will be held against you.

Don't be timid—speak up—express yourself and promote your ideas. Every young man should read Emerson's essay on "Self Reliance." Too many new men seem to think that their job is simply to do what they're told to do, along the lines laid down by the boss. Of course there are times when it is very wise and prudent to keep your mouth shut, but, as a rule, it pays to express your point of view whenever you can contribute something. The quiet mousey individual who says nothing is usually credited with having nothing to say.

It frequently happens in any sort of undertaking that nobody is sure of just how the matter ought to be handled; it's a question of selecting some kind of program with a reasonable chance of success. This is commonly to be observed in engineering-office conferences. The first man to speak up with a definite and plausible proposal has better than an even chance of carrying the floor, provided only that the scheme is definite and plausible. (The "best" scheme usually cannot be recognized as such in advance.) It also happens that the man who talks most knowingly and confidently about the matter will very often end up with the assignment to carry out the project. If you do not want the job, keep your mouth shut and you'll be overlooked, but you'll also be overlooked when it comes time to assign larger responsibilities.

Before asking for approval of any major action, have a definite plan and program worked out to support it. Executives very generally and very properly will refuse to approve any proposed undertaking that is not well planned and thought through as regards the practical details of its execution. Quite often a young man will propose a project without having worked out the means of accomplishing it, or weighing the actual advantages against the difficulties and costs. This is the difference between a "well-considered" and a "half-baked" scheme.

Strive for conciseness and clarity in oral or written reports. If there is one bane of an executive's existence, it is the man who takes a half hour of rambling discourse to tell him what could be said in one sentence of twenty words. There is a curious and widespread tendency among engineers to surround the answer to a simple question with so many preliminaries and commentaries that the answer itself can hardly be discerned. It is so difficult to get a direct answer out of some men that their usefulness is thereby greatly diminished. The tendency is to explain the answer before answering the question. To be sure, very few questions admit of simple answers without qualifications, but the important thing is to state the crux of the matter as succinctly as possible first. On the other hand, there are times when it is very important to add the pertinent background or other relevant facts to illuminate a simple statement. The trick is to convey the maximum of significant information in the minimum time, a valuable asset to any man.

An excellent guide in this respect may be found in the standard practice of newspapers in printing the news. The headlines give 90 percent of the basic facts. If you have the time and the interest to read further, the first paragraph will give you most of the important particulars. Succeeding paragraphs simply give details of progressively diminishing significance. To fit an article into available space, the editor simply lops off paragraphs from the rear end, knowing that relatively little of importance will be lost. You can hardly do better than to adopt this method in your own reports, presenting your facts in the order of importance, as if you might be cut off any minute.

Be extremely careful of the accuracy of your statements. This seems almost trite, and yet many engineers lose the confidence of their superiors and associates by habitually guessing when they do not know the answer to a direct question. It is certainly important to be able to answer questions concerning your responsibilities, but a wrong answer is worse than no answer. If you do not know, say so, but also say, "I'll find out right away." If you are not certain, indicate the exact degree of certainty or approximation upon which your answer is based. A reputation for dependability and reliability can be one of your most valuable assets.

This applies, of course, to written matter, calculations, etc., as well as to oral reports. It is definitely bad business to submit a report to the boss for approval without first carefully checking it yourself, and yet formal reports are sometimes turned in full of glaring errors and omissions.

In Relation to the Boss. *Every executive must know what's going on in his bailiwick.* This principle is so elementary and fundamental as to be axiomatic. It follows from the very obvious fact that a man cannot possibly manage his business successfully unless he knows what's going on in it. It applies to minor executives and other individuals charged with specific responsibilities as well as to department heads. No one in his right mind will deny the soundness of the principle and yet it is very commonly violated or overlooked. It is cited here because several of the rules which follow are concerned with specific violations of this cardinal requirement.

Do not overlook the fact that you're working for your boss. This sounds simple enough, but some engineers never get it. By all means, you're working for society, the company, the department, your family, and yourself, but primarily you should be working for and through your boss. And your boss is your immediate superior, to whom you report directly. As a rule, you can serve all other ends to best advantage by working for him, assuming that he's approximately the man he ought to be. It is not uncommon for young engineers, in their impatient zeal to get things done, to ignore the boss, or attempt to go over or around him. Sometimes they move a little faster that way, for a while, but sooner or later they find that such tactics cannot be tolerated in a large organization. Generally speaking, you cannot get by the boss; he determines your rating and he rates you on your ability to cooperate, among other things. Besides, most of us get more satisfaction out of our jobs when we're able to give the boss our personal loyalty, with the feeling that we're helping him to get the main job done.

Be as particular as you can in the selection of your boss. In its effect upon your engineering career, this is second in importance only to the selection of proper parents. In most engineering organizations the influence of the senior engineer, or even the section head, is a major factor in molding the professional character of younger engineers. Long before the days of universities and textbooks, master craftsmen in all the arts absorbed their skills by apprenticeship to master craftsmen. It is very much as in the game of golf; a beginner who constantly plays in company with "dubs" is very apt to remain a "dub" himself, no matter how faithfully he studies the rules, whereas even a few rounds with a "pro" will usually improve a novice's game.

But, of course, it is not always possible to choose your boss advisedly. What if he turns out to be somewhat less than half the man he ought to be? There are only two proper alternatives open to you; *(a)* accept him as the representative of a higher authority and execute his policies and directives as effectively as possible, or *(b)* transfer to some other outfit at the first opportunity. A great deal of mischief can be done to the interests of all concerned (including the company) if some other alternative is elected, particularly in the case of younger men. Consider the damage to the efficiency of a military unit when the privates, disliking the leader, ignore or modify orders to suit their individual notions! To be sure, a business organization is not a military machine, but it is not a mob, either.

One of the first things you owe your boss is to keep him informed of all significant developments. This is a corollary of the preceding rules: An executive must know what's going on. The main question is: How much must he know—how many of the details? This is always a difficult matter for the new man to get straight. Many novices hesitate to bother the boss with too many reports, and it is certainly true that it can be overdone in this direction, but in by far the majority of cases the executive's problem is to extract enough information to keep adequately posted. For every time he has to say, "Don't bother me with so many details," there will be three times he will say, "Why doesn't someone tell me these things?" Bear in mind that he is constantly called upon to account for, defend, and explain your activities to the "higher-ups" as well as to coordinate these activities into a larger plan. In a nutshell, the rule is therefore to give him promptly all the information he needs for these two purposes.

Whatever the boss wants done takes top priority. You may think you have more important things to do first, but unless you obtain permission it is usually unwise to put any other project ahead of a specific assignment from your own boss. As a rule, he has good reasons for wanting his job done *now* and it is apt to have a great deal more bearing upon your rating than less conspicuous projects which may appear more urgent.

Also, make a note of this: If you are instructed to do something and you subsequently decide it isn't worth doing (in view of new data or events) do not just let it die, but inform the boss of your intentions and reasons. Neglect of this point has caused trouble on more than one occasion.

Do not be too anxious to follow the boss's lead. This is the other side of the matter covered by the preceding rule. An undue subservience or deference to the department head's wishes is fairly common among young engineers. A man with this kind of psychology may:

1. Plague the boss incessantly for minute directions and approvals.
2. Surrender all initiative and depend upon the boss to do all of his basic thinking for him.
3. Persist in carrying through a design or a program even after new evidence has proved the original plan to be wrong.

This is where an engineering organization differs from an army. In general, the program laid down by the department or section head is tentative, rather than sacred, and is intended to serve only until a better program is proposed and approved.

The rule therefore is to tell your boss what you have done, at reasonable intervals, and ask his approval of any well-considered and properly planned deviations or new projects that you may have conceived.

Regarding Relations with Associates and Outsiders. *Never invade the domain of any other division without the knowledge and consent of the executive in charge.* This is a very common offense, which causes no end of trouble. Exceptions will occur in respect to minor details, but the rule applies particularly to:

1. The employment of a subordinate. Never offer a man a job, or broach the matter at all, without first securing the permission of his boss. There may be excellent reasons why the man should not be disturbed.
2. Engaging the time or committing the services of a subordinate for some

particular project or trip. How would you feel, after promising in a formal meeting to assign one of your men to an urgent project, to discover that some other executive had had the gall to send him on an out-of-town trip without attempting to notify you? Yet it has been done!

3. Dealings with customers or outsiders, with particular reference to making promises or commitments involving another division. In this connection bear in mind especially that, when you are in the "field" or the "districts," you are in the premises of the district manager or local office, and that all transactions must be with the manager's permission just as if you were in his home.

4. Performing any function assigned to another division or individual. Violations of this law often cause bitter resentments and untold mischief. The law itself is based upon three underlying principles:

   (a) Most people strongly dislike having anyone "muscle" into their territory, undermining their job by appropriating their functions.

   (b) Such interference breeds confusion and mistakes. The man in charge of the job usually knows much more about it than you do, and, even when you think you know enough about it, the chances are better than even that you'll overlook some important factor.

   (c) Nine times out of ten when you're performing the other fellow's function you're neglecting your own. It is rarely that any engineer or executive is so caught up on his own responsibilities that he can afford to take on those of his colleagues.

There is a significant commentary on this last principle which should also be observed: In general you will get no credit or thanks for doing the other fellow's job for him at the expense of your own. But it frequently happens that, if you can put your own house in order first, an understanding of and an active interest in the affairs of other divisions will lead to promotion to a position of greater responsibility. Many a man has been moved up primarily because of a demonstrated capacity for taking care of other people's business as well as his own.

In all transactions be careful to "deal-in" everyone who has a right to be in. It is extremely easy, in a large corporation, to overlook the interests of some division or individual who does not happen to be represented, or in mind, when a significant step is taken. Very often the result is that the step has to be retracted or else considerable damage is done. Even when it does no apparent harm, most people do not like to be left out when they have a stake in the matter, and the effect upon morale may be serious.

Of course there will be times when you cannot wait to stand on ceremony and you'll have to go ahead and "damn the torpedoes." But you cannot do it with impunity too often.

Note particularly that in this and the preceding item the chief offense lies in the invasion of the other man's territory without his knowledge and consent. You may find it expedient on occasions to do the other man's job for him, in order to get your own work done, but you should first give him a fair chance to deliver the goods or else agree to have you take over. If you must offend in this respect, at least you should realize that you are being offensive.

Be careful about whom you mark for copies of letters, memos, etc., when the interests of other departments are involved. A lot of mischief has been caused by young men broadcasting memoranda containing damaging or embarrassing statements. Of course it is sometimes difficult for a novice to recognize the "dynamite" in such a document but, in general, it is apt to cause trouble if it steps too heavily upon someone's toes or reveals a serious shortcoming on anybody's part. If it has wide distribution or if it concerns manufacturing or customer difficulties, you'd better get the boss to approve it before it goes out unless you're very sure of your ground.

Promises, schedules, and estimates are necessary and important instruments in a well-ordered business. Many engineers fail to realize this or habitually try to dodge the irksome responsibility for making commitments. You *must* make promises based upon your own estimates for the part of the job for which you are responsible, together with estimates obtained from contributing departments for their parts. No one should be allowed to avoid the issue by the old formula, "I can't give a promise because it depends upon so many uncertain factors." Consider the "uncertain factors" confronting a department head who must make up a budget for an entire engineering department for a year in advance! Even the most uncertain case can be narrowed down by first asking, "Will it be done in a matter of a few hours or a few months—a few days or a few weeks?" It usually turns out that it cannot be done in less than three weeks and surely will not require more than five, in which case you'd better say four weeks. This allows one week for contingencies and sets you a reasonable bogie under the comfortable figure of five weeks. Both extremes are bad; a good engineer will set schedules which he can meet by energetic effort at a pace commensurate with the significance of the job.

As a corollary of the foregoing, you have a right to insist upon having estimates from responsible representatives of other departments. But in accepting promises, or statements of facts, it is frequently important to make sure that you are dealing with a properly qualified representative of the other section. Also bear in mind that when you ignore or discount another man's promises you impugn his responsibility and incur the extra liability yourself. Of course this is sometimes necessary, but be sure that you do it advisedly. Ideally, another man's promises should be negotiable instruments, like his personal check, in compiling estimates.

When you are dissatisfied with the services of another section, make your complaint to the individual most directly responsible for the function involved. Complaints made to a man's superiors, over his head, engender strong resentments and should be resorted to only when direct appeal fails. In many cases such complaints are made without giving the man a fair chance to correct the grievance, or even before he is aware of any dissatisfaction.

This applies particularly to individuals with whom you are accustomed to deal directly or at close range, or in cases where you know the man to whom the function has been assigned. It is more formal and in some instances possibly more correct to file a complaint with the head of section or department, and it will no doubt tend to secure prompt results. But there are more than a few individuals who would never forgive you for complaining to their boss without giving them a fair chance to take care of the matter.

Next to a direct complaint to the top, it is sometimes almost as serious an offense to mark a man's boss for a copy of a letter containing a complaint or an implied criticism. Of course the occasion may justify such criticism; just be sure you know what you're doing.

In dealing with customers and outsiders remember that you represent the company, ostensibly with full responsibility and authority. You may be only a few months out of college but most outsiders will regard you as a legal, financial, and technical agent of your company in all transactions, so be careful of your commitments.

11.2 Relating Chiefly to Engineering Executives

The following is a partial list of basic commandments, readily subscribed to by all executives but practiced only by the really good ones.

Individual Behavior and Technique. *Every executive must know what's going on in his bailiwick.* This is repeated here for emphasis, and because it belongs at the head of the list for this section. Just remember that it works both ways, as regards what you owe your associates and subordinates as well as yourself.

Obviously this applies primarily to major or significant developments and does not mean that you should attempt to keep up with all the minor details of functions assigned to subordinates. It becomes a vice when carried to the extent of impeding operations. Nevertheless, the basic fact remains that the more information an executive has, the more effectively he can manage his business.

Do not try to do it all yourself. This is another one of those elementary propositions that everyone will endorse and yet violations are quite common.

It's *bad* business; bad for you, bad for the job, and bad for your men. You *must* delegate responsibility even if you *could* cover all of the ground yourself. It isn't wise to have so much depend upon one man and it's very unfair to your men. It is often said that every executive should have his business so organized that he could take a month's vacation at any time and have everything go along smoothly. The most common excuse for hogging the whole job is that subordinates are too young or inexperienced. It's part of your job to develop your men, which includes developing initiative, resourcefulness, and judgment. The best way to do this is to load them up with all the responsibility they can carry without danger of serious embarrassment to the department. Any self-respecting engineer resents being babied, to the extent where he cannot act on the most trivial detail without express approval of the department head.

On the other hand, it must be granted that details are not always trivial and it may sometimes require a meeting of the management committee to change the length of a screw in a critical piece of mechanism in high production. It's simply a matter of making sure that all items are handled by men of appropriate competence and experience.[1]

Put first things first, in applying yourself to your job. Since there usually isn't time for everything, it is essential to form the habit of concentrating on the important things first. The important things are the things for which you are held directly responsible and accountable, and if you aren't sure what these are you'd better find out mightly quick and fix them clearly in mind. Assign these responsibilities top priority in budgeting your time; then delegate as many as possible of the items which will not fit into your schedule. It is a good general rule never to undertake any minor project or chore that you can get someone else or some other department to do for you, so long as it is not an essential part of your job. For example, if your job is building motors it's a mistake to spend time designing special vibration or sound meters for testing them if you can get the laboratory to do it for you.

In handling special problems of this sort, it is usually good diplomacy to let some local office do the job, if they can, before importing experts from another plant or company.

The practice of drawing upon all available resources for assistance can frequently be applied to advantage in respect to your major products, as well as in minor details. This is especially true in a large organization where the services of experts, consulting engineers, laboratories, and other departments are available either at no cost or for much less than it would cost you to get the answer independently. In fact, there may well be cases in which it would be

[1]"Administrative Organization for a Small Manufacturing Firm," by Willis Rabbe, *Mechnical Engineering,* Vol. 63, 1941, pp. 517–520.

wise for you to limit yourself, personally or as a business manager, to performing only those functions to which you can bring some special talent, skill, or contribution, or in which you enjoy some natural advantage. Some companies, for example, have achieved outstanding success by virtue of their special genius for merchandising the products of others, or by concentrating on the manufacture of a standard competitive article so as to capture the market by lowering the price. Likewise the aircraft companies generally exploit their special aeronautical skill, leaving development of engines, superchargers, propellers, and other components to specialists in these fields. Few of us are versatile enough to excel in more than one or two talents.

Cultivate the habit of "boiling matters down" to their simplest terms. The faculty for reducing apparently complicated situations to their basic, essential elements is a form of wisdom that must usually be derived from experience, but there are marked differences between otherwise comparable individuals in this respect. Some people seem eternally disposed to "muddy the water," or they "can never see the woods for the trees," etc. Perhaps a man cannot correct such an innate tendency simply by taking thought, but it appears to be largely a matter of habit, a habit of withdrawing mentally to a suitable vantage point so as to survey a mass of facts in their proper perspective, or a habit of becoming immersed and lost in a sea of detail. Make it practice to integrate, condense, summarize, and simplify your facts rather than to expand, ramify, complicate, and disintegrate them.

Many meetings, for example, get nowhere after protracted wrangling until somebody finally says "Well, gentlemen, it all boils down simply to this, . . .," or "Can't we agree, however, that the basic point at issue is just this, ...," or, "After all, the essential fact remains that. . . ."

This sort of mental discipline, which instinctively impels a man to go down to the core to get at the crux of the matter, is one of the most valuable qualities of a good executive.[2]

Do not get excited in engineering emergencies—keep your feet on the ground. This is certainly trite enough, and yet an engineering group will sometimes be thrown into a state of agitation bordering on panic by some minor crisis. This refers especially to bad news from the factory or the field regarding some serious and embarrassing difficulty, such as an epidemic of equipment failures. Most crises aren't half as bad as they appear at first, so make it a point to minimize rather than magnify a bad situation. Do not ignore signs of trouble and get caught napping, but learn to distinguish between isolated cases and real epidemics. The important thing is to get the facts first, as promptly and as directly as possible. Then act as soon as you have enough

---

[2]See also *Psychology for Executives,* by Elliott Dunlap Smith, Harper & Bros., New York, N.Y., 1935.

evidence from responsible sources to enable you to reach a sound decision.

Engineering meetings should not be too large or too small. Many executives carry their aversion for large meetings to the point of a phobia. This is reflected in the common saying that nothing worthwhile is ever accomplished in a large meeting. It is true enough that large meetings frequently dissipate the subject over a number of conflicting or irrelevant points of view, in a generally superficial manner. But this is almost entirely a matter of the competence of the chairman. A considerable amount of skill is required to manage a sizable meeting so as to keep it on the proper subject, avoiding long-winded digressions or reiterations of the arguments. It should be the function of the chairman, or the presiding senior executive, to bring out the pertinent facts bearing upon the matter, in their logical order, and then to secure agreement upon the various issues by *(a)* asking for general assent to concrete proposals, or *(b)* taking a vote, or *(c)* making arbitrary decisions. Engineering meetings may degenerate into protracted wrangles for lack of competent direction. The danger in this respect seems to be about in proportion to the size of the meeting.

Small meetings, three or four persons, can usually hammer out a program or dispose of knotty problems much more effectively. The chief drawback lies in the possibility that all interested parties may not be represented, and considerable loss or mischief may result from failure to take account of significant facts or points of view. Apart from the actual loss involved, strong resentment or discouragement may be engendered in the neglected parties. (The Revolutionary War was brought about largely as a result of the fact that the Colonies were not represented in the British Parliament.)

There will doubtless be cases in which it is neither feasible nor desirable to have all interested parties represented in engineering discussions, particularly if the participants are well informed. But in general it is fitting, proper, and helpful to have the man present whose particular territory is under discussion.

An excellent expedient for avoiding the objections to either extreme in this respect is to keep the meeting small, calling in each key man when his particular responsibility is being discussed.

In any kind of a meeting the important thing is to face the issues and dispose of them. All too often there is a tendency to dodge the issues, postponing action until a later date, or "letting the matter work itself out naturally." Matters will always work out "naturally" if the executive function of control is neglected but this represents a low order of "management." Count any meeting a failure which does not end up with a definite understanding as to what's going to be done, who's going to do it, and when. This should be confirmed in writing (minutes).

Cultivate the habit of making brisk, clean-cut decisions. This is, of course, the most difficult and important part of an executive's job. Some executives have a terrific struggle deciding even minor issues, mainly because they never get over being afraid of making mistakes. Normally, facility comes with practice, but it can be hastened by observing a few simple principles.

1. Decisions will be easier and more frequently correct if you have the essential facts at hand. It will therefore pay you to keep well informed, or else to bring out the relevant facts before attempting a decision. However, it is sometimes said that anybody can make decisions when all of the facts are at hand, whereas an executive will make the same decisions without waiting for the facts.[3] To maintain a proper balance in this respect, when in doubt ask yourself the question: "Am I likely to lose more by giving a snap judgment or by waiting for more information?"
2. The application of judgment can be facilitated by formulating it into principles, policies, and precepts in advance. The present paper is an attempt to formulate experience for this purpose. Make up your own code, if you will, but at least have some sort of code, for much the same reason that you memorize the axioms of Euclid or Newton's laws of motion.
3. You do not have to be right every time. It is said that a good executive needs to be right only 51 percent of the time (although a little better margin would obviously be healthy).
4. The very fact that a decision is difficult usually means that the advantages and drawbacks of the various alternatives are pretty well balanced, so that the net loss cannot amount to much in any event. In such cases it is frequently more important to arrive at some decision—any decision—promptly than to arrive at the best decision ultimately. So take a definite position and see it through.
5. It is futile to try to keep everybody happy in deciding issues involving several incompatible points of view. By all means give everyone a fair hearing, but after all parties have had their say and all facts are on the table, dispose of the matter decisively even if someone's toes are stepped on. Otherwise the odds are that all parties will end up dissatisfied, and even the chief beneficiary will think less of you for straddling the issue.

The following criteria are helpful in choosing a course of action when other factors are indecisive; ask yourself these questions:

(a) Does it expedite and progress the undertaking, or does it smack of procrastination and delay?
(b) Is it fair and square and aboveboard?

[3] See "Definition of an Executive," by H. S. Osborne, *Electrical Engineering*, Vol. 61, August 1942, p. 429.

(c) Is it in line with established custom, precedence, or policy? A good reason is generally required for a departure.

(d) Is it in line with a previous specific decision or understanding? Even a good reason for making a change will sometimes not offset the unfortunate impression of apparent instability. "He can't make up his own mind" is a common reaction. (Observe, however, that this criterion is suggested only "when other factors are indecisive." By all means have the courage of your convictions when the change is justifiable.)

(e) What are the odds? Can I afford to take the chance? How does the possible penalty compare with the possible gain, in each of the alternatives offered? Very often you can find a solution wherein the worst possible eventuality isn't too bad, in relation to the possible gains.

Do not allow the danger of making a mistake to inhibit your initiative to the point of "nothing ventured, nothing gained." It is much healthier to expect to make mistakes, take a few good risks now and then, and take your medicine when you lose. Moreover, there are few mistakes that cannot be turned into profit somehow, even if it's only in terms of experience.

Finally, it should be observed that having "the courage of your convictions" includes having the courage to do what you know to be right, technically as well as morally, without undue regard for possible criticism or the necessity for explaining your actions. Many seemingly embarrassing situations can readily be cleared up, or even turned to advantage, merely by stating the simple, underlying facts of the matter. It boils down to a very straightforward proposition. If your reasons for your actions are sound, you should not worry about having to defend them to anyone; if they're not sound you'd better correct them promptly, instead of building up an elaborate camouflage.

Do not overlook the value of suitable "preparation" before announcing a major decision or policy. When time permits, it is frequently good diplomacy to prepare the ground for such announcements by discussing the matter in advance with various key men or directly interested parties. This is, in fact, an elementary technique in diplomatic and political procedure, but it is all too often ignored in engineering practice. Much embarrassment and bad feeling can be caused by announcing a major change or embarking upon a new program or policy without consulting those directly affected or who are apt to bring up violent objections, with good reason later on.[4]

Handling Design and Development Projects. *Beware of the "perils of security" in planning your engineering programs.* It is one of the fundamental anomalies of human experience that too much preoccupation with the pursuit

[4]See also *The Technique of Executive Control,* by Erwin Haskell Schell. Fifth edition, Book Co., Inc., New York, N.Y., 1942.

of security is very apt to lead to greater danger and insecurity. In a competitive world you *must* take chances—bold and courageous chances—or else the other fellow will, and he will win out just enough often to keep you running, all out of breath, trying to catch up. So it behooves you as an engineering executive to "stick your neck out," and keep it out, by undertaking stiff development programs, setting a high mark to shoot at, and then working aggressively to realize your objectives. With competent direction any representative engineering organization will work its way out of a tight spot, every time, under the pressure of the emergency. If you do not like such "emergencies," just remember that, if you do not create your own emergencies in advance, your competition will create them for you at a much more embarrassing time later on.

In order to minimize the risk it is good policy to hedge against the failure of a new project by providing an alternative, or an "out" to fall back on, wherever practicable. You can go after bigger stakes with impunity when you have suitably limited your possible losses in such a manner.

Plan your work, then work your plan. The following formula for carrying out a development or design project seems to be standard in the best engineering circles:

(a) Define your objectives.
(b) Plan the job, by outlining the steps to be accomplished.
(c) Prepare a definite schedule.
(d) Assign definite responsibilities for each item.
(e) Make sure that each man has sufficient help and facilities.
(f) Follow up; check up on progress of the work.
(g) Revise your schedule as required.
(h) Watch for "bottlenecks," "log-jams," and "missing links"; hit lagging items hard.
(i) Drive to a finish on time.

Plan your development work far enough ahead of production so as to meet schedules without a wild last-minute rush. In the nature of things it seems inevitable that the group responsible for design engineering is also in the best position to take care of development projects. This is due to the intimate contacts of the designers with the practical problems of production, performance, and market requirements. But it is also true that very considerable foresight is required to offset the natural tendency of designers to become preoccupied with immediate problems of this nature, at the expense of the long-range development program, which is not so urgent and pressing. It is therefore the function of management to exercise sufficient "vision" to anticipate trends and initiate research and development projects before the demand becomes uncomfortably urgent. This means starting such projects soon enough, i.e., six months, a year, or even two years in advance, to allow sufficient time to carry out all of the necessary steps in a well-ordered program.

Even when the development of new designs simply means a rehash of old fundamentals in new dress, it is important to plan the program early enough and to provide for all stages in the process of getting the product on the market. For example, the following steps may be required to carry through the development of a typical peacetime product:

(a) Market survey.
(b) Preparation of commercial specifications (features and ratings agreed upon jointly by commercial and design divisions).
(c) Preliminary design.
(d) Build and test preliminary sample.
(e) Final design.
(f) Build and test final samples.
(g) Preliminary planning and costs.
(h) Engineering release of final drawings for production.
(i) Final planning and costs.
(j) Ordering materials and tools.
(k) Preparation of manufacturing and test instructions; application, installation, operating, and service manuals; replacement-parts catalogue, publicity releases.
(l) Initial production.
(m) Test production samples.
(n) Minor design changes to correct errors and expedite production.

Obviously, some of these activities can be carried on concurrently, but unless they are all suitably provided for there is very apt to be some awkward stumbling and bungling along the way.

Be careful to "freeze" a new design when the development has progressed far enough. Of course it is not always easy to say how far is "far enough" but, in general, you have gone far enough when you can meet the design specifications and costs, with just enough time left to complete the remainder of the program on schedule. The besetting temptation of the designing engineer is to allow himself to be led on by one glittering improvement after another, pursuing an elusive perfection that leads him far past the hope of ever keeping his promises and commitments. Bear in mind that there will always be new design improvements coming along, but it is usually better to get started with what you have on time, provided only that it is up to specifications as regards features, quality, and cost.

Constantly review developments and other activities to make certain that actual benefits are commensurate with costs in money, time, and manpower. Not infrequently developments are carried along by virtue of Newton's first law of motion long after they have ceased to yield a satisfactory return on the investment. The occasion for vigilance in this respect is obvious enough; it is cited here simply as a reminder.

Make it a rule to require, and submit, regular periodic progress reports, as well as final reports on completed projects. However irksome such chores may seem, your business simply isn't fully organized and controlled until you have established this practice, as regards reports to your superiors as well as from your subordinates. There appears to be no other regimen quite so compelling and effective in requiring a man to keep his facts properly assembled and appraised.

It is further true that, generally speaking, an engineering project is not really finished until it is properly summarized, recorded, and filed in such a manner that the information can readily be located and utilized by all interested parties. An enormous amount of effort can be wasted or duplicated in any engineering department when this sort of information is simply entrusted to the memory of individual engineers.

Notes Respecting Organization.[5] *Do not have too many men reporting directly to one man.* As a rule, not more than six or seven men should report to one executive in an engineering organization. Occasionally a strong energetic leader will deal directly with fifteen or twenty engineers, in which case he is usurping the positions and functions of several group leaders, burdening himself with too much detail, and depriving the men of adequate supervision.

Assign definite responsibilities. It is extremely detrimental to morale and efficiency when no one knows just what his job is or what he is responsible for. If assignments are not made clear there is apt to be interminable bickering, confusion, and bad feeling. Do not keep tentative organization changes hanging over people. It is better to dispose of a situation promptly, and change it later, than to hold up a decision simply because you might want to change it. It is again a matter of facing issues squarely; it is easier to "just wait and see how things work out" but, beyond the minimum time required to size up personnel, it's not good management.

In so far as possible, avoid divided responsibility for specific functions. Ideally each man should have full authority and control over all of the factors essential to the performance of his particular function. This is commonly

[5]For a more authoritative discussion of this subject, see the excellent series of papers on "Organization and Management of Engineering," *Electrical Engineering*, Vol. 61, August 1942, pp. 422–429.

expressed in the aphorism that authority must be commensurate with responsibility. In practice this is seldom possible of fulfillment; we must all depend upon the contributions of others at some point in the process. Still the amount of dependency should be kept to the practical minimum, for it is extremely difficult for a man to get anything done if he must eternally solicit the voluntary cooperation or approval of too many other parties. This is what is known as being "organized to prevent things from getting done."

The logical answer to the problem of divided responsibility (or "division of labor") is coordination. If any activity, such as the design of a product, must be divided into development, design, drafting, and production engineering, these functions should obviously be coordinated by a single responsible engineer.

If you haven't enough legal authority assume as much as you need. During the Civil War a Confederate officer one evening found that his supply train was held up by a single Union battery which was dropping shells accurately into a narrow mountain pass. Without even changing his uniform, he rode around to the rear of the battery, and coming upon them suddenly, sharply ordered them to swing their guns around to another point. He was obeyed with alacrity because he acted as if he expected to be obeyed. He rode off to rejoin his command, and led them through the pass before anyone discovered that he had exceeded his authority.

Of course such tactics are not recommended for general use, but the story illustrates the fact that quite a lot can be accomplished, on occasions, without full administrative sanction. The important thing is to exercise sufficient care to avoid running afoul of the interests and authority of others.

This injunction is based upon three elementary facts of experience:

1. A man will frequently be held responsible for a good deal more than he can control by directly delegated authority.
2. A very considerable amount of authority can be assumed with complete impunity if it is assumed discreetly, and with effective results. People in general tend to obey a man who appears to be in charge of any situation, provided that he appears to know what he is doing and obtains the desired results.
3. Most executives will be very pleased to confirm such authority in their subordinates when they see it being exercised effectively. Executives in general have much more trouble pushing their men ahead than in holding them back.

Do not create "bottlenecks." Coordination of minor routine affairs is sometimes carried too far, when a single individual must pass upon each transaction before it can be carried out. Such rigid control can easily cause more trouble than the original liability. Fortunately, bottlenecks are usually recognized early in the game, and it is easy to avoid them by designating alternates, or by allowing freedom of action in emergencies, with the proviso that the proper party be notified at the first opportunity.

Assign responsibilities for technical subjects, as well as for specific products, in setting up your engineering organization. This is a practice which could be used to advantage in design sections more frequently than it is. The idea is to assign dual responsibilities to each engineer, *(a)* for a particular product or line of apparatus, and *(b)*, for a technical specialty, such as lubrication, heat transfer, surface finishes, magnetic materials, welding, fluid flow, etc. These assignments should be made known to all members of the group, with the request that all pertinent material on each subject be referred to the proper specialist, who will act as consultant and as contact man with laboratories, etc., for the entire section. It may, of course, be desirable to assign full-time specialists to important subjects when the business can afford it; the main point is to establish pools of specialized knowledge rather than to expect each designer to know all that he needs to know about the principal arts and sciences which are common to the various products of the department.

What Every Executive Owes his Men. *Promote the personal and professional interests of your men on all occasions.* This is not only an obligation, it is the opportunity and the privilege of every executive.

As a general principle, the interests of individual engineers coincide with the company's interest, i.e., there is, or should be, no basic conflict. The question of which should be placed first is, therefore, rarely encountered in practice, although it is clear that, in general, the company's interests, like those of the state or society, must take precedence. It is one of the functions of management to reconcile and merge the two sets of interests to their mutual advantage, since they are so obviously interdependent.

It should be obvious that it is to the company's advantage to preserve the morale and loyalty of individual engineers, just as it is common policy to maintain proper relations with the labor unions. The fact is that attempts to organize engineers into unions have failed simply because the engineers have been confident that their interests have been looked after very conscientiously and very adequately by responsible executives.

Morale is a tremendously important factor in any organization. It is founded primarily upon confidence, and it reaches a healthy development when the men feel that they will always get a square deal plus a little extra consideration on occasions.

Specific injunctions under this principle are cited in succeeding items.

Do not hang onto a man too selfishly when he is offered a better opportunity elsewhere. It's a raw deal to stand in the way of a man's promotion just because it will inconvenience you to lose him. You are justified in shielding him from outside offers only when you are sincerely convinced that he has an equal or better opportunity where he is. Moreover, you should not let yourself get caught in a position where the loss of any man would embarrass you unduly. Select and train runners-up for all key men, including yourself.

Do not short-circuit or override your men if you can possibly avoid it. It is very natural, on occasions, for an executive to want to exercise his authority directly in order to dispose of a matter promptly without regard for the man assigned to the job. To be sure, it's your prerogative, but it can be very demoralizing to the subordinate involved and should be resorted to only in real emergencies. Once you give a man a job, let him do it, even at the cost of some inconvenience to yourself. Never miss a chance to build up the prestige of your men. And more than a little mischief can be done by exercising authority without sufficient knowledge of the details of the matter.

You owe it to your men to keep them properly informed. Next to responsibility without authority comes responsibility without information, in the catalogue of raw deals. It is very unfair to expect a man to acquit himself creditably when he is held responsible for a project without adequate knowledge of its past history, present status, or future plans. An excellent practice, followed by many top-flight executives, is to hold occasional meetings of section heads to acquaint them with major policies and developments in the business of the department and the company, so that all will know what's going on.

An important part of the job of developing a man is to furnish him with an ample background of information in his particular field, and as a rule this involves a certain amount of travel. There are occasions when it is worthwhile to send a young man along on a trip for what he can get out of it, rather than what he can contribute to the job.

Do not criticize one of your men in front of others, especially his own subordinates. This obviously damages prestige and morale.

Also, be very careful not to criticize a man when it's really your own fault. Not infrequently, the real offense can be traced back to you, as when you fail to advise, or warn, or train the man properly. Be fair about it.

Show an interest in what your men are doing. It is definitely discouraging to a man when his boss manifests no interest in his work, as by failing to inquire, comment, or otherwise take notice of it.

Never miss a chance to commend or reward a man for a job well done. Remember that your job is not just to criticize and browbeat your men into getting their work done. A first-rate executive is a leader as well as a critic.

The better part of your job is, therefore, to help, advise, encourage, and stimulate your men.

On the other hand, this does not mean mollycoddling. By all means get tough when the occasion justifies it. An occasional sharp censure, when it is well deserved, will usually help to keep a man on his toes. But if that's all he gets, he is apt to go a bit sour on the job.

Always accept full responsibility for your group and the individuals in it. Never "pass the buck," or blame one of your men, even when he has "let you down" badly in dealings with outsiders. You are supposed to have full control and you are credited with the success as well as the failure of your group.

Do all that you can to see that each of your men gets all of the salary that he's entitled to. This is the most appropriate reward or compensation for outstanding work, greater responsibility, or increased value to the company. (Any recommendation for an increase in salary must be justified on one of these three bases.)

Include interested individuals in introductions, luncheons, etc., when entertaining visitors. Obviously, this can be overdone, but if you're entertaining a visiting specialist, it is good business, as well as good manners, to invite the corresponding specialist in your own department to go along.

Do all that you can to protect the personal interests of your men and their families, especially when they're in trouble. Do not confine your interest in your men rigidly within the boundaries of "company business."

Try to get in little extra accommodations when justifiable. For example, if you're sending a man to his home town on a business trip, schedule it for Monday, so that he can spend Sunday with his family, if it makes no difference otherwise.

Considerations of this sort make a "whale" of a difference in the matter of morale and in the satisfaction an executive gets out of his job. The old-fashioned "slave driver" is currently regarded in about the same light as Heinrich Himmler. Treat your men as human beings making up a team rather than as cogs in a machine.

In this connection, it is sometimes advisable to talk things over with a man when you become definitely dissatisfied with his work, or recognize a deficiency which is militating against him. To be sure, it is not always easy, and may require much tact to avoid discouraging or offending the man, but it may well be that you owe it to him. Bear this in mind; if you ultimately have to fire him, you may have to answer two pointed questions: "Why has it taken you five years to discover my incompetence?" and, "Why haven't you given me a fair chance to correct these shortcomings?" Remember that when you fire a man for incompetence, it means not only that he has failed, but also that you have failed.

11.3 Purely Personal Considerations for Engineers

The importance of the personal and sociological aspects of our behavior as engineers is brought out in the following quotation (1):[6]

> In a recent analysis of over 4000 cases, it was found that 62 percent of the employees discharged were unsatisfactory because of social unadaptability, only 38 per cent for technical incompetence.

And yet about 99 percent of the emphasis in the training of engineers is placed upon purely technical or formal education. In recent years, however, there has been a rapidly growing appreciation of the importance of "human engineering," not only in respect to relations between management and employees but also as regards the personal effectiveness of the individual worker, technical or otherwise. It should be obvious enough that a highly trained technological expert with a good character and personality is necessarily a better engineer and a great deal more valuable to his company than a sociological freak or misfit with the same technical training. This is largely a consequence of the elementary fact that in a normal organization no individual can get very far in accomplishing any worthwhile objectives without the voluntary cooperation of his associates; and the quantity and quality of such cooperation is determined by the "personality factor" more than anything else.

This subject of personality and character is, of course, very broad and much has been written and preached about it from the social, ethical, and religious points of view. The following "laws" are drawn up from the purely practical point of view based upon well-established principles of "good engineering practice," or upon consistently repeated experience. As in the preceding sections, the selections are limited to rules which are frequently violated, with unfortunate results, however obvious or bromidic they may appear.

"Laws" of Character and Personality. *One of the most important personal traits is the ability to get along with all kinds of people.* This is rather a comprehensive quality but it defines the prime requisite of personality in any type of industrial organization. No doubt this ability can be achieved by various formulas, although it is probably based mostly upon general, good-natured friendliness, together with fairly consistent observance of the "Golden Rule." The following "do's and don'ts" are more specific elements of such a formula:

1. Cultivate the tendency to appreciate the good qualities, rather than the shortcomings of each individual.

[6]Numbers in parentheses refer to the Bibliography at the end of the paper.

2. Do not give vent to impatience and annoyance on slight provocation. Some offensive individuals seem to develop a striking capacity for becoming annoyed, which they indulge with little or no restraint.

3. Do not harbor grudges after disagreements involving honest differences of opinion. Keep your arguments on an objective basis and leave personalities out as much as possible.

4. Form the habit of considering the feelings and interests of others.

5. Do not become unduly preoccupied with your own selfish interests. It may be natural enough to "look out for Number One first," but when you do your associates will leave the matter entirely in your hands, whereas they will be much readier to defend your interests for you if you characteristically neglect them for unselfish reasons.

   This applies particularly to the matter of credit for accomplishments. It is much wiser to give your principal attention to the matter of getting the job done, or to building up your men, than to spend too much time pushing your personal interests ahead of everything else. You need have no fear of being overlooked; about the only way to lose credit for a creditable job is to grab for it too avidly.

6. Make it a rule to help the other fellow whenever an opportunity arises. Even if you're mean-spirited enough to derive no personal satisfaction from accommodating others it's a good investment. The business world demands and expects cooperation and teamwork among the members of an organization. It's smarter and pleasanter to give it freely and ungrudgingly, up to the point of unduly neglecting your own responsiblities.

7. Be particularly careful to be fair on all occasions. This means a good deal more than just being fair, upon demand. All of us are frequently unfair, unintentionally, simply because we do not habitually view the matter from the other fellow's point of view, to be sure that his interests are fairly protected. For example, when a man fails to carry out an assignment, he is sometimes unjustly criticized when the real fault lies with the executive who failed to give him the tools to do the job. Whenever you enjoy some natural advantage, or whenever you are in a position to injure someone seriously, it is especially incumbent upon you to "lean over backwards" to be fair and square.

8. Do not take yourself or your work too seriously. A normal healthy sense of humor, under reasonable control, is much more becoming, even to an executive, than a chronically soured dead pan, a perpetually unrelieved air of deadly seriousness, or the pompous solemn dignity of a stuffed owl. The Chief Executive of the United States smiles easily or laughs heartily, on appropriate occasions, and even his worst enemies do not attempt to criticize him for it. It is much better for your blood pressure, and for the morale of the office, to laugh off an awkward situation now

and then than to maintain a tense tragic atmosphere of stark disaster whenever matters take an embarrassing turn. To be sure, a serious matter should be taken seriously, and a man should maintain a quiet dignity as a rule, but it does more harm than good to preserve an oppressively heavy and funereal atmosphere around you.

9. Put yourself out just a little to be genuinely cordial in greeting people. True cordiality is, of course, spontaneous and should never be affected, but neither should it be inhibited. We all know people who invariably pass us in the hall or encounter us elsewhere without a shadow of recognition. Whether this be due to inhibition or preoccupation we cannot help feeling that such unsociable chumps would not be missed much if we never saw them again. On the other hand, it is difficult to think of anyone who is too cordial, although it can doubtless be overdone like anything else. It appears that most people tend naturally to be sufficiently reserved or else overreserved in this respect.

10. Give the other fellow the benefit of the doubt if you are inclined to suspect his motives, especially when you can afford to do so. Mutual distrust and suspicion breed a great deal of absolutely unnecessary friction and trouble, frequently of a very serious nature. This is a very common phenomenon, which can be observed among all classes and types of people, in international as well as local affairs. It is derived chiefly from misunderstandings, pure ignorance, or from an ungenerous tendency to assume that a man is guilty until he is proved innocent. No doubt the latter assumption is the "safer" bet, but it is also true that if you treat the other fellow as a depraved scoundrel, he will usually treat you likewise, and he will probably try to live down to what is expected of him. On the other hand you will get much better cooperation from your associates and others if you assume that they are just as intelligent, reasonable, and decent as you are, even when you know they're not (although the odds are 50:50 that they are). It isn't a question of being naive or a perpetual sucker; you'll gain more than you lose by this practice, with anything more than half-witted attention to the actual odds in each case.

Do not be too affable. It's a mistake, of course, to try too hard to get along with everybody merely by being agreeable and friendly on all occasions. Somebody will take advantage of you sooner or later, and you cannot avoid trouble simply by running away from it ("appeasement"). You must earn the respect of your associates by demonstrating your readiness to give any man a hell of a good fight if he asks for it. Shakespeare put it succinctly in Polonius' advice to his son (in "Hamlet"): "Beware of entrance to a quarrel; but being in, bear it that the opposed may beware of thee."

On the other hand, do not give ground too quickly just to avoid a fight, when you know you're in the right. If you can be pushed around easily the chances are that you will be pushed around. There will be times when you would do well to start a fight yourself, when your objectives are worth fighting for.

As a matter of fact, as long as you're in a competitive business you're in a fight all the time. Sometimes it's a fight between departments of the same company. As long as it's a good clean fight, with no hitting below the belt, it's perfectly healthy. But keep it on the plane of "friendly competition" as long as you can. (In the case of arguments with your colleagues, it is usually better policy to settle your differences out of court, rather than to take them to the boss for arbitration.)

Likewise, in your relations with subordinates it is unwise to carry friendliness to the extent of impairing discipline. There are times when the best thing that you can do for a man (and the company) is to fire him, or transfer him. Every one of your men should know that whenever he deserves a good "bawling out" he'll get it, every time. The most rigid discipline is not resented so long as it is reasonable, impartial, and fair, especially when it is balanced by appropriate rewards, appreciation, and other compensations as mentioned in Part 11.2. Too much laxity or squeamishness in handling men is about as futile as cutting off a dog's tail an inch at a time to keep it from hurting so much. If you do not face your issues squarely, someone else will be put in your place who will.

Regard your personal integrity as one of your most important assets. In the long pull there is hardly anything more important to you than your own self-respect and this alone should provide ample incentive to maintain the highest standard of ethics of which you are capable. But, apart from all consideratons of ethics and morals, there are perfectly sound hardheaded business reasons for conscientiously guarding the integrity of your character.

One of the most striking phenomena of an engineering office is the transparency of character among the members of any group who have been associated for any length of time. In a surprisingly short period each individual is recognized, appraised, and catalogued for exactly what he is, with far greater accuracy than that individual usually realizes. This is true to such a degree that it makes a man appear downright ludicrous when he assumes a pose or otherwise tries to convince us that he is something better than he is. As Emerson puts it: "What you are speaks so loud I cannot hear what you say." In fact it frequently happens that a man is much better known and understood by his associates, collectively, than he knows and understands himself.

Therefore, it behooves you as an engineer to let your personal conduct, overtly and covertly, represent your conception of the very best practical standard of professional ethics, by which you are willing to let the world judge and rate you.

Moreover, it is morally healthy and tends to create a better atmosphere, if you will credit the other fellow with similar ethical standards, even though you may be imposed upon occasionally. The obsessing and overpowering fear of being cheated is the common characteristic of second- and third-rate personalities. This sort of psychology sometimes leads a man to assume an extremely "cagey" sophisticated attitude, crediting himself with being impressively clever when he is simply taking advantage of his more considerate and fairminded associates. On the other hand a substantial majority of top-flight executives are scrupulously fair, square, and straightforward in their dealings with all parties. In fact most of them are where they are largely because of this characteristic, which is one of the prime requisites of first-rate leadership.

The priceless and inevitable reward for uncompromising integrity is confidence, the confidence of associates, subordinates, and "outsiders." All transactions are enormously simplified and facilitated when a man's word is as good as his bond and his motives are above suspicion. Confidence is such an invaluable business asset that even a moderate amount of it will easily outweigh any temporary advantage that might be gained by sharp practices.

Integrity of character is closely associated with sincerity, which is another extremely important quality. Obvious and marked sincerity is frequently a source of exceptional strength and influence in certain individuals, particularly in the case of speakers. Abraham Lincoln is a classic example. In any individual, sincerity is always appreciated, and insincerity is quickly detected and discounted.

In order to avoid any misunderstanding, it should be granted here that the average man, and certainly the average engineer, is by no means a low dishonest scoundrel. In fact the average man would violently protest any questioning of his essential honesty and decency, perhaps fairly enough. But there is no premium upon this kind of common garden variety of honesty, which is always ready to compromise in a pinch. The average man will go off the gold standard or compromise with any sort of expediency whenever it becomes moderately uncomfortable to live up to his obligations. This is hardly what is meant by "integrity," and it is certainly difficult to base even a moderate degree of confidence upon the guarantee that you will not be cheated unless the going gets tough.

A little profanity goes a long way. Engineering is essentially a gentleman's profession, and it ill becomes a man to carry profanity to the point of becoming obnoxiously profane. Unfortunately, profanity is sometimes taken as a mark of rugged he-man virility, but any engineer with such an idea should realize that many a pimply, half-witted, adolescent street urchin will hopelessly outclass him in this respect.

On the other hand, there is no reason why a man should be afraid to say "damn." On appropriate occasions a good hearty burst of colorful profanity may be just a healthy expression of strong feelings. But there is never any occasion for the filthy variety of obscenity, and a really foul mouth will generally inspire nothing but contempt.

Be careful of your personal appearance. Roughly eight out of every ten engineers pay adequate attention to their personal appearance and neatness. The other two offend in respect to one or more of the following items:

1. Suit rumpled or soiled, or else trousers, coat, and vest have nothing in common but their means of support.
2. Shoes, unpolished or dilapidated.
3. Tie, at half-mast or looking like it was tied with one hand. Some individuals seem to own but one tie, which takes an awful beating. Others wear colors contrasting violently with suit or shirt, but this is sometimes a matter of artistic license (if it isn't color blindness).
4. Shirt, frayed at collar or cuffs, or just plain dirty.
5. Hands, dirty.
6. Nails, in deep mourning, chewed off, or else absurdly long. A man doesn't need to be fastidious, but dirty neglected nails immediately and conspicuously identify a careless sloppy individual. (This is especially true in the case of an interview, where first impressions are so important.)

Of course we all know some very good men who are oblivious to such details, so that it cannot be said that all who ignore them are necessarily crude, third-rate, slovenly lowbrows, but it is probably a safe bet that all crude, third-rate, slovenly lowbrows are offensive in most of these respects.

Do not argue that you cannot afford to look your best; you cannot afford not to. Your associates and superiors notice these details, perhaps more than you realize, and they rate you accordingly.

In this connection, note the following quotation from a recent pamphlet on "employee rating" (2):

The "halo effect" simply means that rating of one trait is often influenced by that given to some other trait. Thus an employee who makes a nice appearance and has a pleasant manner is apt to obtain a higher rating on all other traits than he deserves.

Analyze yourself and your men. In the foregoing, it has been assumed that any normal individual will be interested in either:

(a) Advancement to a position of greater responsibility, or
(b) Improvement in personal effectiveness as regards quantity and/or quality of accomplishment.

Either of these should result in increased financial compensation and satisfaction derived from the job.

With reference to item *(a)*, it is all too often taken for granted that increased executive and administrative responsibility is a desirable and appropriate form of reward for outstanding proficiency in any type of work. This may be a mistake from either of two points of view:

1. The individual may be very much surprised to find that he is much less happy in his new job than he thought he was going to be. In many instances young engineers are prone to assume that increased responsibility means mostly increased authority and compensation. Actually, the term "compensation" is well applied, for the extra salary is paid primarily to compensate for the extra burden of responsibility. Of course most people relish the added load, because of the larger opportunities that go with it, but many perfectly normal individuals find it more of a load than anything else. It is not uncommon for an engineer or a scientist to discover, to his dismay, that as soon as he becomes an executive he no longer has time to be an engineer or a scientist. In fact, some executives have time for absolutely nothing else.
2. From the business standpoint, it by no means follows that because a man is a good scientist, he will make a good executive. Many a top-notch technician has been promoted to an administrative position very much to his own and the job's detriment.

These facts should therefore be considered carefully by the man threatened with promotion and by the man about to do the promoting. There are other ways of rewarding a man for outstanding accomplishment.

It is not always easy, however, to decide in advance whether you, or the man in question, would be happier and more effective as an executive or as an individual worker. There is no infallible criterion for this purpose but it will be found that, in general, the two types are distinguished by the characteristics and qualities listed in Table 11.1.

Of course many people represent intermediate types, or mixtures; the attributes given in Table 11.1 delineate the pronounced types. Nevertheless, if most of your attributes lie in the right-hand column the chances are very much against your becoming a successful executive. On the other hand, if you are interested primarily in increasing your effectiveness as an individual worker you would do well to develop some of the strong qualities listed in the left column, to reinforce the virtues on the right.

Two facts stand out sharply in this connection:

1. Whatever your position, and however complacent you may be about it,

TABLE 11.1   Characteristic Qualities for Executive or Individual Workers

Executive	Individual Worker
Extrovert	Introvert
Cordial, affable	Reserved
Gregarious, sociable	Prefers own company
Likes people	Likes technical work
Interested in people	Interested in mechanisms, ideas
Interested in:	Interested in:
Business	Sciences
Costs	Mathematics
Profit and loss	Literature
Practices	Principles
Ability to get many things done	Ability to get intricate things done
Practical	Idealistic
Extensive (broad perspectives)	Intensive (penetrating)
Synthetist	Analyst
Fast, intuitive	Slow, methodical
Talent for leadership	Independent, self-sufficient
Uses inductive logic	Uses deductive logic
Has competitive spirit	Prefers to "live and let live"
Bold	Modest
Courageous	Retiring
Noisy	Quiet
Aggressive	Restrained
Tough, rugged	Vulnerable, sensitive
Confident	Deferential
Impulsive	Intellectual
Vigorous, energetic	Meditative, philosophical
Opinionated, intolerant	Broad-minded, tolerant
Determined	Adaptable
Impatient	Patient
Enterprising	Conservative

there is always room for improving your effectiveness, usually plenty of room.

2. Whatever your natural handicaps may be, it is alway possible to accomplish such improvement by study and practice, provided only that you have the will, the determination, and the interest to sustain the effort.

It is very much like the design of a piece of apparatus. Any experienced engineer knows that it is always possible to secure substantial improvements by a redesign. When you get into it you will find that there are few subjects more absorbing or more profitable than the design and development of a good engineer! As Alexander Pope wrote many years ago: "The proper study of mankind is man."

As previously suggested, this applies to the development of your men as well as yourself. It likewise applies to the appraisal and selection of men. After your own character, the next most important factor in your ultimate success is the caliber of your assistants. In fact, there are, doubtless, cases where the character of the executive is not particularly important, provided only that he is smart enough to surround himself with top-notch men to carry the load. In many instances the success or failure of your business will depend upon whether your engineers are slightly above or below the marginal level of competence for the industry.

It is a significant fact that, in the overwhelming majority of cases, the decisive differences in the abilities of engineers are relatively small. In spite of the occasional incidence of a genius or a nitwit, the great majority of personnel in any industry and the backbone of the large organizations are individuals who vary only slightly from the norm. In general, when executives look over an organization to select a man for a better job, those who are passed up have very few actual shortcomings, but the man who is chosen has the least. Likewise, many top executives are distinguished not so much by marked genius as by relative freedom from defects of character. There is nowhere near enough genius to go around.

This should be particularly heartening to the younger men who view the leaders of industry with awe and wonder upon what meat they feed. Nine out of ten of you have "what it takes" as regards native endowments. The problem is to make the most of what you have.

To this end it will be helpful to study some of the employee rating sheets and charts that have been evolved by various industries. Sample forms and a general discussion of the subject will be found in the pamphlet on "employee rating" (2). It is very noticeable that most of these forms are concerned chiefly with acquired rather than inherited traits. The point is that most of the features upon which individuals are rated represent bad habits or plain ignorance, i.e., features that may be controlled and corrected by conscious effort.

Conclusion. The foregoing "laws" represent only one basic element in the general formula for a successful engineering career. The complete list of essential components is as follows:

(a) The written laws (the arts and sciences).
(b) The unwritten laws, of which the foregoing is admittedly no more than a preliminary and very inadequate summary.
(c) Native endowments (intelligence, imagination, health, energy, etc.).
(d) Luck, chance, opportunities ("the breaks").

The last item is included because good or bad fortune undoubtedly enters into the picture occasionally. Broadly speaking, however, luck tends to average out at a common level over a period of years, and there are more opportunities looking for men than there are men looking for opportunities.

About all that we can do about our native endowments is to conserve, develop, and utilize them to best advantage.

The "unwritten laws," including those that are still unwritten, are needed to give direction to our efforts in this latter respect.

The "written laws" receive plenty of attention during our formal schooling, but our studies are not always extended as effectively as they might be after graduation. In many cases, superior technical knowledge and training represent the marginal consideration in the selection of men for key positions.

To anyone interested in improving his professional effectiveness, futher study of both types of laws will yield an excellent return on the investment. Under present conditions, however, most engineering graduates are much closer to the saturation point in respect to the written than to the unwritten variety. A few references are listed in the Bibliography for the benefit of those who may be interested in further excursions into these subjects.

Finally it should be observed that the various principles which have been expounded, like those of the arts and sciences, must be assiduously applied and developed in practice if they are to become really effective assets. It is much easier to recognize the validity of these "laws" than it is to apply them consistently, just as it is easier to accept the doctrines of Christianity than to practice them. The important thing here is to select, insofar as possible, a favorable atmosphere for the development of these professional skills. This is undoubtedly one of the major advantages of employment in a large engineering organization, just as it is advantageous to a young doctor to spend his internship in the Mayo Clinic. Perhaps even more important, as previously mentioned, is the selection of your boss, particularly during those first few years that constitute your engineering apprenticeship. No amount of precept is as effective as the proper kind of example. Unfortunately, there is not nearly enough of this kind of example to go around, and in any event it will behoove you to study the "rules of the game" to develop your own set of principles to guide you in your professional practice.

References

1. *Elements of Human Engineering,* by C. R. Gow, Macmillan Company, New York, N.Y., 1932.
2. "Employee Rating," National Industrial Conference Board, Report 39, New York, N.Y., 1942.
3. "Papers on the Science of Administration," by Luther Gulick and L. Urwick, Institute of Public Administration, Columbia University, New York, N.Y., 1937 (New York State Library, Albany, reference 350.1, qG97).

4. *Principles of Industrial Organization,* by D. S. Kimball, McGraw-Hill Book Company, Inc., New York, N.Y., 1933.

5. *Organization and Management in Industry and Business,* by W. B. Cornell, The Ronald Press Company, New York, N.Y., 1936.

6. *Industrial Management,* by R. H. Lansburgh and W. R. Spriegel, third edition, John Wiley & Sons, Inc., New York, N.Y., 1940.

7. *The Functions of the Executive,* by Chester I. Barnard, Harvard University Press, Cambridge, Mass., 1938.

8. *Human Relations Manual for Executives,* by Carl Heyel, McGraw-Hill Book Company, Inc., New York, N.Y., 1939.

9. "Organization and Management of Engineering Described at Unusual General Session," reviewing by M. R. Sullivan, R. C. Muir, and H. B. Gear, *Electrical Engineering,* Vol. 61, August 1942, pp. 422–429.

10. "Administrative Organization for a Small Manufacturing Firm," by Willis Rabbe, *Mechanical Engineering,* Vol. 63, 1941, pp. 517–520.

11. "Task of the Executive in Modern Industry," by John Airey, *Journal of Engineering Education,* Vol. 32, January 1942, pp. 472–479.

12. *Middle Management,* by Mary Cushing Howard Niles, Harper & Bro., New York, N.Y., 1941.

13. *Management's Handbook,* by L. P. Alford, The Ronald Press Company, New York, N.Y., 1924.

14. *Shop Management,* by F. W. Taylor, Harper & Bro., New York, N.Y., 1911. (This is a classic work in which Taylor is credited with laying the foundations of modern "scientific management.")

15. *Onward Industry,* by J. D. Mooney and A. C. Riley, Harper & Bro., New York, N.Y., 1931.

16. *Personnel Management and Industrial Relations,* by Dale Yoder, Prentice-Hall, Inc., New York, N.Y., 1942.

17. *Industrial Psychology,* by Joseph Tiffin, Prentice-Hall, Inc., New York, N.Y., 1942.

18. "Industrial Psychology, Industrial Relations," by Irving Knickerbocker, *Mechanical Engineering,* Vol. 65, 1943, pp. 137–138.

19. *What Men Live By,* by R. C. Cabot, Houghton-Mifflin Company, New York, N.Y., 1914.

20. *Psychology for Business and Industry,* by Herbert Moore, McGraw-Hill Book Company, Inc., New York, N.Y., 1939.

21. *Industrial Management,* by G. G. Anderson, M. J. Mandeville, and J. M. Anderson, The Ronald Press Company, New York, N.Y., 1943.

22. *Psychology for Executives,* by E. D. Smith, Harper & Bro., New York, N.Y., 1935.

23. *Industrial Relations Handbook,* by J. C. Aspley and E. Whitmore, The Dartnell Corporation, Chicago, Ill., 1943.

24. *The Technique of Executive Control,* by Erwin Haskell Schell, fifth edition, McGraw-Hill Book Company, Inc., New York, N.Y., 1942.

25. *Management of Manpower,* by A. S. Knowles and R. D. Thomson, Macmillan Company, New York, N.Y., 1943.

APPENDIX A

america's top 10 scientists and engineers, 1876 to 1976 *

1. Thomas Alva Edison—1093 patents, including incandescent electric light (1879), phonograph, telephone, microphone, quadruplex telegraph, talking motion pictures, and alkaline storage battery.
2. Benjamin Franklin—efficient heating stove, bifocal glasses, improved street lighting, lightening conductor, and other discoveries about electrical phenomena (1872).
3. Albert Einstein—theory of relativity (1905) and developing the unified field theory.
4. Josiah Willard Gibbs—founder of modern chemistry; responsible for principles of chemical thermodynamics (1876) and vector analysis (1881).
5. Enrico Fermi—directed team that developed first self-sustaining nuclear reaction (1942).
6. Alexander Graham Bell—inventor of the telephone (1876).
7. Wilbur and Orville Wright—first powered airplane flight (1903).
8. Eli Whitney—inventor of cotton gin (1793), interchangeable parts for mass production (1798), and the milling machine (1818).
9. Luther Burbank—experiments in genetics and plant hybridization (1870–1926).
10. John Bardeen—codiscoverer of transistor (1947) and developer of miscroscopic theory of superconductivity (1956).

*V.J. Danilov, "America's Greatest Discoveries, Inventions and Innovations," *Industrial Research 18* (12), November 15, 1976.

one hundred most significant american scientific discoveries, inventions, and innovations through 1976*

Chemistry and Chemical Engineering

1839	Vulcanized rubber	C. Goodyear
1859	Oil drilling process	D.L. Drake
1876	Principles of chemical thermodynamics	J.W. Gibbs
1884	Photographic roll film	G. Eastman
1907	Phenolic plastic	L.H. Baekeland
1909–1957	Surface chemistry and electron theory	I. Langmuir
1913	Petroleum cracking	W. Burton and R. Humphreys
1930–1940	Chemical bonds	L. Pauling
1935	Synthetic fiber	W.H. Carothers
1938	Zerography	C. Carlson
1940–1955	Transuranium elements	G.T. Seaborg
1947	Radioactive dating	W.F. Libby
1947	Polaroid camera	E.H. Land

Agriculture and Food

1793	Cotton gin	E. Whitney
1834	Reaper	C.R. McCormick
1837	Self-polishing steel plow	J. Deere
1870–1926	Plant hybridization	L. Burbank

*V.J. Danilov, "America's Greatest Discoveries, Inventions and Innovations," *Industrial Research, 18* (12), November 15, 1976.

| 1896–1935 | Agricultural chemistry | G.W. Carver |
| 1924 | Quick-freeze food process | C. Birdseye |

Medicine and Biological Sciences

1823	Nature of human digestion	W. Beaumont
1831	Chloroform	G. Guthrie
1846	Use of anesthesia	W.T.G. Morton
1896	Brain surgery	H. Cushing
1902–1912	Suturing, transplants, implants	A. Carrel
1906	Laws of heredity	T.H. Morgan
1912	Vitamins	C. Funk
1913	X-ray tube	W. Coolidge
1938	Blood plasma	C.R. Drew
1943	Antibiotics	S.A. Waksman
1951	DNA structure	J.D. Watson, et. al.
1954	Polio vaccine	J. Salk
1955	Contraceptive pill	G. Pincus
1956	DNA synthesis	A. Kornberg

Physics and Astronomy

1769	Transit of Venus calculation	R. Rittenhouse
1798	Nature of heat	B. Thompson
1802	Astronomical navigation	N. Boroditch
1877	Classification of stars	E.L. Pickering
1889	Spectroheliograph	G.E. Hale
1902–1955	Relativity and other theories	A. Einstein
1909	Existence of electrons	R.A. Millikan
1918	Expanding universe theory	H. Shapley
1923	Compton effect	A.H. Compton
1930	Cyclotron	E.O. Lawrence
1942	Nuclear chain reaction	E. Fermi, et al.
1953	Laser	C.H. Townes

Electricity, Electronics, and Communications

1752	Lightning rod	B. Franklin
1831	Self-induction transformer	J. Henry
1837	Telegraph	S.F.B. Morse

1849	Hydraulic turbine	J.B. Francis
1866	Transatlantic cable	C.W. Field
1876	Telephone	A.G. Bell
1879	Incandescent electric light	T.A. Edison
1886	Electric transformer	W. Stanley, Jr.
1887	Induction motor	N. Tesla
1890	Punched-card data processing	H. Hollerith
1900	Wireless voice transmission	R.A. Fessenden
1906	Triode vacuum tube amplifier	L. De Forrest
1911	Gyrocompass	E.A. Sperry
1918	Superketerodyne AM radio	E.H. Armstrong
1923–1929	Iconoscope T.V.	V.R. Zworykin
1930	Differential analyzer	V. Bush
1940	Color T.V.	P.C. Goldmark
1944	Automatic digital computer	H. Aiken
1944–1946	Computer memory	J. Von Neumann
1946	Electrical digital computer	J.P. Eckert and J.W. Mauchly
1947	Transistor effect	J. Bardeen et al.
1948	Cybernetic theory	N. Weiner
1959	Monolithic integrated circuit	J.S. Kilby
1962	Communications satellite	J.R. Pierce

Metallurgy, Machinery, and Mechanical Engineering

1790	Spinning and carding machinery	S. Slater
1793	Cotton gin	E. Whitney
1800	High-pressure steam engine	O. Evans
1835	Repeating revolver	S. Colt
1841	Wire rope for suspension bridges	J.A. Roebling
1845	Sewing machine	E. Howe
1846	Rotary printing press	R.M. Hoe
1848	Rotary valve steam engine	G. Corliss
1851	Steel converter	W. Relly
1853	Hydraulic passenger elevator	E.G. Otis
1867	Practical typewriter	C.L. Sholes
1876	Barbed wire	J.F. Glidden
1883	Steel frame for skyscraper	W.L. Jenney
1884	Linotype typesetting machine	O. Mergenthaler
1886	Electrolysis of aluminum	C.M. Hall
1888	Adding machine	W. Burroughs

Transportation

1807	Practical steamboat	R. Fulton
1825	First American locomotive	J. Stevens
1865	Luxury passenger railroad car	G.M. Pullman
1868	Automatic air brake	G. Westinghouse
1887	Electric street car	F. Sprague
1892	Gasoline automobile	C.E. Duryea
1896	Experimental airplane	S.P. Langley
1903	Powered airplane	W. and O. Wright
1908–1914	Mass-produced automobiles	H. Ford
1911	Automobile self-starter	C.F. Kettering
1926	Liquid-fuel rocket	R.L. Goddard
1939	Practical helicopter	I. Sikorsky
1969	Manned rocket to moon	W. von Braun et al.

Natural History

1835	Classification of plants	A. Gray
1842–1846	Classification of animals	L. Agassig

INDEX